THE CACTUS AIR FORCE

OSPREY
PUBLISHING

ERIC HAMMEL AND THOMAS
McKELVEY CLEAVER

The Cactus
Air Force

AIR WAR OVER GUADALCANAL

OSPREY PUBLISHING
Bloomsbury Publishing Plc
Kemp House, Chawley Park, Cumnor Hill, Oxford OX2 9PH, UK
29 Earlsfort Terrace, Dublin 2, Ireland
1385 Broadway, 5th Floor, New York, NY 10018, USA
E-mail: info@ospreypublishing.com
www.ospreypublishing.com

OSPREY is a trademark of Osprey Publishing Ltd

First published in Great Britain in 2022

A catalog record for this book is available from the British Library.

ISBN: HB 9781472851079; PB 9781472851086; eBook 9781472851055;
ePDF 9781472851048; XML 9781472851031

22 23 24 25 26   10 9 8 7 6 5 4 3 2 1

Maps by www.bounford.com
Index by Zoe Ross

Typeset by Deanta Global Publishing Services, Chennai, India
Printed and bound in Great Britain by CPI (Group) UK Ltd, Croydon CR0 4YY

Osprey Publishing supports the Woodland Trust, the UK's leading woodland conservation charity.

To find out more about our authors and books visit www.ospreypublishing.com. Here you will find
extracts, author interviews, details of forthcoming events and the option to sign up for our newsletter.

CONTENTS

LIST OF MAPS

LIST OF ILLUSTRATIONS

SBD Dauntless dive bombers and TFB torpedo-attack bombers parked at Henderson Field, late 1942. (US Navy Official)

Most of the Wildcats only lasted a few weeks of operations at Guadalcanal before ending up like this F4F-4. Those deemed too badly damaged to be repaired became the source of parts for others. (US Navy Official)

F4F-4 Wildcat of VMF-121 with ground crew. Pilots at Guadalcanal were effusive in their praise of the ground crewmen who worked under impossible conditions to keep aircraft operational. (US Navy Official)

Japanese dead on Tenaru sandbar after the "Battle of the Tenaru" August 20–21, which saw the destruction of the "Ichiki battalion" during the first Japanese attempt to retake Henderson Field. (US Navy Official)

Marine F4F-4 Wildcats of VMF-121 taxi past USAAF P-38Fs of the 339th Fighter Squadron at "Fighter One" airfield. (US Navy Official)

A file of Marines crossing the Matanikau River with the deep jungle beyond. (US Navy Official)

USS *South Dakota* (BB-57) was sent to the South Pacific to replace USS *North Carolina* (BB-55) that was torpedoed by the same submarine that sank USS *Wasp* (CV-7) on September 15, 1942. (US Navy Official)

USS *Wasp* (CV-7) burning after being torpedoed on September 15 south of Guadalcanal. The carrier sank within 20 minutes of the first torpedo hit. (US Navy Official)

USS *Helena* (CL-50) after the naval Battle of Guadalcanal, November
12, 1942. (US Navy Official)

Rear Admiral Richmond K. Turner (left) commanded the
Guadalcanal invasion fleet while General Arthur A. Vandegrift
(right) commanded the Marines. (US Navy Official)

From left to right: Major John Smith, commander of VMF-221;
Lt. Colonel Richard Mangrum, commander of VMSB-232;
Captain Marion Carl of VMF-221 – the three leading pilots
of the first Marine air group to see action at Guadalcanal.
(US Navy Official)

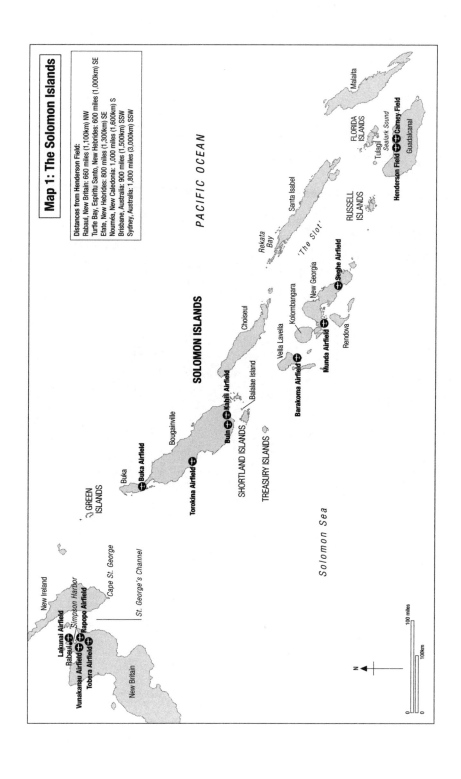

Map 1: The Solomon Islands

Distances from Henderson Field:
Rabaul, New Britain: 660 miles (1,100km) NW
Turtle Bay, Espiritu Santo, New Hebrides: 600 miles (1,000km) SE
Efate, New Hebrides: 800 miles (1,300km) SE
Nouméa, New Caledonia: 1,000 miles (1,600km) S
Brisbane, Australia: 900 miles (1,500km) SSW
Sydney, Australia: 1,800 miles (3,000km) SSW

PACIFIC OCEAN

Malaita

FLORIDA
ISLANDS

Tulagi

Sealark Sound

Henderson Field ⊕⊕ Carney Field

Guadalcanal

Santa Isabel

RUSSELL
ISLANDS

SOLOMON ISLANDS

Rekata
Bay

'The Slot'

Choiseul

New Georgia

Kolombangara

Seghe Airfield ⊕

Vella Lavella

Bougainville

Buin ⊕⊕ Kahili Airfield

Munda Airfield ⊕

Rendova

Barakoma Airfield ⊕

Buka

Buka Airfield ⊕

Balalae Island

Torokina Airfield ⊕

SHORTLAND ISLANDS

TREASURY ISLANDS

GREEN
ISLANDS

New Ireland

Cape St. George

Lakunai Airfield ⊕
Rabaul ⊕ Simpson Harbor
Vunakanau Airfield ⊕ Rapopo Airfield ⊕
Tobera Airfield ⊕

Cape St. George

St. George's Channel

New Britain

Solomon Sea

N

100 miles

100km

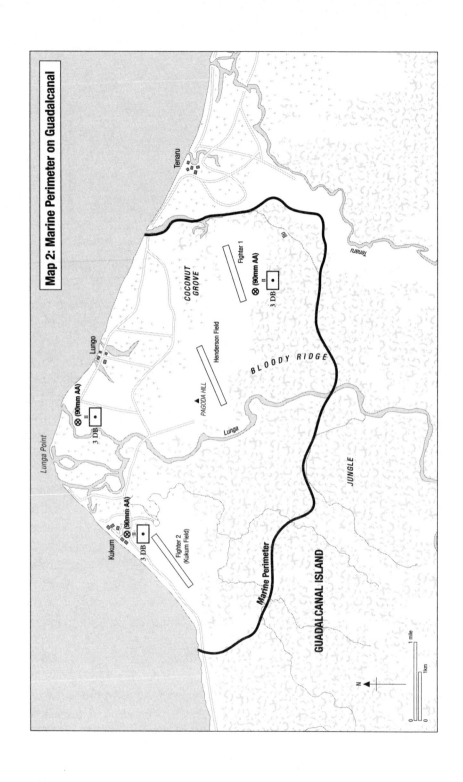

Map 2: Marine Perimeter on Guadalcanal

Lunga Point

Lungo

Tenaru

COCONUT GROVE

Fighter 1

(90mm AA)

3 DB

Henderson Field

▲ PAGODA HILL

(90mm AA)

3 DB

BLOODY RIDGE

Lunga

Tenaru

Kukum

(90mm AA)

3 DB

Fighter 2 (Kukum Field)

Marine Perimeter

JUNGLE

GUADALCANAL ISLAND

N

1 mile

1 km

FOREWORD

Eric Hammel (1946–2020) stands tall among the pantheon of American military historians. A tireless researcher, superb chronicler, and master of extracting the telling anecdote or insightful recollection, "Rick" Hammel devoted almost his entire life to capturing the struggle and sacrifice of free people fighting to preserve their liberty. He began writing military history in his teenage years, inspired by another great popular military historian, Walter Lord. Though he eventually wrote on many different subjects, it was the Pacific War and the resolute and always inspirational history of Marines and their beloved Corps that held his particular interest. Hammel's many works on Marines at war rightly won him both respect and distinction from that very tough audience for his dedication and painstaking scholarship.

Hammel was, at various time, a historian, a publisher, a journalist and military commentator, and an informed student of national security affairs. His broad and profound depth of interests are readily evident in the 40 books and nearly 70 articles that he produced in roughly 60 years of professional research and writing. Like Walter Lord, Samuel L.A. "Slam" Marshall, Stephen Ambrose, Barrett Tillman, and Gordon Prange, he was a master of using oral history interviews to get at the human face of conflict, illuminating the often dry "grand strategic" accounts of the professional military history community.

This book, magnificently edited and completed by Tom Cleaver following Rick Hammel's untimely death in 2020, is vintage Hammel at his best – a riveting "deep dive" look at the first (and most crucial) three months of the Guadalcanal campaign, drawn from years of interviews with veterans of various services, the vast majority of which, like Rick himself, have now passed into that Valhalla of veterans beyond the last great frontier.

Guadalcanal has been the subject of numerous books, many memoirs, and some outstanding official histories, and one might fairly wonder is it really worth yet another book. The answer, as readily evident to the reader, is a resounding "yes." Eclipsed over time by the great and cataclysmic events that preceded and followed it – Pearl Harbor, Midway, the drive across the Central Pacific, the liberation of the Marianas and Philippines, Iwo Jima, Okinawa, and the collapse of Japan, the entire Solomons campaign is now, sadly, far less appreciated, particularly by younger audiences, than it once was.

Guadalcanal set the stage for the Allied recovery of the Solomons, which was pivotal in securing control of the South Pacific, preventing a Japanese takeover of New Guinea, and thwarting Japanese expansion deeper into the South and Central Pacific. With Japan put on the defensive, Allied efforts could turn to building the powerful sea-air forces that would sweep across the Western Pacific in 1944 and secure the island bases from which the Army Air Forces and roving carrier task forces would pound Japan in 1945.

But all that came later: at first, there was Guadalcanal, where America's military cut their teeth in jungle and island fighting. Hammel and Cleaver have once more brought it front and center. Theirs is a harrowing tale of unpreparedness, intelligence, and leadership failures, of learning hard lessons in the furious crucible of war, of sacrifice and loss, of great courage, and, ultimately, of a great victory secured at a fearsome cost, a tale well worth retelling in an era when the spectre of possible Pacific conflict sadly looms before us once again, and Eastern Europe is yet again in flames.

Richard P. Hallion
6 March 2022

AUTHOR'S FOREWORD

If Eric Hammel hadn't been my "brother from another mother," you wouldn't know who I am, dear reader. My career as an aviation author is the result of his cajoling, enthusiasm, and support. He published my first book, *Air Combat Annals* through his company, Pacifica Press. After he read the initial draft of *Fabled Fifteen*, he went out on his own and found a publisher willing to pick it up. He later introduced me to the late Jim Hornfischer, who agented the publication of *The Bridgebusters*. It is not too much to say I literally owe him everything that has brought me to the point where you might have purchased this book because you saw my name on it. It's all due to one of the best people it was ever my privilege to know.

I first met Eric Hammel in October, 1992, at the Aviation Bookstore on Magnolia Boulevard here in Burbank, California. In truth, he wasn't actually there, but there on the shelves were the first volumes of his monumental interview series, *Aces Against Germany* and *Aces Against Japan*. I knew who he was because the late Jeffrey Ethell had once mentioned that Eric was "the best interviewer in our business." As I looked through *Aces Against Germany*, I saw what Jeff meant. I became a fairly accomplished interviewer myself when I first came to Hollywood, where I was fortunate to get freelance magazine assignments and made a reputation for myself for doing good interviews with famous Hollywood people. I had figured out that Steven Spielberg was highly unlikely to spend five seconds talking to "Tom Who?" but he would (and did) spend over an hour talking to Thomas McKelvey Cleaver, interviewer for *Starlog* magazine, about *Indiana Jones and the Temple of Doom*. And he said it was one of the best interviews he'd done; I later learned that it wasn't a "Hollywood compliment" – he's never been known to do that.

So I bought both the books, took them home and devoured them. This author really was a good interviewer! I became more impressed when I found he had done most of the interviews back in the 1960s and early 1970s. That was before many of the then-few "aviation writers" were doing such things. His timing was perfect: the men were still alive, and still young enough to remember what they'd done, and were happy to talk to someone who was interested in them. By the 1990s, their ranks were fewer than they had been, and those of us writing in the field were starting to regret not having done that spadework earlier.

Importantly for history, Eric didn't limit his interviews to the "major names" in any of his books. He interviewed everyone. He was particularly set on getting the interviews of those whose stories were likely to be overlooked: the junior officers, the ground crews, the intelligence officers, the flight surgeons. Everyone! This is why all his books are still considered among the classics in the field, must-reads for any serious student of history.

Twenty years later, in 2011, our mutual friend and fellow aviation history author Jay Stout introduced me to Eric personally. Our first phone call, which he later told me he expected might last as long as 30 minutes, turned into four hours, at the conclusion of which we agreed we must be brothers from other mothers. It was the beginning of one of the best friendships I've ever had.

We spoke at least every other week and generally more frequently over the next nine years. In August 2018, he told me he had received a diagnosis of Parkinson's disease. I was aware of the disease and what such a diagnosis meant, since She Who Must Be Obeyed had received the same diagnosis that spring. A year later, he told me about what he hoped was going to be his last project, a history of the air campaign at Guadalcanal. His four books on the Guadalcanal campaign, all based on first-person interviews, are considered definitive; he hoped this one – which he had planned over several years – would be the capstone of the series. Unfortunately, he was finding that Parkinson's sapped his energy and he was no longer able to put in the several hours a day writing that he had done before.

Almost before I knew what I was saying, I suggested we write it together, with me doing the "grunt work" of putting the words on the page, working from his outline and research files. He took my suggestion under advisement. A few weeks later, he called and said he thought it was a good idea. I contacted Marcus Cowper, my editor at Osprey, and asked if such a book would be of interest; he told me it was. Eric sent me his outline and initial drafts, and I began creating a book proposal. Once I was finished with the first draft, I was quite happy when he read it over and told me he was glad he had decided to do it with me this way because "your sense of drama is just what this needs."

We continued working it over, but things began to change for the worse as the course of his Parkinson's developed. By December 2019, I had to remind him of things we had gone over during the previous meeting. By February 2020, I was reminding him of things we had gone over earlier in that day's conversation. That April, he told me he couldn't continue. "I can't remember the last thing I said to you." Sadly, I let Osprey know the project wouldn't proceed.

That May, Eric's wife of 55 years reluctantly put him in a care home. He died in July 2020.

Several months later, Eric's son Daniel contacted me. He was going through his father's records and had found our e-mails about the project. He wanted to know if I was interested in completing the book. I told him I was. Osprey was happy to hear that the project had a new life.

I was amazed when Daniel sent me the five gigabytes of records and materials from Eric's files. There were interviews with all the "Famous Names" of Guadalcanal, but even more interesting were the interview files of people whose names I was unfamiliar with – and I consider myself knowledgeable on this topic. It was classic Eric: the young kids, the pilots recently graduated from flight school with around 200 hours in their logbooks, who had been the aerial front line of defense. The mechanics who worked miracles keeping the airplanes working, the sailors who had supported the Marines in the bloodiest sea battles the US Navy ever fought. These memories and stories hadn't made it into any other books; I understood why he believed he was going to produce his best work with this project.

How good an interviewer was Eric? One of the interviews in question was done way back in 1962, with Rear Admiral Turner Caldwell, who as a lieutenant 20 years earlier had led Flight 300 from the *Enterprise* to reinforce Guadalcanal. The story he told in his interview was much deeper, with memories of what they did and how they did it that I hadn't read in any of the other histories where he had played a prominent role. And then, when I finished reading the interview, it hit me: Eric was 17 when he did that! Looking over the notes and the questions he'd asked, it was an interview I would have been quite impressed with myself to have done – but not at age 17. Any professional historian with years of experience would have been proud of having done it.

It's been a privilege to put this together. It's been educational for me, because I found memories and stories I'd never known before, and would never have known if I hadn't volunteered to do this.

I hope you find Eric's last work to be as interesting as I did.

Thomas McKelvey Cleaver
Encino, California, 2022

I

BEFORE

The first Marines to be designated Naval Aviators were awarded their Wings of Gold in 1912. During World War I, the Marine-manned Northern Bombing Force compiled an enviable combat record on the Western Front, where such future leaders as then-Captain Roy Geiger first distinguished themselves. In the years between the wars, Marine aviators used their World War I-vintage DH.4s to invent what came to be known as dive bombing and create a system of close air support of Marine ground forces during the "banana wars" in Nicaragua. This battlefield experience led to the development of the organizational and operational strategies for Marine air units in the coming war.

Marine squadrons were removed from Nicaragua in 1932 and Haiti in 1935 following the defeat of the insurgents in both countries, while the words consolidation, contraction, and postponement became the planning strategy for all the American military for the rest of the prewar years. By the time war came in 1941, there were more senior Marine aviators with combat experience than any pilot in the Navy. *This* experience would soon be worth its weight in gold as the Marines faced the strongest opponent in their history.

The most important thing to happen to the Marine Corps in the years before World War II was the establishment on December 8, 1933 of the Fleet Marine Force (FMF), which was placed in the fleet as "an integral part thereof, subject to the orders, for tactical employment, of the Commander-in-Chief US Fleet." No longer was the Corps the "expeditionary force" of the Navy that was involved in limited military actions ashore in a "policing" role; the Marines were now committed to "seizing bases for naval operations in wartime" in major military actions.

This was reinforced with publication of the *Landing Force Manual,* published in early 1934, which became the "bible" of Marine operations throughout World War II. The manual laid out all the steps for conducting an amphibious assault, using elements that were successfully tested in the fleet exercises of the 1930s where the strategy and tactics that would win the Pacific War were proven.

With the proof-of-concept from Nicaragua, close air support of Marines by Marine squadrons trained for the role was an integral part of the overall strategy and tactics for "seizure of bases for naval operations" contained in the manual. In June 1935, Marine aviation was taken from the Division of Operations and Training at Headquarters Marine Corps and established as an independent section reporting to the Commandant as Marine Corps Aviation. Marine Aviation's World War II mission was spelled out by the Navy's General Board in January, 1939: "Marine Aviation is to be equipped, organized and trained primarily for the support of the Fleet Marine Force in landing operations and in support of troop activities in the field; and secondarily as replacement squadrons for carrier-based naval aircraft." In June 1940, of the 10,000 naval aircraft authorized by Congress, the Marines were allotted 1,167. Following the 1941 landing exercises, the Atlantic Amphibious Force recommended that a single division making an amphibious landing required 12 fighter, eight dive-bomber, two observation, and four utility squadrons for proper air support.

Of all US air forces, Marine Aviation experienced the greatest expansion in the years before Pearl Harbor. In 1936, there were 145 Marine aviators wearing Wings of Gold; by mid-1940, that number had only grown to 245. However, by the end of that year, as expansion took hold, there were 425 Marine aviators; most were members of the Marine Corps Reserve, young men entering the service through the Navy's Aviation Cadet (AvCad) program, who committed to four years' active duty upon graduation and designation as Marine aviators. On December 7, 1941, nearly 600 men wore Wings of Gold on their forest green uniforms, manning 13 squadrons equipped with 204 aircraft.

During the first year of the Pacific War, two aircraft would come to define Marine Aviation: the F4F Wildcat and the SBD Dauntless.

The F4F Wildcat began with a 1938 US Navy requirement for a replacement for the F3F biplane fighters that were the first-line equipment of carrier fighter aviation. While the Navy wanted a monoplane fighter that would be similar in performance to the land-based monoplanes that had appeared in Germany, Great Britain, and the United States in the years after 1934 when the first prototypes of the Messerschmitt 109 and Hawker Hurricane flew, the service was also conservative in its planning. Grumman was asked to create another biplane fighter – the XF4F-1 – while Brewster, a manufacturer of horse-drawn buggies in the 19th century that had been reborn as an aircraft manufacturer a year earlier, would build the service's first monoplane, the XF2A-1. Leroy Grumman and his team of experienced designers and engineers saw that the biplane was a dead end; they managed to convince the Navy that, with a few modifications such as an uprated engine, the F3F-2 – already in squadron service – could meet the requirements in the XF4F-1 program. The Navy ordered the upgraded aircraft as the F3F-3, and Grumman was allowed to proceed with its own monoplane design, the XF4F-2.

Brewster, a company known for producing horse-drawn buggies during its hundred years of existence, was virtually moribund as the result of technological change before it was purchased and reorganized by individuals who had never been involved in aviation and had never produced an actual airplane before they decided to become manufacturers of naval aircraft (perhaps the most demanding field of aircraft development). How it was allowed to compete to create the most important aircraft in naval aviation's 20 years of existence, and how it then managed to come in ahead of Grumman, the company that was rapidly becoming the Navy's premier aircraft designer, is one of those mysteries of military procurement that will never be fully known. This failure of a company, which continued to fail in producing aircraft ordered by its customer of choice until the company was finally seized during World War II for mismanagement (an event that happened in the days before there were any MBAs to blame), is a chapter of American commercial development worthy of a US Economic History doctoral dissertation. Nonetheless, the F2A-1 was chosen over Grumman's XF4F-2 and did become the first all-metal monoplane fighter with enclosed cockpit and retractable landing gear to enter US Navy service.

Fortunately for the Navy and history, Grumman convinced the Bureau of Aeronautics to allow them to rework their design a second time, thus creating the XF4F-3. This aircraft had marginally better performance than the F2A-1, which had just entered production. Brewster was demonstrating out the gate that it was unable to meet production schedules, building the airplane in a two-story 19th-century factory that required each airframe to be lifted between floors with a block and tackle to complete the production process, with final assembly completed at the Buffalo, New York airport after the half-finished airplanes were towed there from the factory – a task made even more difficult in the city's well-known winter blizzards. Grumman's demonstrated production capability won the day and the Navy was glad to be able to order the new fighter from the more reliable company.

The first production F4F-3 flew in February 1940, powered by a Pratt & Whitney R-1830-76 Twin Wasp engine with a two-stage supercharger. The second rolled out of the factory that July. These and the next eight F4F-3s were involved in tests by the Navy to change the cooling flaps and exhaust to get rid of exhaust seepage in the cockpit and to improve engine cooling. The F4F-3A was the result of an April 1940 request from BuAer for Grumman to change powerplants to the R-1830-90 Twin Wasp with single-stage supercharger due to fear of production delays with the two-stage supercharger. These 55 airplanes had a lower performance than the F4F-3 and as a result were handed over to the Marines as their first Wildcats in April 1941. Marine aviator Charles Older decided to join what would become the American Volunteer Group because he didn't want to go to war in the F4F-3A after losing a "dogfight" with a US Army Air Corps (USAAC) P-40C while delivering one of the Wildcats from the Grumman factory on Long Island to his squadron at Quantico. The last 100 F4F-3s on order were produced with the R-1830-86 Twin Wasp using the two-stage supercharger. Marine Fighter Squadrons 121 and 211 (VMF-121 and VMF-211) turned in their F3F-2s in September 1941 and re-equipped with F4F-3s while VMF-111 flew the F4F-3As. In November 1941, the F4F received the emotive name "Wildcat." A total of 274 F4F-3 and F4F-3A Wildcats were produced on the Navy contract.

At around the same time the Marines were taking possession of their Wildcats, the British Fleet Air Arm – which had been the first service to take the airplane into combat as the Martlet – prevailed on Grumman to increase the armament from four to six .50-caliber machine guns to increase the weight of fire in their new Martlet II version of the fighter to deal with their German and Italian opponents. The British were also able to prevail on Grumman to use their new Sto-Wing folding wing system that tilted the outer wings almost 90 degrees and turned them back alongside the fuselage. This increased the number of fighters that could be parked on a flight deck by more than a factor of two. However, the wing-fold mechanism also increased weight and further degraded performance so much that Grumman was unable to increase the ammunition load, instead distributing the ammo for four guns among six. While the F4F-3's four .50-caliber weapons each had 450rpg and 34 seconds of firing time, the six guns decreased ammunition to 240rpg, with a firing time of less than 20 seconds; those extra 14 seconds could be a lifetime in combat.

The US Navy ordered the British version of the Wildcat as the F4F-4, despite the fact that speed was reduced from 325 to 318 miles per hour, while the rate of climb was noticeably worse; Grumman's optimistic claim that the F4F-4 could climb at a modest 1,950 feet per minute didn't hold up when pilots found that under combat conditions the F4F-4s were really capable of only 500–1,000 feet per minute, depending on weather conditions. This would be the major problem that squadrons dealt with at Guadalcanal, where they would barely have time to scramble and climb to 20,000 feet to gain the crucial altitude advantage they needed with warnings of incoming raids from the coastwatchers. The first F4F-4 flew in December 1941 and the first squadrons re-equipped in March 1942. The F4F-4 was the "definitive" Wildcat, equipping all Navy and Marine fighter squadrons by the summer of 1942 just before the Marines took theirs to Guadalcanal.

In Pacific combat, the Wildcat was outperformed by the faster, more maneuverable, and longer-ranged Mitsubishi A6M Zero. However, a combination of the Grumman-designed ruggedness, superior tactics such as the "Thach Weave," and hit-and-run maneuvers using altitude advantage, while avoiding the close-in high-G maneuvering combat that the Japanese fighter excelled at, resulted in a claimed air combat kill-to-loss ratio of 5.9-to-1 for the Wildcat in 1942.

By far the most important American technical development in naval aviation during the 1930s was the creation of the scout bomber. Fleet exercises demonstrated that the side that first disabled or sank the opposing aircraft carrier would go on to win the battle. The scout bomber, combining good range with a decent bomb load, allowed aircraft that discovered the enemy carrier the opportunity to put one or two bombs in the flight deck after radioing the location, which could effectively knock the enemy carrier out of the fight at the beginning. Dive bombing provided the best chance for accuracy and had been demonstrated to be the form of attack most difficult for a surface ship to counter.

Design work on what would become the BT-1 scout bomber began in 1935 at the Northrop Corporation in El Segundo, California, owned by Jack K. Northrop, who at the time was responsible for some of the most advanced aircraft construction techniques in the United States if not the world. Northrop hired Ed Heineman, a young aeronautical engineer recently graduated from Cal Tech, to work on the wing design. The BT-1 used all Northrop's advanced technology; the result was an all-metal low-wing airplane with an enclosed cockpit capable of diving nearly vertically to drop a bomb by use of unique Heineman-designed perforated dive flaps to slow the dive and thereby improve bombing accuracy. Unfortunately, the 750hp Wright engine was capable of hauling only a 500-pound bomb load. In 1937, Northrop went bankrupt and Douglas Aircraft acquired the company, which became the Douglas El Segundo Division. Donald Douglas made certain all Northrop's technical staff remained and their active projects continued. The BT-2 was developed with more aerodynamic landing gear and a more powerful engine, with Heineman assuming responsibility for the project as lead engineer.

In response to a BuAer request for a more modern dive bomber than the BT-1 and the Vought SB2U, Heineman's design team created the XSBD-1 (Scout Bomber, Douglas) in the spring of 1939, utilizing the BT-1 wing with its perforated dive brakes. Powered by a 1,000hp Wright R-1820 Cyclone engine, the XSBD could carry a 1,600-pound semi-armor-piercing bomb. The new scout bomber went into production in the summer of 1940; unfortunately it was short-ranged and the 57 produced were passed on to the Marines while the Navy received 87 SBD-2s with increased fuel capacity in the spring of 1941. That September, the SBD-3, which was equipped with self-sealing fuel tanks and had additional fuel capacity, entered production. At the time of the Pearl Harbor attack, the Navy's 14 scouting (VS) and bombing

(VB) squadrons were all equipped with the SBD-2 and SBD-3, which had received the emotive name "Dauntless." Few airplanes would live up to their name as well as the SBD, which turned in a truly dauntless performance during the crucial first year of the Pacific War. In the months after Pearl Harbor, the Marine scout-bomber squadrons (VMSB) were able to re-equip with the Dauntless after the Japanese destroyed most of their horrid SB2U-3 "Vindicator" scout bombers on the ground at Pearl Harbor.

A second Grumman product would make an important contribution at Guadalcanal. While Douglas' TBD Devastator torpedo and level bomber was the most modern carrier-based airplane in the world when it appeared in 1937, with its all-metal construction, enclosed cockpits, and folding wings, the pace of aviation development was such that it was practically obsolete after only two years' fleet service.

Fortunately, development of a replacement had begun in 1939 with a request for proposals issued by BuAer. Vought answered the RFP with the TBU-1 while Grumman presented the TBF-1. Both had a similar layout, but Grumman's design was significantly smaller, as well as faster than Vought's. Grumman's design included a power-operated rear turret of incredibly simple design, while the internal bomb bay could carry four 500-pound general purpose bombs, a 1,600-pound armor-piercing bomb, or a Mark XIV aerial torpedo. The power-operated folding wings reduced the 54-foot wingspan to 18 feet, which meant it could operate from all US Navy aircraft carriers. The XTBF-1 flew in August 1941 and flight tests revealed only a need for an extended dorsal fin for better directional stability.

On November 29, 1941, the prototype was accidentally lost when pilot Hobart Clark and engineer Gordon Israel saw a fine mist of hydraulic fluid from a broken line and incorrectly decided it was an incipient onboard fire; the two bailed out ten miles from Grumman's factory at Bethpage and the airplane went into the ocean. Fortunately, a second prototype was in the process of construction and was delivered on December 15, 1941, by which time the TBF's priority had moved from Very Important to Absolutely Critical. In January 1942, the TBF received the name "Avenger" for obvious emotional reasons.

Avengers quickly began rolling off the production line. VT-8, the attack squadron aboard the brand-new USS *Hornet* (CV-8), commissioned only the previous November, received their first aircraft in April 1942. The carrier had been ordered to the Pacific on March 4, 1942; only a squadron detachment was left behind at Naval Air Station (NAS) Norfolk to convert to the new airplane. Eventually, these four TBFs arrived in Hawaii in May and were sent on to Midway Island in time for a baptism of fire at the Battle of Midway, while their shipboard squadronmates flew into immortality in their lumbering TBDs while attacking the Japanese fleet. Only one of the four TBFs returned from its mission, and that so badly damaged that it never flew again. Despite the inauspicious beginning, Avengers flown by Navy crews in squadrons orphaned by the loss or damage of their carriers that operated from Guadalcanal would demonstrate that the airplane was a ship-killer in their battles against the Imperial Navy transports in "the Slot" (the American name for the New Georgia Sound, a body of open water down the Solomon Islands), even sinking a Japanese battleship.

The 1st and 2nd Marine Air Wings (MAWs), previously designated Aircraft One, FMF, on the east coast and Aircraft Two, FMF, on the west coast, were commissioned in July 1941, with the 1st based at Quantico, Virginia, and the 2nd at San Diego, California. When commissioned, each wing had only one Marine air group (MAG) assigned. By December 7, the 2nd Marine Air Wing's Marine Air Group 21 ("2" indicating 2nd Marine Air Wing and "1" designating the first assigned air group) had 44 aircraft deployed, with the VMF-211 detachment of 12 F4F-3 Wildcats newly arrived at Wake Island and VMF-121's F2A-3s going aboard the carrier *Saratoga* (CV-3) at San Diego for transport to Hawaii. Meanwhile, newly commissioned Marine Air Group 23 had 48 aircraft of various types sitting on the flight line at Marine Corps Air Station (MCAS) Ewa outside Pearl Harbor that Sunday morning, all of which were destroyed by the first Japanese attack wave.

Marine Aviation had always been a small part of overall Naval Aviation, with the Marines joking that when an airplane was assigned to a Marine unit, that proved the Navy was no longer interested in it. In the years before World War II, while Navy units were undergoing rapid modernization, Marine squadrons lagged behind. As late as the summer of 1941, Marine fighter pilots were still flying the tubby Grumman F3F-2 biplane fighter that had been supplanted in Navy fighter squadrons beginning the year before when the Brewster F2A-2 equipped the "Flying Chiefs" of Fighter Squadron 2 (VF-2), while the Grumman F4F-3 Wildcat had gone to sea with the "Red Rippers" of

VF-41 the previous February. The two monoplane fighters first showed up in Marine squadrons that fall. In September, newly designated VMF-211 learned that they would exchange their F3Fs for new F4F-3 Wildcats the next month. By the time a detachment of 12 Wildcats from the squadron went aboard USS *Enterprise* (CV-6) at the end of November, bound for Wake Island, no pilot in the squadron had more than ten hours in the type. When Captain Marion Carl reported to VMF-121 in mid-November after a tour as an instructor at Pensacola, he found himself responsible for giving training to young pilots right out of flight school on the F2A-3, an airplane that was a very considerable step up from the F2Fs and F3Fs they had flown during what passed for "advanced training." The squadron itself was as new as most of the pilots. Marine dive-bomber squadrons in 1941 considered themselves fortunate to be equipped with the Vought SB2U-3 Vindicator, the final development of the Navy's first monoplane dive bomber, which had already been supplanted in Navy dive-bomber squadrons by the new Douglas SBD Dauntless.

The 12 Wildcats at Wake entered combat against Japanese G3M bombers flying from the Marshall Islands four hours after the first strike at Pearl Harbor. Following the raid, only the four Wildcats that had been airborne were still undamaged and flyable, since the other eight had been destroyed or damaged by the bombing as they sat unprotected in the parking area next to the open runway. The detachment had no engine mechanics or other experienced ground crew beyond two ordnancemen, and no spare parts. Yet over the ten days of near-daily battle against the Japanese, the detachment would scrounge parts from the wrecks and manage by dint of ingenuity to keep between two and four Wildcats flyable. In the first Japanese attempt to land on the island, one of the four defending Wildcats managed to sink the Japanese destroyer *Kisaragi* with one of two 100-pound bombs hitting the stern where the depth charges were carried.

Only two Wildcats were left to attempt an interception on December 22 of 33 D3A dive bombers and B5N bombers from a strike flown by the carriers *Hiryu* and *Soryu* that had been detached from the Pearl Harbor strike force to support the second Japanese landing. The six escorting A6Ms made short work of the Marine defenders and the second Japanese landing was made the following day; the 20 surviving Marine Aviators fought to the end as riflemen defending machine-gun positions when the Japanese Special Navy Landing Force troops came ashore. After a four-hour fight, the Japanese accepted the American surrender. In his last report, sent back to Pearl Harbor on the morning of December 20 aboard the PBY Catalina that had arrived the previous evening, detachment commander Major Paul Putnam had closed by stating, "all hands have behaved splendidly."

VMF-121 arrived from San Diego on December 13, going aboard the carrier USS *Lexington* (CV-2) the next day as part of the reinforcements that the Navy planned to land on Wake. On the night of December 22, when Task Force 11 was battling high seas 627 miles from Wake, Vice Admiral Frank Jack Fletcher was ordered to turn back due to intelligence having detected the presence in the vicinity of the two Japanese fleet carriers; the Navy couldn't risk one of its three aircraft carriers in a battle with a more experienced force. Fletcher's staff came close to mutiny at the order, while the Marines aboard the transport USS *Tangier* had to be restrained from taking over the ship and heading on regardless. On Christmas Eve, 1941, Marion Carl and the other pilots of VMF-121 were launched from *Lexington* to take up residence as the aerial defense of Midway Island.

At Guadalcanal, the Marine and Navy pilots would face several Imperial Japanese Navy aircraft. The main aerial opponent at Guadalcanal was the Navy Type 0 A6M2 Model 21 Carrier Fighter *rei-shiki-kanjō-sentōki*, or A6M *Rei-sen*, known as the "Reisen" (Zero) to its pilots and later code-named "Zeke" by its US opponents.

At the time the Zero entered service in 1940, it was the world's most advanced carrier-based fighter. Flown by pilots who were the survivors of the most demanding aviation training program of any air force, the fighter attained legendary status both in its home country and in the minds of those who flew against it.

The A6M's development history begins with "Planning Requirements for the Prototype 12-shi Carrier-based Fighter," issued by the Imperial Navy to Nakajima and Mitsubishi on October 5, 1937. It called for a fighter with significantly heavier armament than any other carrier fighter in existence, with maneuverability superior to that of any potential opponent, and the longest range of any single-seat fighter in existence. The Mitsubishi A5M1, the world's first all-metal low-wing carrier fighter, had just entered service with the initial Imperial Japanese Naval Air Force (IJNAF) squadrons; as good as this was, what was being requested was an order of magnitude superior. Both companies put their top designer on the project and commenced initial design work in anticipation of receiving more definitive requirements. At the end of October, updated requirements were issued: the new fighter must have a top speed of 600 kilometers per hour (370 miles per hour), the ability to climb to 3,000 meters (9,800 feet) in 3.5 minutes, and a flight endurance of two hours at normal power, with six to eight hours at economical cruising speed. Armament was set at two 20mm cannon and two 7.7mm (.303-inch) machine guns. It was to be equipped with radio and with radio direction finder (RDF) for long-range navigation. Additionally, maneuverability should at least equal that of the A5M, with wingspan less than 12 metres (39 feet) for carrier use. The fighter must use an existing engine, a significant but not unreasonable design limitation since mating an unproven airframe to an unproven engine was asking for trouble.

Nakajima's design team concluded that the requirements exceeded the aircraft industry's ability to achieve and withdrew from the competition in January 1938. Mitsubishi's chief designer Jiro Horikoshi, creator of the A5M, concluded that the requirements could only be met if the aircraft was as light as possible. Accordingly, his design took advantage of every possible weight-saving measure. The airframe would use a new top-secret aluminum alloy developed by Sumitomo Metal Industries in 1936, "extra super duralumin" (ESD), which was lighter, stronger, and more ductile than other aluminum alloys though it was more prone to corrosion, making it brittle. This would be dealt with by application of an anti-corrosion coating. To maximize weight saving, there was no armor for the pilot, engine, or other vital points, or self-sealing fuel tanks. Horikoshi's creation was the most maneuverable, longest-ranged single-engine fighter used by any air force in World War II. However, the design tradeoff in weight and construction material used meant it would catch fire and explode when hit by enemy fire.

The airplane was easy to land on either a carrier or a land base with its wide-track landing gear. The airfoil provided high lift at low speeds; with the wing and the overall low weight, stalling speed was under 60 knots. This allowed the Zero to out-turn any contemporary opponent. The large ailerons, which provided amazing maneuverability at lower speeds, required servo tabs because of the increased heaviness of control forces at speeds over 250 miles per hour, while the ailerons became almost completely ineffective at speeds over 350 miles per hour. Allied pilots who survived their encounters with the Zero soon learned to keep their speed up; this design fault was confirmed during tests of an intact A6M2 discovered in the Aleutians in 1942. While wartime propaganda claimed that the Zero was either a copy of or highly influenced by one of several contemporary Western designs, the thorough analysis of the "Akutan Zero" captured on Akutan Island in the Aleutians in August 1942 revealed an incredibly original design, unlike any other.

The Zero entered service in July 1940. On September 13, Lieutenant Saburo Shindo, at the head of 13 A6M2s, attacked 27 Soviet-built I-152s and I-16s of the Republic of China Air Force and shot down all 27 without loss; the event passed without notice in the West. Despite the fact that an early A6M2 Model 11 had been captured in China in early 1941 and thoroughly examined and that a report on the examination and of combat experience against it had been forwarded to the Pentagon by American Volunteer Group founder Claire Chennault in late April 1941, American myopia about Japanese achievements and capabilities was impenetrable before the war (before being quickly replaced by an equally inaccurate belief in superhuman Japanese superiority).

At the outbreak of the Pacific War, 521 Zeros had been produced, with 328 in first-line units such as the Tainan Air Corps and the six big carriers of the Mobile Fleet. The 1,600-mile range of the fighter was extended by the skilled fliers in the Tainan Air Corps who were able to fly to the Philippines from bases on Formosa; MacArthur's command was convinced throughout the campaign that there were two carriers operating off the Philippines when there were none. The Zero's fearsome reputation was the result of attempts by inexperienced Allied fighter pilots to engage it in traditional air combat maneuvering, at which it excelled.

Because the Japanese did not have the ability to quickly construct island airfields, in September 1940 the Imperial Navy issued the 15-Shi requirement for a single-seat floatplane fighter with sufficient performance to allow it to engage in combat with enemy land-based or carrier-based fighters to support amphibious operations and defend remote bases for the coming war. Kawanishi's proposal was adopted as the N1K1 "Kyōfū" (Mighty Wind). However, difficulties were encountered in designing a contra-rotating propeller to use with the Mitsubishi M4KC Kasei-43 engine and the project was delayed. As a temporary measure pending the successful development of the N1K1, in February 1941 the Imperial Navy ordered Nakajima – which was in process of starting additional production of the Zero – to design a floatplane version of the Zero. The design team was led by Shinobu Mitsutake, Nakajima Aircraft Company's chief engineer, and Atsushi Tajima, one of the company's designers. The A6M2-N floatplane fighter was based on the A6M-2 Model 11 fuselage, with a modified vertical fin with a larger rudder and a ventral fin for added stability, equipped with a fixed centerline float and a stabilizing float under each wing. The prototype first flew on December 7, 1941. The first few trials revealed that changes would need to be made to the main float to increase the stabilizing effect of the fins. Three more prototypes were built and underwent intensive testing until March 1942. Production began in April 1942, and a total of 327 were built by the time production ceased in September 1943. Introduction of the A6M2-N, known to the Allies as "Rufe," was rapid. The fighter was first encountered in the Aleutians in June 1942, and over the Solomons by B-17s flying reconnaissance missions over Tulagi in July. While the airplane looked ungainly with its floats, it was nearly as maneuverable as the land-based Zero fighter, with a top speed of 275 miles per hour; this was enough to make it a dangerous opponent to the Wildcat. Once the Allies took Guadalcanal and Tulagi, where the Rufes were initially based, the Japanese had no other airfields in the Solomons. This lack was made up by the decision to base A6M2-N and F1M2 floatplanes from a seaplane base established at Rekata Bay in the Shortland Islands north of Guadalcanal, where they were serviced by the seaplane tender *Kamikawa Maru*. The Rufes confined themselves where possible to attacks on Dauntless and Avenger bombers and Allied patrol planes.

In addition to the Rufe, Marine and Navy flyers in the Solomons would engage with the Navy Type 0 Observation Seaplane Model 11, *rei-shiki kansokuki ichi-ichi-gata (Reikan)*, designated F1M2 and known to Allied pilots as "Pete." The F1M2 was a two-seat biplane floatplane with an elegant look for such a type, and was far more dangerous to opposing pilots in air combat than it appeared to be. First designed in 1934 in answer to an Imperial Navy requirement for a ship-based observation floatplane with better performance than the E8N1 then in service, the F1M2 entered production in 1940, with 342 built by Mitsubishi and 598 by the Sasebo and 21st Arsenals; it became the Imperial Navy's most widely used floatplane during the Pacific War, proving to be structurally tough, easy to maintain, and highly versatile, earning a successful record as an interceptor, dive bomber, convoy escort, coastal patrol, and reconnaissance aircraft. Powered by the Nakajima Hikari MK1 radial engine, delivering 820hp, the F1M2 had a top speed of 230 miles per hour, a range of 650 miles and an armament of two forward-firing and one flexible 7.62mm machine guns. It would be well known to those on Guadalcanal as "Washing Machine Charlie" for its nocturnal missions over the islands. The airplane was highly maneuverable, and several Marine pilots fell victim to it in fights over the Slot, including ace of aces Joe Foss.

The Zero was complemented by the two aircraft with which it shared deck space in the Mobile Fleet. The B5N, designed by Nakajima Aircraft's Katsuji Nakamura in response to a 1935 specification for a torpedo bomber to replace the Yokosuka B4Y, successfully competed with the Mitsubishi B5M for a production contract. The first prototype flew in January 1937 and was quickly ordered into production under the designation Navy Type 97 Carrier Attack Bomber *kyū-nana-shiki kanjō kōgeki-ki* or *kankō* (B5N1). The B5N2 with Nakajima's more powerful Sakae Model 11, 14-cylinder twin-row radial – also used in the A6M2 – appeared in 1940. Like its contemporary the TBD-1, it was the first IJNAF carrier type to feature all-metal monoplane construction with fully retractable landing gear, fully enclosed cockpit, and power-folding wings, with a maximum speed of 206 miles per hour and range of 1,230 miles. While the primary purpose was torpedo bombing, the B5N1 first saw combat in China in 1938 in its secondary role as a level bomber.

At the Battle of the Coral Sea, the ability of the B5N2 with the Type 91 torpedo to execute high-speed higher-altitude attacks astounded US Navy fighter pilots, who expected a low-speed/low-altitude torpedo attack similar to that of the TBD-1. Their ability to outrun the defenders had fatal results for USS *Lexington*. By the Battle of Midway, defending pilots discovered the lack of protection for the crew and fuel tanks, since it – like the Zero – depended on light weight to achieve its performance.

With the US Navy having demonstrated in fleet exercises that surface ships had almost no defense against dive bombing, the Imperial

Navy issued the 11-Shi specification for a monoplane carrier-based dive bomber to replace the existing D1A biplane then in service in 1936, about the same time the US Navy began development of the Vought SB2U dive bomber. Mitsubishi, Aichi, and Nakajima submitted designs, with the latter two asked to design and produce two prototypes each.

Aichi had worked closely with Germany's Heinkel company, with German engineers providing training for their Japanese counterparts. The Aichi design utilized a low-mounted elliptical wing inspired by Heinkel's He-70 "Blitz." Fixed landing gear enclosed in streamlined housings were used for simplicity, while power came from the 709hp Nakajima Hikari 1 nine-cylinder radial engine. The first 11-Shi prototype was finished in December 1937, with first flight trials beginning in January 1938. These initial tests revealed that the aircraft was underpowered and suffered from directional instability in wide turns, while it would snap roll in tight turns. When at their design speed of 200 knots, the dive brakes vibrated badly; the Navy wanted a 240-knot diving speed. The second prototype was extensively modified before delivery. The Hikari was replaced by the Mitsubishi Kinsei 3, with 839hp, in a redesigned cowling. The vertical tail was enlarged to cure directional instability, while wingspan was increased with washout in the outer sections to combat the snap rolls, and strengthened dive brakes were fitted. Tests revealed that the changes cured all the problems except directional instability; it was enough for the D3A1 to win over the Nakajima D3N1. The Imperial Navy ordered it in December 1939 as the Navy Type 99 Carrier Bomber Model 11 *kanjō bakugekiki* (dive bomber), abbreviated to *kanbaku*. The production D3A1 featured a slightly smaller wing and increased power from a 1,000hp Kinsei 43 or 1,070hp Kinsei 44. A long dorsal fin cured the directional instability and the bomber became so highly maneuverable that it could successfully engage enemy fighters.

The D3A1 was qualified for service aboard the carriers *Akagi* and *Kaga* in 1940. The bomber achieved its first major success against the Royal Navy during the Imperial Navy's Indian Ocean raid in April 1942, scoring 80 percent hits during attacks on two heavy cruisers and an aircraft carrier. D3A bombers contributed to sinking *Lexington* at Coral Sea, and *Yorktown* (CV-5) at Midway a month after that. *Enterprise* (CV-6) was seriously damaged at both the Battle of the Eastern Solomons and Santa Cruz while *Hornet* (CV-8) was sunk at Santa Cruz.

The improved D3A2 Model 22, powered by a 1,299hp Kinsei 54, appeared shortly after Midway and entered service in the fall of 1942. The extra power reduced range, so additional fuel tanks, increasing total fuel to 240 US gallons, provided the range needed to fight in the Solomons.

The primary bomber used by the Japanese in the Guadalcanal campaign was the Mitsubishi G4M1, a large twin-engine land-based medium bomber officially designated Navy Type 1 Land Attack Bomber, *Ichishiki rikujō kōgeki ki, Isshikirikukō* (G4M1), Imperial Navy pilots called it *Hamaki* (Cigar), originally due to the cylindrical shape of its fuselage, but by the summer of 1942 for its demonstrated unfortunate propensity to catch fire when its unprotected fuel tanks were hit.

The result of a 1938 Imperial Navy specification to succeed the G3M2 that had entered service the year before, the aircraft was designed by Mitsubishi's Kiro Honjo. The requirements were unprecedented, calling for a twin-engine bomber with a top speed of 247 miles per hour, an operating altitude of 9,800 feet, a range of 2,934 miles without bombs or torpedoes, and a range of 2,300 miles when carrying a 1,800-pound Type 91 torpedo or similar bomb load. The bomber's performance was achieved by structural lightness and a lack of protection, with no armor plating or self-sealing fuel tanks. The first prototype left Mitsubishi's Nagoya plant in September 1939 disassembled and loaded on five ox-drawn farm carts that transported it to Kagamigahara airfield 30 miles away. The first flight was on October 23, 1939, flown by test pilot Katsuzo Shima. Despite successful tests the Navy shelved it in favor of the more heavily armed G6M1 in hopes it could be used as heavy escort fighter for other bombers. When that failed, the G4M1 was officially adopted on April 2, 1941 and ordered into production.

The bomber's first operational success came on the opening day of war during the attack on Clark Air Base in the Philippines where defending antiaircraft guns could not reach its bombing altitude of 10,000 feet; this resulted in the destruction of the majority of USAAC aircraft in the islands, severely limiting the US defense. The next day, G4M1s and G3M2s carrying torpedoes sank the Royal Navy battleship *Prince of Wales* and battle cruiser *Repulse* off the coast of Malaya. Eventually known to the Allies as "Betty," the bomber also hit targets in Australia and was encountered operationally throughout the Pacific.

The G4M1's high speed made it difficult to intercept, while the 20mm cannon in the tail position was much heavier than was carried by other bombers of either side, making an attack from the stern quarter dangerous for an intercepting fighter. If the airplane did not catch fire after being hit in the wings that housed the gas tanks, it could remain airborne despite being badly damaged since the airframe was constructed as a single wing-fuselage unit to give it additional strength and thus allow the lightweight construction, which resulted in its high performance and long range. These qualities made the bomber among the most dangerous aerial weapons fielded by Japan until it came up against determined opposition.

2

WAR COMES TO THE SOUTH PACIFIC

January 4 – August 6

Twelve days after the fall of Wake, aircraft from the Imperial Japanese Navy 11th Air Fleet's land-based 5th Air Attack Force, flying from the Japanese air base at Truk, attacked the Australian base at Rabaul on January 4, 1942. Following the raid, just before dusk, 11 Yokohama Air Group Kawanishi H6K four-engine long-range flying boats bombed Vunakanau Airfield (just outside Rabaul) again; all of the estimated 40 bombs dropped fell far from the airfield. The attacks signaled that war had now come to the South Pacific. Simpson Harbor, the deep-water port at Rabaul, capital of the Bismarcks Protectorate on the island of New Britain in the Bismarck Archipelago northeast of the island of New Guinea, was the best deep-water port for use as a fleet anchorage in the South Pacific. The harbor was surrounded by active volcanoes and the rotting-egg smell of sulfur permeated the atmosphere. The archipelago, due south of the major Japanese Pacific base at Truk Atoll in the Japanese-controlled Caroline Islands of the Central Pacific, was the main barrier between the Japanese islands and New Guinea, with New Zealand and Australia beyond.

Japanese war planners planned to use Simpson Harbor and the two airfields ashore at Rabaul so that Japanese land, air, and naval forces would be able to expand simultaneously into New Guinea and down the 900-mile-long Solomon Islands chain toward the New Hebrides Islands, Samoa, and the Fijis, which would position them to sever the trans-Pacific maritime links between the United States and Australia and New Zealand. Such action might even force an early surrender by the two Pacific nations, leaving the reeling Allies without a regional strategic base from which to mount an offensive to recapture the Philippines and other Pacific territories that were then in the process of falling to the relentless Japanese advance through the western Pacific and Southeast Asia.

The Japanese airmen were in a difficult position. They wanted to cripple the Australian defenses, but they also wanted to avoid wrecking too many vital facilities at a base they expected to own in a few weeks. The Imperial Navy continued to mount large air raids against Rabaul while an invasion fleet escorted by the Pearl Harbor veterans *Kaga* and *Akagi* with seven cruisers and 14 destroyers departed Truk on January 14, bound for Rabaul.

The small Australian Army garrison on New Britain was composed of 1,400 men of the Australian Imperial Force and the New Guinea Volunteer Rifles (NGVR), known as "Lark Force" and commanded by Lieutenant Colonel John Scanlan. The heart of the force was the 700 men of the 2/22nd Infantry Battalion, commanded by Lieutenant Colonel Howard Carr. Personnel from a local militia unit, a coastal defense battery, an antiaircraft battery, and an anti-tank battery rounded out the force. The 2/22nd Battalion Band had been recruited from the ranks of the Salvation Army. The 130-man 2/1st Independent Company, a commando unit, had moved to garrison the island of New Ireland northwest of Rabaul across the Bismarck Sea.

On January 20, 100 A6M2 Type Zero fighters, D3A1 Type 99 dive bombers, and B5N2 Type 99 carrier attack planes launched from the two carriers attacked Rabaul in multiple waves. Eight Royal Australian Air Force (RAAF) Wirraway armed trainers took off to defend the port and in the ensuing fight three of the Wirraways were shot down, two crash-landed, and another was damaged, with six RAAF aircrew killed in action and five wounded. Defending antiaircraft fire brought down one of the attacking Japanese bombers. The raid destroyed the Australian coastal artillery defending the port and town of Rabaul and forced the small force of Australian infantry to withdraw from the town itself.

On January 21, 40 A6M fighters and 20 D3A dive bombers struck the port of Kavieng on New Ireland. At Rabaul that night, the Australian defenders prepared to meet the landing they knew would come, taking up positions along the western shore of Blanche Bay. As they did, the two flyable Wirraways, each with two wounded men in the rear cockpit, and a Lockheed Hudson also filled with wounded, took off from Lakunai airdrome, headed for Lae on the northern coast of New Guinea. Once the planes were gone, the airfield was set afire.

On the morning of January 22, an RAAF Catalina flying boat crew located the invasion fleet off Kavieng as the Imperial Army invaders were wading ashore and managed to send a signal before the Zero Combat Air Patrol (CAP) covering the fleet shot down the big flying boat. The Japanese took the main town of Kavieng without opposition and moved on to the airfield, where after a sharp fight the Australian commandos fell back towards the Sook River. Hours later, aircraft from the two carriers mounted final pre-invasion strikes against Rabaul.

With Kavieng in their possession, the invasion fleet approached Rabaul overnight and before dawn on January 23, the force entered Simpson Harbor. Colonel Masao Kusunose's 5,000 troops of the 144th Infantry Regiment prepared to land. The defenders fought in a series of desperate actions near the beaches around Simpson Harbor, Keravia Bay, and Raluana Point as they attempted to turn back the attackers. Lieutenant Colonel Ishiro Kuwada's 3rd Battalion was held up at Vulcan Beach by a mixed company of Australians from the 2/22nd Company and the NGVR, but elsewhere the other two battalions of the 144th landed at unguarded locations and moved inland, capturing Lakunai airdrome at a cost to the defenders of two officers and 26 enlisted personnel killed in action. Assessing the situation as hopeless, Colonel Scanlan ordered "every man for himself." Soldiers and civilians split into small groups and retreated into the jungle.

In the days following the capture of Rabaul, the Japanese began mopping-up operations. Australian soldiers remained at large in the interior for many weeks, but they had made no preparations for guerrilla warfare. Lacking supplies, their health and military effectiveness declined. The Japanese dropped leaflets from planes stating, "You can find neither food nor way of escape on this island and you will only die of hunger unless you surrender." Over 1,000 Australians were captured or surrendered during the following weeks after a Japanese force landed on February 9 at Gasmata, on the south coast, blocking their line of retreat.

The Japanese were not the only ones taking action in the South Pacific. Escorted by US Navy task forces built around the carriers *Enterprise* (CV-6) and *Yorktown* (CV-5), the US First Marine Brigade, built around the 1st Marine Division's 7th Marine Regiment (7th Marines), arrived in American Samoa on January 23, 1942, to bolster a Marine defense battalion deployed there since early 1941. On the same day, a detachment of Navy light scout planes also arrived in American Samoa, the first American-manned military aircraft to reach the vital stronghold.

On January 29, a US defense force that included the Army's 70th Pursuit Squadron with 25 crated Bell P-39 Airacobra fighters, arrived for duty at Suva, Fiji. That same day, far from the war zone in Washington, DC, the Allied Combined Chiefs of Staff established the ANZAC Area under US naval command. The new defensive region linked the defensive sectors in Australia, New Zealand, and New Caledonia.

On March 8, following the fall of the Bismarcks, the Japanese landed at Lae and Salamaua on the north coast of New Guinea. An attack by aircraft from *Lexington* and *Yorktown* on March 10 sank three transports and damaged several other ships, but by March 13 the Japanese were firmly in command of the region and soon moved A6Ms of the Tainan Air Corps, part of the 25th Air Flotilla, to the airfield at Lae to commence attacks against Port Moresby on the south coast of the big island preparatory to an invasion. The Imperial Navy pilots, including aces Petty Officers 1/c Saburo Sakai and Hiroyoshi Nishizawa, were veterans of the Philippines and Netherlands East Indies campaigns, and very happy to get away from the volcanic stench of Rabaul; they soon found themselves battling jungle diseases in New Guinea as they fought American and Australian defenders in the skies over Port Moresby.

Dale Brannon, who had joined the Air Corps in 1937 after running out of money to stay in school at Ohio State University during the depression, had discovered by 1940 that he liked service life well enough to consider a career, and was granted a regular commission as a first lieutenant. In the summer of 1941, having been one of three Army pilots to fly Bell Aircraft's prototype P-39s and therefore considered "experienced," he was assigned to the 67th Pursuit Squadron, a unit created the year before as a training and replacement squadron of the new 58th Pursuit Group, since they were scheduled to re-equip with the new Bell fighter. Immediately following Pearl Harbor, he reported to Harding Army Airfield at Baton Rouge, Louisiana, where the squadron had relocated, to find himself in command. As he later recalled, "There were only three of us at the time – all first lieutenants – me and Lieutenants Jim Jarmon and Tommy Thompson."

Over the course of December, the squadron was fleshed out with the arrival of a group of brand-new second lieutenants freshly graduated from flight school. During the few weeks until they were ordered to prepare for overseas movement, Brannon was able to scrounge some decrepit P-35s and P-36s from other units on the base so the new pilots could gain as much valuable flight time as possible. They soon departed, traveling aboard what Brannon recalled as railroad cars with wooden bench seats that must have last been used on the Transcontinental Railroad, cooking their meals in the baggage car, to Fort Dix, New Jersey, where they learned they were headed to the South Pacific. On January 24, they departed New York Harbor aboard the transport *Thomas H. Barry*, the former passenger liner SS *Oriental*, as part of a five-ship convoy. Another freighter in the convoy carried 45 disassembled and crated P-400s and two P-39Fs; "P-400" was the designation given to the Airacobra I fighters originally built for the British that were sequestered by the Army Air Forces in the wake of Pearl Harbor. The voyage to Panama was not without danger, since the German U-boat offensive known as Operation *Paukenschlag* (Drumbeat) had just begun, with ships torpedoed and sunk all along the Atlantic coast. Once through the canal, they were escorted across the Pacific by the light cruiser USS *Honolulu* (CL-48) and two destroyers to Melbourne, arriving on February 26, 1942, after 38 days at sea.

After a week in Australia, the squadron went aboard the transport *R.S. Berry*, headed for New Caledonia, arriving on March 15, 1942. The Army's 810th and 811th Engineer Aviation Battalions also unloaded, assigned to improve and build air bases in the region. Dale Brannon learned that the 67th's assignment was to provide air defense for the island, based at the half-completed airfield at Tontuta, 35 miles from Nouméa. The one truck and trailer available on the island took one crated plane to Tontuta every eight hours, alternately groaning and highballing over the mountainous road over two weeks. When the crates and men had all made the move and the crates were pried open, they found the P-400s, and instruction manuals for P-39Ds, Fs, and Ks but none for P-400s. Neither Master Sergeant Foye nor

Technical Sergeant Nebock – the two experienced mechanics in the squadron – had ever seen an Airacobra before. Still, the two noncoms took control of the assembly work. The men slept under shelter halves while the 44 pilots moved into a farmhouse, setting up sleeping bags in the parlor, bedroom, and earth-floored basement. All were soon united in cursing the sudden, unpredictable rainstorms and fighting the mosquitoes.

There were ten kits of simple first-echelon maintenance tools available for assembly. Fuel lines were found plugged with Scotch tape; the electrical circuits of one P-400 had evidently been assembled by a factory maniac: pressing the flap switch resulted in retraction of the main gear, while pressing the gear switch fired the guns. Regardless, in an astounding feat of engineering acuity and a real talent for scrounging what was needed, on the 28th day of assembly, 41 P-400s that had been assembled with the aid of the 65th Materiel Squadron and the construction of an A-frame from coconut tree trunks to raise the fuselages so they could be walked above the wings for mating, stood on the field. Brannon, the pilot with the most P-39 experience, test-flew each as it was completed and checked out the rest of the pilots with only a single accident. Finding that the P-400's flight instruments were inferior, they learned how to fly without them. Spare parts all came from salvage. One Airacobra, named "the Resurrection," was built from parts of four different aircraft that each lacked major components. Once the planes were assembled and found flight-worthy, the ground crews set to painting fierce shark faces on the planes, inspired by photographs of the Flying Tigers in Burma that were featured in the new issue of *Life* magazine which arrived that month.

Fortunately for the 67th, the squadron soon welcomed several fliers who had managed to make it out of the Philippines. Brannon recalled, "They were mostly all lieutenants, along with three captains." One was Captain Thomas J.J. "Jack" Christian, great-great-grandson of Confederate General Stonewall Jackson. Soon thereafter, Captain Jack Bruce took command and Brannon became a flight leader. "I was fine with that, since those guys knew what was what and the rest of us didn't." These men, who had seen combat during the first months of the war, were able to spread their hard-won knowledge of the enemy to the green pilots who formed the rest of the unit. The pilots of the 67th flew as often as possible to become familiar with their new mounts.

With other Japanese air forces in the Dutch East Indies attacking Darwin in Australia, there was much doubt regarding the ability of the Allied forces in the Southwest Pacific to successfully stop the Japanese. One man had no such doubts. So far as Admiral Ernest J. King, Commander-in-Chief US Fleet, and the rest of the top leadership of the US Navy were concerned, they had been forced to enter the Pacific War with one hand tied behind their backs. That was because of the "Germany First" strategy that President Roosevelt and Prime Minister Churchill had agreed to at the Arcadia Conference shortly after the United States began supplying Britain through Lend-Lease, eight months before the Pearl Harbor attack.

Knowing of this decision, when they developed their strategy for the coming Pacific War, Japanese planners worked with the expectation that they would have until early 1943 to prepare for an American counterattack. So far as Admiral King was concerned, "Germany First" be damned; he worked to his own schedule and had no intention of giving the enemy a year to consolidate their victories and fortify their conquered territories while his navy transported the US Army to England, then waited for the defeat of Hitler before rolling back the opponent that the US Navy had been preparing to fight for the previous 20 years.

Following the fall of Rabaul, King moved forcefully in the halls of power in Washington to advocate for an offensive that would move through the Solomon Islands and the Bismarck Archipelago to eventually retake Rabaul, starting that summer. King had a strong ally in his determination not to stand back in the Pacific. General Douglas MacArthur, newly escaped from the Philippines and installed in Australia as Allied supreme commander in the Southwest Pacific, also dreamed of retaking Rabaul as soon as he could convince his superiors in Washington to provide the necessary armed forces. At this time, MacArthur's command included Rabaul, the Bismarcks, and the Solomons. His proposal involved a lightning offensive to retake Rabaul, moving from New Guinea. At this point, traditional Army–Navy rivalry came to the fore; King was adamantly opposed to his navy playing a subordinate role to the Army, which would be the case were MacArthur's proposal to become the US South Pacific strategy, particularly since he had personal experience of just how lacking was MacArthur's knowledge of naval operations. Much of the US Navy's war strategy for 1942–43 was set soon after March 2, when King was named Chief of Naval Operations (CNO) in addition to his ongoing assignment as Commander-in-Chief (COMINCH). The admiral quickly proposed that Efate Island in the French New Hebrides be established as the place "from which a step-by-step advance could be made through the New Hebrides, Solomons, and Bismarcks."

On March 11, the ship carrying VMF-111's 19 F4F-3s arrived at American Samoa from San Diego. The Wildcats were unloaded and based at Tutuila Field, providing air defense for the island. The next day, the 17,500-man US Army Task Force 6814 arrived in Nouméa to secure the defense of New Caledonia. This was the first concrete evidence of a serious American will to contain a potential Japanese move from Rabaul toward Samoa, a move that – if successful – would sever the vital sea lanes linking Australia and New Zealand with the United States.

The Japanese made their next move on March 13, when an invasion flotilla departed Rabaul for Buka, an island off northern Bougainville at the northern end of the Solomons Archipelago. An Imperial Navy landing force swiftly occupied the island; work began shortly thereafter on an emergency airstrip that would later evolve into a major air base, while plans were made for the further development of both Buka and Bougainville.

In Washington on March 14, the US Joint Chiefs of Staff decided to wage the Pacific War with forces already deployed, while building up a much larger combat force in the United Kingdom for service against Germany and its Axis partners in Europe and North Africa. Thus, the Joint Chiefs forced a defensive holding strategy for the Pacific. In the meantime, the buildup of forces continued as King prepared to confront his fellow chiefs with a *fait accompli*.

Units of Army Task Force 6814 arrived at the island of Efate from New Caledonia on March 18. Also on March 18, an independent US Army infantry regiment arrived to defend Bora Bora in the French Society Islands. The Army force was joined by an advance ground detachment of Marine Air Group 24, including VMF-212 ground personnel, on March 25; their first assignment was to help the Army build an advance airfield at Vila, Efate.

On April 2, Marine Air Group 13 headquarters arrived at American Samoa's Tutuila Field, where the air group staff assumed control of regional air defenses. On April 6, VMSB-151's obsolete Curtiss SBC biplane dive bombers were loaded aboard ship at Norfolk, Virginia, and soon departed for American Samoa, arriving there on May 9. On April 14, the newly reorganized VMF-211, which had replaced the squadron lost at Wake Island, departed Hawaii aboard the fleet carrier *Lexington* for duty on Palmyra Island. The pilots, ground crews, administrative troops, and 14 Brewster F2A-3 fighters arrived on April 18. On April 30, Vila Field on Efate was declared operational.

King and MacArthur were forced to put their plans for an offensive on hold in mid-April, when US intelligence discovered the Japanese plan to reinforce their army in New Guinea and undertake an invasion of Port Moresby, while also moving southeast into the Solomon Islands. On May 3, the Japanese landing on Tulagi in the southern Solomons, site of a world-class fleet anchorage, seemed to set the stage for the new enemy offensive in the South Pacific when troops of the Yokohama Special Naval Landing Force came ashore unopposed. In the Imperial Navy's plans, Tulagi was slated for use as an advance seaplane base from which Allied bases in the New Hebrides could be reconnoitered and harassed. The Japanese arrival led to a largely panicked exodus of civilian residents of the Solomons. However, many stayed, chiefly gold miners and religious workers. A fair number of volunteers, mostly former military and government workers, also stayed behind to monitor the Japanese throughout the Solomons under the auspices of the Royal Australian Navy's radio-linked reconnaissance network that would come to be known as the "coastwatchers."

At 0845 hours on May 4, 28 SBD-3 dive bombers and 12 TBD-1 torpedo bombers from *Yorktown*'s Air Group 5 attacked the Japanese invasion flotilla and shore facilities at Tulagi. During this and two follow-on attacks, one destroyer, one small cargo ship, and four landing craft were sunk, and an auxiliary cruiser was damaged and forced aground. The escorting VF-42 F4F pilots shot down two of the new A6M2-N seaplane fighters, then strafed the many H6K flying boats and six A6M2-Ns moored in the harbor. Three SBDs and two F4Fs took hits and made forced landings on nearby Guadalcanal, becoming the first Americans to set foot on that island. They were rescued by Solomon Islanders working for coastwatcher Martin Dempsey and were picked up by a Catalina that flew in from New Caledonia.

Following the strategic victory at the Battle of Coral Sea in May, which saw the loss of the US carrier *Lexington* on May 8 as the price of stopping the planned Japanese invasion of Port Moresby, new Allied forces arrived in the South Pacific. On May 10, Navy Seabee construction engineers commenced work on an advance airstrip at Upolo, in the French Wallis Islands. On May 11, VMF-212's 21 Wildcats arrived at New Caledonia aboard the carriers *Hornet* and *Enterprise*. May 13 saw Army ground forces arrive in Fiji to take over defense of the islands from the Royal New Zealand Army. On May 17, the 68th Fighter Squadron at Tongatabu began a transition from their P-400s to P-40E fighters. On May 26, an advance detachment of VMF-212 Wildcats flew from New Caledonia to Vila Field, Efate.

Within a matter of days after Coral Sea, intelligence revealed that the Imperial Navy was set to make a move in the Central Pacific that – if successful – would gain all of Admiral Yamamoto's original goals in his plan for the Pacific War. This quickly led to the Battle of Midway on June 4–5, in which the Japanese Combined Fleet lost the heart of its carrier striking force – the Pearl Harbor veterans *Akagi*, *Kaga*, *Soryu*, and *Hiryu* – in exchange for the American loss of *Yorktown*. After five and a half months' garrison duty on Midway, Marion Carl and his fellow fighter pilots, along with the crews of VMSB-241 which had been on the island since April, entered combat. By the second day of the battle, both units had suffered losses that left them incapable of engaging in further combat, while Carl had demonstrated his ability as a fighter pilot by shooting down a Zero.

The US Navy had, within a space of 30 days, brought the heretofore unstoppable Japanese offensive to a stop. King saw the Midway victory as his moment to gain official support and approval for his planned offensive. While others in the top naval circles counseled delay until the "new navy" then under construction was ready to enter combat the next year, pointing to the fact that the Imperial Navy was still a major threat to the US Navy as it then existed in the Pacific, King was adamant in his desire to take the offensive.

On May 28, Pacific Area commander Admiral Chester Nimitz had proposed that the US 1st Marine Raider Battalion should seize Tulagi Island as a first step in the projected Allied Pacific War offensive. The first concrete follow-up to the admiral's proposal occurred the day before the Battle of Midway on June 3, when a B-17 of the 19th Bomb Group's

New Guinea-based 435th Bomb Squadron photographed Tulagi. It was the first Allied reconnaissance mission over the area since prior to Coral Sea. For the moment, reconnaissance and some minor harassment were all the Allies could undertake in the Eastern Solomons. It was easy to *imagine* a mission to take Tulagi, but it was another matter entirely to launch an unsupported battalion of heavy infantry into the face of an enemy who could be massively supported in resisting the attack or re-conquering Tulagi.

A meeting in mid-June between King and Army Chief of Staff General George C. Marshall resolved the conflict between King's and MacArthur's proposals for the moment by creation of a three-task plan: Task One was the capture of Tulagi in the Solomons, which the Japanese had turned into an advanced air base capable of interdicting Allied convoys from the United States to Australia; Task Two was an advance by MacArthur's forces along the northern New Guinea coast; Task Three was the capture of Rabaul, which was foreseen as happening in late 1943. As it turned out, this was close to the schedule of what actually happened, other than at the end it was decided to bypass Rabaul.

However, before any further actions could be taken, military politics had to be dealt with. By decision of the Joint Chiefs on March 5, 1942, the Solomon Islands were firmly planted in the kingdom of the Southwest Pacific Theater ruled by General MacArthur, while the Santa Cruz Islands immediately southwest of the Solomons lay in Admiral Nimitz's Pacific domain. MacArthur's protests that he should command were to no avail; George C. Marshall was no "MacArthur Man," having seen the general in action over the previous 20 years, and King held similar views. The two cordially changed the map, shifting the boundary between the Southwest Pacific and Pacific Ocean areas 360 miles west as of August 1, 1942; the Solomon Islands as far north as Bougainville, the New Hebrides, and Fiji were then sub-divided and assigned to the new South Pacific Theater, controlled by the US Navy. MacArthur received orders to place his New Guinea forces in support of the coming Solomons operation. At the same time, he was to develop a plan to retake the northern coast of New Guinea and the island of New Britain, creating a two-pronged attack against Rabaul once the Solomons were under Allied control. Espiritu Santo in the New Hebrides became headquarters for the new South Pacific command.

Admiral Nimitz's personal favorite for the job of Commander South Pacific Theater (ComSoPac) was Admiral William Pye, the interim Pacific Fleet commander prior to Nimitz. The conservative battleship admiral did not meet with King's approval, though the two were 1901 Naval Academy classmates. King's nominee, Vice Admiral Robert Ghormley, was known as an intelligent organizer who could pull together the forces and resources of several branches of service and of several nations. Prior to his return to Washington on April 17, he had been the American naval observer in London. Following the establishment of the command, King named Ghormley commander of the South Pacific Area (SoPac) and, concurrently, commander of the South Pacific Force, with orders to proceed to Auckland, New Zealand, and establish a headquarters. He was to mount an expedition to the Tonga Islands to prepare a forward base that would support a late-summer offensive against an as-yet-undisclosed Japanese base. Nimitz, who also knew Ghormley from their days together at Annapolis, concurred with King's decision, since he knew that Ghormley had a personal connection to President Roosevelt from serving at the White House, which might predispose the president to support the new plan.

At the outset, Ghormley was forced to overcome the problem that he had no troops with which to garrison the Tonga Islands and certainly none with which to mount an offensive. He had no staff. He did not even have adequate charts of the vast realm he was to organize and oversee. It took Ghormley two weeks to assemble a staff from among the best men available.

Most important of these was the appointment of newly promoted Rear Admiral Richmond Kelly Turner to take on the vital task of organizing and commanding the South Pacific Force's transport and logistics, should any of either turn up. A prickly naval intellectual known *sotto voce* as "Terrible Turner," he had just been promoted to rear admiral and relieved as head of the Naval War Plans staff. Aircraft South Pacific (AirSoPac) went to Rear Admiral John S. "Slew" McCain, a peppery Mississippian, who, like Turner, had been at Annapolis at the same time as Ghormley and Nimitz and had belatedly become a naval aviator in the early 1930s. McCain soon established the AirSoPac headquarters aboard the seaplane tender USS *Curtiss* (AV-4), the Navy's first purpose-build seaplane tender, in New Caledonia's Nouméa

Harbor; the ship also provided the major aircraft parts repair shop in the South Pacific.

The first component of the future Cactus Air Force to reach SoPac was the Seventh Air Force's 11th Heavy Bombardment Group, equipped with the Boeing B-17E Flying Fortress. Its members were trained and initially deployed to undertake search-reconnaissance flights and/or maritime long-range bombing missions. On June 20, 1942, the day Brigadier General Willis Hale assumed command of the Seventh Air Force, the count of operational, relatively modern B-17Es was 63: 47 on Oahu and 16 on Midway.

On July 4, 1942, Colonel LaVerne G. "Blondie" Saunders' 11th Bomb Group was selected to supply an advance force of 107 carefully selected ground crew for duty in Fiji and the New Hebrides. The group's flight echelon, 35 B-17Es equipped with the new "ball" turret in their belly as replacement for the useless remote-control turret, was to follow after the ground echelon had reached the new stations, with 27 B-17s based on New Caledonia and eight at Nandi, on Viti Levu, Fiji's main island and administrative center.

On July 15, the 12 B-26A Marauders of the 38th Bombardment Group's 70th Medium Bombardment Squadron arrived from Hawaii at Nandi, while ten other Marauders arrived at New Caledonia. On July 16, a flight echelon of two squadrons of the 11th Bomb Group departed Oahu's Hickam Field.

On July 21, the 11th Bomb Group's 98th Heavy Bombardment Squadron arrived at New Caledonia's new Plaines des Gaiacs airdrome, followed by the 42nd Bomb Squadron. Completing the group's redeployment to SoPac, the 431st Bomb Squadron arrived in Fiji on July 24, and the 26th Bomb Squadron arrived at Plaines des Gaiacs on July 25.

Colonel Saunders later described the unloading facilities at Espiritu Santo as "one barge, a sandy beach and a prayer." A ship unloading heavy equipment could only sling it over the side into a lighter; some of the gear was of such size that the trip to shore was a race to get there before the lighter sank. There were no cranes ashore, while the small finger piers were constructed of coconut logs salted down with coral; they were constantly being rebuilt, since they would wash out to sea and disappear after two or three weeks' use. There was no overall central supply control system to keep track of shipments, which meant that often the first information the group supply officer received regarding arrival dates of supplies was when he learned a ship had arrived in harbor. This meant that crates and boxes accumulated in the coconut groves since there was no way to anticipate storage needs. On Espiritu Santo, there was no question of living off the country for any unit. All food, clothing, and housing had to be brought in from the States. The one thing Espiritu possessed in abundance was a foot-thick covering of soft black dirt that became a quagmire after the frequent tropical rainstorms.

Supplying the B-17 squadrons in SoPac added a whole dimension of challenge. The Navy took on the responsibility to provide aviation gasoline and ammunition. The first shipment was 300,000 gallons of fuel, which was estimated to be enough for two weeks of flying plus a 100-percent overage for emergency use. The entire load lasted just ten days. Realizing that they were vulnerable to the vagaries of shipping schedules, the supply sections anticipated a long wait for more fuel, but 3,000 drums miraculously arrived aboard the cargo ship *Nira Luckenbach* in time to prevent the patrol schedule from going awry. When *Nira Luckenbach* arrived, the steel drums were dumped over the ship's side and floated ashore in nets, where they were hand-rolled up under the trees, then dispersed in dumps of 20–30 drums. They were then loaded on trucks, rolled up on stands, and emptied into the tank wagons which serviced aircraft. There were no gas trucks or trailers.

Loading fuel aboard the bombers was a practical improbability that was nonetheless accomplished, somehow. For the 26th Squadron's August 7 search missions from Efate, all hands – including Blondie Saunders, the group's commanding officer, and Brigadier General William C. Rose, commander of Army troops on Efate and Espiritu Santo – turned out in a heavy rainstorm on August 6 to man a literal bucket brigade that required 20 hours of backbreaking struggle to hand-fill the fuel tanks of the B-17s with 25,000 gallons of avgas.

The 11th Group had no access to field telephones or motor transport, which made operating from any of the group's bases a real test. Likewise, the distribution of the squadrons to their several bases, compounded by inadequate long-range communications, made it almost impossible to schedule planes from more than one squadron for any given mission. Typically, the group was able to get several planes off for each day's scheduled search missions as well as maintaining a mobile force of six bomb-laden on-call strike aircraft on the ground.

Working and living conditions throughout SoPac's front-line holdings were horrific, nothing short of appalling. Nouméa's Plaines des Gaiacs airdrome had been built in the middle of a swamp parked in the middle of a bowl of red earth that produced storms of iron oxide dust, which played havoc with any metal parts built to rub against other metal parts. Engine lubricants had to be changed out after only six flying hours, which put a major strain on parts and fuel inventories designed to last much longer. Nine maintenance men accompanied the nine 26th Squadron B-17s, and they doubled as ground crew. The 26th owed a debt of gratitude to the African-American enlisted men of the 24th Infantry Regiment, who helped service the planes and even improvised spare parts in their machine shop. The airmen on Efate messed with artillerymen, while on Espiritu Santo the entire 98th Squadron, including Colonel Saunders, slept under trees or the wings of their bombers, or in the Forts themselves. In addition to their full flying schedule, the combat aircrewmen undertook a large share of maintenance and servicing of their airplanes.

The aircraft revetments were hacked out of the jungle and were barely deep enough to keep a B-17's nose off the runway. They were so narrow a crewman had to stand at each wing tip to guide the pilots out to the short taxiway, then stay on the wing to keep the bomber from hitting the trees that bordered the taxiway while moving toward the runway. The runway had no lights; for pre-dawn takeoffs, bottles of oil with paper wicks were placed along the runway so their flickering light could mark the runway boundary, while parked jeeps with their headlights on marked the runway's end.

Nandi, most rearward of the 11th Group's bases, was clean and quiet when compared to the forward bases and thus served as a rest area and the only convenient place for engine changes. Conditions at the forward bases were so primitive that Colonel Saunders regularly relieved his units after only one week there.

The machine shop on Admiral McCain's flagship *Curtiss* was enlisted to build an array of replacement parts and devices for the bombers, but complicated tools such as navigation aids had to come from sources outside the combat region, often with long delays and scheduling headaches. Engine changes and other heavy maintenance had to be handled at Nandi, where the port and airfield facilities were reasonably modern and mud free. But there was no way to build new spare engines in-theater, and resupply of new engines from outside SoPac was difficult to contemplate, much less schedule. Improvisation only got the 11th so far; more and more of its B-17s had to be sidelined to await critical replacement parts or cannibalized to keep others flying.

By August 18, the group's supply situation was critical: six ball turret hatches had broken off and there were no spares. There was trouble with turbosupercharger regulators as well as flight and engine instruments. Engine changes were constantly necessary due to the dusty fields, but the 12 spares at Nandi were already in service and the next change at Plaines des Gaiacs would exhaust the entire engine supply in New Caledonia.

While the Air Force reorganized itself for the coming offensive, the Navy was doing the same in the aftermath of Midway. One of the young pilots involved in all this was Ensign Francis Roland Register, who had immediately picked up the nickname "Cash" during his flight training at Pensacola. Register had graduated with his Wings of Gold on December 12, the Friday after Pearl Harbor, with orders to Fighting 3 (VF-3), at the time assigned to the *Saratoga* air group. While aviators like VMSB-232's Commander, Lieutenant Colonel Richard H. Mangrum, lamented in later years that they had followed the Navy-wide order not to keep a diary, Register was one of those who defied the order and kept a concise account of his life in the Navy during the momentous year of 1942.

By the time Ensign Register arrived in Hawaii in January, having taken the opportunity during his graduation leave to get married, *Saratoga* had already been torpedoed for its first time in the war and had recently departed for repair in Seattle. While VF-3 had gone aboard *Lexington* and departed for the South Pacific, Register was stuck at NAS Barber's Point until the squadron returned with *Lexington* in mid-March. The young ensign was assigned as wingman for Lieutenant (jg) Marion W. Dufilho in the VF-3 division led by Lieutenant Edward H. "Butch" O'Hare, now the first Navy ace of the war after his epic defense of *Lexington* against attacking Japanese bombers. Register later assigned all the credit for his survival at Guadalcanal to the on-the-job training he received from O'Hare and Dufilho.

Register was considered too junior and inexperienced to be among the VF-3 pilots who went back aboard *Lexington* to flesh out VF-2 for the Battle of the Coral Sea. He returned to the United States with the remainder of VF-3, now commanded by Butch O'Hare, where they reunited with *Saratoga* when it came out of the repair yard. The carrier departed for Hawaii on May 31, but did not arrive in time to participate in the Battle of Midway. The month of June saw the squadron train hard, and Register was pleased to record in his diary for June 30 that he had been told by executive officer (XO) Lieutenant Albert O. "Scoop" Vorse that he "flew like a veteran." Rumors abounded about what they were going to do. When a request went around for volunteers to move over to VF-8, Register considered doing so, having learned that VF-3 would not be among the squadrons participating in the coming action, but Butch O'Hare counseled him to remain with the squadron.

In Washington, Task One became Operation *Huddle* on July 2, covering the invasion and occupation of Santa Cruz Island in the southern Solomons, followed by Operation *Pestilence* to take the Japanese base at Tulagi and the neighboring Florida Island. On July 8, 1942, all previous plans were cast aside when the photo technicians of the USAAF's 14th Reconnaissance Squadron at Espiritu Santo saw the prints that emerged in the darkroom from the film taken that day by a B-17 sent to photograph Tulagi and the surrounding islands in preparation for Operations *Huddle* and *Pestilence*. A major Japanese airfield capable of supporting long-range bombers was under construction and nearing completion at Lunga Point on the large island of Guadalcanal across Sealark Sound from Tulagi. Such an airfield would allow the Imperial Naval Air Force to interdict and perhaps cut the crucial Allied supply line that passed through the Coral Sea to Australia. *Huddle* and *Pestilence* were quickly forgotten. In a matter of 72 hours, Operation *Watchtower* was hurriedly presented to the Joint Chiefs. The objective now was to land the 1st Marine Division on Guadalcanal and take the airfield before it could be completed. Time was of the essence.

Things moved fast in Hawaii. Register wrote in his diary:

July 5, 1942 – Today was a big day. Much happened and after much work and seeing the right people, I am going to be transferred to Fighting Six with seven other flyers. We will go out on the *Enterprise* in about a week. All the new VF squadrons are to be 36 plane squadrons. Three CV are to go out and I believe we will meet the

Wasp and possibly some Army transports. I think this is the start of our offensive and will probably be the biggest battle of the war so far. Am glad I can be in on it.

The night of July 9, Register was able to take time to fill in his diary for the preceding days:

July 8, 1942 – Today was the big day. In the morning, we prepared to fly our 36 planes out to the *Enterprise* which was about 100 miles out of Oahu. We left about 1300 and landed aboard about 1500. A fighter that landed behind me had a bad crack up, washing his plane out entirely. He came through the barrier and ended up very close to me. Many pilots have been killed while sitting in their planes and the fellow behind running into them. The *Enterprise* is a very nice ship with comfortable quarters. A TBF went over the side while landing.

July 9, 1942 – Today was probably the fullest day I have ever put in and the most tired I have ever been. Got up at 0320 for flight quarters and received a lot of information. At 0630 took off for some tactical maneuvers with 36 VF and 36 US VB. Landed at Maui, then took off again for another problem of bombing the carrier. Flew 6½ hours of very strenuous flying, but learned a great deal. We are rehearsing a coming raid. It is now 2130 and we just secured.

Also aboard *Enterprise* was Scouting 5 (VS-5), late of *Yorktown's* air group but now part of *Enterprise's* air group. Lieutenant Turner Caldwell had taken command at the end of June. Three years earlier, fresh out of Pensacola after winning his Wings of Gold, Caldwell had reported to the squadron as assistant navigation officer. Two weeks after taking command, he led the squadron aboard *Enterprise* with the rest of the air group. He later recalled, "A week after we reported aboard, we learned the ship was headed for the South Pacific, with rumors flying everywhere through *Enterprise* that we would be involved in a 'big operation.' As it turned out, the rumors had no idea how big an operation we were about to become involved in."

Throughout the months after Pearl Harbor, Marine aviators in Hawaii were standing up new squadrons. VMSB-232's commander, Lieutenant Colonel Richard H. Mangrum, who had learned the art of dive bombing flying O2U Corsairs in Honduras as a young Marine aviator back in 1928, had suffered the loss of all his squadron's SB2U-3s during the Pearl Harbor attack, the result of what he later described as "a real first-class strafing attack." Over the months after that, "We were reforming, joining new pilots, splitting squadrons like amoebas, with each half becoming a new squadron. Gradually, very gradually, new aircraft were made available." The effort moved into high gear following the Battle of Midway as it became clear that Marines would soon enter combat in the South Pacific.

Two weeks after Midway, Marine Air Group 23's two fighter squadrons – VMF-223, commanded by Captain John L. Smith, and VMF-224, commanded by Captain Robert Galer – returned to MCAS Ewa from Kauai with the ten F2A-3s they had flown as the sole air defense of northern Hawaii since early January. On arrival, the two squadron commanders were congratulated on their promotions to major and informed that they had six weeks to train the large group of newly graduated second lieutenants waiting for them, before they deployed to the South Pacific. In place of the F2A-3s that had demonstrated their combat inadequacy over Midway, there were brand new Grumman F4F-4 Wildcats on the flight line, to be divided between the two squadrons.

Years later, Robert E. "Bob" Galer – by then legendary as one of three Marine aviators awarded the Medal of Honor for combat at Guadalcanal, the place where they were then unknowingly headed – recalled that of his wartime accomplishments:

> I was most proud of the fact that, with three other experienced pilots, I took 22 kids right out of flight school, and with 40 hours of training, qualified them to operate off an aircraft carrier, to fly their planes in combat, and use their guns effectively – tasks that before the war would have taken 40 hours of training for each. And every one of them acquitted themselves admirably when we got to Guadalcanal.

Smith, born December 26, 1914, in Lexington, Oklahoma, graduated from the University of Oklahoma in May 1936 with a Reserve Officers Training Corps (ROTC) commission as a second lieutenant in the Army Field Artillery and took a Marine commission that July. Entering flight training at Pensacola in July 1938, he pinned on the Wings of Gold of a naval aviator in July 1939 with an assignment to dive bombers.

Over the following three years, he made a reputation for himself in the Corps as a tough, abrasive officer, a moody and sarcastic hard-driving disciplinarian, yet at the same time ambitious and determined. He was lucky to find three survivors of VMF-221 assigned to his unit. Marion Carl, Clayton Canfield, and Roy Corry had flown together at Midway, calling themselves "the three Cs." Carl became operations officer while Canfield and Corry became 3rd and 4th Division leaders respectively. The 22 young pilots they were now responsible for had an average of 180 flying hours in their logbooks. Fortunately, gunnery was a fetish with Smith, who honed the squadron over the next five weeks; under his leadership, the pilots concentrated their efforts on improving their fighting and flying skills.

Dick Mangrum's VMSB-232 had received SBD-2s as hand-me-downs from *Enterprise*'s Bombing 6 following the carrier's return from the Doolittle Raid at the end of April, when that squadron was finally able to re-equip with SBD-3s in preparation for Midway. Mangrum had possession of the well-used Dauntlesses for less than two weeks before they were taken away and sent on to Midway to reinforce VMSB-241 the week before the battle. In the weeks after, Mangrum commanded a squadron without any airplanes. Two weeks after Midway, he thanked the gods for having Captain Bruce Prosser report aboard from having flown SB2U-3 Vindicators with VMSB- 241 in the battle, later describing Prosser as "the backbone of the squadron" while they trained, beloved by the younger pilots for his willingness to impart to them everything he had learned the hard way.

On July 5, VMF-223's Smith and VMSB-232's Mangrum were informed they would be going to war in 30 days, departing Hawaii by the end of the month for the South Pacific to support the Marine landing in the Solomons. Mangrum later recalled:

I was reasonably dumbfounded because my squadron within the month had been divided again. Some 12 new pilots who were fresh out of flight training in Pensacola had joined at the first of the month. Looking at their flight logbooks, I was appalled to discover that none of them had much over 200 hours in the air and that two of then had slightly less than 200 hours of flying of all types in the air, and none in the aircraft which we were equipped. I shall never forget being, of course, admonished that this was of the utmost top secrecy and that no one, NO ONE!, even my executive officer or anyone else in my squadron, was to be told where we were going. We were to be ready for combat, ready for departure on August 1st. So, I left the colonel's office and went back to my squadron's headquarters where I was greeted by my sergeant major, and his first question was, "Major, where's Guadalcanal?" We had one solid month of working as hard as we could, day and night, to try to bring these people up to some degree of combat effectiveness.

On July 8, VMSB-232 received their own airplanes:

When the decision had been made for my squadron to go on the Solomons operation, very rapidly I was provided with 12 new SBD-3 aircraft, which were newly delivered from the United States. This was only two-thirds of the normal strength of a squadron at that time, but there weren't any more available. I left with 12 aircraft and 15 pilots. Only three spare pilots for the 12 aircraft. It was later decided that a full squadron would be 18 aircraft with 53 pilots in order to provide depth.

Mangrum and Prosser led their young pilots in dive-bombing practice every day as they put them and their freshly arrived gunners through a frantic shakedown course, while Smith put his pilots in the air for every available hour they could get for gunnery practice.

Enterprise (CV-6), *Saratoga* (CV-3), and *Wasp* (CV-7) departed Pearl Harbor on July 16. Ensign Register later wrote in his diary:

July 17, 1942 – Our destination for this trip is Tongatabu, southeast of the Fiji Islands. Don't know how long we will be there; probably not very long. I think it will be soon though when we are to see some real action. Possibly the start of our offensive. Position: 0730; Long. 162-34; Lat. N-12-09; Course 195; Speed 16.

July 18, 1942 – Did not fly today. It rained a good part of the time. We are drawing very near to the Equator. Had mock torpedo attacks which were very good and interesting. The fighters strafed the CV. Enterprise can really turn sharp, and really heels over. Long. 196-14; Lat. N-6-38; Course 164; Speed 21 (0630)

July 19, 1942 – We crossed the Equator at 1253 today, then 18 of us took off and flew over it. We lost an SBD today on a search. We all think he got lost as the radar picked him up 90 miles away, but couldn't reach him. 0630 Long. 165-10; Lat. N-1-10; Course 164; Speed 21. Crossed the Equator at 1253 at long. 165-48.

In the Solomons, there were no trained Army personnel or Army photographic equipment available for aerial reconnaissance photographic work. Thus, cameras came from the Navy, while photographers were Marines from newly arrived Marine Observation Squadron 251 (VMO-251). The only USAAF participation in the aerial reconnaissance of the Solomons was the provision of the B-17s that carried the cameras and photographers. The Navy unit at Espiritu Santo responsible for aerial reconnaissance was known as "Quackenbush's Gypsies," for their leader, Lieutenant Commander Robert Quackenbush.

"Quackenbush's Gypsies" flew their first mission on July 23, when two 11th Group B-17s manned by several Marine photographers from VMO-251 flew to Guadalcanal and Tulagi islands to get photos for invasion planning. The B-17s were attacked by Tulagi-based A6M2-N floatplane fighters, but they failed even to damage any of the Flying Fortresses.

Enterprise arrived at Tongatabu on July 24. Ensign Cash Register wrote that it was beautiful, and that he wished he could come back when he had the time to sail around the small islands. The carrier departed the next evening, losing July 25 overnight when it crossed the International Date Line. Register wrote on July 26: "We joined up with two task forces, 16 and 18. We now have over 70 ships in the group. This is the largest congregation of ships the Allies have had. It is a sight one will never forget. Carriers, Destroyers, Cruisers and Battleships, Transports, Tankers, Supply, and Hospital."

On July 28, the crude but functional advance airstrip on Espiritu Santo was declared operational only 28 days after its construction was ordered. On July 30, several 11th Bomb Group B-17s undertook the first search missions out of the new advance airfield, from which they were able to conduct air search and bombing missions in support of the upcoming landings.

On July 31, 11th Bomb Group B-17s based in the New Hebrides opened a seven-day bombing campaign against targets in the invasion area. Though his group's search aircraft had been using the Espiritu Santo airstrip for several days, Colonel Saunders had not yet seen the facility, so, for the first bombing mission, nine B-17s from various squadrons were selected to take part because a radio-compartment auxiliary fuel tank and a bomb-bay fuel tank used for the flight from Hawaii were still installed in each of them. The bomb-bay tanks severely restricted the bomb loads, but a list of alternatives provided no good answers. With Saunders leading, the nine strike bombers took off from Vila Field and flew 710 miles to Guadalcanal through bad weather that helped prevent discovery by Japanese ships and planes. The three lead B-17s dropped 500-pound bombs on the Japanese airfield while the remaining six dropped 100-pound bombs on supply dumps around Kukum. Antiaircraft fire was negligible and inaccurate, and the A6M2-Ns based at Tulagi failed to take off while the bombers were over Guadalcanal.

Colonel Saunders had an opportunity to inspect the Espiritu Santo forward airstrip after landing there on the return flight to Vila Field. He was understandably taken aback by how small and crude the air base looked, the lack of taxiways, roads, docks, dispersal areas, and the minimal presence of ground personnel or adequate supplies or basic standard equipment such as fueler trucks. Nevertheless, given that the advance strip was only 555 miles from Guadalcanal, Saunders considered that six strike bombers and two search bombers could be accommodated there each day.

On a separate July 31 mission, several B-17s from the Fifth Air Force's 19th Heavy Bombardment Group, based in New Guinea, attacked the under-construction airstrip at Lunga Point and beach defenses at Kukum on Guadalcanal.

With the field at Espiritu Santo now operational, after August 1 the B-17s could discard their bomb-bay fuel tanks and carry full bomb loads on Guadalcanal missions, filling their radio tanks at Efate, and refueling at Espiritu on the return leg. On August 1, the "Heavies" thus attacked the Tulagi seaplane base, shooting down two A6M2-Ns.

The August 3 mission was routine; there was no aerial opposition. On August 4, three 11th Bomb Group B-17s based at Vila Field attacked the Tulagi seaplane base. One B-17 was lost when a flaming A6M2-N rammed it. On August 5, several 11th Group B-17s attacked port facilities at Tulagi and Kukum. One B-17 was shot down by an

A6M2-N, demonstrating that while the floatplane might look clumsy, it was dangerous.

The 11th Bomb Group was given August 6 off. The air and ground crews used the time to prepare for a protracted bombing and long-range reconnaissance campaign beginning as soon as the amphibious landings scheduled for the next day were underway.

Meanwhile, even though Navy Catalina patrol bombers had been flying daily search missions over Guadalcanal since July 31 from an advance seaplane base at Ndeni, in the Santa Cruz Islands, there was no evidence that the Japanese in the Eastern Solomons were on alert for the imminent Operation *Watchtower* landings.

3

OPERATION *WATCHTOWER*

August 7

The 1st Marine Division had been hastily organized in mid-1941 as part of the prewar military expansion, moving to brand-new Camp Lejeune in North Carolina after Pearl Harbor, where the "old salts," veterans of duty in the Central American "banana wars" and China, were put in charge of turning newly trained recruits like Private Robert Leckie, freshly graduated from nearby Parris Island, into combat-ready Marines as rapidly as possible. Fortunately for its future, the division was organized as a far larger unit than either US Army or Japanese divisions. In November 1941 the men welcomed Brigadier General Alexander A. Vandegrift, a veteran of service since World War I in Haiti and China, as division commander.

Among the Marines who reported to Camp Lejeune was newly promoted Staff Sergeant James F. Eaton, "jumped up" in rank by wartime need from the lance corporal he had been on return from his tour in China. Eaton was now considered a "salt," expected to pass on what he had learned in China to the new generation of Marines. There were rumors the division might receive the new M-1 Garand semi-automatic rifle that Army divisions were clamoring for; however, the senior levels of the Corps turned down the new weapon, stating that it was not as accurate at long range as the tried and true M1903 Springfield rifle, which was indeed correct but would prove irrelevant in the war to come. As Eaton later recalled:

The Springfield was a wonderful weapon for giving aimed fire against the enemy. We were all Marine marksmen, and could shoot the whisker off the proverbial gnat with that rifle, but when we were in the jungles of Guadalcanal, there weren't any opportunities for aimed fire against the enemy. You pumped as many bullets as you could, as fast as you could, into the trees and bushes where you thought they were, and hoped you hit something. That wasn't easy to do with a bolt-action rifle.

The Marines who fought at Belleau Wood 24 years earlier would have recognized every weapon the Marines who fought at Guadalcanal carried.

In January 1942, the 7th Regiment – the oldest regiment in the Marine Corps – was separated from the division and sent to garrison American Samoa, reinforced with smaller units as the 1st Marine Brigade. The rest of the division was declared ready for operations in May, 1942. Vandegrift was informed that they would soon move to the South Pacific for eventual offensive use. At the time of the move, the 7th Regiment was still manning the defensive garrison in American Samoa. In addition to the 1st and 5th Regiments, both the 1st Raider Battalion, then stationed on New Caledonia, and the 3rd Defense Battalion at Fiji were ordered to rendezvous with the main body when the transport convoy from the United States stopped in Fiji en route to New Zealand. The 5th Marine Regiment was first to arrive in New Zealand in June, where its members engaged in final training.

On July 5 – the same day that Smith and Mangrum learned their futures in Hawaii – in Wellington, New Zealand, General Vandegrift was informed that the 1st and 5th Regiments of his division would land on and occupy Tulagi and nearby Florida islands in the Solomons. At the time, the 1st Regiment was still en route; it did not arrive in Wellington until July 11. On July 12, following the discovery of the airfield on Guadalcanal's Lunga Point and analysis of how close it was to completion, Vandegrift was informed that the entire division would invade what had become the the new focus of the operation, Guadalcanal. Its objective was to capture and hold the airfield. D-Day for the invasion was set for August 7.

On July 26, Vandegrift attended a meeting aboard Vice Admiral Frank Jack Fletcher's flagship *Saratoga*. Also in attendance was amphibious force commander Admiral Turner; Rear Admiral Daniel

J. Callaghan, Ghormley's chief of staff; Rear Admiral McCain, Commander Aircraft South Pacific (ComAirSoPac); and the 11th Bomb Group's Colonel "Blondie" Saunders. The meeting was a singularly cold confrontation in which Fletcher revealed that he had no intention of exposing his precious carriers to Japanese reprisals. Vandegrift had the distinct impression that Fletcher knew very little about the upcoming offensive and didn't care that he didn't know. He had lost one carrier each at the Coral Sea and Midway, losses that weighed heavily on his already very conservative approach to meeting the enemy.

While Ghormley's chief of staff, Admiral Callaghan, who could have invoked the authority of the area commander, silently took notes, Fletcher ignored the arguments and pleas of Vandegrift and Turner. He said that he would leave the Eastern Solomons on the morning of the third day, even though Turner required at least five days to unload the transports. Faced with an immovable Fletcher, Turner was forced to make his stand: lacking carrier-based air cover, the transports would be obliged to retire on the third morning with whatever supplies remained in their holds. Thrown into an operation for which his command was barely prepared, fresh from evolving a plan based on almost zero reliable information, and now faced with the early retirement of his naval support, General Vandegrift managed to leave *Saratoga* with his optimism shaken but intact.

With a dockworkers' strike in Wellington bringing all work in the harbor to a halt, the Marines were forced to load their own transports. There was no "book" to follow, since they were making it up as they went along. Equipment was loaded without thought regarding priority of use since – at that time – no one knew how to "combat load" a ship to support an amphibious operation. Eleven days after the 1st Regiment's arrival, 16,000 Marines loaded aboard the 50 ships of Task Force 62, commanded by Rear Admiral Turner, and departed Wellington. The Marines carried a 60-day combat load that lacked spare clothing, bedrolls, tents, typewriters, unit muster rolls, insect repellent, and mosquito netting. Due to a shipping shortage, their trucks and 155mm howitzers were left behind. Over July 28–30, the Marines participated in landing rehearsals on Koro Island. The event was described in a message from Vandegrift to the commandant of the Corps as "a disaster."

On July 31, Task Force 62 departed New Zealand and crossed the Coral Sea on its way to the Solomons, screened by the US heavy cruisers *Chicago* (CA-29), *Vincennes* (CA-44), *Quincy* (CA-39), *San Juan* (CL-54), and *Astoria* (CA-34) with the Australian heavy cruisers *Canberra*, *Hobart*, and task group commander British Admiral Victor Crutchley's flagship *Australia*, escorted by the destroyers *Blue* (DD-387), *Monssen* (DD-436), *Buchanan* (DD-484), *Patterson* (DD-392), *Helm* (DD-388), *Wilson* (DD-408), and *Jarvis* (DD-393).

The transport convoy was covered by Admiral Fletcher's Task Force 61. *Saratoga*'s polyglot Air Group 3 included Lieutenant Commander Leroy Simpler's 24 Wildcats of Fighting 5 (VF-5), survivors of the loss of *Yorktown*, fleshed out by pilots from the now-defunct VF-8; the SBD-3s of Scouting 6 (VS-6) had been part of *Enterprise*'s air group until after Midway; Bombing 3 (VB-3) was also a survivor of *Yorktown*, fleshed out with the survivors of Air Group 8's dive-bomber squadrons that had gone astray at Midway; a reconstituted Torpedo 8 (VT-8) brought the new Grumman TBF Avenger. Scouting 6's *Yorktown* survivor, Ensign John Bridgers, later recalled that the sunrises and sunsets he saw over the Coral Sea were "the most spectacular I ever saw in my life, completely belying the nature of our reason for being there." Everything the US Navy had in the Pacific was aboard the ships of the two task forces.

Aboard *Saratoga*, the aircrews spent the night of August 6/7 preparing for the coming battle. Among them was Dallas, Texas-born 22-year-old Lieutenant (jg) Elisha Terrill "Smokey" Stover, a section leader in Fighting 5 and veteran of Midway in Fighting 8 who had gained his nickname from a popular 1930s comic, "Smokey Stover." Over the two weeks prior to "D-Day," the squadron's pilots had gone over the coming operation with XO Lieutenant Richard "Chick" Harmer, regarding their targets at Tulagi and Guadalcanal and the general situation they were likely to encounter. Initial intelligence had it that the airfield on Guadalcanal was newly operational and they would encounter Zeros; however, the recent reconnaissance flights flown by the 11th Group's B-17s had revealed that the airfield was still under construction, with a squadron of A6M2-N "Rufe" fighters operating from the seaplane base in Tulagi harbor.

Stover was set to fly with 15 other Wildcats that VF-5 was to launch before dawn. They were assigned to strafe the airfield on Lunga Point at 0630 hours, 15 minutes prior to sunrise and 30 minutes before the Marines landed on Red Beach. After the dive bombers of Bombing and Scouting 3 had worked over the field, the Wildcats would be free to pursue any targets of opportunity they came across. Although Stover had flown at Midway, he had yet to encounter an enemy fighter personally; his sole experience of firing his guns in anger had come on the last day of Midway, when his division strafed survivors of the sunken Japanese cruiser *Mikuma*. On this last night before he faced combat, the reason he had become a naval aviator the year before, Stover had left the pilots in Fighting 5's ready room who were talking too loudly to cover their own fears, and retreated to his stateroom, where he composed what might be his last letter to his wife and wrote his will, placing both in an envelope on which he wrote "To be opened in the event of my death" which he sealed and placed on the small writing desk.

The pilots and gunners of *Saratoga*'s air group were awakened at 0400 hours on August 7. Stover had time to shave, make his way to the wardroom for a full breakfast that he was unable to complete, then make his way to the ready room for a briefing at 0445 hours. At 0500 hours, the 1MC public address system "bullhorn" blared through the ship, "Pilots, man your planes!" Stover made his way to the dark flight deck that was lit only by moonlight through clouds above, managed to find his way through the dark shapes of the aircraft without bumping into one, and quickly pre-flighted his Wildcat. His plane captain was already on the wing when he climbed up, ready to assist him strapping in and preparing for launch. At 0515 hours, "Start engines!" echoed across the flight deck, quickly followed by the coughs of engines first turning over; then the loud roar of 40 aircraft blotted out all other sounds as their engines warmed up.

The flight deck crews signaled the pilots in their cockpit with blue flashlights, first guiding the two Wildcats flown by squadron commander Lieutenant Commander Leroy Simpler and his wingman into position. Each pilot in turn stood on his brakes as he pushed the throttle full forward, then released brakes as the launch officer's flashlight pointed forward, soon disappearing into the darkness ahead of the ship. The next two moved into position and took off; the next division was led by XO Chick Harmer. Stover's division leader, Lieutenant Walter Clarke, and his wingman moved into position and took off. Finally, it was the turn of Stover and his wingman. He moved into position and shoved his throttle forward. The Pratt & Whitney R-1830 Twin Wasp roared smoothly in response to throttle movement and his Wildcat vibrated from the increased power. The launch officer gave his signal and the heavy Grumman fighter rolled forward and quickly lifted off, dropping a bit as it cleared the end of the flight deck. Stover smoothly pulled back on the control stick, following the preceding fighter, identified only by a few faint lights receding into the dark sky. The fighters joined up in the darkness, pilots guided only by the dim running lights of the others.

Once the Wildcats were gone, the Dauntlesses moved up for takeoff. Scouting 3's Lieutenant (jg) Howard "Slim" Russell noticed a blue searchlight playing over the side from the flight deck as he goosed his throttle and moved up into takeoff position, wondering if a submarine had been spotted. Before he could wonder further, his section leader began moving forward and it was his turn to push the throttle forward on his Wright R-1820 Cyclone engine.

Enterprise was only five miles from *Saratoga*, and *Wasp* another three miles away. The sky was now full of airplanes trying to sort themselves out in the darkness and there were momentary mix-ups as pilots joined on the wrong squadron formations, but soon confusion was resolved and VF-5's 16 had joined up in four flights of four. Stover watched their lights as the Dauntlesses appeared out of the darkness below and formed their six-plane division formations. When all were ready, Simpler set course for Guadalcanal, 68 miles away to the north. Stover checked his watch: the hands showed 0555 hours.

Saratoga's strike headed for their target while eight Wildcats from *Enterprise's* Fighting 6 took up their orbits over the fleet as CAP. Other *Enterprise* fighters and dive bombers, with *Wasp's* Fighting 71 fighters and the Dauntlesses they protected, banked toward Tulagi. The pilots did not turn off their running lights until they were 40 miles from the carriers.

It was still dark 30 minutes later when Stover and his squadron mates flew toward Guadalcanal's western end. The moon broke through the clouds overhead as the Wildcats rounded Cape Esperance, bathing the formation in eerie light. Simpler turned east and the formation felt their way along Guadalcanal's northern coast.

At 0615 hours on August 7, 1942, the cruiser *Quincy* announced the American arrival in the Solomons when it opened fire on Kukum.

The Japanese on Guadalcanal and Tulagi were taken completely by surprise when they looked out at Sealark Sound to see US transports drop anchor in what would soon be known as "Ironbottom Sound." The radio station on Tulagi messaged Rabaul: "Large force of ships, unknown number or types, entering the sound. What can they be?" While the Japanese had been aware of Allied movements through signals intelligence, they had interpreted the regional movements as possible reinforcement of New Guinea.

Moments later, Stover saw what he took at first for antiaircraft gunfire ahead. But rather than the fire coming from positions ashore, these flashes rose from the middle of Sealark Sound north of the island. A few tense moments later, he realized that the flashes came from friendly warships that had just opened fire on the shoreline from Kukum eastward to the Marines' landing beach. At regular intervals, bright yellow flashes flared from one of the dark splotches on the water that were becoming more visible as the sun rose higher on the horizon. Each bright flash soon resolved into three tiny white spots soaring aloft in long, glowing arcs before exploding on impact among the coconut palms just inshore. In the cool grey light of pre-dawn, Stover could see little more than the darker silhouette of the island. Further to the northeast, he could make out Tulagi, where five or six fires had broken out along that dark shore.

The fires had been set by the first planes over Tulagi, 11 VF-71 Wildcats led by squadron commander Lieutenant Commander Courtney Shands. Their assignment was to engage any of the float fighters that might be airborne, or destroy them and the other seaplanes and flying boats in the anchorage off Tanambogo and Florida islands. As it turned out, the air was clear of the enemy. While two F4Fs orbited at 5,000 feet to cover the others, three Wildcats strafed a coastal village on Florida while two others peeled off to attack the seaplane anchorage and other targets on Gavutu and Tanambogo islands. Shands led three others as they hunted for possible targets along a stretch of Florida's coast and at nearby Makambo Island. Off the latter island, Shands opened fire at some likely-looking dark objects in the offshore water and set a moored H6K "Mavis" flying boat afire. The rest of the division joined in, setting fire to three other moored Mavises. The pair sent to Tanambogo found four Mavises moored off the north coast, and flamed them. At 0620 hours, Shands and his wingman located six A6M2-N float fighters moored off the village of Halavo on Florida's coast east of Tanambogo. Making a low-level pass, the two Wildcats flamed all six. The Wildcats were followed by 11 SBDs from VS-71 and nine from VS-5 that winged over into their dives, dropping 1,000-pound bombs on targets on Tulagi.

While this happened, Fighting 5 dived on the unfinished airfield at Lunga Point, their bullets whipping the grassy opening and whacking into gear and equipment on the field. Simpler pulled ahead of the pack, forcing pilots in divisions following to add a lot of throttle to keep up. Stover had to push full throttle just to keep sight of division leader Clarke, only two planes ahead. Whenever he got lower, Clarke momentarily disappeared from Stover's view; he was barely visible against the dark jungle below when they were level with each other.

As the formation swept over the field from the west, Stover fired only his four outboard machine guns to conserve ammunition, a standard practice. He fired short bursts, correcting as he saw the fall of bullets that seemed to spray over half the field. He still expected return fire from the ground as he pulled up in a climbing, twisting turn, but there was none. The F4Fs made several passes, shooting up everything they could see as the target became more visible in the dawn light. Stover saw no enemy and there was still no answering fire. On his third pass, Stover streaked across the runway at full throttle and laid his gunfire beneath the roofs of several low metal-walled buildings. Two pilots set a schooner moored offshore afire. As Stover later recalled when writing home of the day, it all seemed too easy.

The strafing fighters were ordered to stand clear by *Saratoga's* Commander Air Group (CAG) Commander Harry Felt, so the 23 Scouting 3 and Bombing 3 Dauntlesses could execute their attack, dive bombing targets along the coast and on the airfield; the rear seat gunners strafed buildings as the pilots pulled out of the bombing runs.

Slim Russell watched the fighters leave, then pushed his stick forward to dive on a dimly perceived gun emplacement 5,500 feet below, firing the two cowl-mounted .50-caliber machine guns to suppress possible return fire. As he neared drop altitude, however, he could see that there was no gun in the emplacement, but decided to drop his 1,000-pound bomb anyway. He pulled the bomb release toggle at 1,800 feet and pulled out. The bomb hit about 100 feet off the beach, in the water, causing no visible damage. Russell castigated himself for the bad drop as he circled and came back at about 60 feet over Kukum, strafing so intently that he almost flew into the water, pulling out close enough that his rear seater later told him back on *Saratoga* that he had seen a wake in the water from their prop blast.

Next, Russell joined several other SBDs over Lunga Point. Flying back over the coconut trees after the first strafing pass, he saw streaks of red tracer coming at him from out of the trees. When he pulled up, the tracers all fell behind and below him. Climbing cautiously while he checked to see if anything vital had been hit, he dived again to strafe the source of the fire. Nothing met him on the way down, but red tracer again chased his tail as he pulled up. Making three more passes, he expended most of his ammunition strafing the coconut groves but was unable to observe tangible results.

Russell finally ran out of ammo and was low on gas at 0720 hours and turned to return to *Saratoga*. As he flew south toward the Coral Sea, he saw how very rough the interior of the island appeared. Rolling hills and mountains covered with dense green foliage were interspersed with occasional meadows where he noticed tiny villages. When he landed back aboard ship, he was met with surprise. Everyone in the squadron thought he had spun into the water on takeoff. The searchlight he had thought was trying to pinpoint a submarine had been trying to locate a Dauntless that had indeed spun in. It turned out that an SBD two places ahead of him had lost power just after clearing *Saratoga's* deck. The pilot and gunner were never found.

Russell grabbed a sandwich and a cup of cocoa while the squadron's SBDs were being rearmed and refueled. With the aircraft again ready, they were launched for a second mission at 0930 hours. The bombers circled over Kukum and Lunga for two hours, during which four of the bombers hit an ammunition dump and blew it up. Russell dropped his second bomb of the day into a wooded area, where it knocked down a frame building and set two large tents on fire. He returned alone to *Saratoga* around noon, and turned in for a nap after lunch. By then, the ground troops ashore didn't appear to need further air support, though flights of SBDs and bomb-armed Grumman TBF Avenger torpedo bombers remained overhead on station in the event they were needed.

By mid-morning, the Marines were ashore at all three landing points. Florida Island was discovered unoccupied and taken without opposition. On Guadalcanal, the enemy had taken to the hills during the first attacks at dawn, and the main force that landed at Lunga Point was in possession of the airfield by mid-afternoon. They were fortunate to capture all the Japanese food supplies; within weeks, the captured rice would be their main sustenance. Tulagi was another matter entirely. The elite veteran troops of the Special Naval Landing Force gave the Marines an introduction to the no-quarter combat they would face on other Pacific islands as they fought to dislodge the tenacious enemy from their caves and bunkers. By noon on August 9, all resistance at Tulagi would end with 70 Americans dead against 476 Japanese. The 20 who surrendered turned out to be Korean laborers from the Japanese construction unit, who had no love for their imperial oppressors.

The decoded message from Tulagi announcing the arrival of the Americans came in from the code room to the desk of Admiral Sadayoshi Yamada, commander of the Imperial Naval Air Force's 5th Attack Force based at Rabaul, at 0800 hours of August 7. Yamada, one of the first Japanese naval aviators, immediately summoned his staff as well as the wing and squadron commanders. As they considered the news, they thought at first that the enemy had come to raid the base. Seeking more information, the admiral ordered an H6K "Mavis" to fly to the southern Solomons and report the situation. However, before any further action could be taken, a message arrived from the commander of Tulagi's now-defunct seaplane detachment: "Enemy forces overwhelming. We will defend our posts to the death, praying for eternal victory." It was now obvious that the Americans had come to occupy Tulagi, and perhaps to destroy the nearly complete airfield on Guadalcanal. The admiral worried that the Americans might attempt a strike by their carriers against Rabaul itself, which could come at any moment. Out on the ramp at Vunakanau airdrome, 27 G4M1 bombers, now known to the Americans as "Betty," were fueled and loaded for a mission against the recently discovered Allied airfield at Rabi in eastern New Guinea. Their orders were quickly changed.

Saburo Sakai and the other Zero pilots of the Tainan Air Corps had arrived at Rabaul from their base at Lae in New Guinea four days earlier. They were already veterans of flying long range over-ocean fighter missions from Formosa during the invasion of the Philippines, which had convinced the Americans that Japanese carriers were present since operating single-engine fighters over such a distance was "impossible."

Among the unit's ranks were the most experienced, highest-scoring fighter pilots in the Imperial Navy, who had cut a swathe across southeast Asia from the Philippines through the Dutch East Indies to New Guinea in the seven months since the opening of the Pacific War. Guadalcanal was a bit further across the Solomons Sea from Rabaul than Manila had been from Formosa. Commander Tadashi Nakajima, leader of the fighter unit, pointed out that a round trip of 1,200 miles would require that the Zeros operate at their claimed maximum range, which had never been done before. Flying such a mission could mean the loss of half his pilots, since there were no Japanese airfields between Rabaul and Guadalcanal where a damaged plane might land. Operating over such a distance meant that the Zeros could fight for only a maximum of 15 minutes over the enemy fleet at full throttle if they hoped to return successfully.

Responding to Nakajima's worry, Admiral Yamada reduced the number of escorts from 36 to 18, with those remaining behind to stay on alert at Rabaul to repel the feared American attack that the admiral believed might be imminent. Because of this, the bombers were sent off with the bombs they already carried, rather than take the time to rearm them with deadly Type 91 torpedoes for use against shipping.

At 0930 hours, Commander Nakajima lifted off the Lakunai airdrome runway on the longest-ever mission yet flown by the Imperial Naval Air Force, followed by 17 of his most-experienced pilots. The 27 G4M1 "Bettys" began taking off from Vunakanau airdrome at 1006 hours. They were led by Lieutenant Renpei Egawa, a nonpilot command officer; each carried two 250-kilogram bombs and four 60-kilogram bombs.

4

TALLY-HO!

August 7–8

At about 1030 hours, Royal Australian Navy Petty Officer Paul Mason, a 41-year-old Australian planter turned "coastwatcher," spotted the formation from his vantage point atop a hill in southern Bougainville 300 miles north of Guadalcanal. He immediately radioed the news in the clear on a priority frequency: "24 bombers headed yours." The message was picked up at Port Moresby, New Guinea, and relayed to Townville, Australia, where the strongest transmitter in the region was located. From Townville, the information was flashed to Pacific Fleet headquarters at Pearl Harbor, which finally re-transmitted the warning to Admiral Fletcher off Guadalcanal at 1130 hours local that the enemy would arrive at approximately 1300 hours. Their target might be the invasion fleet in Sealark Sound or the carriers south of Guadalcanal. The speed of the response astonished the Americans, who had no understanding of the true performance capabilities of their opponents and believed Rabaul was too distant for the enemy to respond, and had thus not factored such an event into their plans.

The pilots of the 17 Zeros (one had aborted) spotted Guadalcanal in the distance, as they passed the Russell Islands, 65 miles from Savo Island. Lieutenant Shiro Kawai, the Tainan Air Corps' senior *buntaicho* (division leader), led his force of five A6M2s, which constituted the "challenge section," as they climbed to 28,000 feet, then surged forward to go in early and draw off the American fighter CAP. The two remaining six-plane sections led by Nakajima and junior *buntaicho* Lieutenant (jg) Junichi Sasai remained at 20,000 feet with the Bettys, which would execute precision high-level attacks on the shipping now becoming visible in Sealark Sound with their antipersonnel and runway-busting high-explosive bombs. Saburo Sakai, leading Sasai's second three-plane section, adjusted his seatbelt and checked his two wingmen, Petty Officers Kenji Kakimoto and Kazushi Uto.

At approximately 1150 hours, radar aboard *Saratoga* picked up the incoming Japanese force, flying at 10,000 feet, 50 miles distant. Several divisions of Fighting 5 Wildcats were quickly scrambled to meet them. The defenders just managed to get into the air and high enough to meet the enemy as they turned on their bomb run. The three VF-5 divisions became quickly engaged, and two Bettys were lost during the attack. The Bettys turned away north after dropping their bombs with the formation still relatively intact. They were jumped by a division of VF-6 Wildcats led by VF-6's commander, Lieutenant Commander Lou Bauer. Bauer's four-plane division was launched from *Enterprise* and joined two other F4Fs that were set to relieve the escorts for *Enterprise* air group commander Lieutenant Commander Max Leslie, orbiting over Guadalcanal in his specially equipped TBF Avenger, which, with its increased communications capabilities, was being used as Ground Support Strike Coordinator. The two escorts had departed for Guadalcanal at 1230 hours while Bauer's division was ordered to head northwest at 8,000 feet. Bauer's departure meant that when the two VF-6 divisions orbiting over the fleet as CAP were forced to land low on fuel, the fleet was temporarily unprotected.

At 1310 hours, Lieutenant (jg) Gordon Firebaugh, an enormously experienced formerly enlisted Chief Naval Aviation Pilot (NAP) and prewar veteran of the elite VF-2, "the Flying Chiefs," who had been commissioned six months earlier, led a division off *Enterprise* as reinforcement CAP to join up with the division led by Lieutenant (jg) Dick Gay, another recently commissioned former Chief NAP. Nine minutes later, *Wasp* launched the first of 16 F4Fs to provide CAP. At the same time, Bauer received orders to turn back to the fleet.

At 1345 hours, Gay's Wildcats spotted the survivors of the Bettys that had been first attacked by the division led by Lieutenant Pug Southerland. The bombers had made their runs over the fleet, though the anti-personnel and high-explosive bombs they dropped had little effect on the ships below. Now Gay and his pilots dived on the eight Bettys, unaware that eight Zeros led by Lieutenant Commander Nakajima were below the bombers. Gay's wingman, Lieutenant (jg) Vincent de Poix, broke formation and made a high-side run on the Betty formation's left side while Gay followed with a high-side run from the right. The second section, NAPs Chief Machinist's Mate Howell Sumrall and wingman Machinist 1/c Joe Achten, followed with their own attack.

After passing over the formation without shooting down a bomber, Gay came around and put his sights on the Betty flying on one engine. This was the bomber flown by Petty Officer Yoshiuki Sakamoto that Pug Southerland had damaged in his attack. Gay took aim at the good engine and set it afire. The fire quickly engulfed the gas tanks in the wing and spread to the fuselage as the Betty fell out of formation and dived into the sea below. The attack on Sakamoto's bomber finally alerted the Zero pilots – who did not have radios – to the presence of the Americans.

Chief Sumrall had recovered from his attack below the bombers. As he banked to turn for a second pass, he saw the Zeros below him and realized he could not attack them from his position. One of the enemy fighters closed as Sumrall attempted a split-S to force a head-on attack, and several 20mm shells struck the Wildcat behind Sumrall's cockpit, knocking out his radio as he attempted to warn the others of the Zeros while a second burst made a large hole in his left wing. Smoke filled his cockpit; when he slid the canopy back he found himself surrounded by four of the enemy. Remembering a story he had heard that the Zero's ailerons froze up at speeds above 250 knots. Sumrall turned in a steep right spiral. As his airspeed indicator climbed above 250 knots, he banked around to catch the enemy but they had already dived away. Now flying on his 27-gallon reserve tank, Sumrall turned back to the fleet.

In the meantime, Sumrall's wingman, Machinist Achten, came under attack from two Zeros as he recovered from his pass against the bombers. One of the Zeros overran him and he put a solid burst into the fighter a moment before he felt the impact of the 20mm shells fired by the wingman behind him. Hit in the engine, Achten dived through the cloud deck to get away, coming out over Florida Island. As he turned back toward the fleet, the engine froze and he ditched near one of the transports, which sent a Higgins boat over to pick him up within minutes of climbing out of the cockpit as the Wildcat sank.

Gay and Sumrall made it back to *Enterprise* and landed safely, while de Poix landed on *Wasp* with his engine dying from lack of fuel as he tried to taxi out of the arresting gear.

Gordon Firebaugh's division spotted the retiring enemy bombers north of Florida Island and set off after them. Firebaugh was glad the Wildcats were each carrying two 42-gallon drop tanks, since it took 15 minutes with the throttles firewalled to finally catch up to the Bettys over Santa Isabel Island, 150 miles from the US fleet. Firebaugh spotted the three Zeros flown by Nakajima and his two wingmen, but failed to spot Lieutenant Kawai's five fighters as he ordered his division to drop their tanks and attack the bombers. Firebaugh and his wingman, NAP Bill Stephenson, went after Nakajima's Zeros while his second section leader, Machinist Bill Warden and wingman Ensign Bob Disque, along with third section leader Chief NAP Tommy Rhodes and his wingman NAP Paul Mankin, dived on the bombers.

Hikotaicho (air group commander) Nakajima and his wingmen had already spotted the American fighters and were climbing toward Firebaugh and Stephenson so fast that Firebaugh was momentarily rattled. Turning toward the enemy, he opened fire on Nakajima at a range of 500 yards and saw hits on the Zero's cowling. At that moment, a burst of 7.7mm bullets fired from below flashed through his cockpit. He looked out to see the other five Zeros that he hadn't previously spotted as they flashed past and banked around. Now surrounded by eight Zeros, he saw Stephenson's Wildcat get hit and catch fire, etching a line of smoke across the sky toward the water below.

As Firebaugh fought for his life, the other four Wildcats attacked the bombers. Rhodes and Disque made a pass against the rear *chutai* (squadron). As they pulled out, one of the Bettys dropped out of the formation, trailing smoke. Disque turned and made a solo run, smoking another Betty. On a third run, he hit the first damaged Betty solidly and it caught fire. Mankin turned and hit the Betty that Disque had smoked on his second pass and it too caught fire and fell out of formation. The two made several other passes at the 23 surviving Bettys before Disque came under attack from Commander Nakajima. Turning to get a head-on pass against the enemy fighter, Disque watched as Nakajima turned too tight for him to follow, then dived out of the fight. Mankin and Disque now turned back for home.

Rhodes and Warden also executed attacks against the bombers, with Warden taking hits from the defensive return fire severe enough that he had to turn away to head home. Before he left, he saw Rhodes come under attack from junior *buntaicho* Lieutenant (jg) Sasai, who hung on Rhodes' tail as he twisted to get away. Only three of Warden's guns would fire but the tracers flashing in front of Sasai's Zero were enough to make him break off and Rhodes dived into the clouds below. Warden too pushed over in a dive to get away. Pursued by one of the Zeros, he pulled out at wavetop height. A final burst of fire stopped his engine and he flopped into the water, knocking himself unconscious against the gunsight on impact. He came too as the fighter began its final dive to the bottom and managed to force the canopy open and swim ten feet to the surface, where he popped his liferaft and climbed in as the enemy fighter flew off.

Firebaugh had managed to get away from his attackers for a few minutes, but soon found himself surrounded by Lieutenant Kawai's Zeros. As Kawai dived on him, he managed to turn and open fire on the Zero, missing it. An instant later, Kawai's wingman, 12-victory ace Petty Officer First Class Motosuna Yoshida, flashed in front of him and Firebaugh's guns stitched the Zero from nose to tail. It nosed over and disappeared into the water. Kawai's second wingman then caught Firebaugh's Wildcat, blowing his liferaft out of its compartment behind the cockpit with a burst of 20mm fire. The next burst set the gas tank beneath the cockpit on fire. Firebaugh banked to the side and threw himself out of the flame-filled cockpit. He delayed opening his parachute to avoid being strafed, holding off so long that when he did pull the D-ring, he only swung twice beneath the 'chute as it deployed before hitting the water with enough force to injure his back.

Mankin made it all the way back to *Enterprise*, along with Rhodes, while Disque touched down on *Wasp* with the last of his fuel. Firebaugh and Warden were picked up by Solomon Islanders and finally made it back to Guadalcanal in September after several close calls evading the enemy.

While these battles took place, Saburo Sakai shot down the SBD flown by VS-71's Lieutenant Dudley Adams, who had spotted the Zero pass by as he pulled out of a dive to escape three other Zeros that had attacked VS-71 squadron commander Lieutenant Commander John Eldridge's division of six Dauntlesses. Adams turned and opened fire, putting a .50-caliber slug through Sakai's canopy before the ace turned on him, killing his rear seater, Aviation Radioman Harry Elliott, and wounding Adams, who was still able to ditch his SBD near a destroyer in Sealark Sound at 1337 hours.

Moments later, Sakai spotted eight Bombing 6 Dauntlesses led by Lieutenant Carl Horenberger that were orbiting over Tulagi to provide on-call air support to the Marines below. Sakai was unfamiliar with Navy aircraft and misidentified them as Wildcats. He and his two wingmen turned toward the new targets. Horenburger's gunner, Aviation Machinist's Mate 2/c Herman Caruthers, spotted the approach of Sakai's threesome. He signaled the approach to his friend, Aviation Ordnanceman 2/c Harold Jones, in another SBD. Jones spotted the three Zeros 800 feet below and a mile astern of the Dauntless formation. Suddenly, one of the enemy fighters broke off, turned left, and approached the dive-bomber formation from underneath. This Zero was flown by Sakai's wingman, Kenji Kakimoto. Jones then saw a second Zero hurtling toward him from dead astern – it was Sakai.

At the same moment, Sakai finally recognized his mistake when he identified the dive bombers ahead; he knew he had made an egregious identification error, but he was committed to the attack. The three SBDs closed up and dropped back slightly astern and below division leader Horenburger's section. With the bombers now concentrated, Horenburger led them in a gradual turn to starboard. Sakai started firing from about 500 feet behind the rear SBD. A 20mm shell hit Ensign Robert Gibson's 500-pound bomb, then ricocheted up and exploded beneath Gibson's armored seat. Several of the other gunners opened fire but Jones could not initially bring his guns to bear on Sakai without shooting the tails of his own fellow-airplanes. Sakai turned to the right and pulled up, which allowed all seven rear seaters to open fire from a distance of about 100 feet.

Jones saw Sakai's cockpit explode with a bright orange flame. The canopy seemed to be torn from its tracks, and Jones got a clear look at Sakai, getting the distinct impression he had been wounded. Sakai's Zero pulled almost straight up, then fell away trailing smoke. Jones lost sight of it as he swung his guns to bear on Kakimoto's Zero, which was closing in from below. As Jones fired at Kakimoto, his pilot, Ensign

Robert Shaw, called "Stand by to bail out," telling Jones the controls were sloppy and he wasn't sure he could keep flying. Shaw fell out of formation and slowed the SBD while Jones surveyed the damage. With great relief, he told Shaw that the right elevator was hit. Shaw decided to fly the 60 miles back to *Enterprise*, where he landed without incident.

By great fortune, Sakai came to with his Zero in a vertical plunge toward the water. He managed to pull out at wave-top height and, despite severe facial and eye injuries that nearly blinded him, he was able to make an epic five-hour 560-mile flight back to Lakunai airdrome. Losing an eye as a result of the battle, he would not re-enter combat for two years.

At 1400 hours, while Gordon Firebaugh's division was still fighting the Bettys and Zeros over Santa Isabel and a total of 44 Wildcats had been launched from the three carriers to cover the fleet, a warning from Admiral Turner's command ship was flashed to the fleet that an attack by Japanese dive bombers was imminent. This was quickly followed by a warning that 25 enemy bombers were attacking from 8,000 feet. Wildcat pilots over Sealark Sound looked desperately for the oncoming enemy but saw nothing. This was because neither message was accurate; there were no Japanese aircraft anywhere near the invasion fleet, but the warnings set all on edge, since the implication was that enemy aircraft carriers were in the vicinity.

In fact, the nine "one way" D3A "Vals" from the 2nd Air Group that had left Rabaul with the others, were at that moment skirting the island chain to the north, flying at 10,000 feet and out of sight of any coastwatcher in the broken clouds. Thirty minutes later, *buntaicho* Lieutenant Fumito Inoue determined he was north of Guadalcanal and signaled the others to follow as he turned south.

Soon, Inoue could see Task Force 62's ships through the clouds. As the dive bombers came closer, he signaled Warrant Officer Gengo Ota to take his three bombers and attack a force of cruisers and destroyers visible to the west while he led the rest of the *chutai* to attack the transports anchored off the Guadalcanal invasion beach. The three bombers banked away and headed for their target.

Lieutenant Albert O. "Scoop" Vorse, who as a member of Fighting 2 had last fought Vals in defense of *Lexington* and *Yorktown* during the Battle of the Coral Sea – where he shot down two of the dive bombers – was the first pilot to realize that an attack was under way, when he spotted Ota's three Vals as they rolled into their attack dives on the warships below while he and two other Wildcats orbited at 11,000 feet over the western anchorage off Guadalcanal.

Vorse immediately banked and dived after the enemy bombers, outpacing his wingmen, who failed to spot the enemy. Vorse's Wildcat vibrated in the dive as he kept his speed up, trying to catch the diving Vals, but the best he could do was open fire from long range. Surprisingly, given the cruisers anchored below, Ota had taken aim at the older Bagley-class destroyer USS *Mugford* (DD-389), which was part of the antisubmarine screen on the western side of the anchorage. *Mugford*'s quartermaster recorded in his logbook that a lookout spotted two fixed-gear airplanes diving out of a cloud astern of the ship and heading right at him at 1447 hours.

When he heard the lookout's shouted warning, *Mugford*'s captain ordered a sharp turn to starboard. Ota and wingman Petty Officer Second Class Koji Takahashi followed their target and each dropped their two 60-kilogram wing bombs. Ota's missed to starboard, but one of Takahashi's bombs struck the destroyer aft, killing 21 men. Vorse managed to get close enough to the third Val, commanded by Petty Officer Second Class Minoru Iwaoka and piloted by Seaman 1/c Seiki Nakamoto, to put a burst into the cockpit. The Val nosed over more steeply and left a trail of smoke across the sky before hitting the water on *Mugford*'s starboard side. In the meantime, the ship's antiartillery (AA) gunners, who had shot down three attackers at Pearl Harbor, hit Ota and Takahashi's bombers, claiming both shot down though the two Vals survived to escape the battle.

As Ota's *shotai* (flight) turned away, Lieutenant Inoue and the other six Vals headed on across the channel between Florida Island and Guadalcanal at 10,000 feet. Minutes later they were spotted by Fighting 5's Lieutenant Hayden Jensen when he looked up and spotted the formation 3,000 feet above. With the radio channel clogged by other pilots, Jensen raced up to Gray and waggled his wings, pointing up. He pushed his throttle "through the gate" and led the others as they climbed after the enemy bombers. One pilot dropped out of the chase when he discovered his guns wouldn't charge. As the Wildcats strained for altitude, climbing at their maximum 1,300 feet per minute, Lieutenant Dave Richardson and his wingman, Ensign Charles Davy, spotted Inoue's bombers from their position to the north at 13,000 feet. Richardson immediately dived after the Vals, hoping to intercept them before they dived on the ships below.

Lieutenant Inoue probably spotted the five Wildcats climbing toward him, which caused him to immediately attack USS *Dewey* (DD-349), another of the destroyers on antisubmarine patrol. The Vals turned back to set up for an attack on the ship when Lieutenant Jensen finally got to them. He turned in his climb and attacked the nearest enemy bomber, which staggered when hit, then smoked and broke off from the formation. Jensen followed it as it dived into the channel, firing all the way till it exploded on contact with the water.

While *Dewey* and the other ships nearby opened fire, filling the sky with 5-inch bursts and ribbons of tracers, Lieutenant Marion Dufilho and his wingman, Lieutenant (jg) Carlton Starkes dived after the attacking Vals, firing into the formation.

Ensign Mark Bright dived so fast that he overran the rear Val. Ignoring the danger from that plane's two 7.7mm nose guns, he pressed his attack on the next one in line. The observer-gunner fired back, but Bright stayed close with his finger on the trigger until flames blossomed from the landing gear and spread back as it nosed over more steeply and went down.

Behind Bright, Gray fired a burst into the rear Val, which smoked; he then pulled up and went high, looking for other attackers, joined by Richardson and Davy.

Inoue and wingman Petty Officer Third Class Seiji Sato reached their drop point over *Dewey* without being hit by antiaircraft fire or the Wildcats. Each dropped their two 60-kilogram bombs, which missed. The two surviving Vals from the rear *shotai* also dropped, but they too missed the twisting destroyer.

At that moment, NAP Machinist's Mate 1/c Don Runyon and the other three fighters of his Fighting 6 division dived into the fight, alerted by the chatter on the fighter channel. Runyon skirted the friendly fire from the ships and attacked one of the Vals, scoring hits before he overran the bomber. NAP Howard Packer, second section leader of Runyon's division, hammered the Val and it fell away, crashing off Lunga Point and exploding on impact. While Packard received full credit for the victory, the airplane had been damaged by fire from Dufilho, Starkes, Runyon, and perhaps Jensen and Bright.

Dulfiho spotted one of the surviving Vals as it completed its recovery. The bomber broke to the south as Dufilho closed and tried to evade by flying across Guadalcanal's mountainous interior. Dufilho, who had first entered combat with Butch O'Hare defending *Lexington* back in February, closed to only 150 feet behind the Val's tail and opened fire. Before he could finish the job, his windshield was covered by oil thrown by his own engine. Cracking the canopy, he leaned out and fired again, trying to adjust his aim on the fall of his tracers. It was hopeless and Dulfiho broke contact, just as Packard tried to close on the enemy. Runyon closed ahead and below, while Packard's wingman, Ensign Shoemaker, closed from the right side. All three were firing when the Val flew into a ravine and blew up. Runyon, the division leader, got the credit.

Warrant Officer Seisuke Nakagaki, leader of the rear *shotai*, was fired on and claimed by both Bright and Runyon as he flew clear. He was then caught by Ensign Shoemaker and Runyon's wingman, Ensign Harry March, as he neared Savo after setting course toward the Shortland Islands. As Shoemaker set up for a high-side run, March closed on the Val's tail and opened fire in the face of a stream of bullets from Nakagaki's observer-gunner. March claimed the Val damaged because he thought his bullets had started a fire, but Lieutenant Hayden Jensen closed on the wounded Val and opened fire from 350 yards as he closed. Nakagaki's Val caught fire and knifed into the water. All defenders involved received full official credit for the lone victory.

In all, the nine Fighting 5 and Fighting 6 pilots who attacked Inoue's six Vals claimed 13 victories, while Vorse claimed one of the three Vals that had attacked *Mugford*, whose gun crews claimed two.

The four surviving Vals reached their pickup point in the Shortland Islands at about 1700 hours. Ota and Takahashi ditched as planned, and all four airmen swam to the waiting Mavis.

Lieutenant Inoue and his wingman Petty Officer Sato ditched near the rendezvous with the seaplane tender *Chitose*. Inoue and his observer were rescued, but Sato and his observer were unable to get out of their bomber before it sank. In return for superficially damaging *Dewey* and killing 21 of its crew with one of 18 bombs dropped in the attack, the 2nd Air Group lost all nine Vals and 12 of 18 pilots and observers.

Around 1730 hours, Fighting 6 pilots Ensigns Shoemaker and Cook, and NAP Nagle, who had landed on *Saratoga* short of fuel, were launched from the carrier to fly a CAP over the transports, before returning to *Enterprise*. There was no reason to send fighters to a distant station so soon before sunset, but the invasion commanders had been badly rattled by the two attacks that day. Shoemaker developed engine trouble on the way out and was almost shot down on the way home by fellow Fighting 6 pilots who only recognized his Wildcat at the last moment and led him home. Cook and Nagle were ordered back to *Enterprise* when they reported on station. Nagle developed a mechanical problem and, though Cook reported that he made a successful water landing, he was never seen again. Cook asked for a radar steer back to the ship, and the carriers even lighted their flight decks to guide him in, but he kept getting wave-offs as he made multiple attempts to land before he finally reported himself out of fuel at 1915 hours. Cook too was never seen again. It was speculated that the *Enterprise* Wildcats were never refueled during their hour-long visit aboard *Saratoga*; on such a busy day it was an understandable omission, but no less tragic in its consequences.

In the first aerial clash of the Solomons campaign, nine of 18 Wildcat fighters and one Dauntless dive bomber of 16 airborne when the attackers arrived were shot down by Tainan Air Corps Zeros, with four Wildcat pilots and one SBD radioman-gunner killed. The Japanese pilots submitted claims for 29 Wildcats and seven SBDs confirmed, and seven damaged Wildcats. The American pilots were credited with shooting down four Betty bombers outright as well as the five Vals, officially credited as 13. Another Betty claimed damaged was crash-landed in the northern part of Buka, and a sixth damaged bomber crashed when it landed back at Vunakanau airdrome. Nineteen of the 21 surviving Bettys sustained varying amounts of battle damage, while 28 4th Air Group pilots and crewmen were killed. Gordon Firebaugh shot down two Zeros, killing their pilots. In addition to Sakai, ten of the 15 surviving Zeros returned to Lakunai, some with many holes but none written off. Five other Zeros, unable to make it to Rabaul, landed on the abandoned Buka airfield, where one crashed.

The significance of this event – the biggest air battle for the US Navy in the Pacific War to that date – cannot be overstated. While half the defending Wildcats were lost in combat, the surviving pilots were all now of the opinion that the Wildcat could "take it" and survive, a confidence-builder that would spread to other squadrons. Because the fighter direction officers (FDOs) had failed to put the defenders in position in numbers sufficient to overcome the enemy, and had sacrificed altitude advantages in several cases, tactics would change as a result. Again, it was shown that the high-frequency radio frequency became overloaded in combat, which eventually led to the adoption of ultra-high-frequency (UHF) radio communications by the end of the Guadalcanal campaign. Pilots now knew of the 20mm defensive tail armament of the Betty, but also that the bomber caught fire easily when attacked. The rumor that the Zero could be defeated by a pilot keeping his speed higher than 250 miles per hour was confirmed, and this knowledge spread throughout the fleet.

However, Admiral Fletcher was concerned over the loss of ten percent of his fighters and was once again worried about declining fuel reserves for his ships. As a result, the admiral announced that the three carriers and their escorts would withdraw from the immediate vicinity of Guadalcanal on the evening of August 8, though he promised to provide "long-range" support for the next three days.

Ensign Register wrote of the day in his diary that evening:

August 7, 1942 – Today was the biggest day of my life. I took off at 0600 and flew in on the attack, but saw no enemy planes; in fact, I saw none all day. The attack was like hell broke loose; the cruisers, destroyers and dive bombers raining death on everything. It was a wonderful spectacle to behold. I flew all day and got in 8½ hours. Opposition was light for us and the ground troops at first. The Japs flew in at 1400 with eight Zeros and 22 heavy bombers and six dive bombers. I missed it as I was over the ship. We shot down eight. Lost four pilots. Cook was lost tonight, a forced landing at sea after dark; might find him tomorrow. Lost six pilots all together. Am dead tired tonight.

The next day, the Marines and sailors worked to bring supplies ashore at Kukum on Guadalcanal while out in Sealark Sound Admiral Turner paced the bridge of his flagship and searched the skies; he set his staff to making sure the unloading went as quickly as possible. The fact the ships had been loaded with no thought of what might be required first became apparent as the men sweated in the holds, searching for the gear most needed.

At midday, what would become the almost-daily noon raid by the 5th Air Group flying from Rabaul approached the southern Solomons.

Twenty-three Bettys and their Zero escort, flying at low level, managed to get within five miles of the fleet before being spotted by radar; this was despite warnings from Australian coastwatchers who had sighted them as they flew down the length of the Solomons Archipelago. At the last minute, they were intercepted by three Fighting 6 F4Fs which shot down three Bettys and a Zero, with NAP Aviation Machinist's Mate 1/c Don Runyon getting the Zero and one of the Bettys. Shipboard gunners accounted for 13 more Bettys shot down in exchange for hits on the transport *George F. Elliot*, which set the ship afire and seriously damaged the destroyer *Jarvis*.

Cash Register's day was exciting but frustrating, as he described it:

August 8, 1942 – Another very big day. Flew eight hours. Missed out on everything again today. I flew more than anyone else today because I volunteered for an extra flight when they thought the Japs were coming but they came after I got back. There is nothing I want more than to shoot some down. Our squadron got six today and lost no men; 12 were knocked down all together. I have volunteered to go ashore with seven other VF to occupy the island. We will have raids everyday and I will have plenty of chances then. I'll need luck, but by God I'm willing, and I know now they will never see me running away. Am afraid Cook has passed on. This is a great blow to me. My best friend here.

With the loss of 23 Wildcats to all causes over two days, Admiral Fletcher decided he lacked adequate air defense and announced that Task Force 61 would withdraw to maximum range. Unloading the transports was proceeding more slowly than planned; as a result of Fletcher's decision, Admiral Turner felt forced to withdraw since the transports would not have air cover; he therefore announced that he would unload as much as possible before departing at dawn on August 9.

5

PUG SOUTHERLAND'S ODYSSEY

August 7–9

Among the pilots launched into combat over what would become known as "Ironbottom Sound" on August 7 was James Julien Southerland II, who had enlisted in the Navy in 1931 and earned a direct appointment to the US Naval Academy, graduating in the Class of 1936. Though he dreamed of being a naval aviator, he had served an obligatory tour as a surface line officer for two years before reporting for flight school at Pensacola, from which he had graduated in 1939. On August 7, 1942, he was VF-5's senior division leader. The coming battle would be the first in which Navy fighters fought in the four-plane division, flying the "finger four" formation. As he later recalled:

> My squadron, VF-5, was assigned the tasks of strafing at Guadalcanal, patrolling over the carriers, and protecting the transports and screening vessels. My first flight, launched just before dawn at 0615 hours, had an ominous beginning when my wingman was caught in the slipstream of the plane ahead and crashed over the port bow of the carrier. I held no hopes for his life, but I later learned that he was picked up by a destroyer and his injuries were not serious.

Southerland, section leader Lieutenant (jg) Charles A. "Tab" Tabberer, and his wingman Ensign Donald "Don" Innis maintained a three-plane patrol, which was uneventful except for one dash after a fictitious Japanese shadowing plane:

> We landed at 0830 hours and were off again at 0915 hours, this time to patrol over the transports. Ensign Bob Price had replaced Ensign Ike Eichenberger as my wingman. This flight also passed without incident, though we were afforded an excellent view of the landing operations on Guadalcanal and the siege of Tulagi, Gavutu, and Tanambogo. The four of us landed aboard at 1130, with our next flight scheduled for 1315.

Southerland was in the wardroom, hastening to devour a buffet luncheon of sandwiches and coffee, when the order came down by messenger for his division to man their planes. He recalled:

> This unscheduled takeoff was explained by the fact that we had information concerning a flight of bombers headed toward us from Rabaul. I told my gang that this looked like the real McCoy and that we must keep as close together as we could, while maintaining of a very keen lookout. I also strapped on my .45-caliber pistol for the first time. Lieutenant Pete Brown's division was scheduled to take off at this time, so I had a flight of eight planes. We were launched at 1215 hours and I reported on station about 1300, requesting calls and instructions. We were told to patrol at 12,000 feet over the transports. Soon after reaching the assigned altitude, I heard the radio send a division out on a vector of 310 degrees at 8,000 feet. I made a weather report, describing visibility, amount of clouds, and bottom and top of overcast which was fairly thick at 11,000 feet; and also reported that visibility was excellent on top. A few minutes later, I went out on 310 degrees at 12,000 feet. Pete Brown's division remained over the transports. Pete was then ordered out on course 300 and shortly thereafter I was given a laconic 'left ten.' As I acknowledged this order, I picked up the enemy horizontal bombers about one-quarter mile away, just forward of my port beam and about 200 to 300 feet above me. I made a contact report as follows: 'Horizontal bombers, three divisions, nine planes each. Over Savo, headed for transports.' Next I sent: 'This division from Pug: Put gun switches and sight lamps on. Let's go get 'em, boys.'

Lieutenant Egawa, the Japanese bomber leader, had ordered his pilot to begin a gentle descent through the clouds from 16,400 feet. He intended to level off just beneath the clouds to attack the enemy shipping from there. The 27 bombers were in a broad vee-of-vees formation as they came through the clouds into clear air at about 1315 and were spotted by Southerland.

The American defenders fell on the formation just as the G4Ms turned to initiate their attack against the transports and opened their bomb bay doors. Southerland dropped into a low side run and picked out Egawa's lead bomber, flown by Petty Officer 1/c Shisuo Yamada; he hit the starboard engine solidly, setting it on fire. It nosed down in flames, tracing a dark line of smoke and flames until it disappeared in Sealark Sound:

> The bombers, Mitsubishi G4M Bettys, were too close to their release point to permit a climb and attack from above and ahead. Consequently, I made a low-side attack from their port quarter. I opened up first on the leading division with all guns, then fired a short burst at the second or starboard division. The range was too great for best results on this shot, but I closed very rapidly and was close aboard the third division when I opened fire on it. At this time I could see the open bomb bays, and it looked as though a total of eight to ten medium bombs were lined up fore and aft on either side of the one plane noted in particular. I hit this plane at the forward end of the bomb bay from below and at close range and saw a burst of flame.

As Southerland banked left and down, 7.7mm bullets cracked the bullet-proof windscreen and an incendiary bullet started a fire behind his cockpit:

> Retiring below and to starboard from this attack, I noted that my fuselage aft had been hit, probably by a bomber's tail gunner, and that it was smoking badly. My bullet-proof windshield had shattered from what was apparently a glancing shot. The smell of incendiary was very noticeable in the cockpit.

Undeterred, he banked around to execute a low-side attack against the right *chutai*.

> Thinking I might have to jump and not wanting to waste any ammunition, I returned to the attack making another low-side run from the starboard quarter on the third section, second division.

He poured all his remaining ammunition into the right engine and wing of the Betty, piloted by Petty Officer 1/c Yoshiyuki Sakimoto, which fell back in the formation.

> I expended all ammunition on this run, scoring one good hit just aft of the starboard engine of one plane and saw this section of his wing go up in smoke. I retired down and to starboard from this attack, still smoking badly in the tail.

Southerland had just shot down the first Japanese airplanes lost in the Solomons campaign.

At that moment, the escorting Zeros fell on the Wildcats. Don "Stinky" Innis managed to climb, scissor, and trade head-on shots with the five enemy fighters of Lieutenant Kawai's "challenge section" before he escaped into a cloud. Southerland's wingman, Ensign Robert L. Price, and Innis' section leader, "Tab" Tabberer, were both shot down. Lieutenant Herbert "Pete" Brown's second section was hit, with Brown's Wildcat so badly damaged he was lucky to land back aboard *Saratoga* in one piece. His wingman, Ensign Blair, managed to take cover in a cloud, then attacked the bombers and damaged one.

Second section leader Lieutenant (jg) Holt and his wingman Ensign Daly managed to confound the Japanese fighter leader, Lieutenant Commander Tadashi Nakajima, through use of the new "Thach Weave" maneuver that allowed them to clear each other's tail. The outnumbered pair of Wildcats engaged the enemy for several minutes, during which Holt managed to break from the Zeros and shoot down a Betty that exploded when its torpedo was hit, then damage a second Betty before the Zeros caught up and exploded his Wildcat. Daly bailed out, landing near Red Beach on Guadalcanal where he was rescued by a whaleboat from *Chicago* and returned to *Saratoga* later that afternoon.

As the others fought desperately, Southerland became engaged in the fight of his life, against Saburo Sakai, already victor over 50 enemy aircraft including the B-17 flown by Captain Colin P. Kelly on the second day of the Pacific War:

> At this time, the Zeros hit me. First one, then two, and finally four joined in what was too obviously the attack on a lame duck. These Zeros were perfectly capable of running circles around me, as I soon

discovered. They employed a system of teamwork in twos, in which one section would attack from above and on each quarter while the other section was getting into position to follow in a similar attack.

From the time I first opened up on the bombers, I never saw another of our fighters, though I knew my boys had followed me in and were also having their troubles.

Southerland, despite being unarmed and unable to fight back, presented a new challenge to Sakai, who later recalled that he had never come across an enemy fighter that could absorb damage like the Wildcat and keep flying.

As Southerland later recalled:

I immediately lowered my seat for better armor protection, and recharged all my guns, hoping that I might have had a jam in previous firing and could still do a little shooting. A Zero was attacking at this time from my starboard quarter, so I pushed over as though diving to escape him, then pulled out immediately, cracking my flaps and whacking off my throttle. He overran me as I'd hoped, and made a climbing turn to the left. I turned inside easily and had the aviator's dream: a Zero at close range, perfectly lined up in my sights for about a one-quarter deflection shot. I pressed my trigger without result and realized sadly that I'd have to fight the rest of this battle without guns.

Fortunately, I discovered a system that minimized the damage done by their fire. This consisted of merely determining which of the two Zeros attacking almost simultaneously on either quarter was about to open fire first, and turning sharply toward him as he opened up. This gave him a full-deflection shot so that he invariably failed to give enough lead when he fired at me, riddling my rear fuselage but doing little serious damage. This quick turn also placed the second plane directly behind me so that I was well protected by my armor plate. When runs were not exactly simultaneous, I would rely chiefly on my armor, placing the attackers directly aft in succession as they made their runs. I am deeply grateful to the manufacturer of our armor plate, for I could hear a steady stream of 7.7mm bullets zinging into it behind me, none of which damaged me in the slightest.

The fight continued for about five minutes, passing from slightly seaward of Savo Island at 11,500 feet down to about 400 feet over the hilltops and approximately 10–15 miles inland from the western tip of Guadalcanal. Sakai grew increasingly frustrated by his apparent inability to bring down this new enemy.

I felt that by working my way in this direction I was accomplishing two things: four Zeros were being drawn well away from the bombers they were supposed to protect and, if I lived to bail out, it would be over land scheduled to be friendly territory if all went well.

My plane was in bad shape but still performing nicely in low blower, full throttle, and full low pitch. Flaps and radio had been put out of commission. I'd tried to call Bob and Tab without success during the descent. The after part of my fuselage was like a sieve. She was still smoking from incendiary bullets but not on fire. All the ammunition box covers on my left wing were gone and 20mm explosive rounds had torn some gaping holes in its upper surface. I did not notice the condition of my right wing. My instrument panel was badly shot up, the goggles on my forehead had been shattered, my rear-view mirror was broken, and my Plexiglas windshield was riddled. The leak-proof tanks had apparently been punctured many times as some fuel had leaked down into the bottom of the cockpit even though the sealing feature was effective and there was no steady leakage. My oil tank had been punctured, and oil was pouring down over my right leg and foot.

Sakai came alongside Southerland and later remembered staring in amazement at the damage the Wildcat had sustained, and the fact that it continued to fly; he was filled with more respect for Southerland's pluck and courage in the fight than that of any other pilot he fought in the war. In a last attempt to put the Wildcat down, he made a run from Southerland's port quarter and put in a burst just under the left wing root with the last of his 20mm ammunition, turning away when he saw the F4F explode:

Good old 5-F-12 finally exploded. I think the explosion occurred from gasoline vapor. The flash was below and forward of my left foot. I was ready for it, having disconnected my radio cord. I opened the hood, and unfastened the chest strap and safety belt. I dove over the right side just aft of the starboard wing root, head first. My .45 holster caught on the hood track, but I got rid of it immediately, though I don't remember how. I did not have sufficient altitude to get out the safest way or to wait the prescribed interval before pulling the ripcord. I fervently asked God to let me live and pulled the ring just as my head was passing below the starboard wing. The plane did a chandelle to the right and went down in a dive, passing about 15 or 20 feet ahead of me.

The ring came out so easily in my hand that I immediately assumed my ripcord had been severed by gunfire. All aviators who bail out want to save the ring. This flashed through my mind as I reluctantly hurled it away and started clawing frantically into the webbing, trying to locate the release end of the rip cord. At this point the parachute opened and I was floating comfortably about 100–150 feet above the trees. Though I had seen the Zeros pull off to the left when my plane exploded, I still feared a strafing attack, so I immediately grabbed the upwind shroud and spilled what air I could from the chute, allowing it to fill about 25–50 feet above the trees. During the end of this drop, I unfastened the chest and leg straps. The trees broke my fall and I came to rest with very little shock. The harness was off and I was 100 yards away in nine seconds flat, a record of some sort, I think. It seemed logical that the Zero pilots might want to strafe my parachute, which presented a nice target stretched out over the trees, and I definitely didn't want to be there at the time. However, I saw no more of the Zeros, so I sat down on a hillside to take stock of the situation.

Sakai, spotting Southerland's parachute when it billowed, had turned away with his wingmen to search for other targets in the cloudy sky.

On Cape Esperance, Lieutenant Southerland discovered that he had not gotten out of the fight unhurt:

A hasty survey revealed the following damage: one large hole in my right foot, which was the most painful of my injuries; three holes in the calf of my right leg; one hole in my left knee; one in my left thigh; three in the upper part of my left arm; one glancing shot through my right eyebrow, which bled considerably but was not serious; and one small piece of shrapnel in my scalp. I also noted two flash burns from the explosion, one on an exposed portion of the right forearm and one on my left wrist between glove and sleeve. Minor abrasions on my left leg from the fall through the trees were of little consequence. Not bad at all, considering!

My right shoe was full of oil, blood, and dirt. I took it off, removed the dirty, oily black sock, stuffed it into the bullet hole to stop the bleeding, tied my shoe on tightly, and headed for the north coast of Guadalcanal. I estimated that my position was about four miles from the north coast and 10–15 miles from the western end of the island. I wanted to get out of this area quickly, as I knew I was in Japanese territory and thought they might have seen me bail out. I tried to make the coast by keeping to the hills, but after about an hour's struggle, with frequent rest periods, I realized that I would have to penetrate the jungle if I wanted to make any headway.

Southerland soon discovered he had been right to worry about the Japanese:

Suddenly I stopped and crept behind a bush to my right. In a high tree, to the left of the lofty dead tree I was using for a bearing, were two Japanese on a wooden platform apparently designed as a lookout post. Fortunately, I saw them first. I continued toward the jungle, keeping as well concealed as possible, and crawled into a discouragingly thick and seemingly impenetrable undergrowth.

There were masses of thick, thorny vines, spider webs with big formidable-looking spiders, and unseen but imagined wildlife of all sorts, mostly poisonous snakes and boa constrictors.

He was the first American to discover the real hellishness of the Guadalcanal jungle the Marines would come to know well.

Southerland had landed on Guadalcanal around 1400 hours, and by what he believed was 1730 hours he had pushed through the jungle, past some buildings that he feared might be occupied but which turned out to be empty, and reached the beach. He went into the water and cleansed his wounds, later tearing up his underwear to bandage them. Spotting some aircraft he identified as SBDs, he took out his signal mirror and managed to attract the attention of two that flew closer.

He ripped off his life vest and waved it, thinking it might be a better identification, then semaphored "SOS" and "Send Cruiser Scout." As he later related, "I didn't think either pilot or radioman could read semaphore, though one plane dropped a smoke bomb, flew low over me rocking his wings, and then headed off with the rest for the carrier." He spent a cold, windy night hiding in some bushes near the beach, hoping for rescue that didn't arrive.

The next morning, Southerland judged his position to be somewhere in the vicinity of Cape Esperance, and that the Marine position as best he understood it was at Kukum, which from what he could remember of his map was around 25 miles distant. He decided to set out along the coast in hopes of gaining US lines:

The going was tougher as my foot had swelled considerably and was much more painful. I soon came to what appeared to be a deserted missionary's home. It was made of wood and corrugated sheet metal with many modern conveniences. There were pigs and chickens in the yard. I investigated carefully, in search mainly of fresh water. This I found in some tanks to the rear. The handle was gone from the valve, but I found an old pump handle with elliptical holes in the shank which I used to turn on the water. I drank just enough to quench my thirst, as there was some danger that the tanks were contaminated.

He found an old truck and his hopes soared that he might find some way to drive to Kukum, but the tank was bone dry. He set off again:

Soon thereafter, I spotted three native boys headed towards me. I raised my right hand and in conventional greeting and they answered in kind. As we neared each other, they extended their right hands to shake in the white man's fashion. They were obviously friendly. I had to assume so anyhow, as they were a formidable looking trio, dressed only in sarongs, with large cane knives at their waists, beaded ornaments on ears and arms, and bracelets made out of boar tusks. They had bushy hair and were black as night. I was unarmed and definitely harmless. I pointed toward Kukum and said, "Japanese." One answered, "No Japanese," whereupon they continued on their way and I on mine.

Southerland continued his odyssey, getting soaked by two passing rain storms:

> About noon, I decided it was time to eat. Having selected a good coconut along the way, I now broke it open, loosening the fiber by pounding on a tree stump and ripping it off with my hands. I broke open two of the holes at the top of the shell with my Eversharp pencil and really enjoyed the cool and refreshing coconut milk. Though I don't like the meat itself, I ate some of it after breaking the shell, in the interest of nourishment.
>
> I slowly continued on my way and soon saw three wild horses coming toward me. Here seemed another opportunity for transportation of a sort. My foot was troubling me to such an extent that any idea to give it a rest seemed good. The horses, however, were teasers. I tried to attract them with some nice, white coconut meat, but they'd only get close then bolt away, and I soon abandoned this idea.
>
> I passed several deserted native villages, each consisting of a number of thatched huts. In one of these villages I found an old high-bowed war canoe, like something out of a movie, stored in a shed about 100 yards from the beach. I cleared a patch through the brush and rocks, and after about a half-hour's labor, with the help of some logs I used as rollers, the war canoe was launched. I made a paddle out of the bottom of a palm frond and climbed aboard. She leaked like a sieve, but I figured this was natural until the wood swelled to close the seams, so I started bailing out with my shoe. This system was doomed to failure as the canoe leaked faster than I could bail. After about a five-minute cruise, I beached the rescue ship just in time, and continued once more on foot.

Southerland continued along the coast, washing his wounds in small freshwater streams he came across. At around 1700 hours, his luck changed for the better:

> I passed more deserted villages, one of which had a little thatched Catholic chapel and schoolhouse. Further on, I located another canoe in a hut. This looked more seaworthy than the first, and I was about to embark on a second launching routine when I spotted two

more natives. They also responded favorably to the raised right-hand greeting. We shook hands. One, who spoke very good pidgin English, said, "Me very sorry," and pointed to my foot. Next he said, "Come with me." Noticing my hesitation, he next said, "Father told me to be good to white man." These were similar in appearance to the natives previously sighted, though the older bushy-haired one had a wooden ornament, like a large, wide fork, stuck in the back of his hair with the handle sticking upward.

I was worn out and figured I had little to lose, so I went with them. We returned first to the Catholic chapel. I told them I was a Catholic, which pleased them greatly. The younger one told me in pidgin English that his Christian name was Joseph, the older one's name was Jonas, and that they had gone to the missionary school for 13 years. Catholic was a magic word. They brought me some more oranges and fussed over me, trying to make me comfortable.

The two took him to their village, where they gave him soap to wash himself and then offered food.

The morning after the battle, Southerland was disappointed to find that when he looked out over Sealark Sound he could see no ships. The natives were reluctant to take him to Kukum for fear the Japanese had returned. Southerland settled in for a long stay in the village.

Joseph had sent one boy into the hills to bring back all the medicine the natives could find. He appeared with three bottles, two small ones labeled APC [aspirin, phenacetin, and caffeine] capsules and aspirin, and one large bottle with no label and about one-half full of a brownish liquid. Joseph pointed to this and said "Iodine." I smelled its contents, however, and noted the odor of plain old household Lysol. I then had Joseph boil me some water, and I soaked my foot in hot Lysol solution. The area of the wound was considerably reddened and swollen, so I figured some disinfectant was badly needed. Joseph also indicated the APC bottle and kept saying "Quinine." Since the mosquitoes and flies had been having a field day with me, and this was known to be malaria country, I decided to take some quinine tablets if Joseph was correct. I laid one of these on the tip of my tongue. The taste of quinine was unmistakable, so I took two of them.

Later that day, Southerland saw two ships approach the island and begin unloading. The natives decided that meant the Americans were still at Kukum, so they decided to resume the trip the next morning. Southerland recalled his final day in the jungle:

The boys came early all right, appearing in the door of the hut about an hour before sunrise. I was anxious to be on my way, so we launched the canoe about a half-hour later, and I took leave of some real friends. Jonas and two other boys came with me, so I left Joseph the only token of appreciation I owned, a penlight, which seemed to fascinate him but was small return for services rendered.

We headed toward Kukum, hugging the shoreline. I tried to persuade them to get farther out, but they were afraid of Japanese planes, and no amount of reasoning could convince them that no plane would waste ammunition on a native canoe. We had, however, passed many Japanese landing boats, all beached and damaged. I felt that Japanese might be encamped near the shoreline and wanted to increase the sniping range. However, we proceeded slowly and without incident until about one mile west of Kukum.

About halfway between us and our destination was a place apparently used for storing fuel and ammunition. Three Japanese flags were still flying. The natives asked me whose flags they were and, when I had to admit they were Japanese, they wanted to go back immediately. However, I told them I thought the village was deserted, so we approached it warily and saw no signs of life.

We then proceeded toward Kukum. Soon I saw men running toward the beach with rifles ready. They wore coveralls and helmets similar to those of the Japanese, so I didn't know who we were running into. The natives also questioned their identity. Taking faith in the evacuation of the village just passed, and realizing we just had to be successful in this campaign, I raised up and waved to them. They waved back, which convinced the natives we were old friends, so they paddled rapidly to the beach. What a relief it was to see our own Marines! I asked them to take good care of the natives, so they handed them food, candy, and cigarettes. I was laid in a blanket while they went for a truck to take me to a first aid station. I kept the natives with me and turned them over to a Marine intelligence officer. These were the first natives contacted since our landing had been made.

The rest is an anticlimax. That night, while I was resting in the medical tent in the woods near the airfield, the Japanese decided to make their first attack from the hills in which they were hiding. Tracers were skimming close aboard when they decided to evacuate the patients. Four corpsmen, who deserve some recognition for devotion to duty, carried me on a stretcher, and we spent from 2330 that night until dawn the next morning jumping in ditches, behind trees, and running like mad toward the beach to avoid gunfire.

Two days later, Southerland flew to Espiritu Santo aboard Admiral McCain's personal PBY.

Southerland's run-in with Saburo Sakai would become the stuff of legend.

6

DISASTER

August 8–16

Air attacks were not the only Japanese response to the invasion. The day of the invasion, Eighth Fleet commander Vice Admiral Gunichi Mikawa, aboard his flagship the cruiser *Chōkai*, in Simpson Harbor at Rabaul with Rear Admiral Mitsuharu Matsuyama's 18th Cruiser Division composed of light cruisers *Tenryū*, and *Yūbari* with destroyer *Yūnagi*, ordered Rear Admiral Aritomo Gotō's 6th Cruiser Division with heavy cruisers *Aoba, Furutaka, Kinugasa,* and *Kako*, en route to Rabaul from Kavieng, to rendezvous with his force near Cape St George that evening. Once joined, the fleet headed southeast toward New Georgia Sound, the body of open water down the Solomons chain that would soon come to be known to Americans as "the Slot;" Guadalcanal lay at the far end. Mikawa's ships heaved to off the east coast of Bougainville at the northern end of the Slot in order to transit the narrow waters late that afternoon. They planned to arrive at Guadalcanal shortly before midnight of August 8–9.

During the day of August 8, the Japanese were spotted by RAAF Hudson patrol planes flying from Milne Bay in New Guinea at 1020 and 1110 hours. The first sighting misidentified them as "three cruisers, three destroyers, and two seaplane tenders." Receiving no acknowledgement when they reported the sighting to the Allied radio station at Fall River, New Guinea, the first Hudson returned to Milne Bay at 1242 hours and reported the sighting in person. The second

Hudson failed to report its sighting by radio and landed back at Milne Bay at 1500 hours; the crew reported sighting "two heavy cruisers, two light cruisers, and one unknown type." The fleet off Guadalcanal did not receive these reports until 1845 and 2130 hours, respectively; by then, the enemy was mere hours distant.

At 1225 hours, two floatplanes that Mikawa had launched that morning to scout Guadalcanal returned and reported that they had spotted two groups of Allied ships off Guadalcanal and Tulagi respectively. As the fleet passed Choiseul Island at 1600 hours, Mikawa informed his captains that "On the rush-in we will go from south of Savo Island and torpedo the enemy main force in front of Guadalcanal anchorage; after which we will turn toward the Tulagi forward area to shell and torpedo the enemy. We will then withdraw north of Savo Island." It was a most daring plan, but the Imperial Navy had spent the past 20 years training for just such a night attack.

Despite Admiral Turner's requests for additional reconnaissance missions over the southern Solomons that afternoon, such missions had not happened; however, Turner was not informed of this and thus mistakenly believed the region was under Allied air observation throughout the day, concluding at dusk that the lack of contacts meant the fleet was safe from Japanese surface attack.

That afternoon, Admiral Crutchley divided the support force to protect the transports while they continued unloading through the night. HMAS *Australia* and *Canberra*, with *Chicago* and the destroyers *Patterson* and *Bagley*, patrolled between Lunga Point and Savo Island to block the entrance to Sealark Sound between Savo Island and Cape Esperance. *Vincennes*, *Astoria*, and *Quincy* with destroyers *Helm* and *Wilson* patrolled between Tulagi and Savo Island to cover the passage between Savo and Florida islands. *San Juan*, HMAS *Hobart*, and the destroyers *Monssen* and *Buchanan* patrolled the eastern entrance between Florida and Guadalcanal. USS *Blue* and *Ralph Talbot* (DD-390), the only radar-equipped destroyers, were west of Savo to give early warning of any approaching Japanese ships, with *Talbot* in the northern passage and *Blue* in the southern passage, 8–20 miles apart. Unfortunately, their primitive radars could be affected by a nearby landmass, which meant they were too far apart to provide full coverage to the west with their uncoordinated patrols. Compounding the error, *Chicago*'s Captain Howard D. Bode ordered the ship's radar turned off at dusk, mistakenly believing that the emissions could reveal his position; the fire control radar would conduct a single sweep every 30 minutes. Because the fleet's crews had been on constant alert for two days, they went to Condition One at dusk with half on duty while the others tried to sleep in their hot and humid berthing compartments or above decks.

At 2130 hours, Crutchley and Vandegrift met with Turner on his command ship to discuss Fletcher's departure and the transports' withdrawal schedule. Crutchley had placed Captain Bode in charge of the southern group, but failed to inform the commanders of the other groups. Turner, Crutchley, and Vandegrift discussed the reports of the "seaplane tender" force, deciding it was not a threat since seaplane tenders did not operate at night. Shortly before 2400 hours, Vandegrift departed to inspect the unloading situation at Tulagi while Crutchley decided not to return to the southern force, neglecting to inform the other commanders of his decision or location.

Approaching Guadalcanal just past 2300 hours, Admiral Mikawa launched three floatplanes for a final reconnaissance. Several Allied ships in Sealark Sound heard or spotted them, but none considered the unknown aircraft a threat; Crutchley and Turner were not informed of the sightings. After launching the floatplanes, the enemy force took up a single column formation led by *Chōkai*, with *Aoba*, *Kako*, *Kinugasa*, *Furutaka*, *Tenryū*, *Yūbari*, and *Yūnagi* following. Spotting *Blue* shortly after midnight, Mikawa ordered his ships to slow to 22 knots to reduce their wakes and turned to pass north of the island. *Blue*'s radar failed to spot anything due to the backdrop of the surrounding islands. Four minutes later, Mikawa's lookout spotted *Ralph Talbot*. Determining they had not been spotted, Mikawa turned to pass south of Savo and increased speed to 26 then 30 knots.

At 0125 hours, Mikawa released his fleet to operate independently. At 0131 hours he ordered "Every ship attack."

At 0134 hours, the ships of the southern force were spotted at a range of 12,500 yards, silhouetted by the burning transport *George F. Elliott*. Four minutes later, the cruisers launched torpedoes at the unsuspecting enemy. At the same time, lookouts aboard *Chōkai* spotted the northern force ten miles away. The flagship turned to face the new threat while the rest of the fleet followed. At 0143 hours, lookouts on the destroyer *Patterson* spotted *Kinugasa* 5,000 yards dead ahead. The captain immediately radioed the fleet: "Warning! Warning! Strange ships entering the harbor!" also sending the warning as he ordered full speed while his gunners fired star shells at the enemy. The order to fire torpedoes was unheard over the gunfire.

As *Patterson* opened fire, the floatplanes dropped flares directly over *Canberra* and *Chicago*. A minute later, *Canberra* opened fire just as *Chōkai* and *Furutaka* opened fire back. *Canberra* took 24 hits within three minutes when *Aoba* and *Kako* joined in, and caught fire. Without power and unable to fire any guns or radio a warning, *Canberra* came to a stop, unable to fight the fires or pump out the water pouring through the side hits.

Aboard *Chicago*, Captain Bode awakened from a sound sleep and ordered his secondary battery to fire star shells, but they were defective. *Chicago* was hit in the bow moments later by a torpedo fired by *Kako* that sent a shock wave the length of the ship, damaging the main battery fire control director. Moments later, a second torpedo hit but failed to explode, while a shell hit the mainmast. *Chicago* steamed west for the next 40 minutes; Captain Bode made no attempt to take command of the battle, though he was technically still Senior Officer Present Afloat (SOPA) as he headed away from the fight.

Patterson engaged in a gun duel, taking a hit aft that caused moderate damage and killed ten crewmen. *Patterson* damaged *Kinugasa* before the ship's lookouts lost sight of the enemy fleet as it headed along the eastern shore of Savo Island and disappeared.

Vincennes, *Astoria*, and *Quincy* were steaming quietly at ten knots, their captains asleep, when the Japanese attacked the southern force. Although they received *Patterson*'s warning and the flares and gunfire were visible, it took precious minutes to go from Condition One to General Quarters. The enemy had already turned toward the northern force at 0144 hours; an inadvertent turn by *Tenryū* and *Yūbari*, followed by *Furutaka*, allowed the Japanese to envelop the northern force and attack from both sides, firing torpedoes, then turning on their searchlights at 0150 hours and firing on the three ships.

Two minutes later, as Japanese shells fell around *Astoria* and the ship opened fire in return, Captain Greenman, awakened by the gunfire, ran to the bridge and ordered a ceasefire in the mistaken belief they were firing on friendly ships. Incoming shells from *Chōkai* – all of which missed – changed his mind but Mikawa's flagship found the range with its fifth salvo, which ripped *Astoria*'s superstructure and started a fire amidships; the sixth salvo set the airplane hangar afire, illuminating it to the Japanese. The next salvo knocked out the No. 1 turret. *Aoba*, *Kinugasa*, and *Kako* joined *Chōkai*; between 0200 and 0215 hours they pounded *Astoria*, bringing the ship to a stop. A final shot from *Astoria* missed *Kinugasa's* searchlight, but hit *Chōkai* in the forward turret, putting the ship out of action and causing moderate damage. At 0225 hours, *Astoria* lost steering control from the bridge. *Astoria* steered a zig-zag course south, but soon the fires spread and the ship lost all power.

Quincy called General Quarters when the flares were spotted. The crew had just manned their battle stations when the Japanese searchlights came on. *Quincy* soon came under cross fire from *Aoba*, *Furutaka*, and *Tenryū* that set the ship afire. As *Quincy* turned toward the enemy, the ship was hit by two torpedoes from *Tenryū* that caused severe damage. *Quincy* fired four salvos, one of which hit *Chōkai's* chart room 20 feet from where Mikawa stood, killing and wounding 36 though he was uninjured. *Quincy's* bridge was hit, killing or wounding all the bridge crew, including Captain Moore. A torpedo fired by *Aoba* silenced the ship's guns. *Quincy's* assistant gunnery officer later reported that he had found the bridge a shambles of dead bodies with only three still alive. The quartermaster reported that the captain had ordered him to beach the ship on Savo Island before he was hit. At that moment, Captain Moore straightened up, moaned, then slumped over, dead. The ship was heeling rapidly to port and sinking by the bow. At 0238 hours, *Quincy* sank bow first.

Awakened with the news, *Vincennes'* Captain Riefkohl ordered General Quarters. When the enemy searchlights illuminated the ship, he hesitated to open fire, fearing the searchlights were friendly. Moments later, *Kako* set *Vincennes* afire; Riefkohl ordered speed increased to escape the attack. At 0155 hours, *Chōkai* fired two torpedoes that caused heavy damage. *Kako* and *Kinugasa* pounded *Vincennes*. *Kinugasa* was hit by an American salvo that damaged the ship's steering. *Vincennes* then took 74 hits from the rest of the enemy fleet before being hit by a third torpedo from *Yūbari* at 0203 hours. With his ship afire and listing to port as *Vincennes* came to a halt with the boiler rooms destroyed, Riefkohl ordered "Abandon ship" at 0216 hours and the cruiser sank at 0250 hours.

Admiral Mikawa's decision to withdraw as *Vincennes* sank saved the Allied fleet further catastrophe. The Allied force covering the transports was reduced to the cruisers HMAS *Australia* and *Hobart*, and

USS *San Juan*, none of which was in position to oppose a further advance by Mikawa in which each would likely have suffered the fates of the others had they joined combat against the Japanese, who had just demonstrated their overwhelming superiority in night fighting.

As Captain Riefkohl ordered "Abandon ship," Mikawa and his staff concluded that with the fleet scattered in the action, it would take time to regroup, in addition to requiring the time-consuming labor-intensive activity of reloading torpedoes. Additionally, the admiral did not know whether there were any surviving enemy warships, or where they might be. Most importantly, he knew the enemy was supported by aircraft carriers and his force had no air cover, though he did not know that Fletcher's withdrawal to maximum range meant he could not intervene. Several officers urged him to continue the attack, but the final decision was withdrawal before daylight to prevent loss to enemy aircraft. Mikawa ordered cease fire. As they passed around the north side of Savo Island, *Furutaka*, *Tenryū*, and *Yūbari* ran across *Ralph Talbot*. Fixed with searchlights, the destroyer was heavily damaged before escaping into a nearby rain squall.

While the Japanese disappeared into the darkness and headed back up New Georgia Sound to return to Rabaul, the survivors fought to save themselves. *Astoria* was still afloat, despite having taken 65 hits. By 0300 hours, nearly 400 crewmen, including 70 wounded, assembled on the forecastle. A bucket brigade battled the fire in the secondary battery while the doctors and corpsmen improvised an emergency sick bay in the captain's cabin. The bucket brigade managed to drive the fire aft on the starboard side of the gun deck.

Patterson came alongside *Canberra* to assist firefighting. An hour later, the fires were almost under control, but Admiral Turner ordered the ship scuttled if it could not accompany the fleet as they withdrew at 0630 hours because Fletcher could not provide air cover, having once again obsessively withdrawn his fleet to refuel. The survivors were taken off and the destroyers *Selfridge* (DD-357) and *Ellet* (DD-398) sank the ship.

General Vandegrift convinced Admiral Turner that the Marines desperately needed more supplies unloaded before he departed. Turner postponed departure until 1500 hours and unloading proceeded.

The destroyer *Bagley* had managed to take off *Astoria's* wounded at 0445 hours. When the ship returned at daylight, it appeared that the cruiser could be saved; a salvage crew of 325 went back aboard and resumed firefighting with another bucket brigade. At 0700 hours, destroyer *Hopkins* was able to secure a towline and swung *Astoria* around to tow the ship to shallow water. At 0900 hours, *Wilson* came alongside *Astoria* to pump water into the fire, but both destroyers departed at 1000 hours when the fleet received warning from an Australian coastwatcher that an enemy air strike was headed down from Rabaul. USS *Buchanan* was ordered to assist *Astoria* and the fleet tug *Alchiba* was sent to tow the ship but the fire increased and several internal explosions occurred before *Buchanan* could arrive. *Astoria's* list increased to ten degrees, then 15; the bow rose as the stern sank. *Buchanan* arrived at 1130 hours but could not come alongside. At 1200 hours, Captain Greenman gave the order to abandon ship. The men went into the water and *Astoria* rolled slowly over on the port beam and sank by the stern at 1216 hours. None of the salvage crew were lost, but 219 men were listed missing or killed in the battle. Fortunately, the expected air attack did not happen. After the war, it was learned that the force had spotted the damaged *Jarvis* south of Guadalcanal and sunk the ship with all hands.

Admiral Turner ordered unloading resumed until nightfall, when the fleet departed and sailed to Nouméa. Despite the extension, much crucially needed equipment never came ashore due to the disorganized loading of the ships.

A measure of revenge was exacted against the victorious Japanese the next morning. During the night, Admiral Mikawa had released *Aoba*, *Furutaka*, *Kako*, and *Kinugasa* to return to their base at Kavieng while he proceeded to Rabaul with *Chōkai*, *Tenryū*, and *Yūbari*. At 0750 hours on August 10, the US submarine *S-44*, one of the ancient World War I-era submarines sent to Brisbane the previous spring to reinforce the surviving submarines of the Asiatic Fleet, came to periscope depth and sighted the four heavy cruisers 70 miles from Kavieng at a range of less than 900 yards. Tracking the enemy ships, *S-44* fired four Mark X torpedoes at 0806 hours at the rear ship, only 700 yards distant. The old Mark Xs were better performers than the defective Mark XIVs carried by more modern fleet submarines. The first struck *Kako* abreast the No. 1 turret on the starboard beam at 0808 hours. The others hit near the forward magazines and boiler rooms Nos 1 and 2. Five minutes later, the cruiser rolled over to starboard and exploded when sea water reached the boilers. The ship sank at 0815 hours, the largest Japanese man-of-war lost to date in the Pacific War.

The withdrawal of the Allied invasion fleet from the Eastern Solomons on August 9 left the approximately 17,000 Marine ground troops ashore in dire straits, without naval, air, or logistical support. Bottlenecks encountered in getting food and equipment ashore had cut anticipated limited supply levels to the bone. There were rations enough for 37 days, and sufficient munitions for about four days of heavy fighting. The troops and their officers were simply stunned by the retirement of the fleet, and, when news arrived, by the defeat off Savo.

The strategic offensive in the Solomons had bogged down as soon as it began. The 1st Marine Division had occupied all of its viable objectives in the area, and at little cost, but it could only sit on them. Everyone expected the Japanese to mount a swift, brutal challenge on land. Steps taken during the first days ashore were in response to that expectation.

In its first night action with the Imperial Navy involving heavy ship units, the US Navy had been thoroughly savaged, the result of its prewar failure to realistically train at night as the enemy had done. The Battle of Savo Island was the worst defeat the Navy had ever suffered in a fair fight. As a result, for the next crucial months supplies sent to Guadalcanal as the Japanese came close to reconquering the island arrived in small convoys during daylight hours, when they could receive air cover. The Marines received barely enough provisions to survive, and just enough ammunition to withstand the repeated enemy attempts to retake the island. Staff Sergeant James F. Eaton recalled the diet of enemy food: "There were no fat Marines in the division when we were finally evacuated in December." Had Mikawa known that Fletcher was out of position and gathered his fleet to go after the transports, the outcome of the Battle of Guadalcanal might have been very different.

While the Marines ashore worked to consolidate their positions, Admiral Fletcher's carriers remained at sea, waiting for the enemy. Ensign Register wrote of the constant refueling, which no one in the fleet other than the admiral liked:

August 10, 1942 – We made no headway today as we met some tankers and at 1730 a tanker pulled up alongside and we started taking on fuel. I think it is a very dangerous situation as we are moving so slow and in a straight line. Hope we don't get a torpedo tonight. Four have crossed our bow so far; hope our luck holds. Long. 164-17; Lat. 16-03; 0630; Course 140; Speed 15.

August 11, 1942 – Task force still is taking on fuel. No sign of sending eight of us into Tulagi. I can't figure out, nor can anyone else, how they can possibly leave the Marines with no air support. They have been raided every day since we started and with no air opposition, they will slaughter them. Very few Jap prisoners were taken as I feel is proper. I swear that no Jap will live that crosses my path. They are not human beings. They can't be, the atrocities they have inflicted on conquered people.

Rumors that the Imperial Navy was on its way spread through the carriers, as Register recorded:

August 12, 1942 – Still taking on fuel. The situation looks very bad for us at the present. Japan is sending everything she has in this area down against us. A lot is coming from Japan itself. 40 Zeros were over Tulagi yesterday. If we would have been ashore there, they undoubtedly would have cleaned us up. Am afraid before this is over, we will be missing at least one carrier and have darn few pilots left. Our air officer says the biggest Naval battle in history is approaching. We have a good fleet, and will take a terrible toll when the time comes.

On August 16, he wrote:

August 16, 1942 – Nothing of excitement today. It seems as if we are in the lull before the storm. From the daily summary reports it looks as if there will be a sea battle pretty soon.

7

THE CAVALRY ARRIVES

August 11–22

Once the Allied fleet had retreated from the Guadalcanal area following the defeat at Savo Island, the primary objective for the abandoned Marines was getting the captured Japanese airfield on the Lunga Plain operational as quickly as possible. Without air support, they were completely at the mercy of Japanese aerial and naval attacks, and highly vulnerable to ground assault. It was fortunate the Japanese were initially nearly as hamstrung as the Americans.

While the Marines were developing a defensive perimeter and rushing to complete their airfield, the Japanese established a routine for keeping the Americans off balance and sleep deprived. From the beginning – the first August 7 air raid – the opposing troops had been undertaking hostile contacts by way of small but persistent land, naval, and aerial hit-and-run engagements. The pressure rarely became very strong, but they plinked away day and night, day in and day out, always testing the resistance, always being bothersome bullies.

The Americans were fortunate that Guadalcanal and the Japanese airfields at Rabaul were separated by more than 600 miles of the Solomon and Coral Seas. Though the Zero was the longest-legged operational fighter in the world, the 1,300-mile round trip between Rabaul and Guadalcanal taxed even its capabilities to the limit, while the twin-engine Betty had fuel for only 15 minutes over the target. The range limitations of the Zero and the Betty meant that missions had to be flown by the most direct route, with no margin for feints or for speeding up the throttled-back engines of the fuel-conserving fighters and bombers. Additionally, the weather in the South Pacific meant that they flew from their bases after the morning cloud buildups had dissipated, which required adherence to a predictable timetable. The route took them from Rabaul to Buka, off northwestern Bougainville, down to Buin, overlooking the Shortland Islands, then straight through New Georgia Sound.

A combat schedule developed since the Japanese could only fly a large formation of bombers from Rabaul in daylight. Weather allowing, the bombers and their escorting fighters would take off from their air bases at Rabaul by 0800 hours, though delays were caused by early morning buildups of weather over the Solomon Sea that could delay departure until as late as 1000 hours.

Before the war, the Australian Navy had recruited Australians living in the Solomons to remain behind if the Japanese appeared and operate a radio warning system when they spotted Japanese naval or air forces. Coastwatcher Jack Read, whose station in the hills of Bougainville overlooked Buka, was generally first to send word of an impending air strike. Paul Mason, near Buin, was next. There were invariably two hours between Mason's warning and the arrival of the bombers over Guadalcanal. This schedule allowed the Marines to count upon several quiet hours after dawn and before dusk for getting work done, with at least two hours during midday in which to find cover and take aim.

The early warning system worked well once defending fighters arrived. As the Japanese formation flew down the Slot, the aircraft were spotted by the Australian coastwatchers on the various islands, who radioed their sightings to Cactus Control at what became Henderson Field, named in honor of Major Lofton R. Henderson, who had been killed leading VMSB-241 in their attack on the Japanese fleet at Midway. By the time they passed Munda, the defenders on Guadalcanal would man their fighters and take off. The Wildcats needed every minute of warning they could get, since it took around 45 minutes for the airplanes to get to 20,000 feet. The enemy formation would finally arrive between 1200 and 1300 hours. Given the variability of weather, which in this equatorial region was marginally predictable and subject to rapid change without prior notice, there were a few times where the clouds over the Slot prevented the coastwatchers from spotting the oncoming Japanese in time to give sufficient warning.

The Japanese at Rabaul lacked the means to mount an immediate ground counteroffensive. They were deeply embroiled in a vicious strategic offensive in Papua New Guinea, which was also being run out of Rabaul. The New Guinea attack restricted the number and type of aggressive actions that the Imperial Navy was free to take against the American castaways in the Eastern Solomons, but the Japanese airmen never let up.

Antiaircraft defense on the island was built around the 90mm antiaircraft guns of the 3rd Defense Battalion, bolstered by the battalion's light automatic weapons batteries and numerous infantry machine guns set up on antiaircraft mounts. The 90mm M1 gun was roughly equivalent in capability to the German 88mm Flak 18. It could fire a 90mm shell 62,474 feet to a maximum altitude of 43,500 feet. Altitudes up to 25,000 feet could be covered regardless of weather or temperature, the two performance variables. Thus, the lone enemy raiders of the early days were usually forced to fly above that altitude, which hampered the accuracy of their bombing and reconnaissance.

Almost as soon as the runway had fallen into the hands of the 3rd Battalion, 5th Marines on August 8, the division air and engineering officers sized things up. They reported that they could put down 2,600 feet of usable runway by August 10, and that another 1,200-by-160-foot section could be completed in the week after that. Rear Admiral Turner promised on August 8 that aircraft would arrive on August 11. Unfortunately, when the fleet was forced to retire following Savo Island, it left with nearly all the 1st Engineer Battalion's equipment, which had yet to be unloaded. Construction of the airfield commenced on August 9 when the 1st Engineer and 1st Pioneer Battalions managed to gather sufficient gear to get started. A miserable 15 percent of their equipment and supplies had been landed, with none of the heavy equipment making it ashore. Thus, they were forced to manhandle 100,000 cubic feet of earth fill to cover the depression in the center of the field that had been left by the Japanese, who had begun their construction at both ends and built toward the center.

The engineers used a huge steel girder as a drag, while a captured Japanese road roller was used to pack the fill. Japanese gear contributed heavily to the small store of engineering equipment available to the Americans, though in general the captured equipment was in poor condition; ingenious American mechanics kept it working hour after brutal hour in their race against time. The only earth-moving equipment was one angle-dozer that the pioneers had managed to land. Dump trucks were nonexistent. The engineers performed incredible feats of improvisation as they overcame monumental difficulties.

On August 11, Major General Millard Harmon, administrative head of Army ground forces in the South Pacific (ComGenSoPac), wrote to Army Chief of Staff George Marshall concerning the situation in the Eastern Solomons: "The thing that impresses me more than anything else in connection with the Solomons action is that we are not prepared to follow up. We have seized a strategic position from which future operations in the Bismarcks can be strongly supported. Can the Marines hold out? There is considerable room for doubt."

On August 12, Navy Lieutenant William Sampson, staff aide and pilot for Admiral McCain, radioed the Guadalcanal-based ground controllers that his PBY-5 Catalina flying boat had developed a serious mechanical malfunction which prevented him from landing in the water off Kukum. He was allowed to land amidst the dust and rubble of the airfield construction effort. Mechanics who checked the plane found no malfunctions. The admiral's aide had conned his way into the history books as pilot of the first plane to land on Henderson Field. Sampson evacuated two wounded Marines, the first aerial evacuation of wounded from a combat zone in the Pacific. He reported the field was in excellent condition, but it was really quite a mess.

That same day, Admiral McCain learned that the transport *William Ward Burroughs*, which carried Air Group 23's equipment and ground crews, had been delayed and could not get to Guadalcanal before August 19. The Marines at Henderson reported that 400 drums of Japanese aviation gasoline had been captured, but there was absolutely no equipment with which to service the aircraft. In response, McCain ordered Major Charles "Fog" Hayes, XO of VMO-251, to leave for Guadalcanal with elements of his squadron's ground staff to prepare for Air Group 23's arrival.

At noon on August 13, the five officers and 118 enlisted men of the Navy's Advanced Base Aviation Construction Battalion 1 (CUB-1) were in the midst of debarking at Espiritu Santo when unit commander Ensign George Polk was informed that they would depart in two days for service at Guadalcanal. CUB-1 had to unload, repack, and reload as much of their gear as they could aboard four old World War I-vintage four-stack destroyers converted to transport amphibious troops such as Marine Raiders. Each could carry only 30 tons of cargo, which meant that only absolutely essential gear and equipment was taken. Since the most essential materials had been stowed in the holds of the ship that brought CUB-1 to Espiritu Santo, the men barely had time to transship 400 drums of aviation gasoline, 32 drums of lubricants, 282 bombs of various sizes, belted machine-gun ammunition, and miscellaneous tools and spare parts. CUB-1 boarded the destroyer-transports carrying light packs and small arms, but not one tent, and no food. The VMO-251 ground staffers joined them on the ships. Lieutenant Hugh MacKenzie, an Australian naval reservist (RANVR) assigned to operate a forward radio station at Guadalcanal, embarked with the CUB-1 and VMO-251 men. His job on the island was to end the rash of garbled transmissions and lost messages that had been plaguing the coastwatcher network since the American arrival in the Solomons.

The convoy disembarked men and cargo at Kukum after dark on August 15. The next morning, CUB-1 and the VMO-251 Marines moved to Henderson Field, where they learned that the Marine quartermaster could not make good all of the personal gear they had left at Espiritu Santo. Lieutenant MacKenzie had to settle for a narrow five-foot-high dugout on exposed ground north of the runway as the site for his radio station.

On August 18, eight Betty bombers arrived over Henderson in the largest air strike since August 9 as the 25th Air Flotilla began the aerial assault leading up to the first Japanese effort to land troops and retake the island. Forced to remain above 25,000 feet by antiaircraft fire, the bombers did little harm. But it was clear to all that the enemy was resuming work and would be back. As yet, nothing stood in their path. A three-ship convoy from Nouméa arrived after the Japanese departed. The ships brought five days of food, which, along with captured Japanese provisions, gave the Marines a two-week food supply. To stretch the supplies as far as possible, the Marines were limited to two meals per day.

In the aftermath of the American invasion, Imperial General Headquarters assigned the Imperial Army's 17th Army, a corps-sized command at Rabaul commanded by Lieutenant General Harukichi

Hyakutake, the task of retaking Guadalcanal. The 17th was at the time part of the campaign in New Guinea; thus only a few units were available: the 35th Infantry Brigade under Major General Kiyotake Kawaguchi at Palau; the 4th (Aoba) Infantry Regiment in the Philippines; and the 28th Infantry Regiment commanded by Lieutenant Colonel Kiyonao Ichiki, which was already aboard transport ships near Guam. Ichiki's regiment, the closest, arrived first. Shortly after midnight on August 19, 916 soldiers from the unit's advance echelon landed from destroyers at Taivu Point, east of the Lunga Defensive Perimeter, hiking nine miles west that night toward the Marine perimeter.

On August 19, CUB-1 and the 1st Engineer Battalion reported that Henderson was fit to support air operations. The airfield was now a 3,800-foot strip 150 feet wide, covered with gravel, with a dirt taxiway and parking area destined to become fields of mud in the many rain storms. The airfield was surrounded by a tenuously held defensive line extending from Point Cruz on the west to the Ilu River on the east, leaving the field only a quarter mile from a mile-long piece of high ground that would come to be known in Marine history as "Bloody Ridge." There were no protective revetments and aircraft maintenance would test American ingenuity throughout their time on the island. The only structure on the field was a wooden tower that the Japanese had constructed which became known as "the Pagoda." *Time* magazine reporter Robert Sherrod, who landed with the Marines, described living conditions at the field as "appalling" with sleeping choices limited to mud-floor tents or dugouts, with slit trenches close by. Malarial mosquitos were numerous. The fliers would be issued Japanese mosquito netting, something the "mud Marines" could only hope for. The facilities were crude, but Henderson Field was ready. It was just in time.

The sky over the Coral Sea was a deep blue with a few clouds on the morning of August 20, when a 14th Air Group H6K "Mavis" operating from the advance patrol base in the Shortland Islands began tracking a cruiser and two destroyers at 1020 hours, transmitting news of the sighting. At 1130 hours, the Mavis reported that the three warships were escorting an aircraft carrier when it sighted the auxiliary aircraft carrier USS *Long Island* (ACV-1), the deck loaded with aircraft. The strange-looking ship had begun life on January 11, 1940 as the C-3 cargo liner *Mormacmail*. Taken over by the Navy on March 6, 1941, the ship had emerged from the yards with the superstructure removed and replaced by a 362-foot flight deck, becoming the first of a new class of aircraft carrier – Auxiliary Escort Carriers – which would over the next few years become the most numerous class of aircraft carriers in the world, by then known as CVEs, which their crews would claim stood for "combustible, vulnerable and expendable." When the message from the Mavis revealing the presence of *Long Island* was received by Combined Fleet headquarters at Truk, Japanese commanders were elated, but they missed the significance of the carrier that the Mavis had sighted, since they knew nothing of the existence of US "auxiliary carriers." To Admiral Yamamoto's staff, it appeared that *Long Island* was stalking Admiral Tanaka's slow Reinforcement Group, which was steaming steadily toward Guadalcanal after departing Truk in two forces on August 16 and 17. *Long Island* was beyond the range of any Japanese strike aircraft, but Tanaka's fleet was in range of the unidentified American carrier. Vice Admiral Nishizo Tsukahara ordered Tanaka to turn away from Guadalcanal and turn directly toward Rabaul. If the Americans knew where he was, they might chase him and in so doing come within range of the 5th Air Attack Force's Bettys.

At 1340 hours, Yamamoto's headquarters received a message from the Mavis in the next search sector over from first, reporting the presence of a second aircraft carrier and several surface escorts; in fact, this was *Enterprise* with escorts. The big flying boat was unnoticed by any American radars, and eased within 40 miles of the carrier as the ship continued tracking its course. At 1334 hours, *Enterprise*'s CXAM air search radar finally picked up the Mavis, and two VF-71 Wildcats flying CAP nearby were vectored out to investigate.

Before the Wildcats could reach the Mavis, a patrolling VS-71 SBD piloted by Ensign Harlan Coit spotted it, and was in turn spotted by the Japanese pilot moments later. The Mavis turned toward home at full power. Coit caught up with it and made several firing runs in the face of heavy defensive machine-gun and cannon fire, but he was unable to hit it in a vulnerable spot. The Mavis escaped while Ensign Coit turned back to make an emergency landing on *Wasp*. The Dauntless was full of holes and its hydraulic system was out of commission, but both Coit and his gunner were safe. The Japanese had missed spotting *Wasp*.

At 1400 hours *Long Island* reached the launch point off the tip of San Cristobal Island, 200 miles south of Guadalcanal. *Long Island's* captain, Commander Donald Duncan, ordered full speed ahead. Black smoke poured from the horizontal funnels on the starboard side as *Long Island's* single diesel engine strained to bring the ship to the maximum speed of 16.5 knots – half that of a fleet carrier.

For *Long Island* and the precious cargo of F4F-4 Wildcats of VMF-223 and SBD-3s of VMSB-232, this was their second attempt to get to Guadalcanal. After less than a month in preparation following notification on July 5 that they were deploying to the South Pacific, the pilots and gunners had packed themselves aboard the little carrier in Pearl Harbor on August 2 and *Long Island* set sail unescorted into the great unknown of the war-torn Pacific. Their ground crews and other key personnel from Marine Air Group 23, and all the necessary ordnance, fuel, and supplies needed to begin air operations, departed separately aboard the transport *William Ward Burroughs*.

On August 9, 1942, completely unaware of conditions on Guadalcanal, *Long Island* had neared the launch point when Captain Duncan learned of the disaster suffered in the Battle of Savo Island the night before. Duncan turned around and headed for the American base at Suva, Fiji, to await clearance to launch his cargo of precious aircraft and pilots. Upon arrival, he informed Admiral Robert Ghormley that most of the pilots were too green to be committed to combat. Ghormley bucked the matter to Admiral McCain, who ordered eight more-experienced pilots transferred to VMF-223 from the well-trained but unblooded Vila-based VMF-212, which would take 223's least-experienced pilots in trade and train them further. On August 14, *Long Island* departed Suva for Efate to make the swap, but the VMF-212 pilots did not come aboard until the day before the ship departed for Guadalcanal on August 18.

On the way out from Pearl, the Marines had worried about getting off the carrier while in the Pacific "doldrums" where there was no wind over the deck. Dive-bomber leader Dick Mangrum recalled: "We had no idea how far south this equatorial condition would be found, and considered ourselves fortunate to discover our destination was far enough south to be well away from this situation." With the southeast tradewind adding another ten knots to the breeze over the flight deck, the crews in the 12 new SBD-3 Dauntless dive bombers checked the gear and equipment – spark plugs, starter cartridges, tool kits, even spare tires – they had stuffed in their cockpits the night before to support themselves for the two weeks they would be on their own before their ground crews arrived. The squadron was six airplanes short of its authorized strength because these 12 had been the only Dauntlesses available in the Ford Island fleet pool when Mangrum learned of their coming deployment. Each Dauntless carried a 500-pound bomb to supplement the small supply on Guadalcanal. According to Mangrum, "receiving orders to bomb-up our airplanes was an eye-opener to just how difficult things were where we were going." Mangrum later recalled that: "Our launch was delayed to the afternoon since the Japanese visited Guadalcanal at midday, and thus, arriving later, we were less likely to get an unfriendly reception from our fellow Marines."

Second Lieutenant Eugene Trowbridge noted in his officially illegal diary (that he kept regardless): "A lot of excitement today as there are enemy subs all around, and today we get the new experience of being catapulted from the ship as the flight deck is too short to fly off. We are all set to leave. Engines warm and tested, baggage all secured, everything all set. Finally we're off."

The flight deck crew pushed Mangrum's SBD into position and attached it to the catapult. The launch officer spun his flag while Mangrum stood hard on the bomber's brakes and pushed the throttle forward. The R-1830 Cyclone ahead of him roared at maximum power just before the catapult shot forward and flung the blue-grey airplane into the sky.

Two minutes later, Second Lieutenant Lawrence Baldinus, a Polish expatriate and former Marine enlisted pilot who had been commissioned after Pearl Harbor and was the most experienced pilot in the squadron after Mangrum, stood on his brakes and ran up his engine, then soared up to join his leader. Second Lieutenant Henry "Hank" Hise, a 22-year-old Texan who had graduated from flight school the previous May with a shade over 200 hours in his logbook, maneuvered his scout bomber on the deck as the crew hooked the airplane to the catapult. He and the other nine "nuggets" (new lower-ranking officers) had never seen a Dauntless before they reported to the squadron in late June. A minute later, the force of the catapult caused Lieutenant Hise to forcibly pull back on his joystick, pulling the Dauntless' nose high enough to nearly stall. He quickly jammed the stick forward and fought to keep the bomber out of the water. Regaining control, he joined up on Mangrum and Baldinus.

A few of the squadron's pilots were survivors of Midway. Captain Bruce Prosser, now XO, had attacked the Japanese fleet in an ancient Vought SB2U-3 Vindicator, during which he was wounded when attacked by a Zero and returned to the island with a critically wounded radioman-gunner. First Lieutenant Danny Iverson had survived 242 bullet and shrapnel hits in his SBD-2, landing back at Midway following the attack on one wheel and no flaps between rows of parked aircraft.

At 1425 hours, the last of the Dauntlesses left *Long Island's* deck. They formed up and orbited to await the shorter-legged F4F-4 fighters of VMF-223.

The first of the 19 blue-grey fighters was pushed into position on the catapult. Squadron commander Major John L. Smith made a last-minute check of his engine and controls. Extremely intelligent and able, he had a demonstrated ability to adapt quickly to changed conditions; most who knew him said he often appeared to be in a bad mood. He had only been assigned to fighters since a month before the attack on Pearl Harbor, and though he had never trained other aviators and had never been in combat, had worked his young replacements hard since the squadron had been informed they were headed for the South Pacific. He had never trained other aviators and never been in combat. Fortunately, he was a superb natural fighter tactician, a confident innovator who had painstakingly trained his men to survive against the otherwise unbeatable Zero flown by the best fighter pilots Japan ever put in cockpits. He later recalled those weeks spent working to prepare his novices for the unknown rigors of combat:

> We all had to qualify on an aircraft carrier, which we did. We spent as much time as we could flying on Saturdays and Sundays and every other day, doing gunnery and dummy runs and anything that would help to give people quick experience or quick training. It was the first experience that I'd ever had trying to train anybody, but it seemed to me that gunnery was the most important thing, so we concentrated

on gunnery more than anything else, which was a good thing after we found out where we were going.

Smith's Wildcat was hooked to the catapult bridle and he went through the same procedure of standing on his brakes while advancing the throttle to full speed that the preceding dive bomber pilots had used. He was followed in quick succession by Captain Marion Carl, newly promoted to XO, and fellow Midway veteran division leaders Captains Clayton Canfield and Roy Corry and their young charges.

With the Marine aircraft launched, the vulnerable carrier reversed course and headed out of range at full speed. At 1455 hours, Yamamoto's staff received a report from the second Mavis that the carrier and its escorts were retiring south. Neither of the big flying boats had seen the launch of Marine Air Group 23 to Guadalcanal.

Finally, shortly after 1500 hours, the 31 Dauntlesses and Wildcats turned north. Henderson Field on Guadalcanal was 190 miles away. The formation droned over the Coral Sea. As Marion Carl later recalled, "Not one of us had the faintest idea what we would find there."

Despite all the effort, Henderson Field could barely be described as an airfield. It was an irregularly shaped blob cut out of the island growth, half in and half out of a coconut grove, with a runway that was too short and too few revetments to protect the aircraft from shrapnel. In mid-September, several weeks after their arrival on the island, Marine Air Group 23's group XO Lieutenant Colonel Charles Fike finally wrote the August 20 entry in the group's War Diary:

> Upon arrival it was found that a servicing detachment of approximately 140 men, commanded by Ensign Polk, of CUB-1, were available for fueling, rearming, and servicing of aircraft. All fueling was done by means of hand pumps directly from drums. Rearming was done without the aid of bomb-handling trucks, bomb carts, or bomb hoists. The enlisted men of CUB-l, although willing and intelligent, had, for the most part, less than four months' service, as a result of which they required the closest supervision. Considering the attending difficulties, Ensign Polk handled this situation remarkably well. His attitude was at all times cooperative.

Second Lieutenant Hank Hise was surprised by the height of the hills on Guadalcanal as he flew up Lengo Channel on Lieutenant Colonel Mangrum's right wing and banked around in a 180-degree turn to begin his approach to the field from the east. The diamond-shaped formation of four elements of three SBDs each broke up with practiced ease. Mangrum broke first to the left, followed three seconds later by Baldinus, and three seconds after that by Hise. Landing gear was lowered at 1,000 feet as the pilots flew the down-wind leg, then flaps were lowered as they turned cross-wind. Mangrum spotted VMO-251's Fog Hayes, who was a qualified carrier landing signal officer (LSO), standing on the hood of a jeep at the near end of the runway, his arms held straight out to the sides at shoulder height – the "Roger" position for a carrier landing that indicated it was okay to land.

When Mangrum was 20 feet from touchdown, he saw himself drifting from the centerline and went around again. Finally in good position on the second try, he chopped throttle and his Dauntless dropped to the runway. Baldinus made his usual perfect landing. Intent on his instruments, Hise nearly plowed into the high stand of trees that were too close to the end of the runway; he pulled up reflexively, gave a last squirt of power, chopped back on the throttle, and plunked onto the ground in a cloud of dust.

While Smith's Wildcats flew cover, the rest of the SBDs landed. Mangrum followed a ground-control jeep to the dispersal area and jumped to the ground as soon as his plane's engine stopped. He had his hand wrung profusely by General Vandegrift, while thousands of thankful Marines shouted themselves hoarse and pounded one another black and blue in a thundering release of emotion. The cavalry had arrived.

Lieutenant Gene Trowbridge later wrote in his diary:

[We] sight the [air]field at 1600. We are really welcomed by the troops as the Japs have been taking their time bombing them and they figure we will help them quite a lot. We are all bedded down for the night and get ready for a nice sleep when, *bang*, the whole world seems to explode. The Japs are coming and some of their cruisers and destroyers are shelling us and the troops... It was a trying first night.

We are nervous and jumpy as there are snipers all around us, just waiting for someone to stick [his] nose out.

The destroyers that shelled the newly arrived pilots would come to be known by the Americans as "the Tokyo Express" for their regular appearances off the island. Imperial Navy Destroyer Squadron 2, commanded by Rear Admiral Raizo Tanaka, had taken up residence in the Shortland Islands, just beyond the range of the Dauntlesses, but close enough that the ships could approach Guadalcanal after dark, execute their bombardments, and be back out of range by daylight. Tanaka would come to be admired by friend and foe alike for his exploits in the Solomons, and was known by Japanese and Americans alike as Tanaka the Tenacious. Having made his career concentrating on torpedo warfare and participating in the creation, testing, and training for use of the deadly Type 93 torpedo, Tanaka became the greatest exponent of its use in combat. Unlike many Japanese officers, the admiral was highly critical of both the decision to go to war to begin with and his superiors' conduct of the war in the South Pacific, though he nevertheless carried out his assignment with great skill and daring.

Admiral Yamamoto was finally able to make sense of the day's events when he received an evening message from one of the infantry units on Guadalcanal, reporting the arrival of a force of Navy-type fighters and light bombers at the Lunga airfield. A permanent force of American aircraft on Guadalcanal radically changed the strategic equation. While the American carriers were still important, the Guadalcanal force on the Lunga airfield was all-important.

Yamamoto ordered another radical change in plans. All combat commands in the region were told to set their sights on the Lunga airfield; it was to be pummeled into submission by air and naval bombardment and then overrun by the ground troops already ashore on Guadalcanal and soon to arrive aboard Tanaka's Reinforcement Group.

The next day, August 21, Admiral Fletcher's carriers gave cover so that two transports could slip into Sealark Sound and unload supplies at midday. Marine Air Group 23's senior mechanics were a welcome addition when they came ashore from the destroyer that had brought them up from Efate.

Coastwatcher Jack Read warned that a Japanese bomber strike force was on the way down the Slot. Lieutenant Hugh MacKenzie, the coastwatcher liaison officer at Lunga, patched into the Marine communications net, known as "Texas Switch," and for the first time was able to pass the news to American aviators who could rise to the challenge. Major John Smith's four-plane F4F division responded to the call.

The Americans were over Savo Island at 1207 hours, climbing through 14,000 feet, when they spotted six Zeros 500 feet higher and on a reciprocal heading. Smith opened fire head-on at the leading Zero as the two aircraft roared toward one other at a combined speed well in excess of 600 miles per hour. The Japanese pilot flinched first. He pulled up, exposing his belly to Smith's six .50-caliber machine guns, and then fell away as the Marine squadron leader was engaged by a pair of Zeros that had latched onto his tail. Smith quickly discovered that the Wildcat could disengage by diving away, if there was sufficient altitude, saving himself when he used the F4F's greater weight and superior diving speed to swoop beneath friendly antiaircraft fire. His wingman, Sergeant John Lindsey, was hit in the fight but managed to make a dead-stick wheels-up landing at Henderson Field, with his Wildcat becoming the squadron's first loss, while Smith became the first pilot to claim a Zero shot down. In a second fight later that afternoon, Lieutenant Trowbridge claimed two more, though the Japanese recorded all planes returned. Over the next two days, the Marines claimed two more Zeros and proved they could stay in the same air with their more experienced opponents.

On August 22, the two Marine squadrons were reinforced by five P-400s from the 67th Fighter Squadron led by newly promoted Captain Dale Brannon in command of the detachment. Equipped with hard-to-find 75-gallon belly tanks, the five P-400s left Plaines des Gaiacs on August 21, flying 325 miles to Efate, then 180 more to arrive at Espiritu Santo before darkness. The next day, accompanied by a B-17 to provide navigation support, with their gas tanks topped off after warming up, the five fighters tackled the 640 miles to Henderson. Brannon later recalled that gas consumption was predicated on low engine speed, a lean mixture, a 15-mile tail wind, and a landing on the proverbial fumes.

Contending with poor tropical weather, the Airacobras flew in close formation on the B-17 at 200 feet, through mist and low-hanging clouds while the pilots struggled to keep each other in sight. Whenever the weather cleared, they spread out until they spotted storm clouds ahead, when they would again snuggle under the navigating B-17's wing. They were followed by a second B-17 carrying life rafts to be dropped to the pilots if they were forced to bail out. After 30 hours in the air after departing from Plaines des Gaiacs, all five set down on Henderson Field.

8

ADMIRAL YAMAMOTO'S REPLY

August 9–24

Following the disaster at Savo Island, Guadalcanal experienced a lull. The Navy was able to run small reinforcement convoys to the island, but Admiral Fletcher's task force operated well south of the island, beyond the range of Japanese search planes. The lack of opposition allowed the enemy to seize the opportunity to reinforce Guadalcanal. Imperial Navy destroyers and cruisers shelled the Marines nightly without opposition; the beginnings of the "Tokyo Express" were discernible.

The Japanese high command had been taken by surprise with the advent of the Allied offensive in the Solomons. Staff planners had been unanimous that the Allies would not respond offensively before the summer of 1943. That the Allies had managed to go on the offensive in the Solomons a year early followed the rude awakening of Midway, where Admiral Yamamoto's prewar prediction that he would "run wild for six months" had been proven prescient. The defeat at Midway resulted in an immediate decision by the Imperial military leadership to discard their planned offensive operations in order to substitute a defensive line that would be held at all costs. The American offensive in the Solomons was seen as the first step of a direct threat to Rabaul; thus, opposing it became the Imperial Navy's top priority. This policy drove Japanese actions over the six months following the arrival of the Marines at Guadalcanal.

The Imperial Navy's 25th Air Flotilla of the 5th Air Attack Force, based at Rabaul, had been reinforced only days before the Allied incursion into the Solomons as part of a general buildup preparatory to occupying Guadalcanal and supporting a further Japanese drive into the New Hebrides. On August 9, Vice Admiral Nishizo Tsukahara activated the 11th Air Fleet at Rabaul and assumed control of regional air operations. The one-armed senior aviator, who had lost his arm to a spinning propeller, advocated a policy of strong reprisals against the Americans. However, since his bomber force had taken severe losses during the first two days of aerial combat, the admiral was restricted to planning harassment and reconnaissance missions to the island. Fresh bomber and fighter units were on the way, but it would be weeks before they would make good the losses of August 7 and 8.

Despite the loss of the heart of the Imperial Navy's carrier strike force with the sinking of *Akagi*, *Kaga*, *Soryu*, and *Hiryu* at Midway, their remaining carrier fleet was still formidable when compared with the carriers the US Navy could bring to action. The 1st Carrier Division now formed the heart of Japanese naval aviation, composed of the fleet carriers *Shōkaku* and *Zuikaku*, and the light carrier *Zuihō*. The light carriers *Junyō*, *Hiryo*, and *Ryūjō* of the 2nd Carrier Division were a worthy second line. *Shōkaku* and *Zuikaku* were of the same class as *Enterprise* and *Hornet*, while *Zuihō*, *Junyō*, and *Hiryo* were equivalent to the newly arrived *Wasp* regarding capability and performance.

By mid-August, Japanese strategy and tactics in the Solomons began to take form. The Imperial Navy had bases in the Buin-Faisi area of Bougainville, at Vella Lavella on Kula Gulf and at Rekata Bay on Santa Isabel, where they established a seaplane base, all of which were supplied from Truk and Rabaul. Japanese troops and supplies were loaded on destroyers or cruisers that landed men and supplies, then took position off Henderson Field and shelled it. Meanwhile, air attacks on Henderson were carried out almost daily from Rabaul, depending on the constantly changing weather. Additionally, various other harassments were maintained against the Americans on the island, which were ingenious sleep-destroyers. "Oscar," a submarine, surfaced nightly in the dark off Lunga to throw a few shells at either Tulagi or Guadalcanal. After midnight, an airplane from the Rekata Bay seaplane base, variously named "Louie the Louse," "Washing Machine Charlie," or "Maytag Mike" for the way the pilot operated his throttle to create strange engine sounds, would lay a stick of bombs across the field.

Probably because it's what *they* would have done, the Japanese assumed through the first month of the American occupation of Tulagi and Guadalcanal that the invasion force was small – approximately 2,000 troops – and that its purpose was to destroy the Lunga airfield. The Imperial Army's underestimate of American troops on Guadalcanal resulted from a reconnaissance mission flown with one of General Hyakutake's senior staff officers aboard. Only a few US troops were sighted on the island, while there was no shipping in Sealark Sound. The staff officer's report led the rest of the 17th Army staff to conclude that most of the troops had been withdrawn following the Imperial Navy's successful response at the Battle of Savo Island. The fact was that no troops had been withdrawn, and the reason no shipping was spotted was because the mission had been flown on one of the few days during which at there were no transports present unloading additional supplies (normally there were at least one or two). Thus, it was not a large leap in imagination for the Imperial Army to conclude that they could send a few thousand troops to remind the Americans who still controlled the South Pacific.

Responsibility for the campaign in the Eastern Solomons passed from the Imperial Navy, in the person of 11th Air Fleet commander Vice Admiral Nishizo Tsukahara, to the Imperial Army, in the person of 17th Army commander Lieutenant General Harukichi Hyakutake, on August 13. The general was 52, as was his opponent General Vandegrift, and had been in active service since 1909, as had Vandegrift. He did not relish the idea of pulling the Imperial Navy's chestnuts from the Solomons fire. He saw the Eastern Solomons problem as a potential diversion from the main campaign in New Guinea for which he was also responsible. He wanted the Solomons over and done with long before two fresh infantry divisions earmarked for autumn operations in northeastern New Guinea staged through Rabaul in late September, easily visualizing those fresh troops diverted to extinguish the brushfire in the Eastern Solomons. In Hyakutake's view, and that of his superiors at Imperial General Headquarters, New Guinea was by far the greater prize. Hyakutake would give the attention required to the Eastern Solomons, but the real effort and the best troops would be saved for New Guinea. To help Imperial Army troops launch the burgeoning air, ground, and naval offensive now known as Operation *KA*, the Imperial Navy offered the 5th Yokosuka Special Naval Landing Force, which Hyakutake snapped up.

Unfortunately, retaking Guadalcanal would require a high degree of coordination between the Imperial Army and Navy. While there is inter-service rivalry in all militaries, the rivalry between Army and Navy in Japan was the most extreme example. The leaders of neither service understood or respected the other, and there was virtually no history of cooperation past the Imperial Navy providing transport for Army troops to distant battlefields. The Imperial Navy knew little of the plans made by the 17th Army to move troops to Guadalcanal, while the Army failed to insure any reliable communication with the Navy. So certain were both of their coming victory that the plan that was developed assumed that each service would achieve the necessary success in intermediate steps without developing a contingency plan should this not be the case.

On August 16, three transports carrying the rest of the 28th "Ichiki" Infantry Regiment and the 5th Yokosuka Special Naval Landing Force, escorted by the redoubtable Rear Admiral Raizo Tanaka's destroyers, with cover by Vice Admiral Mikawa's four heavy cruisers that had been victorious at Savo Island, departed Truk bound for Guadalcanal. Tanaka planned to land the troops on Guadalcanal on August 24, in coordination with planned strikes against Henderson Field by the Japanese carrier force which would prevent the American air units there attacking the landing. There were flaws aplenty in the concept of landing troops at Guadalcanal. No matter how quickly troop-laden destroyers could get there, much time would be lost to disembarking and ferrying soldiers and equipment to the beaches. During that time, the amphibious force would be vulnerable to naval or aerial forces operating in support of the American Lunga garrison.

Tanaka needed the dark hours to cover his approach and retirement as well as to cover the landing operation itself. If he entered the Slot just after sunset at any point southeast of Bougainville, he would have sufficient time and the cover he required, even if the Allies had air or naval support, which reconnaissance reports indicated they did not possess. The danger of not being out of range by daylight was demonstrated on August 19, when a light cruiser involved with the nightly reinforcement mission failed to depart Guadalcanal soon enough. Shortly after dawn, it was spotted in Sealark Sound by a searching B-17. The Flying Fortress banked for a bombing run and delighted Marines ashore watched columns of dark brown smoke pour from a hit abaft the cruiser's mainmast. It made for the open sea beyond Savo with its fantail afire, and later sank.

Despite the fact that the 916-man advance echelon of Ichiki Battalion that landed at Taivu Point the night of August 19 had orders to wait on the beach for the second half of the truncated regiment to be delivered, General Hyakutake, who was still operating on the belief that the enemy forces were smaller than they were, ordered the advance force to immediately attack and retake the airfield. Lieutenant Colonel Ichiki had originally been ordered to scout the Marine positions and await the arrival of the rest of the regiment before taking any offensive action. However, the colonel was so confident that he wrote in his journal, "19 August, landing; 20 August, March by night and battle; 21 August, enjoyment of the fruit of victory." His plan was simple: March down the beach to Lunga Point and penetrate the American defenses. At that point, the Marines were unaware of the presence of Ichiki's force on the island.

At 1200 hours on August 19, a 60-man patrol from Company A, 1st Battalion, 1st Marines, was east of the Tenaru River when it ran head-on into a Japanese reconnaissance patrol. Both reacted instantly. The Marines prevailed in the firefight, while the Japanese who could retreated. As the Marines collected souvenirs and documents from the dead, one officer noticed that there were too many map cases, swords, binoculars, and documents for so small a patrol. There were far too many officers present: four out of 34 men. The corpses were too clean and well dressed to have been anything but freshly landed; their helmets bore the red enamel star of the Imperial Army. The lieutenant leading the patrol turned around and returned to the Lunga Perimeter, where he turned over the haul of intelligence material. When he received word of the patrol skirmish, Colonel Ichiki decided to launch his attack forthwith.

The patrol's report on the aftermath of the firefight fit with a warning the Marines had recently received from Solomon Islanders led by coastwatcher Martin Clemens regarding the presence on the island of the Ichiki Battalion. The evening of August 20, the 1st Marine Regiment dug in on the western side of the body of water mistakenly called the Tenaru River (which was actually several miles further east). Later called "Alligator Creek," this was actually a tidal lagoon separated from the ocean by a narrow sandbar. The Japanese would be forced to cross through the water and over the sandbar to get at the Marines.

The Ichiki Battalion arrived at the eastern side of the lagoon shortly after 2400 hours. At 0130 hours on August 21, they moved out to attack. They were met by machine-gun fire and cannister grapeshot rounds that slaughtered the Japanese troops as they attempted the crossing, turning the water red. The attack was broken around 0200 hours when the few enemy troops who had made it across were killed. At 0230 hours, Ichiki ordered a second attack in which nearly all the 200 soldiers were killed when they attempted to cross the lagoon. A third attack was also blocked at around 0500 hours.

An almost-fatal incident involving six pilots from VMF-212 occurred in the midst of the battle. During the late afternoon of August 20, the six – five inexperienced second lieutenants and a warrant officer with years of flight time – boarded a destroyer-transport (APD) loaded with aviation gasoline, bombs, and bullets for the units at Henderson. When the unescorted APD closed on Guadalcanal in the afternoon, several unidentified bombers appeared high overhead and had no sooner passed the ship than a lookout yelled, "Torpedoes!" The ship picked up so much speed it went down by the bows just as a torpedo passed close astern.

The APD waited for the sun to go down to allow it to sneak up to Kukum and land the munitions, fuel, and pilots. Moving along the coast after sunset, the ship sailed came to an abrupt stop. The six pilots climbed over the side into rubber boats, each carrying a parachute bag filled with clothes and their toothbrushes. They hadn't gotten five yards up the beach when they heard gunfire. Dark forms grabbed them and pushed them down. After the shooting stopped, they were shoved into a vehicle and driven to a pitch-dark coconut grove. Sentries kept stopping the driver until someone finally told him not to go any farther in the dark. The pilots settled in for the night right there, falling asleep on their parachute bags.

Dawn found the surviving Japanese holding their position. The 1st Battalion, 1st Marines, moved inland around the lagoon and enveloped the enemy. As the enemy troops tried to escape down the beach, they were strafed by newly arrived VMF-223 Wildcats flown by Smith, Carl, Canfield, and Corry who flew two strafing missions that convinced any still alive to get away. All resistance ended by 1700 hours. When some wounded Japanese opened fire on the Marines, they went through the battlefield and shot every enemy soldier they came across whether dead or alive, except for 15 taken prisoner. Thirty Japanese survivors escaped to tell the tale to their comrades at Taivu Point. Food, equipment, weapons, and ammunition were taken from the 871 dead. Victory cost the Marines 34 dead and 75 wounded. Late that evening, Colonel Ichiki buried his unit's colors, drew a ceremonial dagger, and disemboweled himself in the soft sand beside Lengo Channel.

While the battle continued through the day, the six VMF-212 pilots were finally sent back to Henderson Field. There, they learned they had come ashore during the opening of the battle. It had been expected that Japanese raiders might land on the beach – just as the VMF-212 pilots had done! – or that infiltrators would attempt to get at the airplanes lined up near Henderson Field – just as the VMF-212 pilots had done! They were indeed fortunate that the Marines who had run across them had not decided to shoot first and make enquiries later.

On August 21, the Imperial Navy's main force composed of *Shōkaku*, *Zuikaku*, the light carrier *Ryūjō*, and their screening force, commanded by Vice Admiral Chuichi Nagumo in *Shōkaku*, departed Truk headed for the Solomons to support General Hyakutake's planned August 24 assault on Henderson Field. Rear Admiral Hiroaki Abe commanded the "vanguard force" of two battleships, three heavy cruisers, one light cruiser, and three destroyers, while Vice Admiral Nobutake Kondō commanded the "advance force" of five heavy cruisers, one light cruiser, six destroyers, and the seaplane carrier *Chitose*. Operational support was provided by 100 land-based bombers, fighters, and reconnaissance aircraft of the 25th Air Flotilla at Rabaul. As it turned out, the major combat action would again take place at sea, in the third clash of aircraft carriers since Coral Sea, known to history as the Battle of the Eastern Solomons.

The Japanese plan called for the 1st Carrier Division to provide a more thorough air assault on Henderson Field than could be achieved by the dozen or so Betty bombers in the typical mission from Rabaul, with the additional hope on the part of the admirals that such a move would draw out the US carrier force so they could avenge Midway.

To provide reason for the US carriers to come out, "bait" was provided by the light carrier *Ryūjō* which operated with the Advanced Force. Nagumo's plan was that, once the enemy took the bait, *Shōkaku* and *Zuikaku*, operating 60 miles north with full deckloads ready for launch, would close the trap and attack the US carriers. Sinking or badly damaging the enemy carriers would eliminate the air cover provided to Allied supply convoys and cut off Guadalcanal from reinforcement.

Throughout the morning of August 22, Admiral Tanaka's slow Reinforcement Group, which was escorted by Admiral Mikawa's four Outer Seas Force cruisers and three destroyers, continued to zigzag toward Guadalcanal at nine knots. At noon, the force was 350 miles north of Guadalcanal. The admiral was intent on landing the troops on the night of August 24. By noon, as the convoy continued to close on Guadalcanal, the Support Force, composed of a battleship and three destroyers, had split and taken stations near Tanaka's flanks; Admiral Kondō's Advance Force of four heavy cruisers, two light cruisers, a seaplane carrier, and six destroyers was 120 miles northwest. Admiral Nagumo's Carrier Striking Force was 200 miles northeast.

During the course of the day, Kondō's and Nagumo's forces refueled under way while two cruisers and a destroyer of the Outer Seas Force headed to the Shortland Islands at high speed to refuel. Vice Admiral Nishizo Tsukahara asked Admiral Yamamoto to release Nagumo's Carrier Striking Force for an attack on Henderson Field the next day and to provide air cover over Taivu Point on August 24 when Tanaka put troops ashore there. Supporting Tsukahara's request, Admiral Tanaka expanded it by requesting that carrier aircraft cover his final approach to Guadalcanal. However, Admiral Yamamoto would only risk *Shōkaku*'s and *Zuikaku*'s air groups in an attack against the American carriers. He would only authorize a strike against Henderson Field by the carrier air groups if it was demonstrated that the American carriers had withdrawn.

For the Japanese, the morning searches on August 23 by Bettys from Rabaul and Mavises from the Shortlands failed to find Task Force 61. When one Betty did not return, no thought was given to it being victim of American Navy fighters, since weather in the region was so stormy. Farthest to the north was Admiral Kondō's powerful Advance Force, while Nagumo's Carrier Striking Force was only some 60 miles distant, both beneath storm clouds. Both intended to attack Task Force 61 on either August 23 or 24, once the enemy was located. In the meantime, it was imperative that Nagumo's carriers remain undiscovered and beyond the range of Allied searches. However, time now worked against this strategy, since the Reinforcement Group transports were scheduled to arrive off Guadalcanal the night of August 24. Since Admiral Yamamoto had stipulated that the *Shōkaku* and *Zuikaku* air groups were not to attack land targets so long as Task Force 61 remained a threat, the only force available for an attack on the airfield was the small *Ryūjō* air group, with its nine B5N "Kates" and 24 Zeros. Since the scheduled 5th Air Attack Force mission against Henderson was scrubbed because of bad weather, use of *Ryūjō*'s small force on August 24 became inevitable. The strike would be launched as soon as the ship and its escorts were within range.

Certain his force had escaped detection through the day, Nagumo turned north to kill time and remain near Tanaka's transports, while also staying beyond the reach of American searchers. Admiral Kondō was also obliged to turn north in order to keep station on Nagumo. Both commanders planned to turn again at 0700 and dash south to cover the landing at Guadalcanal, which they hoped would be contested by the Americans. When Admiral Tsukahara checked with Admiral Tanaka to be sure the transports were on schedule, Tanaka responded that he had lost time and miles due to his turn to the north, and could not get to Guadalcanal as scheduled. Tsukahara agreed and the landing at Taivu Point was delayed to the night of August 25.

At 2200 hours, Admiral Yamamoto ordered that if the morning searches failed to find the American fleet, Nagumo and Kondō were to close on Guadalcanal with their surface battle forces and shell Henderson Field to destruction to ensure the safe passage of the Reinforcement Group.

At 0145 hours, Nagumo ordered the sacrificial diversionary force built around *Ryūjō* to break away from *Shōkaku* and *Zuikaku* and head for Guadalcanal at high speed. Its escorts were the heavy cruiser *Tone* and fleet destroyers *Amatsukaze* and *Tokitsukaze*. The force was commanded by Rear Admiral Chuichi Hara.

At 0600 hours on August 24, Nagumo's Carrier Striking Force turned southeast, into the wind, and *Shōkaku* and *Zuikaku* launched the first search patrols of the day. Kondō's Advance Force, 120 miles southeast, also turned to remain in position to guard Nagumo's eastern flank.

Starting at 0615 hours, the two carriers launched 19 Kates on searches out to a distance of 250 miles. No one really expected to locate the Americans, since the Japanese carriers had sailed out of range during the night. As soon as the searchers were away, Admiral Nagumo ordered that three strike forces comprised of all the Val dive bombers, all the remaining Kate torpedo bombers, and many of the Zero fighters be readied for immediate launch if the enemy were spotted.

At 0830 hours, 24 Bettys escorted by 14 Zeros departed Rabaul bound for Henderson Field. The weather between Rabaul and Guadalcanal over the northern Solomons was still as bad as it had been the previous day.

9

HIDE AND SEEK IN THE SOLOMON SEA

August 19–24

On August 12, Admiral Ghormley received intelligence reports of enemy naval concentrations at Rabaul and Bougainville. A week later, similar concentrations were reported in the Buin-Faisi area, and on August 20 ComSoPac warned the 11th Bomb Group's Colonel Saunders that task forces committed to retaking Guadalcanal were already en route from Truk and Ponape. For the Flying Fortresses, the grinding routine of sea search became their most important assignment. The B-17s would take off from Espiritu Santo in darkness at 0300 hours, fly over Tulagi at sunrise and scour the Bismarck Sea to the northwest, logging 1,600 miles of open-water flying on each search mission.

Daily action had already taken its toll on the bombers and their crews. Over the course of the month from July 21 to August 20, 11 B-17s were lost, eight to operational accidents and two at sea, while only one was lost in combat. Men and equipment had so far stood up well against the enemy. Japanese opposition in terms of flak and intercepting fighters was uniformly poor. Enemy pilots had shown little eagerness to close with the Flying Fortresses. During the intensive operations over the eight days preceding the invasion on August 7, enemy fighters had attempted to engage on all but two missions to the Guadalcanal–Tulagi area; other than in the "ramming" incident, no B-17 had been lost to the A6M2-Ns, though three crew members had been slightly wounded. Bad weather, not the enemy, was the chief antagonist. The lack of homing facilities and radio direction-finding equipment had brought down more B-17's than had the enemy.

Aboard *Saratoga* on August 16, "Smokey" Stover noted in his diary:

August 16 – Fortieth day on this cruise, and I'm ready to hit a port. My longest cruise so far. Haven't flown in a week and would like to get in the air again, even on a four-hour inner air patrol. We have been circling around north of New Caledonia and about 300 miles from Tulagi, waiting for the Japs to make a counterinvasion, I suppose. They have been bombing there about every other day, with no opposition since we left.

The "Battle of the Tenaru" that saw the destruction of the Ichiki force alerted the Allied command to the threatened Japanese offensive. Admiral Fletcher's carriers turned toward Guadalcanal at 0640 hours on August 21.

Search missions to find the enemy began at dawn. VS-71's Lieutenant (jg) Charles Mester and wingman Ensign Robert Escher, assigned a search sector that included the Santa Cruz Islands, discovered a seaplane tender, two destroyers, and several patrol planes in Graciosa Bay on Ndeni Island. Upon receiving no recognition signals from the vessels, Mester identified them as Japanese and the two SBDs initiated an attack. When he was already well into his dive, Mester recognized stars on the wings and fuselages of the patrol planes in the bay and realized they were friendly PBYs! While Mester pulled up and broke off his attack, Escher completed his attack, dropping his 500-pound bomb which landed just off the beam of the seaplane tender as he recovered from his dive and retired under heavy antiaircraft fire.

The ship they had attacked was the USS *Mackinac* (AVP-13), a small Barnegat-class seaplane tender nicknamed "the Mighty Mac" by its crew, which had been operating an advanced seaplane base in the bay since arriving from Nouméa the day before. Ensign Escher soon learned that his bomb had wrecked two OS2U-2 observation floatplanes, damaged the *Mackinac*'s gasoline system, and injured several islanders who happened to be in nearby canoes.

Despite the damage suffered, the seaplane tender was able to maintain operations providing PBYs with support for patrols in the Coral Sea and southeastern Solomons for another two months.

At 0807 hours that day, 26 torpedo-armed Misawa Air Group and 4th Air Group Bettys, escorted by 13 Tainan Air Corps A6M2s, took off from Vunakanau and Lakunai airfields on Rabaul to search for and attack Task Force 61. The strike force searched the Solomon Sea toward the last known position of the American carriers, but at 1140 hours the bomber leader decided they must be beyond range. Vice Admiral Nishizo Tsukahara agreed that the Americans were not a threat when he received the message, and ordered Admiral Tanaka to turn the hovering Reinforcement Group toward Guadalcanal again to land the 1,500 troops aboard his ships on August 24, to join the now-extinct Ichiki Battalion advance echelon.

The Bettys weren't the only Japanese planes searching for the American carriers. At 1045 hours, a Yokohama Air Group H6K "Mavis" out of the Shortland Islands advance patrol base spotted and reported the presence of five surface warships heading a bit south of west at 20 knots. Thirty minutes later, VS-72 Dauntless pilot Lieutenant Robert Ware spotted the Mavis, which turned for home at top speed when it spotted Ware's bomber. The SBD was barely faster than the big flying boat, which was diving to pick up speed, and it took Ware 15 minutes to catch up and move within range. Ware squeezed his trigger and fired his two .50-caliber nose guns as he closed till he was forced to break off 50 feet from the Mavis, which had caught fire. The big flying boat steepened its dive as fire spread to the two engines on the left end of the big parasol wing, mounted on a pylon above the hull. A moment after Ware broke off his attack, the wing folded up and the left end fell off. The Mavis turned on its side and went straight in, exploding when it hit the ocean. At the time of its demise, it was only 15 miles from Task Force 61. Minutes later, Ware spotted four VF-5 Wildcats that had arrived to investigate the source of the black smoke rising from the ocean.

That evening, "Smokey" Stover recorded the event in his diary:

General Quarters all day as we are rather close in [to Guadalcanal]. Finally got a flight. Combat air patrol from 1015 to 1345. Started out as dull as preceding ones, but three of four vectors had something at their ends. First one was a blank, but on the second we got about 20 miles from the fleet to see a tall column of smoke on the water. Saw one SBD leaving in the direction of the fleet. Found nothing but an oil patch on the water and a little smoke cloud drifting away. Two minutes later, a wing section and a lot of other debris came up and was very thick around the slick. The wing was very broad with a large red circle (solid) toward the rounded tip and a float close to the other end, where it had broken off. Saw neither bodies nor survivors. Found out later that a *Wasp* SBD had shot down a four-engine Jap patrol plane. He beat us to it by only five minutes, at the most. On the third vector we found a B-17 streaming along at about 150 knots. After identifying it, we flew up alongside and waved in return to their greetings. Found an SBD about 15 miles out on our last vector. Apparently he hadn't turned on his IFF transmitter. LCdr Roy Simpler found a PBY, and Lieutenant Dick Gray's division found a couple of B-17s. I hear the Japs have made a landing on Guadalcanal to the east of our Marines, who are hollering for help. Don't know if we will go in.

Stover's wingman, Ensign Foster Blair, vented his frustration in his diary: "Wish the damn scouts would tend to their own business." The frustration was understandable, since the carrier's two SBD squadrons had now downed two Mavises in two days, while the fighters had not scored a single victory since August 9.

Over the next two days SBDs from the three carriers flew search missions to find the enemy. While no enemy carriers were found, an alarming number of Japanese submarines were spotted and one sinking was claimed. Sailors who learned of the submarines' presence started calling the waters south of Guadalcanal "Torpedo Junction."

"Smokey" Stover noted in his diary: "Plan of the day for tomorrow says, 'Clear Ships for Action.' We're going north!"

Scouting 3's Lieutenant (jg) "Slim" Russell was also a diarist. On August 20, he wrote:

Tulagi bearing 303 [degrees], distance 228 [miles]. On August 18, we fueled from the tanker *Platte* and received mail. The mail was from June 21 to July 7. Yesterday morning, three destroyers and one submarine were reported to have shelled Tulagi. This past week we have done little except go around in circles. Yesterday, I flew nine hours. One 200-mile search with Ens Bob Balenti, and I flew [wing] on Lt M.P. MacNair for a 250-mile hop in the afternoon. Supposedly an enemy force out there, but no could find. Did sight two islands. Also two PBYs. This morning we had battle stations and stripped the ship for action. One [Japanese] heavy cruiser, one light cruiser, and three destroyers were reported shelling Tulagi at 0600. The *Wasp* sent search planes out at 0800. Three destroyers and one light cruiser reported 30 miles, bearing 270 [degrees], from Savo Island on course 330 degrees at a speed of 25 knots. Leaving us in a hurry!

We were then 258 miles from them. A heavy cruiser was reported in Tulagi Harbor, possibly damaged by a B-17. Since that time, I have not heard anything more. The ship has been at General Quarters all day. This afternoon, we had quite a few bogies reported. Believe at least one of them was a Jap floatplane.

The Japanese also sought the Americans, but neither found the other despite intense efforts.

On August 22, *Enterprise*'s search radar picked up a bogey at 1048 hours. Ensign "Red" Brooks' division of Fighting 6 Wildcats was vectored out by the FDO to investigate. However, neither Brooks, a highly skilled former enlisted pilot, nor anyone else in his division received the message, since they were flying through a heavy rain squall at that moment. The FDO next ordered Don Runyon's division to investigate, but weather prevented Runyon or any of his pilots getting the message. Finally, Scoop Vorse got the message on the third try at 1055 hours, and his four F4Fs proceeded on vector 270 degrees at 10,000 feet. After five minutes, they were ordered to turn to 200 degrees at 8,000 feet. Moments later, the course was again corrected to 180 degrees. Soon they spotted the big enemy flying boat, the same one that had first spotted *Long Island* on August 20. This time, the snooper was only 15 miles from the fleet.

Vorse and wingman Ensign Dix Loesch climbed to make an overhead attack while Lieutenant (jg) Larry Grimmell and wingman Cash Register turned to perform a below-opposite simultaneous attack. At 1105 hours, Vorse banked over and made his overhead run. He had fired only a short burst when the Mavis caught fire, Loesch, Grimmell, and Register pulled out of their attacks when they saw the flying boat nose over in its fatal dive.

To the south at 8,000 feet, Torpedo 3's Chief NAP Wilhelm "Bill" Esders, who had been one of the few Devastator pilots to return to his carrier after attacking the Japanese at Midway, was returning to the task force from his morning patrol when he glanced north and saw the fighters chasing the large seaplane. He later remembered, "The fire started in the fuselage and quickly spread to the midwing section. A moment later, the giant parasol wings collapsed upward, and the fuselage and wings fell separately into the sea." Esders did not see any parachutes, but Register confided to his diary that night that he had seen one man jump from the burning plane without a parachute. "What a horrid fate." Vorse reported: "Red Base [*Enterprise*] from Red-5 [Vorse]. Enemy plane shot down in flames."

While the earlier loss of the Betty had not caused an alert, the failure of the Mavis to return to the Shortlands alerted the Japanese that American carriers were in the Coral Sea, though they had no idea the size of the force.

While all this was happening, *Saratoga's* air group commander, Commander Don Felt, flew to Henderson Field to assess the facilities in the event that large numbers of carrier aircraft needed to land and refuel there; use of the base could double or even triple the range of the carrier air groups. As Felt was completing his business the midday Japanese attack arrived, with the Bettys bombing the field from 22,000 feet. Felt later reported to his pilots that he saw one of the Bettys trailing smoke from a 90mm antiaircraft hit as it left the area. Four VMF-221 Wildcats tried to get through the Zeros escorting the bombers and were shot up for their effort, though no Marine pilot was injured. However, one of the precious Wildcats cracked up on landing. The Marines were credited with downing a bomber, but the Japanese did not record that any airplanes were lost over Guadalcanal.

At 1745 hours, USS *Portland* (CA-33), holding station on the starboard side of *Enterprise's* Task Force 16, reported that a torpedo was passing from port to starboard; it had been spotted broaching about 1,700 yards off *Portland's* starboard beam at 240 degrees. At the same time, destroyers in *Wasp's* Task Force 18 reported a sonar contact and dropped depth charges. A search failed to find any submarine targets, but there was certainty that the carriers were being shadowed by enemy submarines.

At 1930 hours, Admiral Fletcher ordered Task Force 61 to turn northwest. Malaita Island was to port with open waters ahead. If enemy carriers were out there, the admiral was ready for them. Unfortunately, Pacific Fleet Intelligence was unable to provide information on the enemy force, since the Japanese had just phased in a revision to the Imperial Navy's JN-25 code for the third time since Midway. The American code breakers were now shut out of any opportunity to crack JN-25, and would remain "deaf and blind" for the rest of the Pacific War when it came to reading the enemy's mail. The only intelligence that could be provided was based on traffic analysis, which could reveal gatherings of enemy forces, but could not reveal their makeup. The Imperial Navy had taken the extra precaution of sending the veteran radiomen of *Shōkaku* and *Zuikaku* whose "fists" were recognized by American listeners to Kure Naval Base, where they maintained the kind of broadcast associated with a ship in port. So far as HYPO, the USN code breakers at Pearl Harbor, knew, the carriers were still in Japan.

Admiral Fletcher had no inkling that Fleet Intelligence was now unable to read the enemy's radio messages, but his gut told him anyway that enemy carriers were close at hand, and he acted accordingly. There were other complications. Fletcher was constantly concerned about the fleets' fuel state. Shortly after he turned north, he notified Admiral Ghormley's headquarters that he needed to fuel the carriers and their escorts on August 25, and requested that the three fleet oilers hovering off Efate rendezvous with the task force then.

Shortly after Fletcher's message went out, a message from Ghormley arrived, warning Fletcher that the enemy might attack Guadalcanal any time between August 23 and August 26. Pacific Fleet's traffic analysis had determined that two battleships, ten heavy cruisers, five light cruisers, and many destroyers and submarines were moving into position in the region. Further, it was estimated that 80–100 bombers and more than 60 fighters were at Rabaul. While the code breakers had not mentioned enemy carriers, Ghormley's warning stated that the presence of carriers was "possible but not confirmed." The message also stated that Pacific Fleet Intelligence did not believe that the enemy had spotted Task Force 61 during the past ten days, which was accurate. Ghormley's message concluded with a recommendation that only one carrier at a time be released to refuel from the two fleet oilers being sent the next morning.

Acting on Ghormley's suggestion, Fletcher notified Rear Admiral Leigh Noyes aboard *Wasp* that Task Force 18 would be released for refueling the next evening if there were no contacts made by the day's search patrols. With this decision, Fletcher reduced his force by a third at exactly the wrong time.

At 0555 hours on August 23, *Enterprise* launched nine Avengers and 15 Dauntlesses in 12 two-plane search teams to reconnoiter from northeast to northwest to a distance of 180 miles.

At 0725 hours, Scouting 5 commander Lieutenant Turner Caldwell sighted a surfaced submarine headed southeast at a high speed. Turner attacked and dropped his bomb close aboard the submarine, but was unable to observe any results before the submarine dived. At 0815, in a nearby search sector, Scouting 5's flight officer Lieutenant Birney Strong and wingman Ensign John Ritchey surprised a second submarine also running at full speed on the surface on a south-southwesterly course. Their attack caused no observable damage as the submarine crash-dived, though it surfaced twice and they strafed it both times. The enemy battle groups known to be in the area were beyond range or in other sectors.

Finally, shortly after the last *Enterprise* search team reported negative results, American luck changed when the first contact was made at 0950 hours. Despite the heavy rainstorms and poor visibility over the southern Solomons, a VP-23 PBY piloted by Lieutenant Leo Riester from the Ndeni forward base sighted Tanaka's Reinforcement Group transports and their Outer Seas Force escorts heading toward Guadalcanal. The tender *Mackinac* relayed the report to Fletcher at 1012 hours. Fletcher immediately ordered *Saratoga's* skipper, Captain Dewitt Ramsey, to prepare the air group to strike the troop-laden transports or the enemy carriers, if they turned up while there was still time to strike.

Riester's PBY had been spotted by lookouts aboard Tanaka's ships at 0930 hours, 20 minutes before he first sighted them. Tanaka maintained his course and speed, south-southwest at 17 knots, until Reister was forced by his fuel state to return to base at around 1030 hours. As soon as the Catalina was beyond visual range, the Reinforcement Group turned north-northeast at 1040 on Admiral Mikawa's order. The transports were still 300 miles from Guadalcanal, but a little foot dragging would not upset the overall schedule, while the turn away would make the transports hard to find if a carrier strike force searched for them along their last known course from their last known position.

At 1140 hours, Admiral Fletcher received an additional sighting report from a B-17 that had overflown Faisi in the Shortland Islands and reported spotting two destroyers and two transports in the harbor. These were the destroyers from Mikawa's Outer Seas Force, which were refueling. However, Fletcher saw the report as proof that the enemy was prepared to mount a two-pronged amphibious assault against the Lunga Perimeter; this was exactly what every American at every level had feared since August 10.

Fletcher conferred with Noyes at 1203 hours as to whether Task Force 61 should continue north and strike the oncoming transport force or go after the transports in Faisi Harbor. Noyes suggested that *Wasp* should move forward with *Enterprise* to attack Tanaka's transports as soon as possible, but Fletcher demurred on the grounds that *Saratoga's* air group was fresh and he planned to use *Enterprise* for the afternoon searches.

At 1445 hours, *Saratoga* launched 31 SBDs and six TBFs led by CAG Felt to locate and attack an enemy force of two cruisers, three destroyers, and four transports, 275 miles from Task Force 61. He was ordered to return to Guadalcanal after the attack and rendezvous with *Saratoga* east of Malaita in the morning. Shortly after *Saratoga's* aircraft disappeared in the distance, *Enterprise* began launching scouts to search for the missing carriers. There was hope they would be found while Felt's attack group could be diverted to strike them.

Saratoga's strike force flew into dreadful weather with poor visibility because of rain showers and heavy cloud cover, while a heavy weather front was dead ahead. Felt dropped to the surface and spread the force into a line of three-plane sections a mere 100 feet over the sea, and they flew into the front an hour after launch. Section leaders flew on instruments while their wingmen tucked in tight. The wind and rain bounced the planes, making it difficult to maintain the formation's integrity. The effort was difficult for less-experienced pilots like Bombing 3's Lieutenant Paul Holmberg, a 1939 Naval Academy graduate, who later recalled that staying in formation and not flying into the ocean while trying to keep track of his position and navigation was most difficult, particularly since he flew with his cockpit open while rain poured in so that he could see the Dauntless flown by his division leader, Bombing 3's CO Lieutenant Commander DeWitt Shumway.

Even experienced pilots had trouble staying in the air. VB-3 XO Lieutenant Syd Bottomley remarked to his rear seater, Aviation Machinist's Mate 1/c David Johnson, about what a nerve-wracking flight it had turned into, flying in formation with so many planes, in and out of rain squalls, beneath low clouds, with poor visibility. Pilots frequently lost sight of one another when they entered a particularly intense cell, but they kept at it for an hour before they finally flew out of the weather. Commander Felt noted with considerable satisfaction and relief that all were still present.

While *Saratoga's* force struggled through the weather, Henderson Field had launched nine SBDs escorted by 12 F4Fs at 1615 hours, but that effort was a bust owing to the heavy rain and low ceiling.

Felt continued his search for 275 miles with no contact, since the transports had reversed course. Finally, he passed the word: "Return to base." They still faced a 250-mile flight through bad weather in decreasing afternoon light to reach Henderson Field. The force broke out of the bad weather in the light of a three-quarter moon as they made landfall on Malaita Island. By the time they finally arrived over Henderson Field, it was completely dark and they had to turn on their running lights. When they finally touched down, they had been airborne for four hours and 20 minutes, all but an hour in appalling weather.

As he turned to final approach on the field, Johnson remarked to Bottomley that he could see fireflies in the mahogany trees to port. Slim Russell immediately realized they were being fired on by machine guns in the trees, but rather than feel concern, he considered how pretty all those tracers were as they rose toward his SBD. Scouting 3's Lieutenant Commander "Bullet Lou" Kirn felt that the gunfire might have resulted from the uncertainty that prevailed at Henderson – that the fire was possibly from *friendly* guns. Fortunately, there was no damage, though several pilots landed in the wrong direction, later reporting that they had done so to fool the gunners, rather than because they had not realized they were doing such.

Given the limited experience of a majority of his pilots under such trying conditions, Felt believed that the air group had accomplished some marvelous flying. He later recalled, "More than ever, I had complete faith in the ability of the experienced section leaders under extremely difficult instrument-flying conditions, and in the fine discipline of all crews."

Since the enemy carriers were still undetected at the end of a busy day, Admiral Fletcher assumed that this meant they were at Truk. Thus, at 1823 hours, the admiral, whose fleet fuel state was always uppermost in his mind, detached *Wasp* and the rest of Task Force 18 for the trip south to refuel, telling Noyes to get back by August 25. *Wasp's* air group would soon be missed, since Fletcher's decision left Task Force 61 with 153 aircraft: 28 TBFs, 68 SBDs, and 57 F4Fs. Nagumo's Carrier Striking Force had at its disposal 173 aircraft: 45 Kates, 54 Vals, and 74 Zeros.

Once on the ground and having secured their airplanes, Slim Russell and several other Scouting 3 pilots were led through a coconut grove to a tent about a mile from the runway. There, they were each given a mess kit piled high with stew, hardtack, peas, and pears. Though they were used to dining off china and being served by mess stewards aboard ship, Russell later recorded in his diary that "All were extremely glad to get at the Marines' rough but hearty fare." Syd Bottomley was able to sample what he called "an attempt at a form of boilermaker," which consisted of a small bottle of California Lejon brandy and captured Japanese Asahi beer.

Lou Kirn was less fortunate than the others. After seeing to the dispersal of the squadron's Dauntlesses, which would have to be refueled in the morning light, he was unable to break for dinner until long after the Marines' mess had closed down. All he could get was some Japanese hardtack.

Later, Russell's group listened as their Marine hosts told stories about the landings. The Japanese had been so surprised that they ran for the bush just ahead of the Marines, leaving their radios on, food on the tables, and fires in the stoves. It started raining later, but pilots and aircrew had to sleep in or beside their planes in case the enemy mounted an early-morning attack. Russell later wrote in his diary that he thought the foxholes the Marines slept in looked like graves with only one blanket over them, a fern under them, and their clothing and helmets on. Before the night was over, he learned why they stayed in the foxholes, when a Japanese destroyer or submarine (it was the destroyer *Kagerō*) closed on the beach at about 0200 hours on August 24, and fired 15 5-inch rounds in the direction of the parked Navy TBFs and SBDs. The shells landed close but did no damage. After recovering from his initial shock, Russell recalled thinking it was kind of fun to listen to the shells whistling through the air. However, he found little sleep the rest of the night.

The *Saratoga* air group was held at readiness at Henderson to launch a strike against the enemy transports they had missed the previous day. While Marine SBDs searched northward along New Georgia Sound, Marine ground crewmen finished the laborious task of refueling 39 airplanes from 55-gallon drums. Each required the contents of five drums, all of which had to be pumped by hand. Marine mechanics and Navy rear seaters tinkered with engines and other systems in the waiting airplanes. To reciprocate the Marines' hospitality and fuel, all bombs were removed from the bombers and left behind.

The absence of *Saratoga's* strike group kept Fletcher's force tethered to Guadalcanal, staying about 170 miles east of Tulagi. Between 0555 and 0630 hours, 20 *Enterprise* air group SBDs were launched in pairs to cover sectors from northwest to due east out to a distance of 200 miles.

The *Enterprise* searchers found nothing, with the last reporting a negative search at 0947 hours; all were back aboard by 1010 hours. By then, Task Force 61 was abuzz with news that *Enterprise* had intercepted a message from a VP-23 PBY from the advance seaplane base at Graciosa Bay flown by Ensign Gale Burkey, that he had sighted a carrier, two cruisers, and four destroyers sailing due south at 04°40' south longitude, 161°15' east latitude. It was *Ryūjō*. The report was detailed enough for an accurate fix. *Ryūjō* was 281 miles from Task Force 61, beyond strike range.

At 0955 hours, 20 minutes after dispatching his initial sighting report, Burkey's PBY was attacked by two *Ryūjō* Zeros. Burkey tried at first to hide in a cloud, but was forced by persistent attacks to dive down just above the waves, forcing the Zeros to cut off diving attacks to avoid splashing into the sea. They kept it up until Burkey was able to hide in a heavy cloud formation at 1105 hours. The Catalina was not badly damaged and, with the crew far from subdued, Burkey moved to relocate and shadow *Ryūjō*.

At 1012 hours, Fletcher ordered Admiral Thomas Kinkaid aboard *Enterprise* to ready a strike force. Felt's arrival back on *Saratoga* was just in time. The deck crews worked overtime to refuel and rearm the bombers. Pacific Fleet was not reporting any signs of Japanese carriers, but Fletcher now believed they were "out there."

Following interception of Burkey's sighting report of *Ryūjō*, several other reports came in both of sighting of enemy surface warships and of attacks by fighters that were rightly surmised not to be from carriers. Then, at 1030 hours a message was intercepted from the VP-23 PBY flown by Lieutenant Leo Riester, who had found the Reinforcement Group the day before. Reister was flying the easternmost of the six patrols flown by Catalinas from Graciosa Bay. The message read "Attacked by aircraft planes fighting type Zero." Shortly after 1000 hours, Reister's crew had spotted two heavy cruisers and two destroyers, the vanguard detachment of Kondō's Advance Force. The ships had fired on Reister, but no damage was done until three F1M "Pete" float biplanes dispatched by the seaplane tender *Chitose* showed up and chased the Catalina. The Petes were armed with a pair of cowl-mounted 7.7mm machine guns and they riddled the PBY, killing Reister's co-pilot. Misreported as Zeros and far from any known Japanese land base, Fletcher and his staff saw the report as confirmation that a second enemy carrier might be present. Twenty minutes later, at 1050 hours, Lieutenant (jg) Robert Slater's Catalina reported that "enemy planes" had attacked it. Slater's patrol sector was immediately west of Riester's. This bolstered the staff's sense that a carrier or carriers were somewhere due north of Task Force 61.

At 1115 hours, *Saratoga's* radio room intercepted a second message from Ensign Burkey, reporting that at 1110 hours, five minutes after shaking an hour-long pursuit by two *Ryūjō* Zeros, a carrier, two cruisers, and one destroyer were now located at 04°40' south latitude, 161°20' east longitude, headed due south toward Guadalcanal. This second report of *Ryūjō* placed it only 245 miles from Task Force 61, and closing.

At 1116 hours, *Saratoga* received a relayed message from *Mackinac*, reporting a garbled sighting report from Lieutenant (jg) Slater's PBY of a cruiser and four unidentified ships at 05°00' south latitude, 162°05' east latitude, on course 140 degrees. The muddled report had actually originated from the PBY in the sector between Burkey and Slater, flown by Ensign James Spraggins. Apparently, Spraggins' report was regarding one of the surface forces screening the *Ryūjō* group. As Task Force 61's staff tried to incorporate Spraggins' report, Ensign Theodore Thueson, who was flying the westernmost patrol and had previously reported an attack by Zeros, reported the sighting at 1125 hours of two heavy cruisers and a destroyer at 05°12' south latitude, 158°50' east longitude, on course 355 degrees (nearly due north) at 20 knots. These were probably the ships of Misawa's Outer Seas Force, rushing to rejoin the Reinforcement Group after refueling at the Shortlands.

Events appeared to be coming to a head. Admiral Kinkaid recommended an immediate launch against the known carrier revealed by Burkey's sighting reports. Fletcher still believed there were other forces as yet undiscovered, due to the variety of sighting reports he had; given his limited air power, he wanted to delay launch. Fortunately, a few minutes later *Saratoga's* missing strike force appeared overhead. They had departed Guadalcanal at 0930 hours after the dawn search failed to find Tanaka's transports. Fletcher now had the strike force he needed. Flight deck crews turned to with a vengeance once the planes were back aboard, refueling and rearming them while the crews sought momentary respite in their ready rooms. Briefed on the situation by the staff as they knew it, Felt advocated delay because the enemy was still at maximum range for his force. Fletcher, hoping to hear further sighting reports from the PBYs that might tell him if the other carriers were present, agreed with Felt. The admiral remembered too well sending out a premature strike against what turned out to be a minor target at Coral Sea, while the same two carriers he was – unknowingly – up against again managed to slip into range without being discovered, leading to the loss of his flagship, *Lexington*. Caution was the word for the moment.

Minutes later, the situation appeared to possibly change. At 1143 hours, *Saratoga's* FDO ordered Fighting 5's Lieutenant Dave Richardson to respond to a bogey with his four Wildcats. Fifty miles from the task force, they found an H8K "Emily" flying boat, headed straight for the American fleet. Spotting the four Wildcats, the Emily's pilot dived for the ocean's surface and leveled off 50 feet above the wavetops as he turned for Rabaul. Each Wildcat made a firing pass, knocking parts from the Emily until the inboard left engine caught fire. The big flying boat finally fell into the waves at 1211 hours. While no sighting report had been heard, indicating that the enemy had apparently not seen Task Force 61, the possibility that it had done so meant that Fletcher would have to make a decision to launch a strike sooner rather than later. While Richardson's Wildcats were dealing with the Emily, *Saratoga* had intercepted another PBY position report on *Ryūjō* and its escorts, placing them at 04°40' south latitude and 161°15' east longitude, heading due south. It was moving closer into range.

By now, the Task Force 61 staff believed they were under almost constant observation by enemy search planes. In addition to the Emily, *Enterprise* and *Saratoga* had picked up several bogeys during the morning on their air search radars. As in the battles of Coral Sea and Midway, these Japanese searchers appeared to have detected a US carrier force without being detected or challenged. In fact, there were no Japanese search aircraft anywhere near Task Force 61 when the "contacts" were made. Combined with the numerous sightings of surfaced enemy submarines both that morning and over previous days, Fletcher's staff concluded that the enemy probably had received frequent reports of the location, speed, and heading of Task Force 61.

Feeling that the Japanese were indeed present and planning to fight this day, Fletcher asked Kinkaid at 1204 hours how many and what types of aircraft *Enterprise* would have aboard if the 20 searchers were launched, as Kinkaid recommended. Before he could reply, at 1210 hours Fletcher ordered *Enterprise* to launch its second long-range search of the day "as soon as possible." They were to cover an arc of ten-degree sectors from 290 degrees (west-northwest) to 90 degrees (due east) out to 250 miles, the mission profile Kinkaid had recommended at 1129 hours. *Enterprise* turned into the wind at 1229 hours and launched 16 SBDs from VB-6 and VS-5, as well as seven VT-8 TBFs. Sixteen Wildcats were also launched to reinforce the CAP.

Unknown to Fletcher, at noon *Ryūjō* finally came within range of Guadalcanal and launched six bomb-laden B5N2 "Kates" and 15 A6M2s – six escorts and a nine-plane "raiding force" – at 1220 hours. The plan was for the air group to attack Henderson Field in conjunction with the attack by the 25th Air Flotilla from Rabaul. Unfortunately, the Rabaul aircraft didn't show up since they had encountered severe weather over the northern Solomons and had returned to Rabaul at 1130 hours.

At 1234 hours Kinkaid was finally able to respond to Fletcher's question: after all aircraft had been recovered, the *Enterprise* air group would have one command TBF, six TBFs armed with torpedoes, 12 SBDs carrying 1,000-pound bombs, and 20 Wildcats available for a strike. Fletcher responded at 1244 hours: "Will hold your attack group in reserve for possible second carrier. Do not launch attack group until I direct you."

At 1235 hours, *Saratoga's* FDO vectored Lieutenant Dick Gray's VF-5 division against a single bogey coming in from the south. At 1253, 20 miles from the ship, Gray spotted what he thought at first was a B-17 just above the waves below. At 1255, he reported that the bogey was a G4M Betty. In fact, it was one of the four Misawa Air Group Bettys dispatched from Rabaul at 0625 hours that morning. All four F4Fs went after it. The Betty's crew was unaware of the threat until Gray's bullets began hitting it. He set the bomber aflame on his first pass, but the others also had their way with it. The Betty finally crashed only seven miles from the nearest American ships. No one on *Saratoga's* flag bridge believed the crew could have missed seeing and reporting Task Force 61's presence and position. In fact, this crew too had missed their target. Despite the anxieties of Fletcher and his staff, their position and composition was still a mystery to Nagumo. Based on his experience at Coral Sea and Midway, Fletcher remained reluctant to commit to a strike on *Ryūjō*, but he was also aware that the force that struck the first blow in a carrier battle was most likely to prevail. The admiral definitely did not want to end up in the position in which Nagumo had found himself at Midway, with his decks full of fully fueled and armed aircraft when the enemy made their attack. In addition, the hour was growing late if there was to be a strike, if the aircraft were to be able to return and land aboard in daylight.

Faced with all of the above, Fletcher made his decision and ordered CAG Felt to lead a strike that would take off at 1340 hours. Felt and his crews manned their aircraft and a force of 30 SBDs and seven TBFs disappeared from sight at 1400 hours. Fletcher had done what he could.

Unknown to Felt, 20 minutes before his strike force departed, the *Ryūjō* force had been picked up at 1320 hours by *Saratoga's* CXAM air-search radar, which was able to track it after picking it up almost due north of Task Force 61, 112 miles away, but long enough to be certain of its identity, purpose, or origin. The last firm sighting of *Ryūjō* had been at 1105 hours, when Ensign Burkey's PBY was forced to return to Graciosa Bay. As Felt's bombers sped down *Saratoga's* deck and lifted off, a VP-23 PBY flown by Lieutenant Joseph Kellam spotted *Ryūjō* and its escorts. Twenty minutes after Felt's force had disappeared over the horizon, *Saratoga* received the PBY's sighting report at 1405 hours, locating a carrier, two cruisers, and two destroyers at 05°40' south latitude, 162°20' east longitude, course 140 degrees. This put the enemy force 60 miles from the coordinates that Burkey had sent. For a moment, Fletcher's staff wondered if perhaps this was the second carrier they feared was out there. But from the fact that the force was reported with the same composition reported by Burkey, it was determined that this was Felt's target. The strike force was proceeding to the wrong coordinates. If the new sighting was correct, and the enemy was 60 miles from the coordinates Felt had – an extra 120 miles of flight – the strike could fail. Fletcher could do nothing beyond transmitting the new coordinates to Felt. There was no reply.

10

BATTLE OF THE EASTERN SOLOMONS – KILLING *RYŪJŌ*

August 24

Because there was as yet no operational radar at Henderson, and since coastwatcher sightings had proven to be less than completely reliable due to the vagaries of weather in the region that prevented formations being spotted, Air Group 23 XO Lieutenant Colonel Charlie Fike had begun launching one or two divisions of Wildcats at "Tojo Time," 1100–1500 hours, when it was most likely that an incoming strike might appear. Thus, when the small *Ryūjō* attack force arrived at 1415 hours, a division of Wildcats led by Marion Carl was waiting at 20,000 feet, with another 12 Wildcats and P-400s from the newly arrived 67th Fighter Squadron on alert at the field. Carl's wingman was Technical Sergeant Johnny Lindley; Second Lieutenant Fred Gutt was flying section leader with VMF-212's Marine Gunner Tex Hamilton on his wing.

The *Ryūjō* force approached Guadalcanal from the direction of Florida and Malaita islands at 10,000 feet. Lieutenant Murakami led the six Kates, along with the six escorts led by Warrant Officer Shigemi, in one formation, while the formation of nine "attack" Zeros led by *Ryūjō*'s *hikotaicho* Lieutenant Notomi flew about 1,600 feet to the right of the bombers.

Carl spotted the force over Tulagi. As he wheeled his four Wildcats into position, he radioed a warning to Henderson Field. When the

Condition One flag went up in response, the pilots scrambled to man all the available Wildcats, followed by a further scramble down the main runway. While they were supposed to take off in order of divisions and sections behind the flight leader, in practice everyone rushed to get airborne to gain the altitude advantage over the incoming bombers. Because of performance differences between the individual planes, the system of elements and divisions broke down, and everyone joined up on whomever was closest. Leading the dash was Captain Rivers Morrell, VMF-223's XO.

At 1423 hours, Carl led the way as the four Wildcats dived on the *Ryūjō* force. Carl saw only "bombers," lining up on six airplanes in the larger formation that turned out to be Shigemi's six escort Zeros. Firing from overhead and diving through the formation with Technical Sergeant Lindley glued to his wing, Carl was certain he had set one of the "bombers" on fire for his first victory over Guadalcanal and second of the war. Close behind, Hamilton and Gutt fired at the same formation. While Hamilton was drawn into a protracted dogfight with three of the "escort" Zeros, Gutt was able to shoot one of the Kates and dive through the formation behind Carl and Lindley, who became separated as they zoomed to regain altitude for a second attack.

The Kates came directly over the beach and lined up on the four 90mm antiaircraft guns of Battery E, 3rd Defense Battalion. At 1428 hours the guns opened fire while the Kates released their 36 60-kilogram bombs in a group drop at 1430 hours. A Betty was claimed by the overexcited gunners, who actually hit nothing. The drop was equally ineffective, with no damage inflicted even though the bombs detonated on either side of the guns.

Notomi's attack formation had more success. The three *shotai* formations attacked from three directions just as the bombs were dropped, strafing the runway with impunity. Notomi's threesome caught up with a Wildcat that had just lifted off and shot it up. Wounded in the head and shoulder, the pilot managed to keep the airplane airborne long enough to ditch reasonably well off Florida, where he was rescued by islanders and returned to Tulagi the next day.

67th Fighter Squadron skipper Captain Dale Brannon and his wingman, Second Lieutenant Deltis Fincher, dashed for their Airacobras when they saw the Condition One flag go up. Both remembered that they could hear the drone of the enemy overhead by the time they were in their cockpits and starting up. As they raced in echelon along the runway, they could hear the explosions of the bombs over the roar of their engines. Just as they lifted off and retracted their gear, a Zero swooped in front of them. The two aircraft turned toward each other and let fly with everything: eight .30-caliber machine guns, four .50-caliber machine guns, and two 20mm cannon, disintegrating the Zero. They flew through the debris as they clawed for altitude but were attacked in turn by the *shotai* leader and wingman of the fighter they had just destroyed. The enemy fighters made one pass and disappeared. Both P-400s were hit by 7.7mm bullets, but Brannon and Fincher were undeterred. Unfortunately, as Brannon later recalled, "When we got up to Guadalcanal, one of the first things that we found out was that the British had put a high-pressure oxygen system in our airplanes. The Marines had oxygen, but it was low pressure. I remember we managed to get all the way up to 16,000 feet on our first fight. We were really woozy. And of course the Zeros were way up above us."

Three Wildcats took on the retiring attack Zeros at low altitude over Lengo Channel. VMF-212's Second Lieutenant Bob McLeod got good hits on one that he claimed destroyed. In fact, the pilot – Lieutenant Notomi's wingman – was able to nurse his stricken fighter back over Guadalcanal, where he crash-landed, was found by Japanese troops, and was eventually evacuated off the island. In return, VMF-223's Second Lieutenant Elwood Bailey was shot down. Last seen in his parachute, descending toward the water near Tulagi, he never made it home.

Lieutenant Murakami's Kates executed a wide formation turn to the north after they dropped their bombs, in an attempt to retire from the area. At 1433 hours, Marion Carl downed a Kate on the formation's left side. Lindley and Gutt also fired on the Kates. As they did so, reinforcements began arriving. Captain Morrell, flying what was probably the best Wildcat on the island, was in the lead followed by five second lieutenants. All six attacked the five surviving Kates and five escort Zeros from below. As they did so, two attack Zeros arrived to help ward off the offenders. Second Lieutenant Ken Frazier destroyed a Kate on the right side of the formation on his first pass while Carl shot a Zero off Lindley's tail; however, he did not destroy it, as credited. Gutt was shot up and wounded in the left arm and left leg by another Zero, but made it back to Henderson Field. Lieutenants Rex Jeans and Red Taylor teamed up to disable a Kate, but Taylor – one of the six VMF-212 reinforcements – was immediately shot down and killed by a Zero. Last of all, VMF-212's Second Lieutenant John King fired on a Kate that blew up. After King's victory, the Wildcats withdrew.

Later, a bullet-riddled Kate that was most likely the one shot up by Jeans and Taylor dropped out of formation and crash-landed on a small island north of Malaita, from where the crew was rescued the following day by an Imperial Navy destroyer.

Altogether, the Marines claimed 20 confirmed victories: 12 Kates, a non-existent Betty, and seven Zeros. However, the Japanese lost only four Kates, including the one that crash-landed, and three Zeros, including the one Brannon and Fincher had blown up. Marion Carl was credited with four victories, including the phantom Betty, and was immediately recognized as the first Marine Corps ace. In fact, he was actually two kills shy, but would make up the difference two days later.

At 1430 hours, the destroyer *Amatsukaze* picked up a message from Lieutenant Murakami, flying the only Kate equipped with a radio, in which Murakami claimed that the Guadalcanal bombing had been successful. Captain Tadao Kato, *Ryūjō's* captain, recorded that his air group "delivered a strong attack on the airfield at Guadalcanal, destroying 15 enemy fighters in the air, bombing antiaircraft and machine-gun emplacements, and silencing them," claiming also that "having been thoroughly deceived by this maneuver, the enemy believed this small force to be our main strength." In fact, the Japanese had caused little damage on the ground, while three defending Wildcats were shot down with two pilots killed. This was hardly the crippling blow Yamamoto had ordered in support of the troops slowly approaching aboard Admiral Tanaka's transports.

While *Ryūjō's* air group challenged the Marines over Guadalcanal, the carrier and its escorts were spotted at 1440 hours by VT-3 CO Lieutenant Commander Charles M. Jett and his wingman, Ensign R.J. Bye. After sending a sighting report, Jett and Bye slowly climbed to 8,000 feet. As they overflew the destroyer *Amatsukaze*, they were recognized as enemy and the destroyer opened fire with its AA guns.

Amatsukaze's fire was taken up by the cruiser *Tone* and destroyer *Tokitsukaze*. As the Avengers closed in on *Ryūjō* from up-sun, the carrier launched three Zeros and a Kate. Warned by its escorts, it then turned toward the approaching bombers as the four ships attempted to present the worst targets – head-on and approaching the attackers. At 1445 hours, Jett and Bye leveled off at 12,000 feet and opened their bomb bay doors. Jett's radioman-bombardier, Aviation Machinist's Mate 2/c Herman Calahan, had the ships in his Norden bombsight as they and the ships came at each other. At 1458 hours, Calahan dropped the bombs, and Bye's bombardier, Aviation Machinist's Mate 3/c W.E. Dillon, salvoed his when he saw his leader drop. Both Avengers immediately banked away after dropping the two 500-pound bombs they carried. *Ryūjō* turned hard to starboard as the bombs were dropped and all four hit the water 500 feet astern of it. Although he broadcast his sighting report twice, Task Force 61 did not receive Jett's message.

Ten minutes later, at 1510 hours, Scouting 5's Lieutenant Stockton B. Strong and wingman Ensign John Ritchey spotted enemy ships on the horizon. Strong led Ritchey in a shallow dive to investigate. As the two Dauntlesses flew through the haze, he counted three surface warships. When they got within five miles of the enemy, he finally recognized *Ryūjō*. Rear seater Aviation Radioman 2/c Gene Strickland flashed a sighting report: "Position latitude 06-25S, longitude 161-20E, course 180, speed 15 knots." Though he repeated the message in plain language for six minutes, *Enterprise* did not acknowledge. Finally, their gas state forced the two Dauntlesses to turn back. Unknown to them, Felt heard Strickland's position report when he was 55 miles south of the reported position. Unfortunately, Strong's navigation was slightly off; when the *Saratoga* force arrived at the coordinates, they were forced to spend precious minutes and fuel searching for the carrier, which was actually further west.

As the Americans sought the Japanese, so the Japanese sought the Americans. Two Aichi E13A Type Zero observation floatplanes, known to the Allies as "Jake," were launched from *Tone's* sister ship *Chikuma* in the Vanguard Force at 1100 hours to search for the enemy fleet. They reached the limits of their search empty-handed. Fortunately for the Japanese, a third Jake had been added to the search mission at the last minute and launched 20 minutes after the first two.

Enterprise's radar picked up the third Jake as a bogey at 1338 hours. FDO Lieutenant Hank Rowe vectored two Wildcat divisions on CAP led by VF-6 CO Lieutenant Commander Lou Bauer toward the bogey at 1341 hours. The Wildcats were at 15,000 feet and got ahead of the Jake; Bauer was unable to see it, but at 1355 hours, Ensign Douglas Johnson, second section wingman in NAP Doyle Barnes' division, finally spotted it at 3,000 feet over Stewart Island northwest of *Enterprise* and its escorts and closing on the ships. At 1356 hours, Barnes radioed, "The bogey is a bandit, apparently a slow seaplane type."

Barnes' division attacked, but the Jake pilot entered a cloud, then threw off the Wildcats, out-maneuvering them as they made their first pass. On his second pass, section leader NAP Chuck Brewer killed the Jake's rear gunner with a well-aimed burst. At 1400 hours, Barnes set it on fire and it nosed over into the sea just 28 miles from *Enterprise*. But the CAP was late. Just before Barnes made his successful gunnery pass, the Jake had transmitted its crucial sighting report: "Spotted large enemy force. Being pursued by enemy fighters," just as *Saratoga* began launching its strike.

Admiral Nagumo had the Jake's report by 1425 hours. Though the message had no coordinates and did not mention carriers, Nagumo and his staff knew it for what it was. "Enemy fighters" could only refer to carrier fighters. The Jake's search route and speed were known; it was nothing to determine the enemy position. As soon as the calculations were made, Nagumo ordered *Shōkaku* and *Zuikaku* to launch their waiting deckloads without delay. The first wave of 27 D3A1 Vals and 15 Zeros, under command of *Shōkaku*'s *hikotaicho*, Lieutenant Commander Mamoru Seki, one of the most experienced dive bomber pilots in the Imperial Navy, was on its way by 1450 hours. The best estimate was that Task Force 61 was 260 miles away on a bearing of 153 degrees. With luck, the strike force would be over the enemy by 1630 hours.

At roughly the same time as Nagumo's carriers launched their strike, Bombing 6 XO Lieutenant John Lowe and wingman Ensign Bob Gibson, who had been launched to search out to 250 miles north of Task Force 61 rather than the usual 200 miles, found five enemy cruisers at the extreme limit of their search, at 1430 hours. Lowe's radioman sent a contact report that never reached *Enterprise*, then he and Gibson executed an unsuccessful dive-bombing attack on the heavy cruiser *Maya* of Admiral Kondō's Advance Force before turning back. This failure in important communications was soon followed by one even more significant, when Bombing 6 CO Lieutenant Ray Davis and wingman Ensign Bob Shaw, also flying a 250-mile search, sighted a large Japanese task force at 1515 hours. This was Admiral Abe's Vanguard Force, which was only 40 miles ahead of Nagumo's carriers. When Davis and Shaw climbed from their search altitude of 1,500 feet to 12,000 feet to execute an attack on this new target, Davis spotted a "large" carrier in the distance through the haze. A moment later, he spotted another behind that one. The first carrier he spotted was *Shōkaku*, still with a deckload of strike aircraft. Unfortunately, *Zuikaku*'s strike had already disappeared over the southern horizon, so there was no opportunity to give Task Force 61 a warning of what was coming. Davis immediately radioed a contact report of two large carriers, four heavy cruisers, six light cruisers, and eight destroyers on course 120 degrees, speed 25 knots. They received no reply.

Davis and Shaw immediately set to attack *Shōkaku*. Arriving over Nagumo's fleet at 1540 hours apparently unspotted, they initiated an attack from upwind and out of the sun at 1545 hours. In fact, the rudimentary air search radar *Shōkaku* had recently been equipped with had spotted them on their approach, but word had not been passed to the bridge or to the patrolling Zeros. *Shōkaku* was warned of the imminent threat when other ships in the task force opened fire on the two dive bombers. The carrier executed a sharp right turn with the Dauntlesses in their dives; Davis' bomb hit the ocean five feet from the carrier's bow, while Shaw's struck 30 feet further out. A few flight deck crewmen were injured, but otherwise the attack had no effect on *Shōkaku*. As they initiated their pullout, the two Dauntlesses were low enough that Shaw's gunner, Aviation Radioman 3/c H.D. Jones, could count 20 planes on *Shōkaku*'s deck. While the two SBDs made their escape at low altitude, both were hit by flak from the ships, then the Zero CAP caught up with them. One of the Zeros made a run on them, but pulled up in the face of shipboard AA fire.

Davis' and Shaw's rear seaters repeatedly broadcast that the enemy carriers had been found, but *Enterprise* did not receive the messages.

Other ships in Task Force 61 did pick up the messages, but weather affected radio communications, and the garbled report with only the presence of the two carriers but not their position did not reach Admiral Fletcher until 1615 hours.

In the meantime, Nagumo, fearing that an American strike was minutes away, ordered *Shōkaku* to launch its strike. It was estimated they would arrive over the American fleet at 1800 hours.

Saratoga's strike force arrived at the position Strong had reported at 1545 hours, but the ocean was empty, since Strong's navigation was off. Precious minutes were lost but fortunately Felt chose to search to the west. At 1606 hours, he spotted *Ryūjō*, headed southeast at 20 knots toward its pickup point for the Guadalcanal strike. He ordered the 15 Scouting 3 and six Bombing 6 SBDs to attack in coordination with the five Torpedo 8 Avengers; among the VT-8 pilots was Ensign Bert Earnest, sole survivor of the VT-8 detachment which had attacked the Japanese fleet at Midway. While the enemy aircraft maneuvered overhead for 15 minutes to get into position, the Japanese made no move to launch any defensive aircraft until 1620 hours, when *Ryūjō* turned into the wind to launch its remaining Zeros. The SBDs, led by Lieutenant Dick Shumway, attacked from multiple directions in an effort to counter the carrier's maneuvers. Felt watched, frustrated, as the first ten bombs scored only a few near misses. Only Ensign Roger Crow, who lowered his landing gear when he deployed his dive brakes, slowing his dive from 240 to 160 miles per hour, giving him time to see the others' misses, managed to hit the ship; his bomb penetrated its forward elevator and started a fire among the aircraft in the hangars below the flight deck. The fire spread quickly when it got to the tanks storing aviation gasoline.

Seeing only Crow's hit, Felt directed the Bombing 6 SBDs led by Lieutenant Syd Bottomley, which had turned to attack *Tone*, to attack *Ryūjō*. Bottomley pulled out of his dive and moved over to attack the carrier. Bottomley managed to line up with the ship in its turn; Lieutenant Gordon Sherwood, who was following him, saw Bottomley's bomb explode on the flight deck squarely amidships. Sherwood dropped his own bomb, which hit several yards toward the stern from Bottomley's hit, while Lieutenant (jg) Roy Isaman's bomb hit between the two. As Bottomley pulled out low over the water, his rear seater, Seaman 1/c Bob Hansen, saw heavy black smoke curling and rolling over the deck in a streaming curtain while a lick of flame appeared from amidships. He later remembered:

> The water cut by the bow was high enough to attract my attention from the ship itself. I surmised that her skipper was turning his speed up to full. From out of the smoke near the after end, flickering spurts of rapid-fire antiaircraft were showing. I marveled at the pluck and downright guts of the gunners sticking to their tasks against such strong and horrible odds.

Commander Tameichi Hara, captain of the destroyer *Amatsukaze*, later reported what he saw:

> Two or three enemy bombs hit near the stern, piercing the flight deck. Scarlet flames shot up from the holes. Ominous explosions followed in rapid order. Several more bombs made direct hits. Water pillars surrounded the carrier, and it was engulfed in thick, black smoke. This was no deliberate smoke screen. Her fuel tanks had been hit and set afire.

As the SBDs attacked, five of the seven Torpedo 8 Avengers set up in a "hammer and anvil" ahead of *Ryūjō*'s bow, with three led by Lieutenant Bruce Harwood going to the left and Ensigns Hanson and Katz going to the right. The carrier circled twice as the Scouting 3 and Bombing 6 SBDs dived on it. When it came around the second time, Harwood saw that its speed was reduced to ten knots as a result of the hits. The ship was broadside on to him when Harwood dropped his torpedo. At almost the same time, Ensign Hanson dropped his Mark XIV from the opposite side. Harwood's torpedo hit, lifting the bow and pushing the ship to the left with its explosion. *Ryūjō* lost its engine room and fire room in the blast. It quickly lost headway and was soon dead in the water.

As they made their escape from their attacks, the last sight most of the pilots and crewmen had of *Ryūjō* was a huge pillar of oily black smoke billowing skyward as it spread across the horizon. As the last *Saratoga* bomber pulled away from the burning *Ryūjō*, Felt received a message from Fletcher informing him of the presence of Nagumo's force with an estimated location and directing him to divert to the more important target. It was too late.

Felt stayed back, alone, to be sure the carrier was dead. He loitered in the clouds until 1620 hours and later reported: "Carrier continued to run in circles to the right, pouring forth black smoke which would die down and belch forth in great volume again."

When the surviving *Ryūjō* strike aircraft returned from Guadalcanal, they found they had no carrier deck to land on and joined the remaining Zeros circling overhead. A message had been sent directing them to land at the emergency strip on Buka, but at that point none had the fuel remaining to do so. The only airplane that did reach Buka was the Kate that had been launched just before Strong and his wingman had made their attack. Over the next hours, the carrier's crew fought for their crippled ship. Its three escorts circled the stricken carrier. As *Amatsukaze* approached the burning carrier, three airplanes suddenly popped out of the clouds. The Zeros were the last survivors of the Guadalcanal strike. They circled *Ryūjō*, then one of them ran out of gas and glided toward the water, where it ditched beside *Amatsukaze*. The other two ditched near *Tokitsukaze* when their engines stopped a few minutes later. All three pilots were rescued, but the rescue took valuable time from setting up the rescue of *Ryūjō's* 700-man crew. However, the flaming, smoke-shrouded carrier remained afloat. Finally, the flames abated and *Tokitsukaze* eased in to evacuate the wounded. *Amatsukaze* closed on the carrier at 1810 hours, when suddenly two American B-17s emerged from the clouds. A moment later a third came into view. *Tone* and *Amatsukaze* were forced to turn away with the arrival of the 11th Bombardment Group formation, while *Tokitsukaze* had to back away from the carrier to gain sea room. All three opened fire at the bombers, which each dropped strings of 300-pound bombs from high altitude. They claimed one hit, but all bombs fell in the sea wide of their targets. The last three Zeros which had been circling to protect the ships attacked one of the B-17s, whose gunners erroneously claimed a kill. It was dusk by the time they flew away.

There was barely enough light left to conduct the long-overdue rescue. The flames were dying, but the carrier had no power. Captain Hara was struck by the damage he saw as he maneuvered *Amatsukaze* near *Ryūjō*. Fire had gutted it and grotesque corpses could be seen on the decks. The carrier had a 40-degree list to starboard and was sinking lower with each minute.

Hara maneuvered his ship close. The carrier's superstructure brushed against it. He held the destroyer close while 300 survivors made their way aboard. An officer told Hara that there were no more survivors, and he began backing away. *Amatsukaze* was only 500 yards away when *Ryūjō* suddenly took its final plunge beneath the waves. The three escorts turned on their searchlights and began gathering in oil-soaked swimmers. As the sun began to set, the last airplanes ditched and their crews swam to the ships. The little formation turned northeast to rejoin Nagumo's fleet.

SAVING *ENTERPRISE*

August 24

Defense of the American fleet centered on the fighter direction officers (FDOs) of each carrier, due to the fact that current doctrine had been developed during the 1930s before the Navy was able to operate multi-carrier task forces. *Enterprise*'s FDO, Lieutenant Commander Ham Dow, was at this time the most experienced FDO in the fleet. A 1926 Naval Academy graduate and veteran pilot, he had defended *Enterprise* successfully at Midway. Assisting Dow was Lieutenant Hank Rowe, a 1937 Annapolis graduate and pilot who had been trained in fighter control by the Royal Air Force in 1941. Following his stint with the RAF, Rowe had helped establish the US Navy Fighter Direction School in Hawaii and was temporarily assigned as a working evaluator to the *Enterprise* fighter-direction staff for the Guadalcanal invasion. Given the expertise of the *Enterprise* team, the carrier was designated central control for radar-assisted fighter direction once the enemy was spotted, with both Fighting 5 and Fighting 6 under their direction. This was the first time such centralized control had been attempted by the US Navy.

The major problem with US fighter control at this time was that the fleet used high-frequency (HF) radio, which limited the number of channels; both fighter control and the fighters were on the same circuit, which had already demonstrated its limitations at Coral Sea and Midway when the circuit became overloaded with traffic from excited pilots in the midst of combat. Additionally, the CXAM air search radar in use at the time was not accurate in height determination; accurate height could not be gauged until the enemy was within the 12-mile range of the Mark 3 antiaircraft radar. Thus, it took real skill and luck to place the defenders at best advantage far enough out from the fleet for the initial confrontation, while later control during the fight was nigh on impossible due to the overloaded radio circuit.

Knowing that the Japanese had either launched a strike, or would soon do so after Davis and Shaw had spotted them and made their attack, Fletcher gave orders to prepare for the enemy's attack. *Saratoga* and *Enterprise* launched reinforcements for the overhead CAP, with 14 VF-6 Wildcats taking up position over *Enterprise* while the 12 from VF-5 joined up over *Saratoga*.

At 1502 hours, *Enterprise*'s radar picked up a bogey approaching at low altitude, bearing 340 degrees. Rowe immediately vectored Lieutenant Dick Gray's Fighting 5 division to look it over. Gray reported at 1514 hours that the stranger appeared to be a PBY. Suspicions were raised further, since it appeared to Gray that the PBY was trying to close on the task force. Rowe directed Gray to follow it and at 1530 hours directed Scoop Vorse's VF-6 division to close on the intruder. At 1535 hours, Vorse confirmed it was a PBY. Since there were rumors that the enemy had captured several PBYs in the Netherlands East Indies, Rowe directed Vorse to take a closer look; at 1540 hours he reported that the PBY looked okay.

In fact, the VP-23 PBY-5 was flown by Lieutenant Joseph Kellam, who had spotted a carrier and several surface ships at 1405 hours, before having to return to Graciosa Bay. Having not received confirmation that the report was received, Kellam had diverted to Task Force 61 to personally deliver his message. Vorse escorted Kellam's PBY to *Enterprise*, where the message was sent by blinker: "Small enemy carrier bearing 320 True distance 195 miles." This was *Ryūjō*. Kellam then provided new information, the spotting of a cruiser, two destroyers, and three transports 50 miles from the small carrier. This was the first news of Admiral Tanaka's Reinforcement Group. Unfortunately, Kellam and his PBY were still doubted by Fletcher's staff and by the time confirmation of his identity was received from *Mackinac*, it was too late to do anything about Tanaka's ships.

Over the next hour, Fletcher vacillated about committing the remaining strike aircraft on his carriers to a second strike against

Cactus Air Force aircraft at Henderson. (US Navy Official)

Damaged F4F of VF-11. (US Navy Official)

F4F-4 Wildcat of VMF-121 with ground crew. (US Navy Official)

Japanese dead on Tenaru sandbar. (US Navy Official)

F4F-4 Wildcats of VMF-121. (US Navy Official)

Guadalcanal patrol. (US Navy Official)

USS *South Dakota* underway. (US Navy Official)

USS *Wasp* burning. (US Navy Official)

The Japanese troopship *Kyushu Maru*. (US Navy Official)

Admiral Nimitz (left), and Admiral Halsey (right). (US Navy Official)

USS *Northampton* trying to tow the mortally damaged USS *Hornet* during the Battle of Santa Cruz. (US Navy Official)

USS *Russell* comes alongside USS *Hornet*. (US Navy Official)

USS *Smith* is hit during the Battle of Santa Cruz. (US Navy Official)

USS *South Dakota* with Kates at the Battle of Santa Cruz. (US Navy Official)

TBF-1 of VT-10 launches. (US Navy Official)

USS *Enterprise* at Santa Cruz. (US Navy Official)

Marines fire on torpedo plane. (US Navy Official)

Smoke rises from two enemy planes shot down, November 11, 1942. (US Navy Official)

USS *President Jackson*, November 11, 1942. (US Navy Official)

USS *San Francisco* after the naval Battle of Guadalcanal, November 12, 1942. (US Navy Official)

USS *South Dakota* at Nouméa. (US Navy Official)

USS *Helena* (CL-50) after the naval Battle of Guadalcanal, November 12, 1942. (US Navy Official)

Rear Admiral Richmond K. Turner (left) and General Arthur A. Vandegrift (right). (US Navy Official)

Left to right: Major John Smith, Lt. Colonel Richard Mangrum, Captain Marion Carl. (US Navy Official)

Nagumo's force, now that he had strong intimations they were "out there." However, the fuel state of the fighters overhead came to dominate operations.

Enterprise had been unable to land aircraft, since the reserve strike was spotted aft for takeoff, and *Saratoga* had been taking CAP fighters aboard for refueling. At 1600 hours, Fletcher ordered *Saratoga*'s task force to turn into the wind so it could launch 16 Fighting 6 Wildcats which were now fully fueled. As soon as these were airborne, orders were given that five TBFs and two SBDs be taxied forward so 12 Fighting 5 F4Fs could come aboard for refueling.

At 1602 hours, Task Force 61 ran out of time.

Enterprise's CXAM radar picked up *Zuikaku*'s inbound strike at 1602 hours; they were only two minutes behind their own estimated time of arrival (ETA). A minute later, Dow's information was confirmed by *Saratoga*'s radar. The bogey was 88 miles from *Enterprise* and 112 miles from *Saratoga*, bearing 320 degrees. Immediately after the initial pickup, the bogey faded from the screens at a distance of 85 miles from *Enterprise*, providing an altitude estimate of 12,000 feet. At the moment, its 14 Wildcats were overhead at 8,000–15,000 feet, while *Saratoga*'s dozen were at 10,000–15,000 feet. Dow assumed overall fighter control and ordered both formations to climb to 14,000 feet and "buster" (fly at best speed). The two carriers turned into the wind and *Enterprise* launched 16 more Wildcats, while *Saratoga* launched its 15 remaining fighters. By 1637 hours, 53 Wildcats – 25 from VF-5 and all 28 from VF-6 – were airborne, the largest fighter force yet to defend an American task force. While the ship continued into the wind, *Enterprise*'s air officer, Lieutenant Commander John Crommelin, ordered the nine SBDs and seven TBFs still on deck launched immediately, telling VS-5's commander, Lieutenant Turner Caldwell, to take lead, fly north, and hit any target he found. Once airborne, the formation was joined by five Torpedo 8 Avengers led by Lieutenant "Swede" Larsen, launched by *Saratoga* to clear its deck. The quick action likely saved *Enterprise*, since the fully fueled and armed dive bombers were parked right where the ship would be hit only minutes after they were launched.

VF-5 XO Lieutenant "Chick" Harmer's division had been launched at 1400 hours and ordered to climb and maintain station at 20,000 feet. By 1600, he noted that his fuel state was at one-third full. Two minutes later, Dow asked if he could delay landing to refuel and ordered the Wildcats to descend to 10,000 feet.

After a few moments, Dow ordered Scoop Vorse's division to investigate an incoming bogey at 1,500 feet. Rowe followed that by diverting three other VF-5 and VF-6 divisions to follow Vorse. When the bogey closed to 30 miles of *Enterprise*, Rowe diverted the 16 Wildcats that had just been launched as CAP reinforcement to oppose the possible enemy strike. The bogey turned out to be two Torpedo 3 TBFs with their IFF gear turned off inbound from their fruitless search patrol. Thirty of the 53 defending Wildcats were now out of position at low altitude. Rowe hurried to reposition the defenders.

Just as the *Zuikaku* bogey went off the screens at 85 miles, it made a course correction. Rowe estimated that they were planning to attack from the west out of the sun, rather than from the northwest. He ordered VF-6 CO Lieutenant Commander Lou Bauer, leading the 16 CAP-relief Wildcats, to intercept as far west as possible. Vorse's division was also sent west. Lacking full information, Rowe couldn't know that only Vorse's four had any hope of arriving in the right position in time.

The big bogey reappeared on the screens at 1618 hours, 44 miles distant. At 1625 hours, VF-5's CO Lieutenant Commander Leroy Simpler brought his four F4Fs aboard *Saratoga* with the last of their fuel. The refueling of the four would set a record, since they were able to take off at 1706 hours and join the battle in the time it took the *Zuikaku* force to arrive overhead.

Lieutenant Commander Mamoru Seki spotted *Enterprise* and its ring of surface escorts at 1620 hours, 40 miles ahead beneath clear skies. Several minutes later, he spotted *Saratoga* and its escorts 25 miles beyond *Enterprise*. At 1627 hours, he signaled "Assume attack formation."

Immediately, Lieutenant Shigematsu's four "offensive" *Shōkaku* Zeros surged ahead of the Vals to take on American fighters; this left only six "defensive" *Zuikaku* Zeros with the 27 Vals.

The first Americans to spot the incoming raid were the four pilots in Chief NAP Doyle Barnes' VF-6 division, who spotted the *chutai* of nine *Zuikaku* Vals led by Lieutenant Reijiro Otsuka at 1629 hours and 25 miles distant from *Enterprise*. Otsuka's *chutai* was the left wing of Commander Seki's 27-plane formation. Barnes led his division in a frantic climb to reach the enemy's altitude, which had been incorrectly estimated by the *Enterprise* FDOs. The fully loaded F4F-4 Wildcat's climb rate was so poor that before they could gain sufficient altitude for an attack, the division had to reverse course and pursue them; their effort was fruitless given the enemy's speed. Unfortunately, Lou Bauer and the other 11 Wildcats were out of position to attempt an interception and saw nothing of the enemy.

Scoop Vorse, whose four Wildcats intercepted the errant Avengers at 2,000 feet, strained for altitude. As they climbed through 8,000 feet at 1633 hours, Vorse spotted the formation of Vals against the clear sky in a vee-of-vees formation. The Wildcats were hanging on their props as they struggled to get at the enemy. A minute later, Vorse's section leader, NAP Howell Sumrall, spotted what he first thought were a dozen Zeros – they were Lieutenant Shigematsu's four *Shōkaku* Zeros. To Sumrall the fighters appeared to be using their considerable altitude advantage to close on the Wildcats, which weaved and maneuvered as they continued to climb toward the Vals.

Sumrall, who was flying in the number four position to protect the division's two inexperienced wingmen, saw the number four Zero roll inverted as its pilot took in the formation. Realizing the enemy pilot expected the number four man to be an inexperienced wingman, Sumrall gave him what he expected, slowing slightly and lagging behind the others like a newcomer. As he climbed through 10,000 feet, he saw the enemy pilot waggle his wings, telegraphing his coming attack. As the Zero dived toward him, Sumrall kicked full right rudder and pulled his nose as high as possible, firing a short burst to make his opponent steepen his dive. The Zero did so and as he dived beneath Sumrall, the Wildcat's wings sparkled with gunfire and heavy .50-caliber bullets blew off the rear of the Zero's belly tank, setting it afire, and passed through the cockpit. The burning fighter entered a long, shallow glide and flew all the way into the ocean. Sumrall's wingman, Ensign Cash Register, fired at the Zero and thought he hit it as he followed the burning fighter despite Sumrall's orders to rejoin; he saw the pilot bail out at 6,000 feet.

As Sumrall dealt with the fourth Zero, Vorse and his wingman, Ensign Dix Loesch, finally leveled off at the Vals' altitude. As Vorse executed a reverse to make a pass on the dive bombers, Shigematsu's three remaining Zeros closed to protect their Vals. Number three turned and dived on Sumrall; spotting this, Vorse tacked onto him. The enemy pilot opened fire out of range and continued to snap bursts as he closed on Sumrall, who held his course since he saw Vorse on the opponent's tail. Loesch had to remind Vorse to drop his wing tanks as he closed to firing range and executed a low-side pass on the enemy, which caught fire. The enemy pilot pulled up and the fire died, then he executed a wingover. Thinking their opponent out of control, Vorse and Loesch followed it down to 1,000 feet and claimed a victory as it continued its dive, but the pilot actually made it back to *Shōkaku* and landed his damaged fighter successfully.

At this point, Dow and Rowe lost their struggle to control the battle, as the radio frequency was quickly overloaded with elated cries of "Tally ho" and worried calls of "There's a Zero on your tail" as the pilots spotted the enemy and made their attacks.

Three Fighting 5 Wildcats led by Lieutenant Dave Richardson with Lieutenant Marion Dufilho and Ensign Leon Haynes – none of whom had ever flown together before – had been launched from the *Enterprise* at about 1545 hours. Originally briefed to escort a strike force against Nagumo's carriers, Richardson received an order on a chalkboard as he and the other two moved into position to launch to orbit the fleet at 10,000 feet and await further contact. They had been vectored onto the three Torpedo Three Avengers that got everyone mixed up and then vectored against the large bogey that Rowe thought was setting up to attack from the west.

After chasing around at full throttle and searching high and low for the enemy, they finally spotted the Val formation at a good distance and at 15,000 feet, headed toward *Enterprise* at 1638 hours. Richardson led them in a climbing turn toward the bombers, but they were suddenly bounced by all six of Lieutenant Saneyasu Hidaka's six defending *Zuikaku* Zeros. Coral Sea veteran Haynes turned in to meet the two Zeros executing a direct attack from astern; the two enemy fighters passed him, then turned to engage from head-on. Both passed again, then one reversed and opened fire from dead astern. Haynes dived away, recovered, climbed back into the fight, and caught one of the Zeros from the left rear. It smoked when he hit it and was last seen diving through 6,000 feet.

Meanwhile Richardson evaded the two that attacked him from ahead, then turned into them. They disappeared but he dived to 4,000 feet before he was sure they weren't on his tail. He climbed back to find the others but only Haynes joined up. Marion Dufilho, who had entered the record books back in February when he and Butch O'Hare defended *Lexington* against Japanese bombers, was never seen again, apparently the victim of the third pair of *Zuikaku* Zeros.

Lieutenant Dick Gray and Ensign Frank Green had been airborne since they launched from *Enterprise* at 1445 hours. Earlier, with an attack imminent, the two had been turned away from a fueling stop aboard the *Saratoga*. Though low on fuel, they had attempted to engage the attackers. As they climbed toward the Vals, Gray spotted Richardson's fight and dived in to help. He managed to outmaneuver one of the Zeros and put so many rounds into it at such close range that he saw the pilot slump over when hit. As it spun violently out of control, a second Zero attacked him and Gray was forced to dive away, taking himself out of the battle altogether.

At 1638 hours, strike leader Seki passed the order, "All forces attack." He waggled his wings and the other 17 *Shōkaku* dive bombers took up a line-astern formation and followed Seki in a sharp turn south, lining up on *Enterprise*. Lieutenant Otsuka's nine *Zuikaku* Vals continued on their original course so as to skirt Task Force 16's antiaircraft umbrella and attack the more distant *Saratoga*. *Enterprise* was making 27 knots when Seki started down on its port side at 1640 hours.

Chick Harmer had never been able to receive a vector from the FDO due to the deluge of traffic on the radio frequency. Suddenly, he saw Seki's formation silhouetted against a cloud on the far side of the task force. His division was at 5,000 feet and the enemy was at 12,000 feet still 15–20 miles from their attack point. Harmer pushed full throttle and the other three followed him as they strained to get to the enemy's altitude in time to blunt their attack. Just as Seki and his nine bombers reached their dive position, the four Wildcats achieved an attack position 1641 hours, just as Seki banked and entered his dive.

Harmer was closing on Seki when his wingman, Ensign John McDonald, flashed past him and opened fire on Seki. Harmer was forced to fall back and not open fire to avoid hitting McDonald. McDonald followed Seki through the intense antiaircraft fire from *Enterprise* and its escorts. Although McDonald was unable to hit Seki, the *hikotaicho's* concentration was rattled, keeping him from an accurate dive. As *Enterprise* twisted through a tight starboard turn, Seki was unable to follow his aiming point and when he dropped his

250-kilogram bomb at 1,500 feet, it missed to port. *Enterprise* gunners reported Seki's Val plunged into the sea, but he got away at very low level, as did McDonald, who faced as much danger from the gunners as any of the enemy.

As McDonald went after Seki, Harmer caught the second Val and followed it through the beginning of its dive. The observer-gunner fired several bursts at Harmer but was silenced by Harmer's initial burst of fire. Though the Val did not burn, it suddenly steepened its dive. Unable to match the dive, Harmer pulled out. The enemy pilot dropped too high, and his bomb missed *Enterprise* by a wide margin. Moments after he pulled out from chasing the second Val, Harmer was hit solidly by a defending Zero that closed on him, wounding him in his left leg. He managed to jink away from the Zero.

Lieutenant Sandy Crews, Harmer's section leader, managed to catch the third Val and hit it in its wings, fuselage, cowling, and engine. There was no return fire. He followed it, firing, but it did not catch fire. Crews pulled out at 3,000 feet as antiaircraft fire from *Enterprise* and other ships got too thick. The third Val also released too high and its bomb hit the water 200 yards off the carrier's port quarter, then it started burning and spiraled into the water 600 yards off *Enterprise*'s port beam. Crews climbed back toward the oncoming dive bombers and was able to make one opposite-course pass at another, without any observed results.

The lead *Shōkaku shotai* had scored no hits for three tries, but there were no Wildcats to oppose the next four Vals, the three in the middle *shotai* and the lead Val of the rear *shotai*. Fortunately, all four bombs missed *Enterprise*.

Moments after Harmer waded in, Fighting 6's NAP Aviation Electrician's Mate 1/c R.W. Rhodes claimed a Val, while NAP Aviation Machinist's Mate 1/c L.P. Mankin discovered just how maneuverable the Val was when one turned inside his plane and peppered his tail. Six Wildcats tried to corner one Zero at 17,000 feet, but the pilot evaded with a series of elegant aerobatics before flying off. Ensign R.M. Disque shot a Zero off the tail of an SBD of the inner air patrol, following up with a second Zero when it tried to attack four other Wildcats.

Almost all the attackers concentrated on *Enterprise*. Defending Wildcats followed the Vals in their dives, disregarding the intense antiaircraft fire. Marine Sergeant Joseph R. Schinka, commanding *Enterprise*'s No. 4 20mm antiaircraft battery, spotted a puff of smoke overhead as a Val was hit by a Wildcat. He opened fire even though the Vals were out of range. The tracers guided fire from the screening ships. A barrage of 20mm, 1.1-inch and 5-inch antiaircraft fire filled the sky as *North Carolina* (BB-55), *Portland* (CA-33), *Atlanta* (CLAA-51), and the escorting destroyers all came to the carrier's defense.

NAP Chief Machinist Barnes caught up with the nine Vals of the second *Shōkaku chutai* over *Enterprise* as they prepared to enter their dives. At 1640 hours, he yelled over the radio, "Okay, let's go give them hell!" It was one of the few clear messages on the fighter channel. Barnes and his wingman, Ensign Ram Dibb, attacked the three Vals of the second *chutai's* third (rear) *shotai* as they waited to dive. Dibb hit one and drew smoke, but it did not fall away as he thought. He flew through "friendly" antiaircraft fire to try to get another Val, but pulled up short and did not try to follow any of the enemy bombers into the friendly fire.

Barnes' section leader, NAP Chuck Brewer, overshot the second *chutai* as he dived from 15,500 feet and overtook the two rear Vals of the rear *shotai* of Seki's lead *chutai* just after they simultaneously pushed over. He set the first on fire; the pilot dropped his bomb too high and it exploded 2,000 yards off *Enterprise's* starboard bow, while the bomber hit the water 1,000 yards from the carrier. Brewer shifted his aim to the other Val as the pilot maneuvered to give the observer-gunner a better shot. Brewer fatally damaged the Val, but he was forced off at 4,000 feet by extremely heavy antiaircraft fire. The Val, on fire from nose to tail, continued its dive toward the tightly turning *Enterprise* and the pilot dropped his bomb at 2,000 feet and stayed in the dive, probably in the hope of crashing into its flight deck.

Aboard the carrier, *Enterprise* gunnery officer Lieutenant Commander Orlin Livdahl, in his post in Sky Control atop the island, later remembered that he tucked his head into his shoulders as the flaming dive bomber appeared to dive straight at him. The bomb missed *Enterprise* just to starboard and the Val screamed in and exploded when it hit the water only a short distance away. The double impact threw up a huge geyser of water and a smelly black substance that fell over Sky Control, 110 feet above the ship's waterline. Both hits were so close, and so close together, that Livdahl thought for a moment the ship herself had been hit, and other Japanese observers credited the crew with crashing into *Enterprise* with the bomb still aboard.

Even as Brewer hit the last two Vals of the lead *Shōkaku chutai*, the three Vals of the lead *shotai* of the second chutai, led by Lieutenant Keiichi Arima, the *Shōkaku* bomber squadron *buntaicho*, who was riding as the observer in the lead Val of the lead *shotai*, flown by Petty Officer First Class Kiyoto Furuta, were already diving toward the twisting carrier below. NAP Barnes followed the dive bombers into the cauldron of fire. At 1642 hours, his Wildcat was hit head-on by a 5-inch shell that blew off its wings and tail. The fuselage, with Barnes still in the cockpit, plunged into the water 2,000 yards off the port quarter of the destroyer *Balch* (DD-363). Barnes' was one of four Wildcats shot down by "friendly fire" in the battle.

Furuta had started his dive over the port quarter of *Enterprise* as it swung into a left turn, expertly guiding his dive bomber through intense antiaircraft fire, following the carrier in a twisting turn of his own. He released his bomb at low altitude and recovered smoothly just above the water. In the rear seat, Lieutenant Arima saw a definite hit.

The first bomb ever to strike *Enterprise* did so at precisely 1644 hours. The delayed-action bomb angled into the teak flight deck at the forward starboard corner of the after elevator, penetrating 42 feet through three steel decks before it detonated in the chief petty officers' quarters below the waterline. The concussion whipsawed *Enterprise* from stem to stern, first upwards then side-to-side, as hundreds of crewmen were jerked from their feet. The explosion killed 35 and wounded 70, wiping out a damage control team stationed in the chief's' quarters. Six-foot holes were ripped in its hull at the waterline and the carrier listed to starboard as seawater poured in. The hangar deck bulged upwards a full two feet from the blast, rendering the aft elevator useless.

Thirty seconds later, Arima's wingman's bomb hit 15 feet from the first, on top of the two starboard aft 5-inch gun mounts of the ship's Gun Group 3. Arima's bomb had set off the ready powder for the port aft 5-inch guns, but this second bomb set off a sympathetic detonation of Gun Group 3's 65 ready powder casings. Observers on other ships, including a Navy movie cameraman who caught the whole event on film, saw the blast of the second bomb quickly followed by a very large magnitude secondary blast. The blast's tremendous heat, in addition to the huge orange ball of flame followed by heavy black smoke, ensured the instantaneous death of 41 of Gun Group 3's 50 crewmen. The nine survivors and four bystanders were severely injured. Those not ripped to shreds by the force of the blast were burned beyond recognition; many were reduced to grotesque charcoal caricatures of the men they had been. The blast threw large chunks of metal and pieces of bodies as far as the destroyer *Monssen*, a mile from *Enterprise*'s starboard quarter.

Petty Officer Kazumi Horie, pilot of the third Val of Arima's *shotai*, was hit in his dive by a 20mm round that hit his bomb and set it off. The flaming bomber hit the flight deck forward of the first two hits and created a ten-foot hole that disabled the central No. 2 elevator.

The first two Vals of Lieutenant Arima's second *shotai* both missed, but one pilot dropped his bomb close enough to the carrier's starboard side that the explosion drenched many on the island. Both bombers survived the gauntlet of fire and recovered low over the water. The third bomber in the *shotai* took multiple hits as it reached the release point. Many observers saw it stagger in the air and fall apart. However, its bomb fell free and dropped toward the flight deck below.

Boatswain's Mate First Class Al Gabara, gun captain of the No. 4 1.1-inch mount, was looking at his friend, Boatswain's Mate Second Class Arthur Davis, when the bomb hit close by the aft elevator at 1646 hours, exploding in a relatively low-order detonation incorrectly thought by many to be the result of a defect. Davis, standing in the open, was blown apart by the full force of the blast. A large piece of him landed in the gun pointer's lap. Bosun Gabara went into shock until one of the loaders yelled into his ear, "Gabby, you're hit!" He later recalled not feeling a thing, but when he saw the loader's shocked look, he looked down and discovered a steel sliver had pierced his right arm just below the elbow. He had spent a few lost moments absently sweeping shell casings from the mount.

Photographer's Mate 3/c Robert Read was standing in an exposed vantage point on the island as he followed the third bomb in his viewfinder all the way to impact. Read snapped the moment of explosion, one of the most memorable photographs of the entire Pacific War, but shrapnel from the blast killed him.

Seaman 1/c Willie Bowdoin, a loader on the No. 3 1.1-inch gun crew, was wounded in his leg and posterior by tiny steel shards and knocked to the flight deck. When he recovered his senses, he realized that a small fire had broken out behind the gun. When he moved to grab a fire extinguisher, he was confronted by a screaming Seaman 1/c Joyce Lamson, the pointer, whose abdomen had been torn open by shrapnel, exposing his intestines and shredding his right leg. Two flight deck crewmen carried him to the aid station under the flight deck, while Bowdoin fought the fire, and won.

As Bosun Gabara's attention expanded beyond his own injuries, he realized that every man in his gun crew had been peppered by flying steel slivers and was injured. He finally turned and saw that the starboard after 5-inch gun gallery, the station of his best friend aboard ship, was a smoking ruin where men struggled to cover the dead with canvas and carry the bodies away.

Fortunately for *Enterprise*, the final three Vals from Arima's last *shotai* were unable to obtain position to mount an attack on the carrier, and they diverted instead to an attack on *North Carolina*, which was steaming to *Enterprise*'s rear and adding its numerous 5-inch/.38-caliber AA mounts as well as its 1.1-inch and 20mm batteries to the defense of the "Big E." At 1645 hours, the battleship was struck by several errant "friendly" antiaircraft rounds from other ships. The three Vals diverted to line up on it, having been thrown off their mark by the last-minute attack by NAP Barnes' Wildcat division. Fighting 6's Ensign Douglas Johnson, who had just pulled off from a gunnery run on the Vals, followed them into their dive despite the sky being filled with explosions of shells from the fleet below.

North Carolina's luck held as two bombs missed to port, while the third missed to starboard. The enemy strafed its decks as they recovered from their dives. The ship's AA batteries blew the lead Val out of the sky 1,500 yards off its starboard quarter, while the second was shot down by converging AA fire from *North Carolina* and the antiaircraft light cruiser *Atlanta*, and fire from Ensign Johnson, who received a full victory credit. Johnson's Wildcat was struck in the wings and rear fuselage by shell fragments from below, and the radio antenna was shot away, but Johnson himself was unscathed. The lucky third Val was able to recover and escape the immediate vicinity of Task Force 16.

Eighteen *Shōkaku* Vals had attacked *Enterprise* and *North Carolina*. Five were shot down over *Enterprise* by fighters or antiaircraft fire, with two downed over *North Carolina*, also by a fighter or antiaircraft fire. Of eight Fighting 5 and Fighting 6 Wildcats that intercepted the Vals, one was shot down by "friendly" antiaircraft fire. The *Shōkaku* airmen who survived claimed six hits on *Enterprise* but had scored only three. They were plenty.

Enterprise was saved from being rapidly engulfed in flames because flammable paint had fortuitously been chipped from the compartment around the impact zone during the previous week, while Chief Machinist Bill Fluitt, the ship's gasoline officer, had ordered and overseen the draining and venting of the nearby aviation fuel lines, which had all been filled with carbon dioxide literally minutes before the bomb struck.

The carrier's battle to survive wasn't over. Two minutes before Seki led the *Shōkaku* dive bombers into their attack on *Enterprise*, Lieutenant Reijiro Otsuka, who had led his nine-plane *Zuikaku chutai* to attack *Saratoga*, which was about ten miles beyond *Enterprise* when Seki chose the "Big E" as his target, found his formation under strong attack from defending Wildcats.

Lieutenant Saneyasu Hidaka's six *Zuikaku* Zeros had fallen behind the Vals when they engaged Lieutenant Dave Richardson's three-plane Fighting 5 division and were unable to protect the dive bombers.

Just as Otsuka gave the order to move into line-astern to commence attack, three Fighting 5 Wildcats led by Lieutenant Hayden Jensen that had been chasing Otsuka since spotting the formation at 1632 hours, initiated a diving attack from 20,000 feet while the Vals descended from 15,000 feet to their attack altitude. Jensen concentrated on the three bombers of the center *shotai*. He made a high-side run on the nearest of the three and claimed a victory when he saw the bomber fall out of the formation in flames. Jensen and wingmen Ensign John Kleinman and Lieutenant (jg) Carlton Starkes made several independent passes, claiming seven destroyed.

A moment after Jensen initiated his attack, Don Runyon's four-plane Fighting 6 division joined the fight with a dive from 20,000 feet out of the sun. Runyon's attack convinced Otsuka that his formation stood very little chance of reaching *Saratoga* and he turned his formation toward the nearer *Enterprise*. Runyon's Wildcats made repeated firing runs and Runyon claimed two victories as well as forcing two of the enemy bombers to break off their attack and turn for home.

Runyon's division was jumped by four *Zuikaku* Zeros that likely shot down Runyon's second-section leader, NAP Bill Reid, who was never seen again. The intervention by the four Zeros broke up the one-sided battle as they forced Jensen to dive away while Starkes and Kleinman defended themselves. Runyon broke off his attack on the bombers and took on a Zero, which he claimed.

Ensign Frank Green, who had become separated from his section leader, Lieutenant Dick Gray, dived into the melee and attacked a Val from dead astern that emitted smoke and then fell flaming from the formation. He attacked a second bomber but was forced to dive away when a third Val turned on him and opened fire on him with its cowl guns.

Lieutenant Jim Smith and wingmen Ensigns Horace Bass and Ike Eichenberger hit the Vals just as they reached their pushover point, in the midst of the antiaircraft fire from *Enterprise* and its defenders. Eichenberger followed one right into the antiaircraft fire and emerged unscathed, while Lieutenant Smith and Ensign Bass were apparently shot down by the "friendly" fire. Observers aboard several ships saw one Wildcat spin out of control into the ocean and a second flaming Wildcat dive straight into the water about two miles from the destroyer *Balch*. The three Vals did drop their bombs but they missed the carrier, with one hitting the water immediately astern and denting the ship's hull in the explosion, while the other two near-missed to either side. As the third dive bomber recovered from its attack and tried to fly off, Ensign Ram Dibb came upon it and shot it into the sea.

Despite more victory claims than there were Vals or Zeros, only two Vals were downed by the 15 Wildcats. However, the fighters broke up the formation at the critical moment, which forced four of the enemy bombers so far out of position that they were unable to attack the damaged and smoking *Enterprise*. Those four Vals turned away at low altitude and attempted a glide-bombing approach on *North Carolina*, but they were intercepted as they flew up the battleship's wake by Runyon's wingmen, NAP Howard Packer and Ensign "Dutch" Shoemaker. Both attacked the Vals and then escaped *North Carolina*'s defensive fire. At 1646 hours, all four bombs dropped by the Vals missed the ship, though all four bombers managed to escape the task force's fire.

The attack on Task Force 61 was over by 1648 hours when the last Val disappeared, only four minutes after Seki had pushed over to initiate his dive. The fleet ceased firing between 1649 and 1650 hours. Several men aboard *Enterprise* later reported that the abrupt silence was almost painful.

At 1749 hours, 65 minutes after the first enemy bomb had torn its way into *Enterprise*, and while its crew frantically engaged in continuing firefighting and repair efforts below decks, the carrier majestically turned into the wind at 24 knots and LSO Lieutenant Robin M. Lindsey began routine recovery of the air group.

In all, American defenders in the air and aboard the ships claimed 70 of 27 Vals present as confirmed victories, as well as 16 of the ten Zeros present. There were even claims for two non-existent Kates. The real victory total, claimed by fliers and shipboard gunners, was ten of 18 *Shōkaku* Vals, seven of nine *Zuikaku* Vals, one of four *Shōkaku* Zeros, and three of six *Zuikaku* Zeros, 21 of 37 strike bombers and escort fighters. The downed *Shōkaku* Zero pilot was eventually recovered.

In addition, one *Zuikaku* Zero and one *Shōkaku* Zero ditched after they ran out of fuel, with both pilots rescued. One *Zuikaku* Val was rescued when they ditched near a friendly cruiser, while another lost *Zuikaku* Val ditched near Malaita, where the crewmen joined a band of Japanese coastwatchers. Only eight *Shōkaku* Vals, two *Shōkaku* Zeros, and two *Zuikaku* Zeros landed back aboard their carriers safe.

The outlandish American claims were matched by those of the returning Japanese pilots, who reported bombing two carriers, leaving both burning and sinking, as well as a battleship hit and also left burning. The Zero pilots reported shooting down 12 of the five Wildcats that were actually shot down, four of which were the victims of "friendly" fire from surface warships.

12

RESOLUTION

August 24–25

At the same time the Japanese strike found *Enterprise*, VS-3 CO Lieutenant Commander Lou Kirn was leading ten SBDs of Scouting 3 and three from Bombing 5 home after their attack on *Ryūjō*. Kirn spotted 27 Val dive bombers and nine escorting Zeros 2,000 feet below his formation, headed the same way. They were Nagumo's second strike. After warning *Saratoga* of the inbound threat, Kirn and his men could only fly on, since they didn't have enough fuel to engage the enemy and still get home.

When the enemy departed after the first attack, *Enterprise* and its escorts moved to join with *Saratoga's* task force, under the protection of low clouds. With the conclusion of the battle, the defenders still in the air began landing back aboard the two carriers. Several managed to get aboard with the last of their fuel, at least three with their engines dying from fuel starvation before they were able to taxi forward on the flight deck after the arresting wires brought them to a stop. Fighting Five Exec Chick Harmer, who had been wounded attacking Seki's Vals, saw the smoke from the burning *Enterprise* as he searched for deck to land on. A minute later, he spotted *Saratoga*, ten miles distant and headed for his home carrier. Arriving overhead, Harmer saw he was the only airplane in the carrier's landing pattern. He made what he felt was a really good approach, but just as he leveled his wings in anticipation of receiving the "cut," LSO Lieutenant Walter Curtis gave him a "come on" followed an instant later by "cut." The bit of extra throttle Harmer had to give in response to the "come on," sent him into a thoroughly embarrassing barrier crash that flipped the F4F on its back since the airplane was light because it was nearly out of fuel and ammunition. Harmer was not hurt, but the Wildcat was wiped out along with his pride. Once he climbed out of the wreckage and the medics could examine him, it was found that his leg wounds were minor, but the doctor gave him a jolt of morphine and sent him to bed.

The *Enterprise* search planes had been in the air longer than any others in the American force, and were forced to orbit while the carriers brought aboard their thirsty fighters once landing operations started at 1749 hours. Bombing Six's skipper Lieutenant Ray Davis, who had found the Japanese fleet carriers and attacked *Shōkaku*, was forced to orbit during a very long delay and wound up landing aboard *Enterprise* at 1809 with a mere four gallons of fuel remaining in his reserve tank. He was the last of the *Enterprise* searchers to land back aboard. At 1805 hours, Commander Felt's *Ryūjō* strike force began landing aboard *Saratoga*. They had not lost a single airplane during the strike or in several air battles.

Suddenly, at 1810 hours, *Enterprise* veered left. With her collision alarm sounding, the carrier veered through the task force at 24 knots, out of control. When the rudder was at maximum deflection left, it suddenly swung right, and jammed hard to starboard. The "Big E" narrowly missed slicing the destroyer *Balch* in half. Its engines were thrown in reverse and it slowed to ten knots as the breakdown flag went up its truck. The rudder was jammed so far right that control was not regained even when the port screws were put to reverse with the starboard screws full ahead. Just at that moment, the first blips of the second enemy attack wave showed up on the task force radars. After *Enterprise* was first hit, the steering room had been sealed off to keep the crew of seven from being overwhelmed by smoke. Without ventilation, the powerful electric steering motors soon pushed the temperature inside to 120 degrees, then 150, and finally to 170 degrees, at which point both men and machinery failed. As the enemy continued toward the fleet, *Enterprise* circled, helpless, for the 38 minutes it took for damage control parties to fight their way into the steering compartment and start one of the two steering motors. In the Combat Information Center, radar operators breathed a sigh of relief when the enemy passed 50 miles south, then reversed course to the northwest, missing the fleet entirely. Fortunately, they had suffered from communications problems as had the Americans, and had missed getting Commander Seki's precise position report at 1642 when he first sighted Task Force 61. *Enterprise* quickly resumed landing its chicks aboard.

Lieutenant Rube Konig was perhaps the most worried naval aviator in the air at this time. His six Torpedo 3 Avengers had been launched from *Saratoga* at the last minute with the enemy strike 40 miles out, without any current navigation information, with orders to "find the enemy and attack." He had hoped to meet up with the *Enterprise* aircraft that had been launched minutes before, but hadn't managed to do so. The Avengers were 250 miles from home with the sun low on the horizon when Konig had spotted what he thought might be the wake of an enemy warship. At his signal, the formation split into two groups of three for a "hammer and anvil" attack. As they descended to attack altitude 100 feet above the waves, each formation moved out in line abreast. Straining to see the target silhouetted against the setting sun, Konig was moments from the release point when his wingman exclaimed that the target was a round reef and the "wake" was the pounding surf. Pulling out of his attack run, Konig identified the "target" as Roncador Reef, 100 miles northwest of Santa Isabel. Wherever the fleet might be, the Avengers had arrived at the point where their fuel state required they turn back.

The six bombers rejoined formation and Konig led them west, hoping to see ships in the setting sun. After flying 50 miles and seeing nothing but empty sea, he ordered everyone to jettison their torpedoes to save weight and set throttles for "maximum range." He announced that he didn't think they had enough fuel to get to Guadalcanal and wasn't sure where it was if they did. The others agreed that they should try to find the carriers, and that when the first one ran out of fuel they would all ditch to stay together. With no information on where to look for the fleet on return, Konig eyed the setting sun with alarm and stared long and hard at the gas gauge with its needle dropping toward "empty." He had no charts, no radio call sign to identify his flight, no radio frequency-change schedule, and no way of monitoring news of any changing conditions. Ensign Holley's engine was throwing oil on his windshield so the young pilot hoped they would come across something before it froze. The six flew on into the darkness as the sun disappeared over the western horizon.

Finally after what seemed an age, Aviation Radioman 2/c David Lane came on the intercom: "Mr. Konig – I think I hear an 'N.'" It was *Saratoga's* beacon! Konig turned right 45 degrees in accordance with the "N" signal; 15 minutes later, he spotted wakes below and then saw *Enterprise* steaming into the wind to bring them aboard. NAP John Baker landed first, without incident. Next in line was Ensign Holley. In the darkness, with oil all over his windshield, physically, mentally, and emotionally drained, the young pilot came in too fast and too high and didn't spot the wave-off. The big Avenger missed all the arresting wires, bounced over the barrier, and hit the island. It flopped onto the deck and literally fell apart around the crew; Holley suffered a minor forehead laceration, while his radioman and gunner both crawled out of the wreckage without a scratch. *Enterprise's* deck was closed.

Konig and the other three were ordered by signal lamp to proceed to *Saratoga*. Konig remembered flying his best landing ever. When the deck crew measured Konig's fuel tank with a dipstick, he discovered there wasn't enough gas left to go around again if he had been waved off. The last two planes ran completely out of fuel as each touched down; number three had to be pushed forward to let number four come aboard.

The last Task Force 61 aircraft to return was the Avenger flown by *Enterprise* air group commander Lieutenant Commander Max Leslie. Leslie's TBF had been the last airplane launched from the carrier before the Japanese strike arrived. The airplane was equipped with additional radios as a "command" aircraft, and carried additional fuel tanks in the bomb bay, limiting its warload to two 500-pound bombs. Leslie had attempted to catch up with Caldwell's Flight 300 unsuccessfully, though the formation had been launched only some 20 minutes earlier, and had then searched for the enemy on his own with a continued lack of success.

The last light of day let him spot what looked like the wake of a ship just as he had flown as far as he dared while leaving sufficient fuel to get back to the task force. Leslie had been cheated of bombing the Japanese at Midway when his miswired SBD had dropped its bomb when he checked the manual release after takeoff from *Yorktown* (though he had continued to lead the formation and actually dived on *Soryu* to encourage his young pilots); this might be the chance to change that. Turning to follow, he was again disappointed when the "wake" turned out to be a trick of the waning light that made waves breaking over isolated, submerged Roncador Reef again appear to be the sign of an enemy ship. Breaking off, Leslie took a bearing for Point Option, the spot in the ocean where Task Force 61 was supposed to be, and turned back.

At 1942 hours, he flew within radar and radio range of the task force and picked up a faint beacon indication. The sky above was partly cloudy, which made the ocean below pitch dark. Doggedly, he continued on, hoping that the carriers had survived the attack he had seen in the making as he flew away while Seki's Vals began their dive. Flying low in hopes of spotting a ship's shadow against the faint starlight through the clouds reflecting on the waves, he was finally rewarded with the silhouettes of two small ships beneath his wings. Finally, his earphones crackled with a familiar voice: "Max, this is Ham Dow. Keep coming. Get some altitude."

Leslie flew on as his Naval Academy classmate and close personal friend followed the air boss' progress in *Enterprise*'s Radar Plot, passing on terse commands to bring the Avenger home. At long last, the big full moon rose above the eastern horizon and shone across the ocean through the clouds. Below, Leslie saw silvery wakes and knew he was home, but still not safe. He was on edge since this flight had marked a major increase of his time in a TBF; now he had to make his first night trap, the most dangerous event in carrier flying and something he hadn't done in any airplane in a while, in an airplane with which he lacked easy familiarity. He breathed a sigh of relief when Dow informed him that *Saratoga*, the closest carrier, would flick on its deck lights at the last minute, humbled at the risk his fellow sailors were taking on his behalf. Minutes later, he picked up *Saratoga* and executed a "Roger pass" as the deck-edge lights flickered faintly, putting the big torpedo bomber on the deck in a perfect landing when the tail hook caught the "three" wire. Everyone was home who was coming home.

As night fell, Task Force 61 retreated southeast to join *Wasp*'s Task Force 18 and hopefully avoid the oncoming Japanese. The move was a wise one, since both Admirals Abe and Kondō were steaming south in an attempt to engage the US carriers at night as had been attempted at Midway. By midnight, their failure to make contact with Task Force 61 resulted in an order to turn back. *Shōkaku* and *Zuikaku*, with their air groups much reduced from battle and their escorts low on fuel, also retreated north.

Admiral Nagumo decided to hold his fleet north of Bougainville to see if there was an opportunity to go after the American carriers again, but such did not happen and the fleet returned to Truk on September 5.

Despite the fact that they had not been touched in the battle both *Shōkaku* and *Zuikaku* were not really able to engage in further combat, due to their losses. The Japanese inability to replace their losses with fliers of equal skill degraded the air groups once they arrived back at Truk and received replacement crews. Nagumo was perhaps the only Japanese naval commander at this time to realize and accept that the Imperial Navy was on an unsustainable course with regard to its ability to engage in sustained combat. The Imperial Navy had not been built for this kind of warfare, but rather to fight a quick and limited conflict. While the admiral would continue to give his utmost, the fact that he knew in his heart that there was no likelihood of a victorious outcome for his navy played a role in his enthusiasm for the coming operations and would ultimately lead to his replacement as a front-line combat leader.

On the American side, Fletcher and his staff tended to take the claims of the defenders in the day's battle at face value, despite the fact that they had actually overclaimed by nearly four times what actual enemy losses were. No one said anything, but everyone knew that if Fletcher had been more willing to gamble and less obsessive about his fleet's fuel state, the presence of the *Wasp* air group could have been decisive, since there would have been sufficient aircraft available to make a separate strike against Nagumo's carriers when they were discovered, rather then being limited only to what *Saratoga* had launched. Once again, despite his best efforts not to repeat his past mistake at Coral Sea, Fletcher had launched his main strike at a secondary target and allowed the enemy to escape. This time, though he had not lost a carrier as he had back in May, the damage *Enterprise* had suffered would obviously remove it from the South Pacific at a crucial moment while it underwent repairs. While he believed he had inflicted serious damage on the enemy air units, the fact that neither major opponent had actually been damaged meant that the enemy was free to rebuild his force and come back for another attempt. The admiral had no way of knowing just how bad the situation for US carriers was about to get.

The B-17s of the 11th Group also played a role in the battle. At 1215 hours on August 24, Colonel Saunders was informed of a contact report of an enemy carrier 720 miles from Espiritu. Knowing that sending the B-17s out would involve hazardous night landings, Admiral McCain left the attack decision to Colonel Saunders, who accepted the risk and sent out two separate flights – three B-17s led by Major Ernest R. Manniere and four by Major Sewart. Manniere's three found what they reported as a carrier dead in the water and a cruiser or large destroyer at 1745 hours and commenced an attack. The bombs overshot on the first run and the three bombers banked around for another try, reporting four direct hits. On the bombers' return to Espiritu Santo after dark, the night landing took its toll when a rainstorm drenched the field while they were approaching, which put out the lanterns marking the perimeter of the strip; the darkness was complete. Lieutenant Robert E. Guenther's B-17, with its No. 4 engine failing, fell into a steep bank and crashed into the hillside on final approach. Guenther and four other crew were lost.

Major Sewart's four B-17s surprised a second group of Imperial Navy ships 60 miles east of Manniere's force, reporting a possible small carrier escorted by one battleship, four light cruisers, and four destroyers. The Flying Fortresses steadied on their run and claimed two or more hits on the carrier; final results were observed by a ball turret gunner who stated that the target could not have been a carrier since the 500-pounders had "knocked her turrets off." The four B-17s were then intercepted by Zeros, with the crews claiming five shot down and seven probables. Two B-17s were damaged and the formation was now desperately low on fuel, but Major Sewart led his flight back to Efate intact.

Ensign Register had finally found the combat he longed for on August 24. That night in his cramped stateroom aboard *Enterprise*, he confided to his diary:

August 24, 1942 – The end of my big day. Flew all day. At 1630 we intercepted 55 enemy airplanes; 40 bombers, 15 fighters. I didn't get a chance to hit the bombers. The Jap VF attacked us and I shot down the first Zero off my wingman. Got separated and had gun trouble. Fought several more but due to guns did not get them. Shot at a Zero which just about got me. Just shot him down when another Zero attacked me. Had no ammunition, but pointed my nose toward one and got by him and someone shot the other one off as he was shooting at me. VF-6 got 29 airplanes and lost two pilots, a wonderful record. The *Enterprise* was hit by three bombs. 100 killed, 150 wounded.

The Cactus Air Force was the big winner of the Battle of the Eastern Solomons, because of the unexpected reinforcement produced by the arrival of *Enterprise*'s "Flight 300," the dive and torpedo bombers that *Enterprise* had launched before the Japanese attack. Lieutenant Turner Caldwell later remembered:

> At around 1740 hours, we had been airborne for closing on two hours and were over 200 miles from the ship. I was about to turn back when I got a message from the ship ordering me to take our formation to Guadalcanal. I turned west. As twilight deepened, we passed between Santa Isabel and Malaita islands and Savo loomed beyond. My previous flights over the area now stood me in good stead. A lovely great moon came up. It was full darkness by the time we arrived over Henderson Field, but I recognized the curve of the beach. The field had no lights, but the Marines laid out flashlights along the edge of the runway. Their radio was useless, though we could hear a word or two occasionally. We broke out and landed, each pilot for himself. Without landing instructions, some made passes from seaward. The next morning they realized how lucky they had been – the inland end of the runway was marked by a stand of 200 foot trees!

Flight 300 became a welcome reinforcement when the unit learned the next day that Task Force 61 had withdrawn south to refuel and tend to *Enterprise*'s damage, and was thus beyond their range to fly home:

> We were adopted by Mangrum's squadron. The Marine pilots gave us spare shoes and khakis, and captured Japanese underwear. A couple days later, an Avenger from *Enterprise* landed, came to a stop, opened his bomb bay and dumped our effects, then taxied off with his propeller blast scattering everything before he took off and disappeared back to the ship.

The Navy fliers would make their own mark on history in the desperate weeks to come.

On the evening of August 24, Admiral Tanaka reversed course and the troop convoy headed back toward Guadalcanal, in the belief that the American carriers were out of action and that Henderson Field had been badly damaged. Since his cruiser support had departed, he sent the five covering destroyers ahead to bombard Henderson and keep the American dive bombers on the ground. While the warships prepared to open fire at 0010 hours on August 25, newly promoted Lieutenant Colonel Dick Mangrum led Lieutenants Larry Baldinus and Hank Hise into the night sky in an effort to get at them. Mangrum later explained: "The airfield was only about 3,000 feet, which was short even for my airplanes. We were able to get off at night by positioning a jeep at the far end with its lights on, to give us something to aim at to stay on the strip, and to give us an idea when we would have to lift off."

Once airborne, "We climbed out and there was a sliver of moon left and standing around the end of Florida Island we could make out Japanese ships and we attacked them." When they found the ships and attacked, all three missed, with one dud bomb failing to explode. Mangrum led the others in strafing the destroyers, then headed back home, where the lighted jeep at the far end and a man pointing a flashlight at the near end of the strip allowed them to land successfully. A second three-plane strike, mounted at 0400 hours by Flight 300 SBDs, found the enemy destroyers retiring past Savo. The only hit was scored by Ensign Wilson Brown, who became lost in the darkness and was never heard from again.

At dawn on August 25, the convoy was joined by the five destroyers that had shelled the airfield the night before. At 0800 hours, the fleet was 150 miles from Guadalcanal, plodding along at eight and a half knots, the best speed of the slowest transport. Five minutes later, 18 Marine and Navy dive bombers from Henderson Field led by Mangrum attacked out of the sun. The Dauntlesses had originally been launched in an effort to find and attack the Japanese carriers, but poor weather forced them back. Mangrum recalled, "We pushed through a squall and came out in clear air and there they were." Near misses damaged the light cruiser *Jintsu*, wounding 24 crewmen and knocking Admiral Tanaka unconscious. The SBDs also scored solid hits on the transport *Kinryu Maru*. Just as the destroyer *Mutsuki* maneuvered to come alongside *Kinryu Maru* to rescue its crew and troops, four 11th Bomb Squadron B-17s that had taken off from Espiritu Santo at 0615 hours on a search mission, and had been diverted to support the attack on the convoy after it was discovered, made one of the most successful high-altitude bombing attacks on a moving ship in the entire war, dropping five bombs on or around *Mutsuki* and sinking it immediately, with the ship disappearing into Ironbottom Sound at 1015 hours. A badly shaken but uninjured Admiral Tanaka transferred from *Jintsu* to the destroyer *Kagerō* and ordered *Jintsu* back to Truk. He then gave orders for the convoy to alter course to the Shortland Islands, where they would be out of range of the Americans.

The sooner *Enterprise* could depart for repair at Pearl Harbor, the better. Before it headed north on August 25, *Enterprise* transferred 17 Wildcats and six Avengers to *Saratoga*. The "Big E" would be absent from the South Pacific for seven critical weeks. *Saratoga* rendezvoused with *Wasp* and Task Force 18 on the evening of August 26 and on August 29, *Hornet* and Task Force 17 arrived to replace *Enterprise*, having fortuitously departed Pearl Harbor on August 22 as reinforcement for Fletcher's force.

Ensign Register wrote more of his experience of the battle that evening:

> **August 25, 1942** – Landed on *Saratoga* last night as did most of our pilots. Had a burned out engine, no guns, no gunsight and three gallons of gas. The *Enterprise* has to go back so we were transferred over here and will stay. We think we sank a Jap CV, CA, and an AK. The *Hornet* will join us tomorrow. It is a very odd experience to go through a fight like this. There is no doubt of being scared. My mouth was so dry I couldn't swallow, but as soon as I started firing, I started cussing until he went down in flames. Guess I sort of went out of my head, as I was in a group of Zeros and was shooting at them as fast as I could. Give me a little luck and good guns, and I'll shoot down a lot more. I have one assist also.

Over the next seven weeks, the fighting settled into stalemate as both sides licked their wounds and attempted to reinforce the troops they had ashore while Admiral Yamamoto planned his next attempt to retake the island.

13

REINFORCEMENT

August 26 – September 7

It didn't take long for operations to turn Henderson Field into a mess. It had been jury-rigged and improvised from the start. Nevertheless, conditions were improving by fits and starts, and not a few backward steps. In the beginning, when a bomb blast blew out many cubic yards of runway, engineers, ground crew, and CUBs ran out to the crater and filled it in with carefully premeasured earth fill, which had been loaded in trucks parked on the verges of the open area. When the fill had been dumped, all hands tediously hand-tamped it to create a hard, even surface for the aircraft, which might be circling overhead, using precious fuel. The situation vastly improved with the arrival of several pneumatic tampers. Soon, it took only 30 minutes to fill a crater left by a 500-kilogram bomb.

Even without the Japanese, the ground crews had a rough time keeping the aircraft operating. The earliest method for fueling aircraft involved strapping a 55-gallon fuel drum to the rafters of an uncompleted Japanese hangar, then pumping by hand through a chamois. When fuel trucks were finally landed, the gas still had to be hand-pumped from their storage tanks into aircraft tanks. Most of the aircraft were fairly new upon arrival at Henderson Field, but they could not be adequately maintained. The novel methods employed by ground crews at Henderson Field kept at least a minimal number of aircraft flyable.

Weather was a constant irritant. It rained daily, often several times a day. Each storm turned the runway into a glutinous quagmire. Aircraft designed to land on concrete runways and wooden carrier decks placed enormous stress on their wheels, which had a disturbing propensity for sticking where they touched earth while inertia kept the rest of the airplane moving. Depending upon speed, the weight of the airplane, the viscosity of the mud, and the skill of the pilot, any given airplane might flip over, swerve, ground loop, drop one or both main landing-gear assemblies, lose a wheel, come to a safe stop, or become airborne. Marion Carl observed many years later when asked about operations on Guadalcanal that, "That was the most adventuresome flying I ever did. Every takeoff, every landing, was an adventure."

As Japanese air raids became stronger and more frequent, early warning and fighter direction became problems. A modern SCR-270 air-search radar set and a crew of technicians were included in the August 7 landings, but only the technicians were landed, while the radar set never made it off the ship that carried it. In addition, there was no trained FDO available. Going through the captured Japanese gear revealed a crude radar among the collection, but the technicians were unable to figure out how to get it running. The 3rd Defense Battalion's 90mm antiaircraft batteries included one outfitted with an outmoded, unreliable radar, originally designed to guide searchlights. The other antiaircraft batteries lacked even that crude radar. The impressive record of the battalion in knocking down roughly half the enemy aircraft lost over Guadalcanal can be attributed only to its very high standard of training.

Thus, Cactus Air Operations was forced to rely exclusively upon timely coastwatcher reports of enemy air activity. While this generally worked, there were times when weather was such that the Japanese flew above the clouds unseen, or when weather conditions created radio problems. Two hours' warning from the coastwatchers was barely enough to get the airplanes organized and off the ground and for the slow-climbing F4Fs to be bullied up to 25,000–27,000 feet in order to successfully attack the enemy formations. The Zero was a fast climber and highly maneuverable at lower speeds; it outclassed the F4F in all but two vital categories: diving speed and ability to take punishment. These differing characteristics dictated the tactics each side employed. It was essential for the Marines to attack Zeros or Zero-escorted bombers from above and dive through the Japanese formation before the Zeros could follow. The Zero was the better airplane, and Zero pilots were the more experienced airmen, so the Grumman's higher diving speed was often all that kept VMF-223's CO John Smith's youngsters from a dunking or death.

Japanese raids from Rabaul appeared overhead almost daily. The Betty lacked armor and self-sealing tanks, and nearly always lived up to its reputation with Japanese aviators as "a flying cigar." If a pilot could put a two-second burst into either engine or into the wing gas tanks, the result nearly always was that the bomber would quickly catch fire. Another fatal target was the pilot's cockpit, just ahead of the wing. After attacking, the Wildcats would continue their dives to throw off any of the escort, then zoom climb back to altitude if they could, or return to Henderson if they were damaged or unable to achieve an altitude advantage.

Tactically, the Marines soon learned that the Zero's fabled maneuverability rapidly fell off at speeds over 250 miles per hour. The fighter's large ailerons had no power boost; at higher speed, the ailerons progressively froze up to the point that above around 320 miles per hour they were so close to unmovable that the airplane lost all maneuverability. Marion Carl remembered, "So long as we didn't stick around to fight the Zeros on their terms, and dived fast, they couldn't keep up with us and their ailerons got heavy enough that even a Wildcat could turn with them if you had to." This was later demonstrated in air combat tests with an intact Zero found in the Aleutians, which were performed in the United States at the same time the Cactus pilots were making their own less-formal but more useful tests. Additionally, the radio in the A6M2 operated at a frequency close to that of the operation of the engine, which led to so much static that the radios were useless; many Japanese pilots simply removed them as useless and to save weight. The result was that the enemy could not warn each other of attacking enemy aircraft or organize themselves to face new threats, as the Marines could with their superior communications. Regarding the merits of the Wildcat, Marion Carl was once asked after the war if he was glad he hadn't had to fight at Guadalcanal with the Brewster F2A-3. He replied that he believed the outcome would have been the same:

> The F4F-4 Wildcat was much heavier than the F4F-3 with the additional guns and ammo, and had no increase in power. It was only marginally less bad in performance than the F2A-3, which was also

underpowered due to additional weight without a power increase. Using the same tactics, we could have been as successful with the F2A as we were with the F4F. There might have been a few more pileups on the runway, since the F2A's gear wasn't as strong.

The other advantage the Marines had was that they operated over or close to home. While maintenance facilities were crude, shot-up aircraft could be nursed home and made airworthy again, or at least parts could be scavenged to keep others flying. Japanese cripples, and their valuable crews, were often lost on the very long ride home. The crews of shot-down or shot-up aircraft had no chance of survival to get back to their units. This put the enemy into an ultimately unsustainable situation regarding their losses. Though nearly 100 American aircraft were lost during the campaign, a high percentage of Allied airmen who had to parachute stood a good chance of rescue by other Americans or Solomon Islanders. Smith, Carl, and many of the other original pilots as well as those who came after would have the opportunity to walk or swim home. Such possibility of survival was an important morale factor in an effort that seemed to hold no end of frustrations for the Americans.

The inadequacies of the ground-support effort were graphically illustrated on August 25 when the fighters could not be rearmed quickly enough to intercept 21 Bettys that arrived overhead at 1155 hours. Forty bombs fell in a tight pattern around the Pagoda, the captured building that served as control tower and air operations center. All but three aircraft on the field managed to get airborne, and damage to the runway was minimal, but the inability to counter the attack was unsettling and infuriating.

The raid signified that the enemy was being reinforced. In five days of combat, Smith's 19 Wildcats had been whittled down to 11 – three shot down, one crash-landed, one destroyed in a test flight, and three grounded for lack of spare parts. Only nine of Mangrum's 12 SBDs were operational, with one lost in a water landing and two awaiting spare parts. The 11 *Enterprise* SBDs of Flight 300 were available, but no one knew for how long. The P-400s looked as if they might be useless in air defense operations, even though seven more had flown up on the afternoon of August 25. Stocks of ammunition, aviation gasoline, oxygen bottles, lubricants, bombs, and spare parts were rapidly dwindling. In a message to Admiral Ghormley sent that afternoon,

General Vandegrift warned that he would be out of aircraft in a short time unless Guadalcanal received replacement pilots and airplanes: "Present rate attrition aircraft Cactus makes imperative present numbers be augmented earliest date. Recommend rear echelon MAG-23 arriving Samoa late August be sent Cactus with spare aircraft earliest practicable date. Urgently need oxygen replacement bottles filled."

At 1203 hours on August 26, while SBDs and P-400s scrambled eastward out of range, Smith managed to get 12 F4Fs into position over Henderson Field to intercept 16 enemy bombers that had been reported approaching Cactus from over New Georgia at 1136 hours. However, before the Wildcats were able to engage, the Bettys plastered Henderson, dropping an estimated 50 high-explosive, fragmentation, and incendiary bombs that damaged equipment and set fire to 2,000 gallons of precious aviation gasoline. Smith and XO Major Rivers Morrell teamed with two of the VMF-212 pilots to down three confirmed Bettys, while Marion Carl scored two Zeros. In all, eight Bettys and five Zeros were confirmed destroyed against the loss of Midway survivor First Lieutenant Roy Corry, who was shot down and killed.

Lieutenant Eugene Trowbridge wrote of the mission:

Usual raid. I got my fourth Zero fighter and was also shot down. While I was firing, I saw tracers start by my port side just as my victim burst into flames. I felt a terrific jolt and the controls were wrenched from my hands. I started to spin but recovered shortly after and found that the engine was out of commission and the covering for my port flipper was almost completely gone. The windshield was almost completely covered with oil, obscuring my vision. As I was directly over the field, I made a crash-landing and came out okay. When the landing gear collapsed, I found out that they had also shot that out too. Big day.

A reported Japanese raid on August 27 failed to materialize, while on August 28 the incoming raid was forced to return to Rabaul due to bad weather over the northern Solomons. At 1700 hours, VMSB-232's Lieutenants Danny Iverson and Hank Hise and Flight 300's Ensign Jesse Barker were over the Russell Islands, when Hise spotted four destroyers silhouetted against the setting sun only 70 miles from Cape Esperance. Flight leader Iverson did not react to Hise's message and he reasoned that Iverson had failed to see the enemy. Iverson had seen them but he had assumed they were Americans. He dropped down so his gunner could flash a recognition signal; the Japanese answered with flak. After climbing above a thin cloud layer, Iverson pitched through a hole in the clouds. Startled, Hise followed. The enemy destroyers were maneuvering to avoid attack. Hise selected one and dropped his bomb at 2,500 feet, certain he had missed by a half-mile. Unable to find Iverson, he headed home while Ensign Barker scored a hit on the rear destroyer.

At Henderson, Hise taxied straight to the Pagoda to report his find. Soon, Iverson arrived home to report how he had been unable to get lined up during either of two dives, while Barker also arrived safely. Mangrum led a mixed formation of six Marine and five Navy SBDs that took off at 1730 hours to find the enemy. Turner Caldwell bored through the failing light to score a direct hit on one destroyer while Ensign Chris Fink planted a 1,000-pound bomb directly amidships on the destroyer *Asagiri*, which exploded and sank within 60 seconds. A third destroyer was damaged by near misses, and Marines Second Lieutenant Oliver Mitchell and Private First Class Frank Schackman were lost while strafing the fourth destroyer, which escaped unscathed in the bad weather and low-light conditions.

At 0940 hours on August 29, coastwatcher Paul Mason on Bougainville warned Henderson that 18 B5N2 bombers and their Zero escort were passing over the southeastern end of Bougainville. The Japanese aircraft belonged to the *Shōkaku* and *Zuikaku* carrier air groups. Later that morning, the transport *William Ward Burroughs* finally arrived and anchored off Kukum at around 1100 hours. The VMF-223 and VMSB-232 ground crews were the most welcome reinforcement to date. However, before any of the precious aviation-oriented cargo could be brought ashore, *Burroughs* upped anchor when coastwatcher Donald Kennedy on New Georgia reported spotting the incoming Japanese strike, with a promise to return the next day. Unfortunately, the ship ran around on a coral reef in the entrance to the Tulagi anchorage, making it a sitting duck with its valuable cargo of aircraft supplies.

On receiving Kennedy's warning, ten F4Fs and all 12 P-400s were scrambled; by 1115 hours all flyable aircraft had taken off to avoid the incoming attack. The P-400s were in three flights of four; they climbed to 14,000 feet where, according to the squadron historian, "they staggered around, looking closely at all spots within their vision to make sure they were just spots and not enemy formations." The Kates reached the airfield about noon, before they could be intercepted. The Airacobras never got close, but Wildcats accounted for four Kates and four escorting Zeros. VMF-223 commander John Smith downed two B5Ns to become the first Cactus ace, followed minutes later by Second Lieutenant Kenneth Frazier who downed a Kate and a Zero to become "second ace." The discouraged P-400s returned to find the runway swarming with men while the strip seemed to have sprouted bushes; the ground crews were using them to mark bomb craters. Ammunition exploded while grass, hangars, and aircraft burned. One F4F landed in such bad shape that it was set aside to be cannibalized for spare parts.

The Japanese continued to bring troops to Guadalcanal. The 35th Independent Infantry Brigade, then at Palau, was notified on August 13 that it would move to Guadalcanal. Initially, this was scheduled to coincide with the Imperial Navy's foray to the Solomons that resulted in the Battle of Eastern Solomons, but due to difficulty in transporting troops, the half of the brigade carried to the island by Admiral Tanaka's "Tokyo Express" was forced to wait while the other half, coming in troop-carrying barges that could only move at night, made its way to Guadalcanal. Overall command on Guadalcanal was now in the hands of Major General Kiyotake Kawaguchi. On the afternoon of August 29, five of a force of seven troop-laden Japanese destroyers, carrying the 750 troops of the advance echelon of Kawaguchi Battalion, were spotted heading for Taivu Point.

That night, Mangrum led a flight of SBDs launched at 0030 hours on August 30 in hopes of catching the enemy unloading, but the ships were not found. The troops were landed at Taivu Point while the Dauntlesses searched fruitlessly. After depositing the soldiers safely on the beach, the flotilla commander was so unnerved by the sound of aircraft engines in the dark that he fled without bombarding the Lunga Perimeter or Henderson Field, or attacking the stranded *Burroughs.* On arrival back at Rabaul, he was summarily relieved of command by Admiral Tanaka for disobeying new standing orders to attack American surface vessels whenever found. This was the first official mission of what would come to be known to the Marines as the "Cactus Express" before it was named "the Tokyo Express" by the war correspondents.

The P-400s flew a dawn mission to provide a CAP over four destroyers in Tulagi harbor, with additional relieving flights through the morning. At 0930 hours, word came from Paul Mason on Bougainville that a large formation of Japanese single-engine aircraft was heading to Guadalcanal. These were 18 Zeros sent to the tiny Buka reserve strip the day before from *Shōkaku* and *Zuikaku*. Their mission was to mount a fighter sweep to destroy the American fighters that came up to intercept. Because they flew too high for positive identification from the ground, observers assumed they were Zero-escorted D3A dive bombers or B5N level bombers and their target was either the four destroyers at Tulagi or the stranded *Burroughs*. Seven Wildcats and 11 P-400s were in commission. At 1100 hours, the Zeros were above the clouds over eastern New Georgia; their progress was reported by coastwatcher Donald Kennedy, who only heard them.

On receipt of Kennedy's warning, four Airacobras took off, assigned to patrol over Tulagi and hit the dive bombers as they pulled out from their attacks. John Smith led the seven serviceable F4Fs and the other seven P-400s aloft at 1105 hours. The sky over Henderson Field became overcast as SBDs took off to get out of the way of bombs and Zeros. The Wildcats climbed to 15,000 feet and orbited over Sealark Sound, expecting to intercept Kates or Vals, while the seven P-400s orbited below the F4Fs at 14,000 feet and the first four airplanes took position at 14,000 feet over Tulagi and *Burroughs*.

At 1145 hours, the seven-plane P-400 flight was jumped from out of the low clouds by Zeros roaring in from below and behind. Woozy from lack of oxygen, the Airacobra pilots were slow to react, but nevertheless turned gamely toward the threat. They started to turn into a defensive Lufbery Circle but in moments there were more Zeros than Airacobras in the circle. The P-400s were simply outclassed and their pilots were forced to dive into the clouds, where they had to rely upon their inadequate instruments to get them out in one piece.

Suddenly, the weather over the channel and island turned from marginal to poor. The cloud cover dropped to a mere 1,000 feet and visibility dropped to a quarter-mile. When the four P-400s over Tulagi straggled out of the rain, they were bounced by six Zeros that tore them apart. All four P-400s and two pilots – First Lieutenant Robert Chilson and First Lieutenant Keith Wythes – were lost, while six of the other seven Airacobras returned to Henderson riddled beyond repair.

Nonetheless, the Army pilots claimed six kills and were credited with four; these were not recognized in enemy records.

The Marines fared better. At first they didn't realize the P-400s had been hit, the result of incompatible radio equipment. Smith went after the remaining 12 Zeros of the flight, which he spotted as they dived on the grounded *Burroughs*. Ever mindful that his pilots had a tendency to switch targets too quickly in hopes of getting a piece of everything in the sky, Smith ordered them to choose one target and stay with it. Then he led them for a bounce out of the sun. Six of the enemy were shot down on the first pass, an incredibly satisfying result. Smith pulled up, then quickly turned back when he saw that his green wingman had a Zero on his tail. Smith destroyed the enemy fighter while his wingman ran for the protection of clouds over the channel. As he was about to head for the clouds himself, Smith was obliged to make a head-on pass at a Zero boring in from below, and it exploded under his fire. Seven Marines had downed eight of Japan's best carrier pilots in three minutes, and two badly damaged Zeros were lost on the return leg to Buka. Among the victorious Marines was Second Lieutenant Zenneth Pond, who achieved acedom when he added a fifth Zero to his previous score. Unfortunately, though VMF-223 had no pilot losses, three more F4Fs were bound for the boneyard from damage they received in the fight.

That evening, the five remaining operational Wildcats at Henderson were caught refueling when 18 Bettys appeared at 1800 hours and sank the destroyer-transport *Colhoun* as it was unloading supplies. *Burroughs*, still high and dry off Tulagi, was untouched, but a good deal of its valuable cargo was jettisoned during attempts to refloat it while the Lunga Boat Pool rushed to unload it. *Burroughs* was refloated on September 2, but it ran aground again that same day. It was refloated again on September 3 and eventually unloaded most of its cargo at Kukum, including such "luxury" items as prefabricated heads (toilets), pipes, frozen meat, and liquor. It finally got under way on September 5, bound for Espiritu Santo with 241 survivors from *Colhoun* and two other destroyer-transports that had been sunk by Japanese gunfire from the "Tokyo Express" off Tulagi just after midnight that day.

The battle proved that the P-400s on Guadalcanal could not be used as interceptors. The 67th Fighter Squadron had early been aware of the limitations of its planes and the report of the action of the 30th convinced General Harmon, who immediately asked Washington for

P-38s and P-47s, or the P-40F with the Rolls-Royce Merlin engine. In the meantime, since the P-39 type was the USAAF's mainstay in the theater, ways were sought to improve its performance. Since .50-caliber bullets were deadly against Zeros, consideration was given to replacing the heavier cannon in the airplane's nose with a .50-caliber machine gun while removing the four .30-caliber wing guns to lighten the fighters. In Washington, Air Force Commander General Hap Arnold was concerned about the Airacobra's performance, but the best that could be done immediately was to hasten the delivery of P-39Ks to the South Pacific to replace the P-400s. By the end of September, the newly delivered P-39Ks had their wing guns removed, reducing weight by 650 pounds and giving the airplane a service ceiling of 27,000 feet. The 37mm cannon that the standard P-39 was armed with was heavier than the 20mm cannon carried by the P-400s, but was kept for its destructive power in the ground attack role for which the P-39 had in the meantime proven itself well suited.

The most important occurrence of that busy August 30 was the departure of 19 new F4Fs and 18 new SBDs from Fila Harbor, Efate, where Marine Air Group 23's VMF-224 and VMSB-231 had arrived on August 28 aboard the aircraft transports *Kitty Hawk* and *Hammondsport*.

VMF-224 commander Bob Galer later recalled that the *Hammondsport* had originally been a train ferry that operated between Florida and Cuba. "We taxied our airplanes onto this ferryboat. The top speed on our voyage south was about eight knots."

Accompanying the two squadrons was Marine Air Group 23's commanding officer, Colonel William Wallace, who later recalled:

In forming at Ewa, I went up on gunnery exercises with [the young pilots], and we had no high-altitude oxygen equipment or anything else in the planes, and they had no gunnery practice to speak of, practically none. When we went down to the South Pacific Area, I put all that in a letter to Admiral Turner. I went to see him. I said, "Admiral, we aren't ready to go into combat. These boys haven't even fired the guns." He said, "Bill, you're going down to Efate and Espiritu, and you'll have all the time in the world to train." We went down to Efate on a ship, and I was transferred to the *Long Island* and catapulted at the dock. We stayed on Espiritu overnight and, next morning, flew to Guadalcanal.

Shepherded by a pair of B-17 pathfinders, Wallace led the second half of his four-squadron group to Henderson Field for a mid-afternoon arrival. When he climbed down from the cockpit of his F4F, he was uncharacteristically embraced by General Vandegrift, whom he had known for 20 years. "Bill," an elated Vandegrift exclaimed, "I was never so glad to see anybody in my life."

Fighting 224's 2nd Lieutenant George Hallowell, one of those young lieutenants on Colonel Wallace's mind, remembered:

> After being launched, we flew to the nearby airfield (code named Roses), which was commanded by Lieutenant Colonel Harold "Joe" Bauer, the commanding officer of VMF-212. At Roses, we mounted wing tanks on our aircraft and tested them. The next day, August 29, we flew to Espiritu Santo and landed at the airfield code named Buttons. This was the home of VMO-251, which was commanded by Lieutenant Colonel John Hart. VMF-224 and VMSB-231 remained overnight at Buttons and took off at 0700, August 30, for the flight to join up with VMF-223 and VMSB-232 on Guadalcanal. I had a total of 47 hours in the F4F on the day I landed on Guadalcanal. This included carrier qualification aboard the USS *Hornet* on August 14, 1942, and the flight to Guadalcanal from Efate.

During the flight to Guadalcanal, two young VMF-224 pilots passed out from unfamiliarity with using oxygen, and were lost. The safe arrival of VMF-224 and VMSB-231 brought the totals up to 86 Marine pilots to fly 64 operational F4Fs and SBDs.

Following the initial arrival of the Marine flyers at Henderson, the Japanese had reinforced their position in the southern Solomons by basing a squadron of A6M2-N "Rufe" floatplane fighters and F1M2 "Pete" floatplane scouts at Rekata Bay in the Shortlands. The base was out of range of the Americans, but the Japanese aircraft could operate over Guadalcanal.

On August 31, the naming of the area south of the Solomons in the Coral Sea as "Torpedo Junction" was proved right when the submarine *I-26* torpedoed *Saratoga*, hitting the ship's starboard side just aft of the island. Admiral Fletcher and 12 crewmen were injured and a fireroom was flooded. *Saratoga* took on a four-degree list with the turbo-electric propulsion system damaged by multiple electrical short circuits caused by flooding, leaving the carrier dead in the water for an hour while the heavy cruiser *Minneapolis* (CA-36) prepared to take the ship in tow. Damage control parties were able to correct the list and the electrical system was restored by noon, which allowed *Saratoga* to steam under the ship's own power by late afternoon. *Saratoga* arrived at Nouméa harbor on the evening of September 1; the next morning, after the damage was examined, the ship was ordered stateside for repairs and three of the four veteran air squadrons were flown off.

Ensign Register was seeing more action than he had expected, as he described in his diary:

August 31, 1942 – Had General Quarters at 0400 then we went to bed until 0530 when we had it again. Subs have been after us and sure enough, they got us today at 0730. I was in the ready room when a terrific explosion just about knocked me out of my seat. We were hit on the starboard side in the middle. At least two more missed us. We started to list quite badly, and lost our way. At 1400 got some way on, corrected list, and launched planes for Espiritu Santo. The ship is headed back. Don't know where or what will happen to VF-6. Wouldn't doubt if we were hit again tonight.

On September 1, AirSoPac commander Admiral McCain fired off a confidential report to Admiral Nimitz, requesting significant reinforcement on Guadalcanal. He concluded presciently: "Cactus can be a sinkhole for enemy air power and can be consolidated, expanded, and exploited to [the] enemy's moral hurt. The reverse is true if we lose Cactus. If the reinforcement requested is not made available, Cactus cannot be supplied and hence cannot be held."

Shortly after midnight on September 1, eight destroyer-transports led by Admiral Tanaka carried General Kawaguchi and his 35th Brigade main body from the Shortlands to Guadalcanal's Taivu Point, where they landed without incident and were met by the surviving haggard Ichiki Battalion base troops. They moved down the beach to the deserted native village at Tasimboko.

On September 1, the 11th Air Fleet was reinforced by 24 Bettys and 20 Zeros from the 26th Air Flotilla. The Japanese bases at Rabaul and Kavieng were now coming under increasing pressure from the

B-17s of the New Guinea-based 19th Bomb Group, which damaged a number of the aircraft and drew precious fighters off escort duty in order to protect the bases. However, these units were not immediately employed against Cactus, since there was an eight-day respite from Japanese attacks between September 1 and 8 while the enemy units at Rabaul provided air cover for the Japanese Army in the Kokoda Track campaign in New Guinea.

The bombing break allowed the engineers to finish a second airfield, "Fighter One," half a mile from the main strip at Henderson Field on the Lunga Plain. They were aided by the arrival on September 1 of the Navy's 6th Naval Construction Battalion, soon to become famous as "Seabees," which landed with its equipment at Kukum and went to work on the new airfield, a task that would be completed in seven exhausting days. The fighter pilots would soon call the hastily scraped-out dirt field "the Cow Pasture" when the incessant rainstorms turned it into a muddy bog.

The early battles had recorded approximately equal results: between August 26 and September 2, the Americans suffered 15 losses while claiming 19 enemy aircraft.

On September 2, VF-6 transferred from Espiritu Santo to Efate, as Ensign Register described:

> **September 2, 1942** – 28 VF flew into Efate at 0930 today. The field is all dirt, but not too bad considering everything. Have seen quite a few old friends here. The Marines and Army are located here. Quite a few have Malaria. We moved over to a little island in the Bay of Efate called Iririki. The tents are on the sides of the hill and it is pretty rugged living. The old Boy Scout days only much tougher.

With *Saratoga* now out of the fight, in response to McCain's candid message, Nimitz signaled Admiral Ernest King, in Washington, requesting that *Saratoga's* valuable aircraft be transferred directly to McCain's command for possible deployment on Guadalcanal. King agreed and McCain received permission from Nimitz on September 3 to send the squadrons to Guadalcanal.

An hour after sunset on September 3, a Marine twin-engine R4D – the Navy designation of the C-47 – landed at Henderson following a nine-day flight from California by way of Hawaii and New Caledonia.

Flying it was Lieutenant Colonel Perry Smith, commander of Marine Air Group 25's only active unit, Marine Transport Squadron 253 (VMR-253), the first Marine Corps air-service unit deployed to the South Pacific. Aboard was Brigadier General Roy S. Geiger, commander of the 1st Marine Air Wing, who arrived with his staff to assume command of air operations at Cactus.

Perry's co-pilot, 2nd Lieutenant Arthur Adams, recalled the flight:

That was quite a historic flight in my book. We took off from New Caledonia and went up to Espiritu Santo, [where Colonel Perry Smith] spent a considerable amount of time. I think we were there about a day, speaking with people at the [new 1st Marine Aircraft Wing] headquarters... and then we finally took off.

We timed our arrival at about dusk on Guadalcanal. General Roy Geiger was a passenger on that flight. They didn't worry much about safety belts in those days, and I noted that he spent most of his time sitting on a keg of nails in the cargo compartment near the cargo door, which I presume he did because that was probably pretty comfortable and also it was the nearest exit in the event of some problems.

The flight to Guadalcanal was the first one made by an R4D, and there were very limited navigational aids, of course. As we got closer to Henderson Field, the navigator kept a pretty close watch through the navigation bubble in the top of the aircraft, looking for friendly or unfriendly aircraft. It got dark a little earlier than we thought. Communications with Henderson Field were pretty sketchy, and we weren't exactly sure where we were. So we flew down the northeast coast of the island after having made landfall, thinking that we had missed Henderson Field. This was with landing lights on, and we were calling for assistance from anyone who saw the landing lights. We got down to the end of the island, turned around, and came back doing the same thing. We finally spotted the flare pots that had been put up for us at Henderson Field as we approached.

It wasn't much of a strip there, and Colonel Smith misunderstood the instructions and lined up to land on the wrong side of the flare pots. Fortunately he saw the error in time to take a wave-off and go around. We finally did land in darkness, and immediately the flare pots were put out and Condition Red [highest readiness] was declared because "Washing Machine Charlie" was overhead. So that was our introduction to Henderson Field.

Stocky, silver-thatched 57-year-old Brigadier General Roy S. Geiger was Naval Aviator No. 49 and Marine Aviator No. 5. He had won the Navy Cross as a member of the Marine Corps' Northern Bombing Force in Flanders during World War I, the unit that made the major American contribution to "strategic bombing" in the war's final offensive. Between the wars he was a leader in the development of Marine aviation, commanding the squadron that was the first to develop dive bombing as an operational tactic in Nicaragua. He was now commander of 1st Marine Aircraft Wing and commander of Aircraft Guadalcanal (ComAirGuadalcanal). That name was quickly overshadowed when the radio code name for Guadalcanal – "cactus" – was adopted as "Cactus Air Force," which became the name for all US air forces on the island during the desperate weeks to come.

Geiger and Vandegrift went back to both having graduated in the same class at Marine Basic School and having been commissioned Marine officers together 33 years earlier. Geiger's arrival had an immediate and dramatic positive effect upon the course of the Solomons air war, since he had the experience, know-how, intelligence, rank, commitment, and perseverance to make things work. As ComAirGuadalcanal, Geiger's plan was to turn the defense-oriented Cactus Air Force into an offensive weapon. It didn't hurt morale and his personal prestige among the men he commanded that his leadership style was best summarized as "Follow me!"

Further reinforcement for Cactus became available following *Saratoga*'s torpedoing. On September 4, Lieutenant Commander Leroy Simpler's 24 Wildcats of Fighting 5 and the 18 SBD-3s of Scouting 6 were launched from *Saratoga* while it was under tow, catapulted into the air one at a time, and flown to Efate. After *Saratoga* arrived in Efate's Tongatapu Harbor, ground crew from the squadrons were assembled and senior men with experience learned they would accompany the aircraft to Guadalcanal as reinforcement for the Marines.

On the same day, Colonel W. Fiske Marshall, Marine Air Group 25's commanding officer (CO) was appalled at what he found on landing at Henderson, stating it "looked like a Doré drawing of hell."

Lieutenant Colonel Charlie Fike, Marine Air Group 23 forward echelon commander during the unit's first ten days ashore on

Guadalcanal, wrote a revealing summary of the living conditions in the air group's official war diary after resuming his role as the air group's XO:

> Air operations at Cactus during the period August 20–30, 1942, were carried out under the most primitive operating conditions and despite an acute shortage of personnel. Food was prepared over open fires, washing and bathing was done in the Lunga River, and practically all hands kept their clothes on continuously except when at the river bathing. The full cooperation of ground forces was extended to aviation units at all times; however, the fact that ground forces were already short of much of their equipment and motor transportation due to the unexpected departure of transports from Cactus prior to completion of the unloading placed a definite limit on the assistance these units could extend to aviation forces.

The Americans were not the only ones receiving reinforcements. Following his arrival on Guadalcanal, General Kawaguchi was surprised that the Marines did not attack him while he observed Marine aircraft overhead daily. Finally, word reached the general from Colonel Oka on September 4 that the first of the troop-transport barges that had set out from the Shortlands carrying new reinforcements had reached the southern tip of Santa Isabel Island, on the other side of 60 miles of open water directly north of Cape Esperance, and were waiting there for the rear groups and stragglers to join. It would be several days before the crossing would be made in force, but all was well. General Kawaguchi dispatched an officer-courier to Oka with verbal instructions detailing Oka's role in the upcoming assault.

That same morning of September 4, American patrol planes spotted Oka's barges beached and camouflaged on San Jorge Island, near Santa Isabel's southeastern cape. As soon as General Geiger learned of the discovery, he took direct control of the aerial effort to destroy them. Cactus Air Force F4Fs, SBDs, and P-400s mounted three separate missions to bomb and strafe the barges. Many were seen to sustain direct hits or were smoking when the attackers left.

During the day, the Marine Raiders commanded by Lieutenant Colonel Merritt Edson were brought over to Guadalcanal from Tulagi, with the intention of having them attack the enemy that had been discovered at Tasimboko. Unfortunately, the destroyer-transports that were to take them to the village were sunk by the "Tokyo Express" that night. The next day, the Raiders took up position on a T-shaped ridge half a mile south of the airfield, east of the Lunga River.

Over the night of September 4–5, the surviving Japanese barges ferried 700 infantrymen across the 60 miles of open water separating Santa Isabel from Guadalcanal. Shortly after dawn on September 5, the last 15 barges were only 300 yards from shore at Cape Esperance when they were bounced by the dawn patrol flown by Captain Dale Brannon and Second Lieutenant Zed Fountain in the only two flyable P-400s. After cautioning Fountain to try for only one barge at a time, Brannon led the two Airacobras in a wide turn, chose a target, and throttled back to come in at a steep angle. As he flew toward the enemy, he fired two rounds from his 20mm cannon, then pulled up to view the results of his attack. Only then did he realize he had flown through a storm of small arms and light machine-gun fire. Fountain reported light damage to his airplane but thought he had scored hits.

Brannon lined up his sights on another barge and squeezed off two more rounds from the 20mm cannon. He hoped the cannon would hole the bottom of the barge and his machine guns would kill men shooting back at him. After several more passes, the stricken barges were losing way and Brannon ordered a return to base. The two P-400s were replaced 25 minutes later by six VMF-224 Wildcats. Only one barge was confirmed sunk, but as many as 250 enemy troops were thought killed or injured. VMF-224's Second Lieutenant Robert Jefferies was killed by defensive fire while in a strafing pass. His F4F fell away out of control and crashed into the sea.

In the final air action on September 5, VMSB-231 commander Major Leo Smith led two other SBDs off Henderson Field at 1515 hours and made directly for a cluster of Japanese landing barges on their way to Guadalcanal. When they returned home at 1630 hours, the pilots reported all barges sunk. Hundreds of Japanese were killed or injured during that long September 5, and most of Oka's stores were lost at sea.

Over the course of September 6, Brannon's mechanics managed to bring two more P-400s back from the dead. On the morning of September 7, more barges were discovered off the village of Tasimboko. Brannon led the four P-400, each carrying a 500-pound bomb, to attack the barges. After dropping their bombs on the first pass, the pilots circled around and strafed the enemy troops in the water. Once their ammo was expended, they flew back to Henderson to rearm and refuel while Marine Wildcats replaced them. Two hours later, the P-400s were back over Tasimboko. The relentless attacks left the enemy with little to show for their effort at bringing reinforcements to the island. At the end of the day, one Airacobra pilot reported that he and his wingman had strafed a "bloody X" on the water going after the struggling soldiers. The P-400s had at last found their métier as flying artillery, with their ground crews loading bombs and high-explosive ammunition every night in anticipation of a quick response to the enemy in the morning.

The 67th maintained armed patrols to counter Japanese barge traffic, sometimes flying as many as five missions a day to counter an enemy that was constantly working to land reinforcements. The barges were supplemented during early September by Admiral Tanaka's "Tokyo Express," which made nightly missions to unload troops. With their success, the 67th Squadron gained a new sense of purpose and became known as the "Jagstaffel," a corruption of the German term for "fighter squadron." They painted fierce faces on the noses of their fighters. Squadron armorers devised contact fuses to allow them to drop depth charges on the enemy as the supply of bombs ran low.

14

GROWING INTO THE JOB

September 5–14

Aerial combat began to settle into a routine dictated by the 600 miles that separated Guadalcanal from Rabaul. Depending on the weather, enemy bombers in a vee-of-vees formation of 18–24 Bettys would arrive around midday, high in the sun and escorted by 20 or more Zeros, which still operated in the old prewar formation of a leader and two wingmen. The Japanese were aware of the presence of the coastwatchers on the islands between Rabaul and Guadalcanal, and would make limited course changes around the islands to avoid being spotted, though they could not make wide variations from the direct route due to fuel supply limitations. When the formation came to a point around 150 miles out of Henderson it would have reached maximum altitude in a gentle climb initiated as it passed New Georgia. The bombers would then nose over as Guadalcanal came into sight on the horizon and arrive in a fast shallow dive making as much as 250 miles per hour, aiming for the airfield.

On Henderson, when the word came from the coastwatcher on New Georgia 100 miles north that the enemy had passed his position, a black flag – the signal to scramble – would shoot up at the Pagoda. In response, pilots and crews would man every flyable aircraft and head for the runway without waiting to warm up, making their way through the craters. If a pilot noticed a wind drop amid the dust, he knew his plane had run afoul of a dud hole or a small crater hidden in the tall grass. Takeoff was first come, first serve, and aircraft took off two at a time on the narrow strip.

Once in the air, the F4F pilots would fire a short burst to check their weapons, then pull back on the stick and strain for altitude as fast as the slow-climbing fighter could move. The Dauntlesses and Airacobras would stay low, turning toward the perimeter and heading off over the jungle to work over the Japanese territory.

After the black flag went up, the ground crews would make their way past the taxiing aircraft and take shelter in the foxholes and slit trenches that lined the field. The Army and Navy ground crews shared the hardships with the Marines, even voluntarily manning forward foxholes on nights when an enemy breakthrough seemed likely. Whether Marine, Navy, or Army, there were not enough of them for the job. There were few tools, no hoist equipment, and no new parts. Among the ground crews of the 67th Squadron, only seven armorers were among the men that landed on August 23. VF-5's ground echelon of experienced senior petty officers came as a godsend for all the various units.

Refueling airplanes was difficult, since there were only a limited number of hose lines and pumps, which were attached directly to the fuel containers. Because dirt and dust were ever present, the fuel had to be strained through cheese cloths to insure there was nothing in the tanks that could foul a fuel line and bring an airplane down. Crew chiefs regularly slept under their airplanes with a rifle and pistol beside them in case individual Japanese managed to slip through the Marine lines.

Fortunately, during the weather break in early September, an SCR-270 radar set arrived in a supply convoy and was set up by September 2. An operational radar allowed the defenders to be vectored to the oncoming Japanese from an advantageous position, despite clouds. Over the next week, two more SCR-270s and two SCR-268 fire control radars arrived, along with crews who knew the rudiments of operating them. However, there were still no trained FDOs available, with the result that the radars were only marginally effective; they became more useful as aviation support personnel figured out how to use them. A group of technically inclined officer volunteers banded together under Lieutenant Colonel Walter Bayler, "last man off Wake Island," who was now Marine Air Group 23 communications officer, to learn the SCR-270's secrets. It was nothing like having trained personnel, but over the next several weeks the Bayler group was able to get increasingly useful data from the radar sets as well as find the SCR-270's shortcomings and develop work-arounds.

Marion Carl recalled a typical vectored interception:

> We would be orbiting the island at 20,000 feet or so when ground control would finally get a radar vector on the incoming formation. The bombers were generally flying at 12,000–13,000 feet with the escorts 1,500 feet higher. With good luck, we could be positioned to dive on them out of the sun. The entire fight would be over within 20 minutes.

Air activities were canceled by both sides on September 7 due to terrible weather, though VS-3's Lieutenant (jg) Alan Frank spotted 17 landing barges near San Jorge while flying an evening search. He immediately attacked and sank two.

At 1800 hours, the 1st Raider Battalion's four infantry companies departed Kukum aboard two destroyer-transports and two tuna boats that had been fitted with .50-caliber machine guns and grandly proclaimed as "yacht patrol vessels," headed for the abandoned village of Tasimboko where the enemy was gathering. On arrival, the stillness was shattered when a Raider accidentally discharged his rifle. They were lucky that the enemy had already abandoned the landing beach when they heard the two ships approaching in the darkness.

Once ashore, the Raiders moved on toward Tasimboko at dawn, supported by three P-400s that appeared on station despite one of the hairiest takeoffs any of the pilots had ever experienced. Due to the driving rain the day before, the poorly drained Cow Pasture was muddier than usual. When he was given clearance for takeoff, newly promoted Major Brannon lowered half flaps, stood on his brakes, and ran the straining Allison engine to full throttle. He lifted his feet off the brakes and roared down the runway, throwing mud in all directions with his prop while his wheels sank in the ooze. He just managed to attain takeoff speed and barely get airborne before running out of runway. Second Lieutenant Vern Head followed. He began moving, but could not get free of the mud. As the Airacobra whipped and slid nearly to the end of the runway, Head yanked the stick into his gut and pulled the straining airplane into the air. The fighter momentarily hung on its propeller before it stalled and fell into the mud; the impact broke it in three sections as it burst into flames. Second Lieutenant Deltis Fincher, who had moved into takeoff position when Head began his takeoff roll, had half an instant to decide what to do. Despite his fear that the bomb he carried might explode, Fincher jammed the throttle forward and managed to get off, flying right through the flames. As the fire crew pulled Head out of the cockpit injured but alive, Second Lieutenant Peter Childress popped into the air over their heads. The three surviving Airacobras joined up for the hop to Tasimboko. After dropping their bombs on the village, they remained over the Raiders, providing support for two long hours before returning to the Cow Pasture on the last of their fuel reserve.

As the P-400s headed back to Henderson to rearm at 0730 hours, the two destroyer-transports commenced firing at a 37mm gun that had opened up on the Raiders as they moved down the beach. Edson reported the Raiders had captured two fieldpieces at 0855 hours and were advancing further into the jungle. Aircraft from Henderson provided continuous air cover while the Raiders continued on toward Tasimboko. A terrific rainstorm arrived at noon that stopped flight activities, but the Raiders pressed on and took the village. Finding Japanese food supplies and other material, the Marines took as much food as each man could carry and destroyed the rest before they returned to the beach and went back aboard the destroyer-transports.

On September 8, nine VMF-212 Wildcats were flown up as replacements for the Henderson fighter squadrons. The next day, the weather broke in the enemy's favor.

Kawaguchi's 2,000 infantrymen hacked through dense underbrush over the next four days, measuring progress by the meter and half-meter, scrambling up steep, muddy hillsides and stumbling through seemingly bottomless bogs. The battle-hardened veteran soldiers were constantly in fear of air attack or ambush as they moved through the thick jungle. The water they refilled their canteens with was contaminated and food became scarce. Disease spread as they struggled to reach the positions from which they were to launch their attack at 2100 hours on September 12, with gunfire support from the "Tokyo Express."

To get protection from the air attacks, General Vandegrift moved his headquarters away from Henderson on September 9 and took a position near the ridge south of the airfield. The next day, the Raiders and the Parachute Battalion dug in on the south side of the hill along the crest, only 2,000 yards south of Henderson's runway. The 5th Battalion of the 11th Marines registered their 12 105mm howitzers on the jungle south of the ridge as a precaution, though no one expected an attack from there due to the density of the woods.

When the Japanese resumed their attacks on September 9, Marion Carl led 16 Wildcats to intercept 36 inbound Bettys over the Slot. In his first pass, Carl hit two of the bombers and set them afire. As he slowed to take aim at the second, a Zero slipped in behind and shot out the Wildcat's oil lines, setting the engine on fire. Carl managed to evade this attacker and bailed out, falling free to get away from the enemy fighters and their reputation for shooting pilots in their parachutes for what seemed an eternity before he felt it safe to pull his ripcord. Moments later, shucking his parachute harness as his feet touched the water, he dropped into Ironbottom Sound.

After four hours in the water, trying to swim toward shore against the wind and waves, he was spotted by a passing native in a canoe, who pulled him aboard. Carl didn't know enough Pidgin to explain that he wanted to be taken to the Marine positions on the island and unfortunately the man didn't speak English. Instead, he was put ashore not far from Cape Esperance on the northern end of Guadalcanal. He was right in the midst of the enemy and would have to find his way through them to get home. Over the course of September 10 and 11, he hid from Japanese patrols. At dusk on the 11th, he came across a Fijian medic named Eroni who worked with the Guadalcanal coastwatcher team led by Martin Clemens. Eroni offered to lead him past the Japanese, but they were thwarted in their attempt the next day, when they narrowly missed discovery by a Japanese patrol. Hiding in the jungle for a third night, they found a dilapidated motorboat the next morning which Eroni managed to get running. That night, the two sailed out into Ironbottom Sound, arriving at the Marine lines the next morning. Back at Henderson, Carl discovered that his personal gear had already been doled out to his squadron mates and his bunk assigned to a recently arrived replacement.

The Japanese continued to use barges to reinforce the troops on Guadalcanal. The 67th's Dale Brannon recalled that "They could hide along the coasts of the islands to the north, but when they got to Santa Isabel and set out over those 60 miles of open water to Cape Esperance, they had no defenses if they got delayed during the night and we could catch them out there at dawn." The Airacobras were very successful, since the airplanes performed well at low altitude, while their 20mm cannon and .50-caliber machine guns, and ability to carry a 500-pound bomb on the center rack, turned them into a very effective fighter-bomber against the relentless enemy.

Over the next weeks, defying technical orders regarding dive-bombing methodology, the P-400 pilots developed their own dive-bombing technique. While the instrument panel carried the warning: "Do not release bomb when nose angle more than 30 degrees up or down or when airspeed exceeds 280 mph," the pilots discovered that a bomb would release in a 70-degree dive and clear the propeller arc if the pilot applied quick pressure as he released the bomb to pull the airplane away from the falling bomb. The planes averaged 300 miles per hour and sometimes reached over 400 miles per hour, pulling out successfully. While the Dauntless pilots pushed over at 15,000–17,000 feet and pulled out at 1,500 feet, the Airacobra pilots initiated their dives at 5,000 feet, released at 1,000 feet and pulled out right over the jungle, zig-zagging over the jungle canopy to avoid ground fire, then returning to strafe where the bomb explosion revealed troop positions.

At Efate, September 11 saw several pilots of VF-6 given orders transferring them to Fighting 5 as reinforcement for losses the squadron had suffered over the two weeks since they had been among the first reinforcements to arrive on the island. Among the Fighting 6 pilots who made the transfer was Ensign Cash Register. That day, 24 Wildcats and six SBD-3s, with the ground crews in a Marine R4D that provided navigation assistance as well as transportation, flew up to Henderson, arriving in the afternoon. That evening, Register recorded the day's events in his diary:

September 11, 1942 – Woke up this morning with the news that we are to fly to Guadalcanal today. We left Efate at 0945 and got at Espiritu Santo at 1110. Left there at 1250 and arrived at Guadalcanal at 1645. A 750 mile hop. Fields are very bad, but we didn't lose or damage an airplane. The field is covered with wrecked planes and bomb craters. Once here, I was told by a Marine that cruisers shell us at night and we're bombed during the day, with sniping from the hills. It's a tough, rugged, dirty outfit quartered here.

Among the Scouting 6 pilots was 22-year-old Ensign John Bridgers, survivor of the sinking of *Yorktown* at Midway, and Ensign Niles Siebert, with whom Bridgers would become "closer than brothers" during their six-week stay on the island. Bridgers later wrote of his arrival:

The morning after our first night on the island, we were standing at the flight line when Washing Machine Charlie came over at dawn. We were on one end of the runway while the bombs were dropping on the opposite end. Even at a distance, the exploding bombs seemed close enough for concern and everyone jumped into a large, sandbagged foxhole near the operations tent. A *Life* magazine photographer who had come up to the island with us was the last one in and landed atop the squadron members packed beneath him in the revetment. This cameraman was a stout fellow of nearly 300 pounds and, though we were well missed by the bombs, several of us suffered bruises and painful backs.

While the news he and the reporter had come to cover was slow for the few days they were there, they made the most of being with us, and went on what we thought of as a "milk run" raid the next day. The next spring, just before I finally departed the Solomons, the April 12, 1943 issues of *Time* and *Life*, in both the stateside and the miniature "battlefield editions" featured accounts of our mission. For our visiting journalists, this was the only story in town; thus it was that our "milk-run" received notoriety far beyond its importance to the conduct of the war. At the end of the war, I was probably best remembered by the folks at home for having my picture in *Life* than for the considerable and significant combat action I saw later in the war. For me, my memories of Guadalcanal are mainly of being fallen on by an overweight photographer and the food, which was even worse than what we had been getting back in New Caledonia.

On September 12, *Saratoga* raised its anchor at Tongatapu Harbor where it had been since September 6 while its crew made temporary repairs for their trans-Pacific voyage. Escorted by the battleship *South Dakota* (BB-57), cruiser *New Orleans* (CA-32), and five destroyers, the carrier departed for Pearl Harbor, arriving on September 21. The next day, it entered drydock for more permanent repairs which would take the remainder of the year. The US Navy now had only two carriers in the South Pacific – *Wasp* and *Hornet*.

Over the four days after the Raiders' attack on Tasimboko, it became obvious the enemy was preparing for some major action.

On September 12, coastwatcher Donald Kennedy on New Georgia sent a warning that 25 Bettys and 15 Zeros were on their way from Rabaul. With the guidance of Colonel Bayler's self-taught fighter directors and the newly installed radar, 20 VF-5 and 11 Marine Wildcats shot down four Bettys and one Zero, while the 3rd Marines' 90mm guns shot down two additional Bettys. One of the Bettys was the victim of VF-5's Ensign John Wesolowski, the first of five victories he would score over the island during September, while the Zero was credited to newly promoted Lieutenant (jg) Cash Register. One Navy pilot died when he tried to land his damaged Wildcat dead-stick following the fight.

Wesolowski later recalled what fighting over Guadalcanal was like:

Our function was to repel the Japanese air and sea attacks on the beachhead and to provide air cover for our own land and sea forces. Every day from the time of our arrival, VF-5 stood alert in a tent about 50 yards down the hill from the Pagoda, a Japanese-built structure that was used by the flight-operations people. At first, we had one pilot per plane, so all of us were always on duty. There was nothing else to do anyway. When we got the signal to scramble – a siren or shotgun blast – we all ran or were driven by jeep to our planes, which were parked randomly within a few hundred yards of that tent. As the aircraft attrition went up, we took turns being on alert for a given period, because we then had more pilots than planes. That gave us a chance to take a swim in the Lunga River, wander around within the confines of the beachhead, or play poker. One of our guys, Ensign Foster Blair, even did needlepoint.

Our tactics were adopted from the Marines and were both simple and straightforward: When enemy aircraft were either spotted by coastwatchers or detected on our own crude radar, we would scramble. Typically, as soon as we scrambled, we all made a slow climbing turn around the field so that we could join up and the flight leader could get to the front of the pack. Insofar as possible, we formed into four-plane divisions and made a near-full-power climb to altitude. If we had enough time, we could get to our maximum altitude of about 30,000 feet. We were in radio contact with guys at the base, who gave us whatever information they had on the incoming raid. If there were bombers, they always came in from the same direction and were always in one or more very shallow vee-of-vees formations, flying abreast. They were at 23,000–25,000 feet; their escorts were always well above them, at about 31,000 feet. We tried to get into position for an overhead or high-side run, usually on the left side of the bomber formation. The escorts generally didn't make their presence known until almost all the F4Fs had peeled off into their runs on the bombers. Once we had peeled off, we were on our own. Rejoining was very haphazard.

Some days, there were no bombers, just fighters. Whenever we made contact with Zeros, it was every man for himself as soon as the melee started. It seemed that formation flying was forsaken in the heat of the moment, even though we tried to keep track of things. Some days, we were in combat before we had even joined up. Those were some of the more exciting days.

On the night of September 12, Register confided in his diary:

September 12, 1942 – Today started the war to the end for us. This I believe is the hottest battle front there is now. Twenty-six bombers and 20 Zeros came over today dropping bombs on the field; really raising hell. Again I got separated because of engine trouble and was attacked by Zeros. Got one and was very lucky to get back. There is no way for me to explain the seriousness of our position. We are fighting for our very lives. Everyone is exhausted from fighting day and night. May God give us the strength and help us. We get no help or relief from home. This is beginning to look like another Bataan. We are expecting to be shelled tonight by cruisers.

No one took much note of the fact that, on this mission, the Bettys bombed the ridge south of the runway, rather than the airfield itself. The event could not be laid to navigational error, since the bombers had approached at a right angle to the axis of the runway, overflying the airfield before dropping their bombs. This was despite the fact that Guadalcanal coastwatcher Martin Clemens reported shortly after first light that his Solomon Islander scouts had spotted Japanese troops moving through the jungle east of the Tenaru River. Marine intelligence downgraded their estimate of "several thousand" to "several hundred," despite Clemens having taught his scouts, whose language had only the numbers "one," "two," and "many," to count troops accurately.

That evening, three Scouting 6 Dauntlesses spotted three groups of enemy ships headed for Guadalcanal down the Slot. The most important and dangerous was Admiral Tanaka's flagship, the cruiser *Tenryū* and its three escorting destroyers from the "Tokyo Express," which obviously intended to shell the Marines. Unfortunately, there was not enough daylight left to mount an attack. At dusk, an afternoon Raider patrol returned to the positions they had originally occupied on the south side of the ridge and reported there were "many" enemy soldiers in the jungle to the south. After dark, Colonel Edson called a meeting of his officers that night to plan combat patrols for the next morning.

At the same time that Edson met with his officers, Kawaguchi Battalion finished their preparations to attack; the advance troops moved up to the base of the ridge that blocked their advance. Unfortunately, it was only when the troops began to climb the ridge after dusk that the general first learned that the ridge – which lay between his force and the main runway – was manned by Marines, when runners returned from the front with the information. There was no time to maneuver around the obstacle; the hungry, exhausted troops would have to advance over the defended ground.

The battle broke out at 2100 hours, just as Edson's meeting ended. Shortly before, "Washing Machine Charlie" dropped flares just south of the runway to light the ridge. While the lead elements of Kawaguchi Battalion floundered in the jungle flats below the ridge, seeking the first line of Marine listening posts, the artillery of Ichiki Battalion east of Alligator Creek opened fire. Tanaka's ships arrived off Lunga Point and opened fire to support the attack. Several "shorts" landed in the aviators' bivouac area, killing two pilots from VMSB-232 and one from VMSB-231, but no aircraft were hit and there was no serious damage on the airfield. Unfortunately for the attackers, several "overs" from the ships killed many of the advancing infantry.

The two sides fought to a draw through the night until the Japanese withdrew out of range. The Marines dug in to better advantage. The Raiders and paratroopers held their lines until dawn and saw the enemy

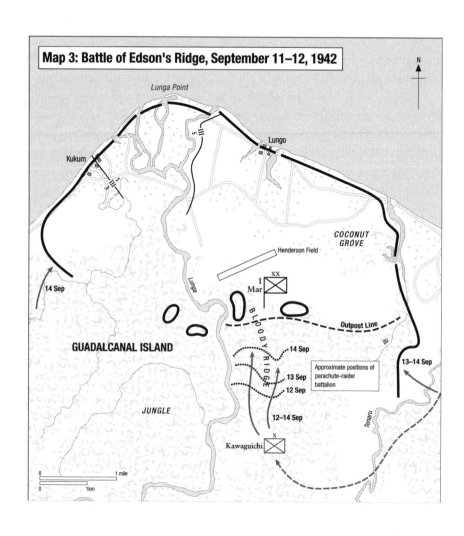

Map 3: Battle of Edson's Ridge, September 11–12, 1942

retreat back into the jungle. At dawn, the Marines moved to recover ground lost in the initial enemy attack. Japanese snipers abounded, which made the advance cautious and slow. Edson advised General Vandegrift, "They're testing, just testing. They'll be back." The Marines continued to pry more ground from the enemy through the rest of the day. Defenses were repaired and improved, and artillery pieces were moved to maximum advantage. The enemy was not ready to quit. General Kawaguchi still commanded about 1,000 troops, double the 500 Marines holding the ridge.

An hour after dawn, 19 VMO-251 Wildcats that had been launched from *Hornet* and *Wasp* arrived at Henderson. The pilots had expected only to deliver the F4Fs, then return to Espiritu Santo for more training, but instead they were quickly introduced to combat. An hour after their arrival, two C5M2 "Babs" reconnaissance aircraft, escorted by nine Zeros, arrived over the airfield to see if it had been captured by the Army. They were spotted on radar and 12 Wildcats from VMF-223 and 224 and the newly arrived VMO-251 took off to make the interception. The Zeros managed to protect the two reconnaissance planes, but the Wildcats shot down four of their number, while the enemy pilots shot down two F4Fs and damaged two others whose pilots were killed when they crashed trying to land back at Henderson.

The daily noon-hour raid didn't show up until 1400 hours, when 27 Bettys and 12 Zeros were picked up on radar and intercepted by Wildcats from VMF-212 and VF-5. Two Bettys were shot down and two others damaged, for the loss of one F4F and a pilot from each squadron. This time, six enemy aircrew bailed out of the Bettys and were pulled out of Ironbottom Sound to become prisoners of war.

Later that afternoon, two Rufes from Rekata Bay came in low over Henderson and caught an SBD from VMSB-231 as it turned to final approach over Lunga Point to land. Second Lieutenant O.D. Johnson and his gunner were killed when their Dauntless hit short of the runway and exploded. As the sun was setting, the last reinforcements from *Saratoga*'s air group – 18 VF-5 Wildcats, 12 Scouting 6 SBDs and six Torpedo 8 TBF Avengers – arrived from Espiritu Santo.

Colonel Edson had been right that the enemy would be back. While 105mm artillery fire from the 11th Marines and mortars on the ridge hammered the enemy, their relentless attack forced the Raiders and paratroopers to retreat halfway back across the ridge. At 2200 hours,

Edson informed Vandegrift that his force was down to 300, and the Japanese had yet to ease the pressure. Isolated groups and individual Marines separated from their units stopped charges and confused the enemy by firing from odd places at odd moments. Nevertheless, the Marines were increasingly outnumbered. Vandegrift ordered the last reserves to the hill and prepared for the worst. If Edson's force couldn't hold, Henderson and the Cow Pasture could fall and the Marines could be driven from the island. By 0230 hours on September 14, Edson reported he was "out of the woods." While the enemy had not yet acknowledged defeat, it was felt they had spent themselves.

At 0300 hours, the 67th Squadron's Captain John Thompson, now in charge while Brannon was felled by an attack of dysentery, was awakened and told to report to the Pagoda, where he was met by a Marine officer from Edson's unit. Thompson later recalled: "He grabbed a pencil and a scrap of paper and drew a rough diagram of the ridge showing the positions of both sides. He said the Japanese were expected to make a big push at daybreak." There was only enough fuel on the field for three airplanes. The Airacobras were fueled and armed.

At dawn, 50 enemy soldiers broke through the southeast corner of the thin defensive line and attacked toward the Cow Pasture. They ran into a strongpoint manned by Marines from the 1st Engineer Battalion. With the sound of nearby gunfire in their ears Thompson led Second Lieutenants B.E. Davis and Bryan Brown as they manned the three Airacobras. They took off, circled the field once, and made their attack. Thompson later recalled: "We came in low over the trees, pulled up and saw the Marine positions. In the clearing below were hundreds and hundreds of Japanese, ready to charge. I lowered the nose, pressed the trigger and just mowed right through them. The other two did the same thing." Brown's P-400 was hit by enemy fire, but he was able to turn the momentum of his dive into sufficient altitude to get back and make a dead-stick landing at the Cow Pasture. While he was touching down, Thompson and Davis came around for a second run. Thompson was hit in his radiator and had to break off and make an emergency landing. Davis made repeated strafing runs until he ran out of ammunition. The 67th's desperate mission had broken up the final assault on the ridge.

The last-ditch attack was hurled back, but in a moment of heart-stopping drama at division headquarters, a sword-wielding Japanese officer with two riflemen headed directly for General Vandegrift, who was in the open, alone and unarmed. Gunnery Sergeant Sheffield Banta, an utterly unflappable old salt, stopped typing a report long enough to unholster his .45-caliber pistol and shoot the officer dead in his tracks. Two more quick gunshots from Banta dropped one of the riflemen practically at the general's feet while the last fell where he stood; a fourth infiltrator was later routed out of Vandegrift's quarters.

The surviving enemy soldiers melted back into the jungle. Many wounded were carried into the rain forest by their comrades. Later that day, Marines counted 600 dead on "Edson's Ridge," as it came to be called, most of them the result of the Airacobras' gunfire. Thompson was called to General Vandegrift's headquarters that evening, where the general told him, "You won't read about this in the newspapers, but you and your flight just saved Guadalcanal." Thompson returned to the squadron with a fifth of the general's Scotch, which the young pilots made quick work of. Brown and Davis were awarded the Silver Star, while Thompson became one of only 11 USAAF pilots awarded the Navy Cross during the Pacific War.

The 1st Raider Battalion lost 31 killed and 104 wounded; the Parachute Battalion lost 18 killed and 118 wounded. Several dozen supporting engineers and artillerymen also died. Many of the wounded were flown to Espiritu Santo aboard the Marine Air Group 25 R4D transports that landed each dawn with ammunition and other supplies.

Register wrote of the battle in his diary:

September 13, 1942 – We were shelled last night as if hell broke loose. Eight of us were in a bomb crater digging like gophers. Shells whistling and bursting all around, with heavy fire from the hills around us. Lost four bomber pilots last night with a direct hit on the bomb shelter. Many more gone. We are standing by now for a carrier attack.

I have never seen, and I don't think this has occurred any other place, the terrific courageous fight the men are making here at Guadalcanal. We have the worst jungle conditions here with the Marines striking out into it hunting out Japs. We only hold a 10 mile radius from the beach. The island is 80 miles long and 30 miles wide and the rest of it is full of Japs. Over 5,000 and more coming in every day and night. They shoot at us on takeoff and landing. Our strategy and leadership has been very poor on this whole invasion.

It has been very disheartening and has discouraged the men terribly. So many mistakes have been made. They have sent us no equipment or reinforcements. For two weeks they ate Jap rice on the island. If the people back home only knew the truth instead of what is put out to them.

Don't know how much longer I can last. Flew over four hours and most of the time at 26,000 feet. Zeros came over this morning with us losing many pilots. Two very good friends were killed, one on the field. This afternoon we intercepted 26 VB and 20 VF. I got one VB, ran out of gas and just made the field. Two were killed like this yesterday. God, I never knew life could be like this; we are like rats in a trap fighting every minute for our lives and knowing it's just a matter of time before we will all go. Very few of my friends I started with are left. We are taking a terrible toll on the Japs, but can't stop them.

15

STALEMATE

September 15–30

General Kawaguchi led his 1,200 surviving troops across the Lunga River, where they linked up with Colonel Oka's battered men; scores of wounded were left by the wayside with the dead. There was no food or medical supplies. By September 19, NCOs were beating the flagging troops and cursing them onward. In the end, the survivors crossed the Matanikau River and emerged from the dense rain forest near Point Cruz, where they rushed to lap up water washing over the beach; many died from ingesting sea water, convulsed in agony. Of the 2,100 men Kawaguchi had led to the foot of Edson's Ridge on September 12, only 1,000 retired safely to Kokumbona. The Imperial Army's inability to support and supply its troops made its contribution to the deadly arithmetic of stalemate on the island.

In mid-September, the 67th Squadron's history reported: "Every airplane in commission soon became an example of the ground crew's ingenuity and resourcefulness." The mechanics still lacked the proper tools and manuals, which made routine maintenance to keep the Airacobras flyable difficult. Since there were no supplies of spare parts for the orphaned ex-RAF P-400s, the wrecks became the only source of replacement parts. The ground crews were forced to take extraordinary measures to keep the airplanes operational as the weeks wore on. They decided to rebuild one Airacobra that cracked up while landing on the muddy strip rather than turn it into parts, taking a left wing from another wreck to replace the crumpled left wing, while the bent propeller blades were turned into a balanced replacement by the expedient of pouring molten lead in them until they "felt right." Over the next two months, the battered P-400, renamed "the Resurrection," provided solid service. The accomplishment of the crews in keeping six to eight Airacobras in sufficiently good shape to allow them to continue strafing and bombing the ubiquitous barge traffic was little short of miraculous and a testament to American ingenuity.

September 14 saw the Cactus Air Force score one of its most successful days. A total of 24 Rufe fighters and Pete bombers from Rekata Bay appeared over Henderson throughout the day. They lost eight to the defenders, who suffered no losses. At midday, seven Rabaul Zeros escorting a C5M "Babs" reconnaissance plane appeared over Lunga Point. The defenders caught them over Cape Esperance and shot down one Zero and the Babs. Henderson's muddy airstrip claimed a VMF-223 Wildcat that skidded out of control on takeoff, with the pilot emerging from the resulting crash seriously injured for the only loss of the day. After 24 very eventful hours on Guadalcanal, the VMO-251 pilots were glad to see the R4D Skytrain that arrived just before dusk to return them to Espiritu Santo.

Conditions on Guadalcanal were hellish for all the pilots and aircrewmen. The cold rice from the captured Japanese stores that was now getting bad, along with the damaged tin cans of sardines, resulted in crippling dysentery that contributed to severe weight loss. Dale Brannon later recalled that between his arrival on Guadalcanal on August 22 and the onset of the rains in mid-September that marked the end of the first phase of the battle, he lost close to 20 pounds. "And there were some in the squadron who were worse off than me." The widespread poor health of both fliers and ground troops came from the poor food and a combination of tropical diseases like dengue fever and the malaria spread by the ubiquitous mosquitos. The island's huge rats, which appeared everywhere, disrupting sleep as they hunted through tents, trenches, and foxholes for food, carried typhus. Water on the island was dangerous to drink without first being treated to kill the microscopic creatures swimming in it. The constant rain led to a fetid, moist environment that meant clothing, boots, and equipment quickly rotted. Daytime temperatures were pushed into the high 90s by the tropical sun, accompanied by humidity approaching 90 percent that quickly enervated anyone involved in any physical effort. The daily driving tropical rain storms turned foxholes and trenches into ponds for breeding even more mosquitos, and made muddy quagmires of living quarters, roads, and airfield taxiways. Marion Carl later recalled that Guadalcanal was "the only place on Earth where you could stand up to your knees in mud and still get dust in your eyes."

Lieutenant (jg) Register was among those suffering. After only four days on the island, he wrote:

September 15, 1942 – Pilots are becoming exhausted and sick; it's a pitiful sight. Everyone is trying so hard and is driving themselves on. Am so tired I can't eat. I didn't get any planes today. I passed out today so had to stay at the field hospital for a day and a half. Lack of food and exhaustion from high altitude were the causes. No planes came over today and no shelling.

During Scouting 6's time on Guadalcanal, John Bridgers experienced the most awful food he found anywhere during the war, later writing of one item in particular:

Throughout the war, the food product manufacturers back in the States were constantly working to improve the foodstuffs they provided the armed forces. One such attempt I encountered during this period was called "canned butter," which had been formulated to withstand melting in the fierce heat of the tropics. It looked like the real thing. When a gallon container was put before us in the mess tent, we all tucked into it. The trouble was that it had a wax base, so when a generous layer was slathered on a piece of bread, it simply coated the hard palate with an immovable layer of wax. No one ever explained to me how, if it didn't melt in the tropical heat of over 95 degrees, it was expected to liquefy at normal body temperature of 98.6 degrees. Anyway, I did momentarily forget my problems with Spam while struggling to free the roof of my mouth of this so-called "butter."

Fighting 5 commander Leroy Simpler remembered standing in line for a meal one day when a Japanese sniper suddenly opened up on the men. "The only ones who left the line were two Marines who'd just been served. Everyone else dropped to the ground till the sniper was finished off, but nobody left that line. We were too hungry to take the chance of coming back and finding they'd run out of food." Simpler also remembered that: "There was no rank in the chow line. That was by order of General Vandegrift. If you got there and there were ten privates in front of you, that's the way it was. I think it was one of his best decisions, because it promoted unity among everyone in such a difficult circumstance."

As things appeared to be reaching the breaking point for men and equipment, Guadalcanal's defenders gained a two-week respite, the fortunate result of a strong storm system that swept across the northern Solomons and the Solomons Sea, starting the afternoon of September 14 and bringing rain to the entire archipelago over the next two weeks. The bad weather prevented the enemy on Rabaul mounting any raids until September 27. The Americans at Henderson Field used the respite to repair and rebuild as many airplanes as they could, cannibalizing those that had been damaged beyond repair. Replacements came in as possible during times when the weather was less forbidding, though both airfields became soggy, muddy bogs while the drenching rain storms remained overhead.

September 15 brought disaster to the Allied forces in the South Pacific. Good weather in the Coral Sea, 150 miles southeast of San Cristobal Island, saw the ocean "like glass" under a clear blue sky. Task Force 18 – composed of the carriers *Wasp* and *Hornet*, accompanied by the battleship *North Carolina* (BB-55), heavy cruiser *Salt Lake City* (CA-25), light cruiser *Helena* (CL-50), and destroyers *Laffey* (DD-488), *Lansdowne* (DD-486), *O'Brien* (DD-415), *Mustin* (DD-413), *Farenholt* (DD-491), and *Anderson* (DD-411) – was covering the transports bringing the 7th Marine Regiment to Guadalcanal from New Caledonia.

At 1215 hours, *Wasp*'s radar picked up a "bogey" 30 miles distant. Minutes later, a Wildcat pilot in the CAP spotted and shot down a Kawasaki H6K Type 97 "Mavis" flying boat. At 1230 hours, the bosun's pipe sounded "watch Condition Two," with the air department at flight quarters. Lookouts manned their stations. In the days since the fleet had left Nouméa, several enemy submarines had been spotted; the waters were well known to all with good reason as "Torpedo Junction."

No one aboard the ships knew it, but the Imperial Navy submarine I-19, commanded by Lieutenant Commander Shogo Narahara, was just over the horizon and on the lookout for them. At 1345 hours, the officer of the deck manning the periscope called Narahara to the control room to report that he had spotted smoke on the horizon. The captain took a quick look for himself, confirming there was more than one source to the wisps of smoke on the northern horizon and ordered the vessel to close on the enemy.

As "duty" carrier, *Wasp* was responsible for launching antisubmarine patrols to protect the force, which constituted the sum total of the Navy's warships in the South Pacific. At 1420 hours, the carrier turned away from the fleet into the wind and launched eight F4Fs and SBDs to relieve the midday search patrol. Once the replacements were airborne, LSO Lieutenant David McCampbell recovered the 11 planes circling overhead waiting to land.

Captain Narahara peered through his periscope and saw *Wasp* heel slightly as the ship executed a starboard turn to rejoin the rest of the ships. Word came from the forward torpedo room that all was ready. At 1443 hours Narahara fired the first of six Type 95 torpedoes at a range of 1,000 yards.

Aboard *Wasp*, lookouts suddenly screamed warnings of inbound torpedoes. Captain Sherman ordered "Hard a' starboard," but he was too late. Two torpedoes passed ahead of the carrier; lookouts aboard *Helena* saw them pass the cruiser's stern. At 1445 hours, three hits in the vicinity of the aviation gasoline tanks and the ship's magazine staggered *Wasp*. At 1448 hours, *Lansdowne* managed to narrowly avoid the sixth of Narahara's torpedoes, which then sped past *Mustin* at 1450 hours as it penetrated *North Carolina*'s screen. The fifth hit *O'Brien* at 1451 hours when the destroyer turned back from maneuvering to avoid the sixth. At 1452 hours, the sixth torpedo hit *North Carolina* just forward of the battleship's No. 1 gun turret, creating a hole 32 by 18 feet, 20 feet below the waterline, killing five men in the explosion. Skillful damage control quickly righted a 5.6-degree list and the battleship was able to remain in formation at 26 knots.

Narahara's spread of six torpedoes was the most successful shot taken by a submarine of any navy during the war.

In the aftermath, *Wasp*'s forward area was ripped by fiery blasts that tossed aircraft on the forward flight deck overboard like toys. Spare airplanes stored in the hangar deck overhead broke free, falling hard enough to snap off their landing gear when they hit the deck. Other planes on the hangar deck caught fire; the flames were sucked below into the crew spaces through open hatches. Ready ammunition stored near the forward antiaircraft guns on the starboard side detonated by the heat blew the No. 1 1.1-inch gun mount overboard. On the bridge, Captain Sherman was spattered by blood from the gun captain's corpse, which the explosion had thrown through the air to land next to him.

Wasp's condition rapidly became even more desperate. Forward, firefighting crews lost their fight when the water was cut off by the failure of the main pumps while ammunition and bombs exploded when the unstoppable fire reached the magazines. At 1452 hours the central damage control station was evacuated when the sound-powered phones went dead. Three minutes later, the fire breached the aviation gasoline tanks and grew in intensity. Water flooding through the ship's gaping wounds brought on a 15-degree list to starboard. The carrier was surrounded by oil and gasoline fires on the water.

Captain Sherman ordered the helm to port and speed reduced to ten knots in hopes that the wind on the starboard bow would blow the flames to port. Three major gasoline vapor explosions wracked *Wasp* at 1508 hours. Captain Sherman saw there was no hope of saving the carrier and notified task group commander Rear Admiral Leigh Noyes, who agreed with his decision to abandon ship. The order to do so was given at 1520 hours; the crew began going overboard as the escorting destroyers maneuvered to pick them up. LSO McCampbell, who had been the Navy diving champion as an Annapolis midshipman, considered a fancy dive off the fantail, but on seeing the wreckage in the water below, "I grabbed the family jewels in one hand and my nose in the other and jumped like a kid going into a pool." Captain Sherman managed to climb onto a mattress that he found in the water before he was rescued by *Farenthold*.

As the flames spread, *Wasp* drifted. *Lansdowne* was ordered to sink her; the two torpedoes the destroyer fired failed to explode. The torpedomen disabled the magnetic exploders and set the last three to run at ten feet. They all exploded on impact, but *Wasp* refused to sink until 2100 hours, taking 193 dead with the ship.

O'Brien survived but the destroyer had suffered severe structural damage. The ship reached Espiritu Santo the next day, where emergency repairs were carried out. Departing for San Francisco on October 8, the destroyer stopped at Suva in the New Hebrides on October 13 for three days of repair. At sea on October 18, the ship was leaking badly and the hull split open at 0600 hours on October 19; the crew abandoned ship 30 minutes later. *North Carolina* also made temporary repairs at Espiritu Santo before departing for Pearl Harbor two weeks later. At Pearl Harbor, the battleship went into dry-dock for major repairs to the hull, finally returning to the South Pacific in January 1943. Narahara had significantly reduced the fighting power of the US Navy in the South Pacific at one of the most crucial moments.

Despite the poor weather that began on the 14th and expanded across the archipelago over the next two weeks, the Cactus Air Force remained active throughout this period.

Just after daybreak on September 16, two SBDs on morning patrol found three enemy destroyers and what the fliers took to be four light cruisers, part of Admiral Tanaka's "Tokyo Express," headed home to their base in the Shortlands after a night delivering cargo and troops and bombarding Henderson. By 0800 hours, Scouting 3's Lieutenant Commander "Bullet Lou" Kirn led 13 VS-3 SBDs and five Torpedo-Eight TBFs to strike the enemy. An hour after takeoff, they found the ships. The TBFs attacked with torpedoes while the SBDs dived on the enemy from 2,500 feet. The lead ship, described as a light cruiser, was hit by a torpedo and near-missed by a 1,000-pound bomb, while another "light cruiser" sustained damage from two near misses; one destroyer was left smoking. Kirn's force all returned safely in the poor weather.

The day ended when two SBDs searching to the northwest reported spotting a heavy cruiser and two destroyers 150 miles from Henderson Field at 1620 hours. Both attacked, but the 500-pound bombs they each dropped detonated too far away to cause damage. At 1755 hours, Kirn, again at the head of 12 VS-3 SBDs, located the enemy force and attacked through flak to score three near misses on the heavy cruiser, and a direct hit and three near misses on one of the destroyers. Ensign Oran Newton and Aviation Radioman 3/c Robert Thornton were last seen as their Dauntless crashed into the sea, hit by defensive fire.

The Imperial Navy made further runs of the "Tokyo Express" with reinforcements while the storms continued. The warships would depart the Shortlands in mid-afternoon, with up to 1,000 troops on the decks. Around 1800 hours, they arrived at the 200-mile range limit of Guadalcanal-based aircraft. If the defenders were fortunate to spot them at that point, there was time to mount one strike, but even experienced Navy and Marine crews frequently claimed a destroyer hit or sunk where nothing had been accomplished. Increasing their speed with nightfall, the destroyers would arrive off Guadalcanal around midnight. Their usual unloading point was eight to ten miles west of Henderson Field, just across the Matanikau River. "Washing Machine Charlie" would arrive to distract the Americans, while one or two escorting destroyers shelled the airfield.

Dick Mangrum remembered that he and other experienced SBD pilots attempted to glide bomb destroyers while they were off the beach, but were never able to make a successful attack, losing several aircraft and crews. The Japanese would finish unloading by 0300 hours and head north at high speed, putting them out of range by dawn.

Action was light on September 17, with only two Japanese aircraft spotted in the air; however, it was a day of small victories by small flights of Cactus warplanes on patrol, an increasingly positive trend. An air-raid warning at 1000 hours saw six fighters scrambled, but there was no contact. At 1405 hours, three P-400s strafed beached landing barges near Morovovo, in western Guadalcanal, but no Japanese were seen. Two SBDs spotted a floatplane on the water in Rekata Bay and strafed it through a hail of antiaircraft fire. Both were shot up, but returned home safe. At 1500 hours, Flight 300's Ensign Hal Buell ran across what he identified as two light cruisers 20 miles off northeastern New Georgia. Responding to his report, four SBDs with 1,000-pound bombs and a TBF carrying four 500-pound bombs went after the ships. One Dauntless' bomb failed to release while the other three missed their targets and the TBF jettisoned its bombs when two unidentified Japanese planes attacked it.

At 1505 hours, an 11th Bomb Group B-17 reported spotting ten H6K flying boats, three Rufes, four cruisers, and many destroyers, cargo vessels, and transports at Gizo. In response, Cactus Control launched 13 Dauntlesses and four Avengers, but they ran into bad weather and turned back. On the way home, VMSB-231's Second Lieutenant Alan Smith and his rear seater went missing in the poor weather.

September 18 saw operations restricted due to weather. Though visibility was poor in many sectors, several patrols were launched. At 1100 hours, VMSB-232's Second Lieutenant Leland Thomas was shot down by "friendly fire" from ships in Tulagi Harbor. Though his radioman-gunner was rescued, Thomas was killed. At 1730 hours, six VT-8 TBFs and crews arrived from Efate to end the day.

September 19 saw more of the same. At 1015 hours, an 11th Bomb Group B-17 was shot up over Gizo and landed at Henderson as a precaution; fortunately, its gas tanks hadn't been hit, so after a short stay for temporary repairs, the big bomber was able to get off and return home without taxing the refueling capability on the field. At 1410 hours, three P-400s bombed and strafed several enemy landing craft at Morovovo, claiming destruction or damage of 15. Right after the Airacobras turned to return to the Cow Pasture, Marines manning a forward observation post reported hearing explosions that could have been from an ammunition dump. Adding to the day's meager gains, a flight of Cactus SBDs escorted by six Wildcats led by Major Smith took off at 1540 hours to attack targets at Rekata Bay. The attack was successful, and all aircraft returned safely. While this was in progress, a VMSB-231 SBD crew flying a search pattern north of Santa Isabel spotted a Mavis and two Rufes passing them on an opposite heading at 1600 hours, but did not attack. At the same time, two Flight 300 SBDs spotted an auxiliary aircraft carrier, a heavy cruiser, three destroyers, ten other vessels, and a dozen patrol boats at Gizo. The SBDs withdrew when they were spotted by two Rufes, due to low fuel. Ensign Chris Fink's Dauntless ran out of gas at 1700 hours and he set down smoothly on the water between Savo and Cape Esperance. Fink and Aviation Machinist's Mate 3/c Milo Kimberlin got in their life raft, but by the time a J2F Duck arrived from Kukum, it was too dark to see anyone on the surface. At 0600 the next morning, Marine Air Group 25 XO Lieutenant Colonel Charlie Fike took off in the J2F-3 utility plane to track them down and spotted them around 0700 hours. He picked them up and returned without further incident.

September 20 literally started off with a bang at Henderson when VS-3's Ensign Roger Crow cracked up taking off 15 minutes after midnight, crashing into a parked R4D and tearing off a wing. Despite his SBD being declared damaged beyond repair, while he had several broken ribs and an injured back, Crow returned to duty the next day. All flyable fighters were scrambled at 1020 hours in response to an air raid alert, but the enemy, if there were any, failed to materialize. At 1435 hours, a cruiser and two destroyers were located 20 miles north of Kolombangara Island. In response, VS-3's Lou Kirn led a mixed attack force of VS-3 and VMSB-231 SBDs that took off at 1600 hours. Spotting the enemy at 1735 hours, they attacked with 1,000-pound bombs and claimed four near misses.

At 1835 hours, a pair of VMSB-231 SBDs bombed and strafed what they thought were enemy personnel and houses on a hill overlooking Gizo Harbor. However, a local coastwatcher reported that the target was Rovianna, a friendly village. Making matters far worse, Captain Ruben Iden radioed that he and Second Lieutenant J.W. Zuber were lost, circling over an island, and running low on fuel. Iden's last report stated that Zuber had run out of fuel and safely ditched. When Zuber was eventually returned to friendly hands several days later, he reported that Iden had run out of fuel, ditched, and had drowned. The day ended on a good note when a coastwatcher reported that VMSB-231's Second Lieutenant Alan Smith and Corporal T.A. Costello, who had crashed in bad weather on September 17, were safe and sound on Santa Isabel. They were picked up by the J2F on September 22, following a day of heavy rain throughout the island chain on September 21.

While rain pelted the Solomons on the 21st, the weather broke over Rabaul and the 26th Air Flotilla, equipped with 72 new Bettys, 60 Zeros, and eight Babs reconnaissance planes flew down from Truk in preparation for the renewed offensive. Admiral McCain was able to scrape together 23 Wildcats and Dauntlesses to reinforce Henderson Field. On September 22, six SBDs in VMSB-141's advance party arrived as replacement for the worn-out VMSB-232. The rest of the squadron, led by skipper Major Gordon Bell, would follow on October 5.

Rain and overcast continued on September 22, with air action confined to Cape Esperance, where Admiral Tanaka's destroyers continued dropping off supplies and reinforcements for the Sendai

Division. At 0045 hours, three SBDs launched on night patrol 90 minutes earlier located what turned out in the light of a flare to be four enemy destroyers. Attacking immediately, the Dauntless pilots dropped their 500-pound bombs and strafed. The destroyers hastily departed on a northwesterly course. The pilots landed back at Henderson Field to rearm and refuel; they took off again at 0230 but failed to relocate the ships in complete darkness.

At 0740 hours, five P-400s took off to attack the enemy around Visale, near Cape Esperance, hitting a machine-gun emplacement and starting several fires before returning. The Airacobras were followed by three Torpedo 8 TBFs and five other P-400s that bombed and strafed the area. The bad weather claimed the 67th's Second Lieutenant Ellery Farnum, who failed to return.

General Geiger followed that attack himself, flying an SBD to Visale where he bombed the supplies the "Tokyo Express" had left behind. He meant his act to set an example. While new pilots and aircraft dribbled in, the air war was still very much in the hands of the few who had arrived at the beginning, who were now slowly folding. Some cracked up when landing or were shot down while others lost all fear and became too reckless in combat. Others burned out from lack of sleep or lack of relaxation. Wildcat pilots avoided fights because they had been too brutally stressed for too long to carry out their primary mission – kill or be killed trying. Dauntless pilots faced similar difficulties. Geiger's mission demonstrated that if a 57-year-old could fight, there was no reason younger men could not better stand the strain. His act also erased the barriers separating order-giver from order-taker; from that point on, the general was seen by his pilots and crews as a combat Marine.

Rainy, miserable weather continued on September 23. Except for a harmless encounter between a B-17 and three Rufes 15 miles northwest of Rekata Bay, there was no combat. Marine Air Group 14's commander, Lieutenant Colonel Albert Cooley, flew in to visit Cactus Air Operations in order to get a feel for operations in advance of the planned relief of Colonel Wallace's Marine Air Group 23, which was increasingly tired and worn down, after a month of intense action. During the day, the first airplanes and crews from Marine Air Group 14's VMSB-141 arrived for service. SBDs and replacement pilots from the squadron arrived in small groups until Bombing 141 was present at full strength on October 6.

The weather continued bad on September 24. Search flights were dispatched all morning and into the afternoon. One VS-3 Dauntless crew spotted a downed P-400 about five miles west of Kukum and about 200 yards from the coast; it was the airplane in which Second Lieutenant Farnum had gone missing over Visale on September 22, but there was no sign of what had happened to Farnum. At 1500 hours, two SBD crews ran across a flotilla they identified as being a light cruiser and four destroyers, 200 miles from Guadalcanal. Both attacked, but one bomb hung up and the other exploded 20 feet from the "cruiser." The Imperial Navy committed only a few light cruisers to the region, but they did deploy large destroyers as a matter of course.

The contact report resulted in a launch at 1600 hours of eight SBDs from VMSB-231 and VS-3 that located the quarry at 1730 hours, bearing due east 150 miles from Guadalcanal. Six Dauntlesses dropped their bombs through heavy antiaircraft fire, but all missed. As this happened, another two-plane VS-3 search team located one enemy destroyer 230 miles east. Both attacked and both missed, then both were attacked by a pair of Petes and one SBD was badly shot up.

VF-5's Cash Register wrote in his diary for September 24 (written October 7):

> Just received some very authenticated true information. This will never get out to anyone back in the States and few in the service. The generals and admirals have thought from the start that it was impossible for us to hold Guadalcanal. They gambled with a very small force hoping that it would do what it has done. No supplies or reinforcements were sent up for a month and even now nothing to help us. The day we were ordered up here this place was in a critical position. We arrived the eleventh. The day of the fourteenth, they gave this place a maximum of 36 hours to hold out. Of course, at the time no one here knew of this. For two days they sent no planes or supplies. Even now they have sent nothing to us. It was our squadron that turned the tide and has held this island. We are getting a raw deal here.

At 0730 hours on September 25, six Airacobras in two three-plane flights arrived over a firefight between Marines and enemy soldiers near the mouth of the Matanikau River. The Marines were equipped with several marker panels, but they displayed only one; one P-400 dropped a 100-pound bomb into a patch of rain forest, but no explosion was heard or seen.

That afternoon, five pilots from Marine Air Group 14's VMF-121 arrived at Henderson aboard an R4D. Small groups of other squadron pilots were slated to join this modest vanguard over the next week to take up the load of the nearly fought-out VMF-223 and VMF-224, to which the new pilots were temporarily assigned.

September 26 dawned rainy and overcast, severely limiting flight operations over most of the region, with many standing patrols aborted early. Nevertheless, eight 11th Group B-17s staged through on their way to attack shipping around Buka. The bombers claimed bomb hits on a heavy cruiser and a troop transport and the gunners claimed three F1Ms and three A6M2-Ns shot down. All eight B-17s overnighted at Henderson before returning to Espiritu Santo the next morning.

September 27 was the day that the 11th Air Fleet resumed offensive operations over Guadalcanal in a big way. At 1045 hours, VMSB-231's Second Lieutenant Dale Leslie was sent to establish a radio link between Marines on the ground west of the Matanikau River and air support. Orbiting overhead when the Marines were surrounded and appeared about to be overwhelmed by the enemy, Leslie radioed for help and directed landing craft dispatched from Kukum by flying low over them in the direction of the beach nearest the Marines. While a Navy seaplane tender laid down a curtain of fire, Leslie helped to effect the Marines' skin-of-the-teeth reembarkation as he strafed the encroaching enemy. During three more flights over the battle area, he helped monitor the enemy forces and guide Marine infantry units.

Following nearly two weeks of unremitting bad weather the coastwatchers reported a flight of 18 Bettys escorted by 27 Zeros headed down the Slot toward Guadalcanal. With the final warning as the enemy passed over New Georgia, 35 Wildcats scrambled at 1312 hours.

Thirty years later, Fighting 5's John Wesolowski, whose first victory, a G4M, had been scored on September 12 with a pair of Aichi E13A

"Jake" reconnaissance seaplanes near Savo Island in the early evening of September 14, wrote of the battle:

> Shortly after 1300 hours on September 27, 1942, we were alerted and scrambled as usual. Marine F4Fs from VMF-223 and VMF-224 also took off. I was the wingman of my squadron commander, Lieutenant Commander Leroy Simpler, and I joined up on him. Behind me was our second section and several more divisions of the squadron. The skipper then proceeded to climb at maximum power, but my plane and several others simply couldn't keep up, even at full power. Believe me, we had the best mechanics in the world, working in almost unbelievable conditions, but some planes just did not perform as well as others. Spark-plug age might have had an effect because we weren't able to perform the routine 30-hour checks on the planes and were scavenging parts here and there. No doubt, Lieutenant Commander Simpler's plane was better tended to than many of the others.
>
> Eventually, I lost sight of the skipper and the rest of the squadron in the clouds, but I knew their altitude and general location by way of my radio, so I kept trying to catch up. There were other stragglers, and we stragglers were loosely joined up a few thousand feet below and behind the main body of the squadron. I soon got ahead of the other stragglers and lost sight of them, too. I was completely alone.
>
> When I was somewhere in the neighborhood of 21,000 feet in an all-out climb at about 105 knots airspeed, I swear I heard machine-gun fire. I looked back in my rearview mirror and saw two Zeros diving on me and firing. Of course, it is not possible to hear machine guns in those circumstances, but I thought I did. More likely, I felt bullets impacting on my plane. By the time I looked back, the two Zeros had already flattened out from their high-side pass at me and were essentially at my altitude. They both were firing; I could see the muzzle flashes.
>
> I immediately nosed over to get some airspeed and, when I did, I saw a third Zero. I believe he had overshot while making a pass on me. When I saw him, he was below, ahead, and pretty close. He was in the process of pulling up, probably to get a new altitude advantage. He was dead in front of me and in my sights, so I fired at him almost reflexively. My pipper must have been at least 50 miles or so in front of him because he was starting up and I was starting down. This was

really a snap shot from someone whose main purpose was to get out of a nasty situation. I had all six of my guns charged and the ammo mix was one tracer every fourth round in each gun. We also had a mix of standard and armor-piercing ammo. I can't say how long a burst I fired, but I think it was quite short. I don't know where I hit him; he just seemed to break apart with little or no fire associated. He was only there for an instant; I may have overshot him before smoke and flames occurred.

I was thinking of the two Zeros that were still on my tail, so I continued to nose down almost vertically. As my speed went up, I did an aileron roll onto my back and started to pull through. That is, I dove away vertically and then, as the speed built up, executed what amounted to a half slow roll, except that I was vertical. When my orientation was 180 degrees from where I had started, I intended to pull out as fast as I could so that my ending direction was the reverse of my starting heading. We had often discussed doing this evasive maneuver; we felt that the Zero was not rugged enough to follow it without suffering structural damage. However, I was having a pretty difficult time myself. I couldn't seem to pull out, because I was going so fast by then. I don't know what the airspeed was since the needle was on its third time around the dial, which was only calibrated for two turns. I was reluctant to use trim tab for fear of pulling too many Gs and breaking up my own plane. I also discarded the idea of bailing out, because I knew that if I opened the canopy the airstream probably would tear the plane apart. So I kept pulling back on the stick and very slowly got my fighter under control. I had long since lost track of the two Zeros.

When I finally got pulled out at about 600 feet, I was going way over 400 knots. I then started to climb back up to join the squadron, whose chatter I could hear on the radio. By the time I got to 16,000 feet, however, the squadron was ordered back to base, so I followed it in.

After landing, I heard the skipper yelling loudly, "Take Wesolowski off my wing; I don't want him there anymore!" He was really angry because I had not stayed with him during the climb, but I was not the only straggler, and the others helped me convince him that I was not at fault. He agreed to keep me as his wingman. He then congratulated me for having survived a brush with three Zeros – which we were all kind of afraid of – and bringing back the airplane with minimum damage.

Writing of the day's events in his diary several weeks later, Cash Register confided:

September 27, 1942 – two Zeros. We scrambled at 1330 today. They told us to expect a torpedo attack so we were at 14,000. Saw the bombers coming at 23,000. I led a division and tried to climb up to them. Got up even with them and very close, still trying to get higher to make a run when Zeros attacked us. Everyone left me as six Zeros attacked me. The first one shot and missed and then I got him. The others were then on my tail shooting like hell. I couldn't shake them and saw their tracers going all around me. Went into a dive and lost them. Just pulled out when another Zero came straight down by me, not hitting me. I got on his tail and shot him down. He dove straight into the ground and exploded. Today was my toughest day. Didn't think I was coming back.

Altogether, the Marine pilots claimed six Bettys and a Zero, while the Navy fliers claimed four Zeros. VF-5's NAP 1/c Lee Mankin gained ace status with the A6M he downed, while Register achieved ace status with his two Zeros.

Only one SBD was lost in the attack, but four others and three TBF Avengers were damaged beyond Henderson's limited repair capability, to become sources for spare parts. The next morning, only 18 SBDs and two Avengers were operational.

On September 28, their Dauntlesses used up and the crews thoroughly exhausted, the last five pilots and all 11 radioman-gunners from Turner Caldwell's *Enterprise* Flight 300 who were among the first of the early defenders of Guadalcanal were airlifted out, thus ending the unit's heroic service on the island. John Bridgers, Hal Buell, and the other surviving pilots and crewmen of Scouting 6 were also on the plane. Lieutenant Turner Caldwell remembered:

Of the 11 planes we brought to Guadalcanal, one flew into the palm trees on a night takeoff – with no injuries, a real miracle! – one was hit on the ground by a Marine plane that landed with no brakes, seven were destroyed or damaged by Japanese bombing attacks, two were shot down. We did a lot of good for the Marines.

The next day, six SBDs from *Wasp*'s Scouting 71 (VS-71) put down on Henderson's muddy runway. They were followed at the end of the month by the squadron's other eight Dauntlesses, led by squadron leader Lieutenant Commander John Eldridge.

Taking off at noon, VS-3's Ensign Neil Weary and VMSB-231's Second Lieutenant Dale Leslie flew as targets for a radar calibration flight before dropping their 500-pound bombs on targets of opportunity along Guadalcanal's northwestern coast. Leslie's SBD suddenly disappeared while flying at 20,000 feet over New Georgia and failed to return. It was believed that he was shot down by a Zero from the midday attack, which started with a scramble instigated at 1258 hours by a New Georgia-based coastwatcher.

Spirits in the 67th Squadron were lifted by a coastwatcher's report that he had the squadron's missing pilot, Second Lieutenant Farnum, safe but in poor health. Natives working with the coastwatchers also returned VMSB-231's Second Lieutenant J.W. Zuber and the two radioman-gunners who had gone down after becoming lost the evening of September 20.

The clear skies allowed the coastwatchers to give sufficient warning for the defenders to get to altitude before the enemy's arrival. The battle took place between 34 Wildcats and 25 G4Ms escorted by 30 Zeros. VMF-212's skipper, Lieutenant Colonel Harold "Indian Joe" Bauer, also known as "the Coach," who had flown up to Henderson to get the lay of the land before his squadron flew in from Espiritu Santo, and three newly arrived VMF-121 pilots flew with VMF-223 and 224. Marion Carl later recalled the fight: "The Marine F4F pilots claimed 14 G4Ms and one A6M over Guadalcanal between 1315 and 1400 hours. VF-5 F4F pilots claimed ten G4Ms. Five F4Fs were damaged but none was lost." Imperial Navy records indicate that only four G4Ms were actually downed over Guadalcanal, while three ditched during the return flight to Kavieng on New Ireland. VF-5's John Wesolowski achieved ace status with a claim for a Betty. John Smith and Marion Carl each claimed one of the seven credited to VMF-223, while Bob Galer shot down three of VMF-224's eight. "The Coach" claimed his first victory.

Cash Register later wrote in his diary:

September 28, 1942 – Left at 1000 on an attack group. We flew 400 miles [round trip] to hit a Jap convoy but made no contact. Just got back when they scrambled the fighters. The four of us that escorted the attack group couldn't get off. 35 [F4Fs] got in the air and got to 25,000. I stood by a dugout and watched it all. I saw eleven bombers go down in flames. Their bombs dropped about a mile from me. Altogether 24 enemy planes were knocked down with no loss to us, although five [F4Fs] were damaged. It was a big day for us; am sorry I missed it; probably could have busted my score. I'm leading the squadron now, but several are close.

With good weather continuing on September 29, the 11th Air Fleet changed its tactics in an attempt to draw the defenders into an ambush. Nine Bettys departed Rabaul and Kavieng with 27 Zeros. The bombers flew only as far as New Georgia before turning back, their job having been to guide the fighters to the area and, by their brief presence, draw the defending fighters up due to their being reported by the coastwatchers. Although 33 F4Fs took off from the Cow Pasture, only 14 VF-5 pilots led by Lieutenant Commander Simpler found the raiders. In a wild, swirling action, the Navy pilots were credited with three kills and three probables against one F4F and its pilot lost before the remaining Zeros broke for home. Ensign Joseph "Dutch" Shoemaker, a VF-6 veteran sent to Guadalcanal to help fill out VF-5, found that the climb to altitude turned out to be too much for his Wildcat, and he had to drop out with a smoking engine. Approaching the airfield on the deck at low speed with his wheels down, several Zeros caught him about three miles west of Lunga Point and shredded his fighter with their fire. Shoemaker was killed when the flaming Wildcat crashed into a stand of trees and exploded. Against this loss, VF-5 added another ace to their ranks when Ensign Mark Bright downed a Zero.

Rainy weather returned on September 30, reducing air operations at Henderson. Though most of those on Guadalcanal didn't realize it at the time, the relentless mathematics of stalemate continued to work in their favor. During the first half of September, the enemy had mounted 12 raids, during which they lost 31 bombers and fighters, while seven

Bettys returned to Rabaul heavily damaged. All crews from the shot-down aircraft were lost. In return, the defenders lost 27 aircraft with nine pilots killed in action, while pilots such as Marion Carl who was rescued once and Bob Galer – who took to his parachute twice and crashed at sea a third time – were rescued to fly and fight another day. In the battles at the end of the month, the enemy had suffered the loss of more crews who could not be replaced.

16

THE SITUATION IS NOT HOPELESS, BUT IT IS CERTAINLY CRITICAL

October 1942

Following the loss of *Wasp*, Admiral Nimitz wrote bleakly of the situation in the Solomons a month later on October 15, 1942: "It now appears that we are unable to control the sea in the Guadalcanal area. Thus our supply of the positions will only be done at great expense to us. The situation is not hopeless, but it is certainly critical."

Born in Fredericksburg, Texas, five months after his father's death and raised in the German-speaking community there, Chester W. Nimitz learned responsibility early. At age eight, he began working after school and on weekends as a meat market delivery boy and later for his mother at the hotel she later owned and ran in Kerrville. High school graduation found him with few prospects. Discovering that there were no appointments to West Point available, he learned that his congressman had one available Annapolis appointment. Believing it was his only opportunity for further education, he passed the congressman's test with the highest score and was appointed to the Naval Academy from Texas' 12th Congressional District in 1901. He graduated seventh in a class of 114 in 1905, a year behind – and therefore junior to – William F. Halsey, Jr.

Following two years' sea duty aboard the battleship *Ohio* (BB-12), he was commissioned an ensign in 1907 and volunteered for submarine duty, where he was assigned as commander of USS Plunger (later A-1) in May 1909. Promoted to lieutenant, he commanded the Atlantic Fleet Submarine Squadron from May 1912 to March 1913; that such a junior officer was in a "senior" position demonstrated how little the Navy's leaders understood submarines and the potential of submarine warfare.

Promoted to lieutenant commander in August 1917, Nimitz served as chief of staff to Captain Samuel Robison, Commander Submarine Force Atlantic during World War I. After the war, while a student at the Naval War College in 1922–23, he developed a plan for a hypothetical Pacific war that became the basis of the operation plan he put to use 20 years later. Promoted to rear admiral in 1938, he commanded Cruiser Division Two in 1938 and Battleship Division One in 1939, then spent the next two years as an assistant to President Roosevelt. On December 17, 1941, the president chose him to become Commander of the Pacific Fleet following Pearl Harbor, an assignment that saw him promoted directly to full four-star admiral over seniors such as Vice Admiral Halsey.

As Pacific Theater commander, Nimitz's philosophy was that an effective senior commander needed to choose competent subordinates, define their objectives, and provide them with the means necessary to meet those goals. He refused to interfere in the conduct of any individual operation, believing that the commander on the scene knew best what tactical measures to take. Calm and affable, Nimitz was not a self-promoter with reporters and got on well with admirals and young staff officers; his concern for enlisted personnel was legendary. Many who dealt with the admiral believed he knew them personally; while he did have a good memory for names and faces, he had learned early to create files on those with whom he served, which he would review with his flag lieutenant before meeting subordinate commanders. He loved a good story and used his collection of such, which was frequently described as "salty," for serious purposes. When planning sessions grew argumentative, he would bring up an anecdote that eased tensions, as President Lincoln had done. He was not a man to flaunt his rank, listening more than speaking, seeking to elicit reasoned opinions of commanders and planners while shepherding all toward consensus. Responsible for managing a multi-service command the admiral was scrupulously even-handed in hearing every point of view; no matter how violent the argument, men left his meetings still on speaking terms.

By mid-September, Nimitz had come to believe that he must interfere in the conduct of the war in the South Pacific, having finally lost confidence in the man he had appointed Commander South Pacific Theater (ComSoPac), Vice Admiral Robert L. Ghormley. In the face of the reverses suffered since the August 7 invasion of Guadalcanal, Ghormley's performance had become lackluster and pessimistic, as reflected in the reports Nimitz received. He had expected that Ghormley would make his headquarters on Guadalcanal or aboard ship in the immediate area. Ghormley had instead moved his headquarters to Nouméa, 900 miles from Guadalcanal, and had not set foot on the island since the invasion or "made himself visible" to the Allied forces there for morale purposes. Far more important, he had not resolved the differences between Admirals Fletcher and Turner before the invasion over how long the carriers would cover the landing forces and supply fleet. Nimitz saw Fletcher's constant concern with the fleet's fuel state as over-cautious and held Ghormley responsible for having not laid down the law with more offensive-minded operational orders. Increasingly, both Nimitz and Admiral King saw their commander as weak and indecisive. Both senior admirals were worried about Ghormley's ability to effectively command what both saw as the most important naval operation of the war.

Nimitz was right to be worried. Following their failure to take Henderson Field in the Battle of Edson's Ridge, the Imperial High Command had ordered that preparations be made for a second offensive, with the date for the attack set at October 20. To reinforce the Imperial Army forces on the island, 17,500 troops of the 2nd and 38th Infantry Divisions were transferred from the Dutch East Indies to Rabaul. They would be transported to Guadalcanal over several runs made by the "Tokyo Express" between September 14 and October 9. The new Japanese commander, General Harukichi Hyakutake, arrived in early October. Support for the operation by the Imperial Navy included increased air attacks on Henderson Field on every day the weather permitted, while the warships delivering troops also bombarded American positions before they departed each night.

To confirm his beliefs, Nimitz visited Ghormley's headquarters, where he found defeatism rampant. He flew on to Guadalcanal to visit

Vandegrift and the other senior leaders, and took time to meet and speak with others in the ranks. He found a force comprised of men who were more than willing to make the sacrifices called for to achieve the goal of defeating the enemy, who also believed they had been abandoned by those in overall command of the war.

On October 1, Admiral Nimitz held a ceremony to award medals to his men. Among those with whom the admiral met and spoke was VF-5's Lieutenant (jg) Register, who later wrote of the event in his diary:

> **September 30, 1942** – Rained very hard all day. Admiral Nimitz flew in at 1600. A few of us will be awarded medals. I have been recommended for some time for the Distinguished Flying Cross.
>
> **October 1, 1942** – This morning I was awarded the Distinguished Flying Cross. Admiral Nimitz pinned the medal on my chest. He read my citation and shook hands and said he hoped to see me with Stars and many more planes. I have never thought of medals as I never dreamed I would get one. I have always done my very best and have flown whenever possible. I am very thankful and joyful. This will give my wife and folks joy; mine comes from my work.

Nimitz left the island convinced the men could hold out – if he could support them. The day after Nimitz's visit, the skies cleared from two days of rain and the Zeros returned, with 36 fighters again escorting nine Bettys that again turned away when they sighted Guadalcanal. The post-frontal weather prevented the coastwatchers on Bougainville and New Georgia spotting the formation and providing warning. Thirty-three Wildcats warned by the island's radar of the enemy's approach were still struggling for altitude when the enemy fighter sweep arrived overhead. The Zeros' first pass cost VMF-223 two Wildcats, while John Smith only escaped by hiding in a cloud. Popping back out, he found himself behind three surprised A6M2s and shot down one; the other two quickly recovered from their surprise and nearly got him. Badly shot up, the Wildcat's engine failed during Smith's return to the Cow Pasture. He crashed six miles short of the field while trying to glide the distance and land dead-stick. The crash site was behind enemy lines, but Smith was able to hike back to his own lines without encountering the enemy. On their return to Rabaul, the Zero pilots claimed six Wildcats shot down over Ironbottom Sound for a loss of one of their own. The VF-5 pilots claimed four Zeros, with one credited to squadron CO Leroy Simpler.

VMF-224's Bob Galer was also shot down over Ironbottom Sound; it was his third and last shootdown in less than three weeks. He recalled the fight:

I was up with six fighters, cruising about at 20,000 or 25,000 feet. Suddenly, 18 Zeros came at us out of the sun, and we took 'em on. The day was cloudy and after a few minutes, the only other Marine I could find was Second Lieutenant Dean Hartley. In the melee of first contact, I heard several bullets splatter against and through my ship, but none stopped me. At about the same moment, Hartley and I started to climb into a group of seven Zeros hovering above us. The fight lasted about four minutes; I shot down two Zeros and Hartley got a possible. The other four were just too many and we were both shot down. Hartley got to a field, but I couldn't make it. The guy that got me really had me boresighted. He raked my ship from wingtip to wingtip. He blasted the rudder pedal right from under my foot. My cockpit was so perforated it's a miracle that I escaped. The blast drove the rivets from the pedal into my leg. I pancaked into the water near Florida Island. It took me an hour-and-a-half to swim ashore. I was worried not only about the enemy but about the tide turning against me, and sharks.

Galer struggled ashore, to come across four Solomon Islanders armed with machetes and spears. Fortunately, they were friendly and took the bedraggled Marine to their village. After enjoying what hospitality his hosts could offer, the men put Galer in a canoe and rowed him across the sound to a Marine camp on a beach five miles away from Henderson. He walked back from there.

Regardless, the defenders had lost the fight, with six Wildcats shot down in return for four Zeros.

That night, Register wrote his impressions of the day's battle:

October 2, 1942 – We scrambled at 1230. Ran into a bunch of zeros, but no bombers. I shot down one zero, getting my own plane shot up pretty badly. Everyone agrees I am very lucky to be back.

We lost five fighter pilots today. Three TBF pilots were lost last night. A few of us are going every day now so it looks as if it's only a matter of a little time before it will be all over. Am becoming so exhausted and disappointed in our relief that we are all losing our spirit and fight. Our planes are in very bad shape and no match for the enemy.

The next day when the enemy returned with another fighter sweep, the skies were clearer and the coastwatchers radioed their warning in time for the Wildcats to get off the field and grab sufficient altitude to meet the 27 Zeros in a hard-fought fighter-versus-fighter battle. Leading six VMF-223 F4Fs, Marion Carl scored what would turn out to be his last victory, bringing his score to 16.5 before his guns jammed. His wingman Ken Frazier was able to shoot down two before the others turned on him and shot up his Wildcat badly enough that he was forced to bail out. His score of 12 put him in third place in VMF-223's "ace race," behind Smith and Carl. Newly arrived VMF-121 pilot First Lieutenant Floyd Lynch dropped one enemy fighter, but the top score of the day went to Coach Bauer, whose four victories made him an ace in only two sorties. This time, Japanese records confirmed that the total of nine Zeros claimed by the Marines was accurate.

That afternoon, the enemy seaplane tender *Nisshin*, accompanied by six destroyer escorts, was discovered 200 miles northwest of Guadalcanal by a patrolling SBD pair. The ship carried an important load of tanks that were to be off-loaded that evening on Guadalcanal. The two Dauntlesses were jumped by the ten Zeros flying cover over the convoy but still managed to report the convoy's position before making an escape. At 1600 hours, three more destroyers were spotted by other searching SBDs. The enemy force had to be dealt with before darkness. A strike force of eight SBDs and three TBFs lifted off Henderson at 1629 hours and spotted *Nisshin* and its escorts an hour later. The wildly maneuvering ships put up a flak umbrella that prevented any hits. The ships were spotted again at 2230 hours, off Cape Esperance. Newly arrived VS-71 skipper John Eldridge led a strike force of four Dauntlesses from four different squadrons into the dark sky. Eldridge and one pilot were successful in spotting the enemy in the darkness, but their bombs missed. The ships were well on their way back to the Shortlands before daylight after successfully unloading the tanks and troops.

Register wrote of the day's operations before turning in that night:

October 3, 1942 – Flew but made no contact. Zeros were over, some strafing the field. The Marines contacted them and got some. Received word that 8 DD and 1 CA were steaming in. Sent bombers out to hit them, but no hits. Expect a big landing and probably some shelling.

Neither landing nor shelling happened on October 4. Register wrote:

October 4, 1942 – Two of our pilots were evacuated today. They were exhausted and in pretty bad shape. The General sent out a dispatch requesting our immediate relief due to our conditions. Probably won't be for some time yet though. No attack today.

Tensions were high on the island as every indication pointed to a major attack at any time. Searching SBDs found destroyers from the "Tokyo Express" waiting near the 200-mile "bomb line" for their run to Guadalcanal that night. Cactus managed to launch a flight of dive bombers that found the ships and attacked. Register recorded the day's results:

October 5, 1942 – There was no attack today although 6 DD are coming in tonight. Our attack group hit one, but they're still coming. Probably will be shelled tonight. Two more men are to be evacuated tomorrow. I'm feeling pretty well compared to most of them.

The 67th Fighter Squadron received a welcome boost when 11 P-39Ns arrived on the evening of October 7 from Espiritu Santo. These new Airacobras outperformed the wretched P-400s in all ways. They were able to operate effectively at altitudes up to 18,000 feet and if they had sufficient warning could even get to 27,000 feet, which allowed them to make interceptions with the Wildcats. However, the most useful thing about these airplanes was the heavy 37mm cannon they carried in their nose. The weapon could have a devastating effect when strafing barges and the ships of the "Tokyo Express;" the tanks that had recently arrived could be taken out with one shot. While the Army pilots remained in the ground support role, they had airplanes which were not held together with baling wire. The next day, the Marine R4Ds brought a full selection of spare parts, spare engines, proper tools and proper maintenance manuals. "Sky high morale" was recorded in the squadron war diary. Register's gloomy diary entry that night showed that all was not well: "October 7, 1942 – Rained very hard today. Field is in very poor shape."

More enemy warships were spotted late the next day, waiting for the protection of darkness to make their run to deliver more troops. The force sent out to attack them ran into Rufes and Petes from Rekata Bay flying cover for the warships. Register wrote than night about the fight, in which he added to his score by shooting down a Pete:

> **October 8, 1942** – At 1700, eleven VF took off to accompany an attack group. One CA and five DD were approaching 120 miles away. We hit them just before dark. One torpedo hit was made on the CA. Encountered heavy fighter opposition. They were biplane two seater VF. Very maneuverable, but not as fast as we are. Shot one down and a probable on another one. Came close to getting it myself though. Lost one pilot Roach; hope we can find him. Started back in the dark 120 miles out to sea. Found the field but we had many crackups on landing. Was the last VF to land; field was foul, with only 5 gallons of gas left. Landed on the fighter strip warn net.

Days were indistinguishable from each other as the enemy maintained their pressure. Register flew with the others on October 9 and wrote about the desire for relief that night:

> **October 9, 1942** – Took off on a scramble at 1100. Climbed to 30,000 but encountered no enemy. My wingman evidently had oxygen trouble as he lost control of his plane and dove into the ocean. He must have been unconscious, as I could not get him on the radio. 20 VF came in today, which looked mighty good. No relief, though, yet. Some of the Marine fliers are going back however. We are the fall guys around here.

Admiral Nimitz returned to Hawaii from his South Pacific tour on October 10. Four days later, while he contemplated the overall situation he was about to write such a bleak assessment of the next day, he called for his friend and former superior, Vice Admiral Halsey, to step in and provide a supporting assessment. Despite his own convictions and the evidence gleaned from his visit, he was still reluctant to step in and order operational changes in the South Pacific. He wanted a second opinion.

Admiral William F. "Bull" Halsey had achieved great acclaim throughout the country in the first months of the war for his aggressive actions in the initial attacks against Japanese forces in the Central Pacific, and for commanding the Doolittle Raid. Just before the Battle of Midway he had been sidelined with an attack of shingles that was the likely result of the stress he had been under since the Pearl Harbor attack. He had finally been released from the Pearl Harbor naval hospital where he was treated for the malady while Nimitz was returning from the South Pacific. His assessment of the situation would be important.

VMF-223's exhausted fliers took off for what turned out to be their last mission from Henderson Field on October 10. Squadron leader Smith led seven Wildcats to escort SBDs and TBFs to New Georgia where more enemy ships had been spotted. Halfway there Smith happened to look back and see 15 Rufe and Pete floatplanes closing on his formation. He called a warning and reversed course; the other six followed. Spotting the oncoming Americans, the enemy formation turned to flee, but the Wildcats caught up and shot down six Petes and three Rufes. Smith's Rufe was his final victory, giving him a total of 19 to make him the leading Marine ace to that point in the war.

October 11 saw the first involvement of the A6M3 Model 32 Zero fighter, known to the Allies as "Hamps" since it was believed they were an altogether different type due to their clipped wing tips. The A6M3 Model 32 used a Sakae 21 engine providing 1,130hp. Due to weight differences with the new engine, the main tank was reduced from the A6M2's 137 gallons to 120; with the A6M2 barely able to operate over Guadalcanal from Rabaul, the new Zero had been unable to take part in the battle until the emergency field at Buin was expanded to allow a permanent force to be based there. This allowed the "Hamp" finally to reach Guadalcanal. Unfortunately for the Japanese, the October 11 sweep of 17 fighters was identified as a fighter sweep by the coastwatchers as they passed over New Georgia, and they were unable to entice any defenders into the air.

A second strike of 55 Bettys and 30 A6M2 Zeros that arrived 55 minutes later did meet American opposition. The enemy recorded that one G4M was shot down while claiming two Wildcats. Bob Galer's VMF-224 pilots claimed seven Bettys and four Zeros. Neither attack inflicted serious damage, but the 11th Air Fleet's two strikes were meant to cover the approach of a major reinforcement effort, and they were successful in delaying the launch of midday scouting flights that could have discovered the oncoming fleet.

Savo Island victor Vice Admiral Gunichi Mikawa's Eighth Fleet had been ordered to make a supply run to Guadalcanal the night of October 11–12. The Reinforcement Group included the seaplane carriers *Chitose* and *Nisshin*, which carried 728 soldiers along with four large howitzers, two field guns, one antiaircraft gun, and ammunition. The force was commanded by Rear Admiral Takatsugu Jojima and included the destroyers *Asagumo*, *Natsugumo*, *Yamagumo*, *Shirayuki*, and *Murakumo* carrying additional troops, covered by *Akizuki*. Rear Admiral Aritomo Gotō's veteran heavy cruisers *Aoba*, *Kinugasa*, and *Furutaka* from Mikawa's force were assigned as cover in case the Americans mounted any opposition, since there had been no effort to interdict operations by any "Tokyo Express" mission since the campaign had commenced.

Jojima's Reinforcement Group had departed the Shortlands anchorage at 0800 hours to start their 250-mile run down the Slot to Guadalcanal. Admiral Gotō departed the Shortlands at 1400 hours that afternoon. To protect them from Cactus-based strikes, the ships were covered by revolving flights of Hamps from Buin; the last flight of the day being ordered to remain on station until sunset, then ditch their aircraft and wait for pickup. All six pilots did as ordered, but only one pilot was found and recovered in the dark waters.

Even though the Henderson flights had been delayed, Jojima's force was spotted by a VP-23 PBY at 1445 hours, 210 miles north of Guadalcanal between Kolombangara and Choiseul islands. The sighting report identified the enemy ships as two "cruisers" and six destroyers. Unfortunately, Gotō's heavy force was not sighted.

With US intelligence indicating that a major reinforcement effort would come in early October, Rear Admiral Norman Scott's Task Force 64, composed of heavy cruisers *San Francisco* (CA-38) and *Salt Lake City* (CA-25), light cruisers *Boise* (CL-47) and *Helena* (CL-50), and destroyers *Farenholt* (DD-491), *Duncan* (DD-485), *Buchanan* (DD-484), *McCalla* (DD-488), and *Laffey* (DD-459), had taken station south of Guadalcanal near Rennell Island on October 9. Scott, an experienced surface warfare commander who had commanded the fire support group in the August invasion, where he saw Japanese night combat capabilities first-hand at Savo Island, had drilled the fleet and conducted a full-scale night battle practice on October 8. Task Force 64 did not possess his opponent's experience of night fighting, but it would be the best-trained American combat unit to fight in the Guadalcanal campaign.

That evening, Lieutenant (jg) Register wrote:

October 11, 1942 – Was grounded by the doctor today. Asked the Captain to let me fly but he wouldn't. Doctor recommended and said I needed a two months rest. Guess I'm in worse shape than I thought. Still think I could fly though. Will try and get flying in a few days. Two Jap CA and 6 DD are approaching. We have a task force close that's supposed to intercept them. Will probably catch hell again as usual.

That night, the Navy fought the Battle of Cape Esperance, the first time the Imperial Navy was defeated in a night engagement. The battle occurred at the entrance to the strait between Savo and Guadalcanal, just to Cape Esperance.

When he received the PBY report at 1607 hours, Scott turned his force toward Guadalcanal to intercept the enemy. His plan for the engagement had his force in column formation with the destroyers at the front and rear of the cruisers. *Helena* and *Boise* would use their superior SG surface radar to gain position advantage. Once engaged, the destroyers were to illuminate the enemy with searchlights and fire torpedoes while the cruisers opened fire as soon as the enemy was spotted.

Task Force 64 passed Cape Esperance at 2233 hours, and assumed battle formation with *Farenholt, Duncan,* and *Laffey* in the lead, followed by Scott's flagship *San Francisco, Boise, Salt Lake City,* and *Helena,* while *Buchanan* and *McCalla* were in the rear. With the moon having already set, visibility in Ironbottom Sound was poor with no ambient light and no visible horizon. At almost the same moment, Jojima's ships rounded

Cape Hunter; at 2200 hours, Jojima had informed Gotō there were no American ships present. The Reinforcement Group proceeded to the usual unloading point east of the Matanikau River. At 2300 hours the floatplane launched by *San Francisco* spotted Jojima's ships and reported them to Scott. Men aboard the ships heard the plane, but no warning was sent to Gotō.

Gotō's cruisers increased speed to 30 knots as they approached Guadalcanal and passed through several rain squalls in the sound. *Aoba* led, followed by *Furutaka* and *Kinugasa*, with destroyers *Fubuki* to starboard and *Hatsuyuki* to port. At 2330 hours, they emerged from a rain squall and were picked up on radar by *Helena* and *Salt Lake City*. Admiral Gotō was unaware that he was headed straight at the Americans, who were positioned to cross the enemy's "T."

Helena's radar showed the enemy 27,700 yards distant at 2332 hours. Scott ordered his ships to turn to 230 degrees as a column movement at 2333 hours, but the lack of American night combat experience led to a mistake. The three lead destroyers executed the movement correctly, but *San Francisco* incorrectly turned simultaneously, followed by *Boise*. This threw the three lead destroyers out of formation. *Helena* and *Boise* reported contacts to Scott at 2342 and 2344 hours, but the admiral believed they were tracking the three destroyers. He then asked *Farenholt* if it was attempting to resume station, to which it replied, "Affirmative, coming up on your starboard side." Scott now believed the reported contacts were friendly.

Farenholt and *Laffey*, unaware of the approaching enemy, increased speed at 2345 hours to resume station. *Duncan's* captain, who had the enemy on radar, thought they were attacking and increased speed to launch a solitary torpedo attack without telling Scott what he was doing. *San Francisco's* SC radar finally spotted the enemy, but Scott was not informed. Gotō's ships were 5,000 yards distant and visible to lookouts aboard *Helena* and *Salt Lake City*. At this point, Scott was in position to cross the enemy's "T." *Helena* asked permission to open fire at 2346 hours, using the general procedure request, "Interrogatory Roger" ("Are we clear to act?"). Scott answered "Roger," meaning message received, not permission to act. *Helena* opened fire, quickly followed by *Boise*, *Salt Lake City*, and *San Francisco*, to Scott's surprise.

The Japanese were taken by surprise. When *Aoba's* lookouts had sighted Scott's force at 2343 hours, Gotō assumed they were Jojima's force. At 2345, when the ships were identified as American, the admiral ordered his ships to flash identification signals. *Aoba* flashed its lights just as the first American salvo smashed into the superstructure; the cruiser was quickly hit by 40 shells from *Helena, Salt Lake City, San Francisco, Farenholt,* and *Laffey* that damaged the radio and demolished two main gun turrets and the main gun director. Several large-caliber projectiles passed through the flag bridge without exploding; the force of their passage killed many and mortally wounded Gotō.

Fearing his ships were firing on each other, Scott ordered cease fire at 2347 hours. When *Farenholt* flashed its recognition signal, he finally realized the destroyers were back in position and ordered fire resumed at 2351 hours. Taking more hits, *Aoba* turned to starboard to get away and made smoke; thinking the cruiser was sinking, the Americans shifted fire to *Furutaka*; the ship's torpedo tubes were hit at 2349 hours, starting a large fire. At 2358 hours a torpedo fired by *Buchanan* hit in the forward engine room. *San Francisco* and *Boise* sighted *Fubuki* and raked the ship with fire; heavily damaged, the cruiser began to sink. Quickly turning to port, *Kinugasa* and *Hatsuyuki* escaped immediate attention.

During this exchange, *Farenholt* took several hits from both Japanese and American ships, killing several crewmen. The destroyer passed to the disengaged side of the American column, escaping further damage. When *Duncan* executed the planned solo torpedo attack, the ship was hit by gunfire from both sides and set afire, turning away to escape.

Gotō's ships attempted to escape, but Scott's force tightened formation and pursued the retreating enemy. At 0006 hours, *Kinugasa* fired two torpedoes which just missed *Boise. Salt Lake City* and *Boise* turned on their searchlights, giving *Kinugasa's* gunners clear targets. At 0010, two shells from *Kinugasa* hit *Boise* in the ship's main magazine; the explosions killed nearly 100 and threatened to blow *Boise* apart. Fortunately, seawater rushing in stopped the fire before it exploded the powder magazines. *Boise* sheered out of formation and retreated. *Kinugasa* and *Salt Lake City* hit each other several times. *Kinugasa* suffered minor damage while *Salt Lake City's* speed was reduced when a boiler was damaged.

At 0016 hours, Scott's ships lost sight of the enemy and firing ceased by 0020. Henderson Field was safe.

Jojima's ships completed unloading while the battle raged and returned passing south of the Russell Islands and New Georgia. The extensively damaged *Aoba* joined *Kinugasa* and they retired north through the Slot. *Furutaka* lost power at 0050 hours and sank at 0228 hours, 22 miles northwest of Savo. *Hatsuyuki* picked up the survivors. Jojima sent *Shirayuki* and *Murakumo* to assist *Furutaka*, while *Asagumo* and *Natsugumo* rendezvoused with *Kinugasa*.

Boise extinguished the on-board fires at 0240 hours and rejoined the task force at 0305 hours. *Duncan's* crew abandoned ship at 0200 hours. Scott ordered the rest to retire towards Nouméa, where they arrived the afternoon of October 13. *McCalla* discovered the burning *Duncan* around 0300 hours but the destroyer finally sank at 1200 hours on October 12. *McCalla* and boats from Guadalcanal picked up 195 survivors. They also found 100 *Fubuki* survivors who initially refused rescue but allowed themselves to be picked up and taken prisoner the next day.

Sixteen SBDs took off from Henderson shortly after dawn to search for any stragglers in the aftermath of the battle. VS-71's Lieutenant Commander Eldridge spotted three destroyers north of the Russell Islands at 0700 hours, two of which were assisting a damaged third. His six Dauntlesses attacked, but they only scored a near miss on *Murakumo*. VS-3's Lieutenant Commander Lou Kirn, leading a strike of SBDs from VS-3, VS-71, and VMSB-241, and TBFs from VT-8, with a strong Wildcat escort, spotted the destroyers *Murakumo*, *Asagumo*, and *Natsugumo* at 0800 hours. The Wildcats strafed before the dive bombers attacked. Three bombs near-missed *Murakumo*, setting the destroyer up for the Avengers. One torpedo brought *Murakomo* to a stop and the ship sank that afternoon. Eleven SBDs and TBFs escorted by 14 F4Fs found and attacked *Asagumo* and *Natsugumo* at 1545 hours. One SBD hit *Natsugumo* amidships while two near misses created severe damage. After *Asagumo* took off survivors, *Natsugumo* sank at 1627 hours. *Murakumo* was hit again and set afire. *Shirayuki* scuttled the destroyer with a torpedo after the crew abandoned ship.

Although the bombardment mission had failed, Jojima's force had successfully delivered the men and equipment. *Aoba* returned to the Imperial Navy base at Kure, Japan; the ship was repaired by February 15, 1943.

Admiral Scott's claim that Task Force 64 had sunk three enemy cruisers and four destroyers was widely publicized in American newspapers. *Boise* required a trip to the Philadelphia Naval Shipyard for repair, where the cruiser was dubbed "the one-ship fleet" in the press and was under repair until March 20, 1943.

Cape Esperance was a tactical victory, but it had little strategic effect on the overall situation. Unfortunately, the victory prevented an accurate assessment of the enemy's night fighting skill. There was no knowledge of the range and power of the Type 93 torpedo, how effective Japanese night optics were, or the fighting ability of Japanese destroyer and cruiser commanders. Instead there was an incorrect belief that radar-directed American naval gunfire was superior to Japanese torpedo attacks. After the battle, a junior officer aboard *Helena* wrote, "Cape Esperance was a three-sided battle in which chance was the major winner."

The day of October 12 saw the survivors of VMF-223 climb aboard an R4D headed for Espiritu Santo. Over their seven-week tour, the squadron claimed 110 victories, including 47 Zeros and 47 Bettys. John L. Smith was credited with ten Bettys while Marion Carl claimed eight, to give both pilots more Japanese bombers in their scores than any other Marine pilots during the war. Nineteen pilots had landed at Henderson Field on August 20; ten paid the ultimate price.

That night, Cash Register wrote:

October 12, 1942 – The Japs turned the trick on us again. We lost two destroyers and a CA damaged. No damage to them as I've heard. This could be wrong though. The Air Force here got them today though. Two DD and one CL. We left 50 men in the water all day and will have to stay there tonight due to the inefficiency of the men in command here.

The next day, VMSB-232, which had arrived on Guadalcanal on August 20, was relieved and the survivors were flown back to Espiritu Santo. The report of Marine Air Group 23's medical officer on the status of the squadron's pilots after seven weeks of combat is a good portrait of what all the aviation personnel faced: of the 15 pilots who had landed at Henderson on August 20, seven had been killed in action, four were wounded, and two were evacuated due to extreme mental and physical fatigue prior to the squadron's final relief. Only three came through without being wounded, though the flight surgeon stated they required prolonged rest due to their mental and physical states. Squadron commander Dick Mangrum recalled:

It was extremely hard on men and equipment. I lost most of my squadron, some to combat in the air, some to shelling on the ground, one to an accident, one to an unfortunate occurrence where ships in the harbor became panicky and somebody shouted, "Enemy aircraft!" and it was one of my planes, and they shot him down. These things happen in war. In short, my unit, my squadron was pretty well used up.

Mangrum was the only one of the three unwounded survivors who was able to climb aboard the R4D on his own. For his service, the skipper received the Navy Cross and the first Distinguished Flying Cross awarded for action at Guadalcanal.

That night, Register wrote in his diary:

October 13, 1942 – learned this morning that three other fellows and myself are to be evacuated tomorrow. They seem to think we are too exhausted and run down to fly. Still believe I'm all right; am the same as before. The doctor found out about my neck and said I was through for awhile. Had the worst raid we have ever had today. 22 bombers came over with us not making interception. They hit the runway and surrounding area very hard. The earth shook and the air howled. An hour later 13 came over and hit us worse. We lost many planes and a lot of material. Runway is in very poor shape. If there ever was a hell on earth, this was it today.

Register was premature in his belief that he had seen the worst. That night, an event took place which every man present would later remember as their single most terrifying experience in all their time on Guadalcanal; it was known universally by the survivors as "the Bombardment."

At 1830 hours, the 150mm howitzers that had been landed on October 11–12 opened up from their position near Cape Esperance. At approximately 1930 hours, "Washing Machine Charlie" arrived and dropped flares for the barrage. At 0130 hours on October 14, "Louie the Louse," the name given a Japanese night-heckler seaplane flown from Rekata Bay, dropped anti-personnel bombs on the field, then dropped a red flare over the west end of the field, a white flare in the middle, and a green flare over the eastern end.

Unknown to the Americans, Vice Admiral Takeo Kurita's battleships *Kongō* and *Haruna* had taken position offshore. Each ship had a main armament of eight 14-inch naval cannons and a secondary battery of multiple 6-inch guns. For this mission, they were armed with special very high-explosive ammunition. At 0138 hours, they opened a barrage that lasted a terrifying 97 minutes. The 900 high-explosive 14-inch shells wreaked destruction throughout the Marine positions. The earth shook and palm trees were splintered. Buildings were set afire and knocked down, while the fuel dump caught fire. Henderson seemed to be a sea of flame. Sergeant James Eaton later recalled the night as the most terrifying in his 20-year Marine career: "Those shells sounded like express trains as they came in, and the ground shook like an earthquake with each explosion." More than 40 Marines were killed. After the battleships departed around 0300 hours, the Army artillery – which had already been nicknamed "Pistol Pete" – resumed their barrage until shortly before first light.

Dawn revealed greater wreckage than anyone imagined possible. The airfield was a shambles, the pierced-steel planking (PSP) on the runway was reduced to tangled, twisted steel. The Pagoda had to be bulldozed before it fell over on its own. Fortunately, the enemy had concentrated on Henderson, leaving Fighter One alone. Thirty Wildcats were still operational, but 39 SBDs at Henderson were either destroyed or so badly damaged they were unflyable, leaving only seven others capable of flying; all the Avengers were gone. Major Bell, VMSB-141's newly arrived commander, his XO, the senior division leader, and two other squadron pilots were among the dead; there was no pilot in the squadron over the rank of second lieutenant left alive. VS-71's Lieutenant W.P. Kephart was also among the dead. Radio communication was wiped out and nearly all the avgas had been set afire; the only fuel immediately available was in the tanks of three badly damaged B-17Es from the 11th Bombardment Group that had arrived on the field the day before.

As if that wasn't enough, the one SBD launched for an early morning reconnaissance discovered two enemy task groups – a transport force of six ships with destroyer escorts, and a bombardment force of two heavy cruisers with two destroyers – heading down the Slot to finish off the work begun by the battleships.

During the day, an R4D was sent up to Henderson Field to collect pilots to fly the eight VB-6 SBDs that *Enterprise* had left behind at Espiritu Santo back to the island. By 1500 hours, the Navy servicing unit had managed to get four of the less damaged SBDs in condition to accompany the seven survivors that had been gassed up with fuel scavenged from the B-17s that Lou Kirn led off the pockmarked runway to hit the enemy at dusk. AA from the destroyers provided a good defense for the transports, with the result that no hits were scored. Fortunately, sufficient repairs were made to the runway that the SBDs were able to land after dark without further loss.

The two undamaged B-17s managed to take off shortly before noon. Among those they took with them was the exhausted Cash Register, who made his final diary entry that night on Espiritu Santo:

> **October 14, 1942** – Last night looked like the beginning of the end. A battleship and cruisers shelled us for two hours. Never thought I would live through the night. Our whole area was wrecked. Gas, material and planes were just about wiped out. Shells rained all around us hitting not more than 30 feet from me. The ground shook all through the shelling. Many people went crazy and many were killed. There never was a hell like this and people will never know what this has been. Got out on a B-17; very lucky as the runway was in very poor shape. Looks very bad for Guadalcanal.

The "Tokyo Express" paid a return visit the night of October 14/15, when the cruisers *Chōkai* and *Kinugasa* dropped 752 8-inch high-explosive shells on the field, severely damaging or destroying all but three of the SBDs. Dawn found the "Tokyo Express" off Tassafaronga, unloading the five transports attacked the day before; the Japanese were so certain of the destruction of Henderson that they continued their work in daylight. Major Joe Renner, Henderson's air operations officer, led the effort to get the three surviving Dauntlesses ready to fly a do-or-die mission. The first to attempt takeoff ran into a bomb crater on the runway just before liftoff and crashed. Renner and First Lieutenant Joe Patterson jumped in a jeep and drove the length of the runway, spotting craters. Armed with that knowledge, Patterson tried to get off in the second bomber but hit a crater and turned the second SBD into wreckage. Neither he nor his gunner were harmed and they volunteered to try again. The third time was a charm and the Dauntless got airborne, at which point Patterson discovered that the landing gear wouldn't retract and the dive brakes didn't work. Nevertheless, he continued on and executed a glide-bombing attack through the defending flak, scoring a direct hit on a transport.

By 0700 hours, two more SBDs were reclaimed. Lieutenants Waterman and Finch took off and bombed the ships, while Major Davis led six VMF-121 Wildcats in a strafing attack. After several hours' work, ten more SBDs were returned to life. A forgotten fuel dump was rediscovered, providing 350 gallons of fuel for the Dauntlesses and seven surviving P-39s to attack the enemy troops that had come ashore. Several more piecemeal attacks were made throughout the day, during which the new P-39s demonstrated their knockout punch with strafing attacks against the transports and destroyers. Around midday, the eight SBDs arrived from Espiritu Santo. With these reinforcements, General Geiger stopped the piecemeal attacks and organized a strike. Fortunately, the 30 Zeros overhead made no attempt to attack while 12 SBDs were bombed-up. Geiger's staff pilot, Captain Jack Cram, had arrived at Henderson the night before with the general's PBY-5A. Loading the Catalina with two torpedoes, he made a torpedo run with the ungainly flying boat, hitting a transport with one torpedo before the Zeros went after him when he returned to Henderson. VMF-121's First Lieutenant Roger Haberman was approaching for an emergency landing on Henderson when he saw the Catalina dodging the enemy fighters and shot down one Zero as Cram landed.

Despite the pounding they had taken from the enemy, by dusk on October 15 the Cactus attacks had set the *Kyushu Maru*, *Sasako Maru*, and *Azumasan Maru* on fire with their attacks, which destroyed most of the artillery ammunition they were carrying. The three ships were beached, while the other three transports were able to make their escape with the escorting destroyers. Only 4,500 troops of the 2nd "Sendai" Division survived to get ashore. Eighty years later, the rusted remains of the three ships are still on the beach.

The enemy was persistent. That night, the heavy cruisers *Myoko* and *Maya* shelled the field between 0025 and 0125 hours on October 16, but this was not as successful as the two previous bombardments had been. Later that morning, Bob Galer flew his last mission, to strafe the beached transports.

Lieutenant Colonel Thomas G. Ennis, XO of Marine Air Group 14, had arrived on Guadalcanal a few days before "the Bombardment." He became General Geiger's adjutant after the event when his predecessor in the position was wounded in the shelling. After the war, he related that a day or so afterwards, General Vandegrift held a meeting of all senior commanders and staff officers, at which he discussed the possibility that the enemy would prevail and take the airfield. "I was shocked when General Vandegrift expressed his belief that we might have to make a fighting retreat into the jungle if the enemy was successful, and take up what would have amounted to a guerilla-style campaign. That was the moment I understood completely just how bad things really were on Guadalcanal."

On October 16, Halsey flew to Nouméa to report on the overall situation as Nimitz had requested. The admiral was surprised to find a fairly lackadaisical attitude on the part of Ghormley's staff toward the desperate situation the Marines faced on Guadalcanal. Halsey's assessment of the command's failure, written overnight and sent to Nimitz on October 17, convinced the Pacific commander that Ghormley and his staff did not have the answers to the many serious questions in need of quick answers. On October 18, CinCPac curtly informed Ghormley he was relieved of command and would be replaced by Halsey. It was one of the most important decisions Admiral Nimitz made during the Pacific War.

Halsey was precisely the man who was needed in the dire situation in which the Allies found themselves at this moment in the South Pacific. "America's Fightingest Admiral" brought his decisiveness and aggressive personality to the task as he quickly took command. Word of his arrival went through every unit in the region like a shot of adrenaline. His fighting reputation sent morale into the stratosphere. After formally assuming command on October 19, the admiral's first act was to fly to Guadalcanal, where he personally assured General Vandegrift that the Navy would provide all possible support and spent time meeting and talking with both officers and enlisted men on the island.

He was faced with an immediate crisis. After seven weeks of combat, there was no serious air power left at Henderson Field. There were shortages of everything and top priority had to be given to resupplying the island as quickly as possible. In the face of the expansion of the Japanese military force on the island with the continued successful landings at Cape Esperance, he needed to find reinforcement for the Marines, and find it now. Most important, a fleet had to be cobbled together to face the Imperial Navy, since it was now apparent that their carriers were at sea and that plans were afoot for the veteran force to provide support for an offensive by the Imperial Army that could come any day. Fortunately, the first regiment of the US Army's American Division had arrived at Nouméa at the end of September. Halsey overrode those who followed the rules, who said he did not have the authority to alter the unit's assignment of defending an airfield under construction in Fiji, and Admiral Turner mounted a special convoy that landed the 164th Infantry Regiment on Guadalcanal on October 20.

October 16 saw the departure of two more of the veteran squadrons. VMF-224 finally saw the end of their time on Guadalcanal, when the squadron's surviving pilots and those of Fighting 5 were evacuated. Galer's pilots had scored 56 victories for a loss of seven, with 14 of those victories scored by Galer. Their comparatively light losses were testament to the Australian coastwatchers and the Solomon Islands natives they worked with who put out into the waters of Ironbottom Sound and the Slot in their canoes to rescue downed American fliers and get them ashore where they could be picked up.

Fighting 5 had scored 13 victories on August 7 during the initial invasion, and 64 more over the course of their six weeks on the island. Ten of the pilots became aces. Of the 36 pilots Lieutenant Commander Simpler had led up to Guadalcanal at the beginning of September, nine had been killed in action, seven were wounded badly enough to be evacuated, 17 had been evacuated for pilot fatigue, and two were missing in action.

Between the two squadrons, there were too many men for all to return to Espiritu Santo by air, so squadron commander Simpler remained behind with those who would leave aboard the destroyer-seaplane tender USS *McFarland* (AVD-14), one of the old World War I "four pipers" that had been converted for use as a seaplane tender for operations in the forward area and had been serving as a fuel transport during the campaign. "I remained behind because as commander, I didn't want to bump one of the men from the flight. Also, I rather relished the thought of several days at sea for our return to Espiritu Santo." *McFarland* had arrived in Lunga Roads at dawn with a cargo of aviation gasoline that had just been offloaded. "There was about 160 of us who came aboard, Marines and Navy. Just after I came aboard, I looked back at the island and saw airplanes taking off. I told the captain that we didn't fly for training, and that there was a good chance we were going to be attacked soon." In fact, what soon arrived was one of the biggest raids the Japanese staged in the entire campaign.

Minutes later, as he stood on the starboard wing of the ship's bridge, Simpler looked up and saw Japanese dive bombers overhead. "One of them did a wing-over and came straight at us." In fact, nine bombers attacked *McFarland*. "The captain had all the lines cut to the unloading barge and got the ship underway." Bombs from the first seven exploded harmlessly around the destroyer. The eighth had better aim as the pilot managed to land his 551-kilogram bomb directly on the fuel barge, which erupted like a volcano. The explosion staggered *McFarland* and the old ship nearly sank. "We'd only moved a few feet when we were hit on the fantail by the bomb. Fourteen of my boys were killed or wounded."

The exploding barge was the first sight Lieutenant Colonel Joe Bauer's 19 VMF-212 Wildcat pilots saw as they arrived overhead from Espiritu Santo. They were nearly out of fuel and "the Coach" ordered them to land at the Cow Pasture. Bauer paid no attention to his gas gauges as he tore into the Vals while they rejoined from their attack dives, dropping four in a long firing pass through the enemy formation.

The ship headed across Sealark Sound toward Tulagi to get help:

I worked with others to take care of the wounded. The ship could only use one engine since the other was damaged by the bomb, and we were only making three or four knots. It seemed to take forever to get across Ironbottom Sound and I kept looking up in fear that we'd be attacked again and wouldn't be so lucky.

In fact, one propeller had been damaged, as well as the rudder and the steering engine, which was why the ship was moving so slowly.

We finally got to Tulagi in the late afternoon. We got the wounded off and then those of us who weren't hurt went on a barge that we rode back to Guadalcanal that night. We then flew out in an R4D the next day. I was heartbroken over our losses, after they'd all survived what we'd gone through.

McFarland shot down one of the attackers, but lost five killed and six missing, with an additional 12 critically wounded from the crew, in addition to the 14 dead and wounded from Fighting 5 and VMF-224, with six other passengers wounded. For this action, the ship was awarded the Presidential Unit Citation.

Those who replaced the originals were about to undergo a trial by fire as difficult as anyone had experienced since August 7.

17

SWIVEL-NECK JOE

October 8 – November 12

On Thursday, October 8, 1942, the Bogue-class escort carrier USS *Copahee* (ACV-12) turned into the wind in the Coral Sea 350 miles southeast of Guadalcanal and launched the first of 20 F4F-4 Wildcats of VMF-121. As the fighters lifted off the little carrier's deck, they climbed toward the others that circled overhead and joined the formation. The Marines had only had the opportunity for limited training in taking off from an aircraft carrier, and Second Lieutenant Robert F. Simpson pulled up too steeply after lift-off and stalled out. Fortunately, the Wildcat fell off to port, and the young pilot was able to get out of the cockpit as the airplane sank without being run over by the oncoming ship. Simpson was picked up by one of the escorting destroyers, no worse for wear. Once assembled in formation, the now-19 blue and grey fighters turned and headed toward Guadalcanal, three flying hours distant.

VMF-121 had been formed on June 24, 1941, with a cadre of pilots from VMF-1, the fighter squadron assigned to the 1st Marine Air Wing at Quantico, Virginia. Newly graduated pilots from Pensacola joined the unit, which was equipped with Grumman F4F-3s in July, in time for the pilots to get familiar with their mounts before they participated with the "Red Force" in the prewar General Headquarters Carolina Maneuvers that fall, a "dress rehearsal" for American participation in World War II. With the maneuvers completed, the squadron received orders to the West Coast and arrived at NAS North Island on December 16, ten days after the beginning of the Pacific War. The unit was one of the first to be based at Kearney Mesa north of San Diego, which later became MCAS Miramar, where they trained for two months while pilots were split into cadres to form Fighter Squadrons 122, 123, and 124 of the newly established Marine Air Group 12.

In March, VMF-121 received a new commanding officer, Major Leonard K. Davis, and the Brewster F2A-2 fighters no one had liked getting as replacements for their Wildcats back at North Island were exchanged for new F4F-4 Wildcats fresh from the Grumman production line. The squadron personnel stopped being used for the formation of new squadrons, and Davis set to work training his pilots for the war in which they would soon participate. Davis later recalled that the majority of his pilots were second lieutenants freshly graduated from Pensacola. "They had gone through the accelerated fighter course at NAS Miami and had about 20 hours each in fighters on average." Second Lieutenant Sam Folsom was one of the new graduates. He remembered the early days in the squadron: "Up until July, when it was clear we'd be sent to the South Pacific, the squadron had 40 pilots and only ten planes, so as you can imagine none of us got much training."

By mid-summer, Davis and his pilots knew they'd be going to the South Pacific, the only questions being exactly when and exactly where. On August 1, the squadron's new XO arrived. Captain Joseph Jacob Foss was 27 years old, two years Major Davis' junior. Examining his new exec's personnel jacket, Davis was gratified to see that Foss had 150 recent hours in the F4F, logged over the previous two months.

Joe Foss had fought hard to get there. Born April 17, 1915 in a farmhouse near Sioux Falls, South Dakota, he'd grown up with the hard work of farming the desolate Dakota plains; he'd also gone hunting quail, pheasants, and jackrabbits with his father, and developed a "shooter's eye." Like many youngsters in 1927 who would grow up to fly and fight in World War II, he had fallen in love with flying when Charles A. Lindbergh visited the nearby Renner, SD, airport on the national tour that he hoped would create a generation of air-minded youth. In 1931, Foss' father Frank had paid $1.50 each for father and son to take a first aircraft ride in a Ford Trimotor at Black Hills Airport flown by famed South Dakota aviator Clyde Ice.

Foss dreamed of going to school and becoming an aviator, but that seemed to come to an end in March 1933, when his father drove over a downed electrical cable in the middle of a storm and was electrocuted as he stepped out of his car. Not yet 18, the boy became the man of the family, working with his mother and brother to keep the farm, an effort made more difficult as the "Dust Bowl" took its toll in the Great Depression.

In 1935, the Foss bothers attended an air show where they watched a Marine Corps aerial team led by Captain Clayton Jerome perform loops and rolls tied together. Knowing his brother's desire to fly, younger brother Cliff took over management of the farm while Joe returned to high school and after graduation was accepted to the University of South Dakota. That summer before heading off to school, he worked at a gas station to pay for books and tuition while also saving up $65 in order to take flying lessons from Roy Lanning at the Sioux Skyway Airfield, soloing after seven hours' instruction. At school, he and a group of other air-minded students convinced the administration to set up a Civil Aeronautics Administration (CAA) flying course; by the time he graduated in 1939 with a degree in business administration, he had 100 hours in his logbook.

Armed with a pilot's license and a college degree, Foss hitchhiked to Minneapolis, Minnesota, where he enlisted in the Marine Corps Reserves, from where he joined the Naval Aviation Cadet program. At Pensacola, his Squadron Five instructor was Marine First Lieutenant Marion Carl. When he graduated in 1941, his demonstrated flying ability resulted in an assignment as a "plowback," instructing in Pensacola's Squadron One. After repeated requests for fighters, he was told that a 26-year-old was "too old" for that assignment. After a year instructing, he went to the Navy School of Photography at NAS North Island, after which he was sent to Marine Photographic Squadron One (VMO-1) on graduation. VMO-1 received F4F-7 photo reconnaissance Wildcats that spring and Foss took every chance to build hours in the airplanes. By that summer, the Marines needed qualified Wildcat pilots; being 27 was suddenly not an impediment to an assignment to a combat squadron. With his orders in hand, Foss married his high school sweetheart, June Shakstad, and reported to VMF-121.

On August 25, the squadron's pilots flew their Wildcats down to NAS North Island, where they were "cocooned" with tape over all openings, in preparation for movement overseas. The ground personnel followed. The afternoon of August 31, the airplanes were loaded aboard

USS *Copahee*, while the men went aboard the troop ship SS *Matsonia*. The ships departed the next morning, headed for New Caledonia. The ships arrived at Nouméa on September 22. The planes were offloaded and towed to the airport, where they were flown by the squadron pilots over the next week learning to take off from *Copahee*. Those that had the least difficulty with this were held back to bring the squadron's planes to Henderson while other groups were sent up to the island aboard R4Ds.

The first group to go up to "the 'Canal" on September 24 included Second Lieutenants Thomas H. Mann, Jr., John S.P. Dean, Floyd A. Lynch, Jacob A.O. Stub, and George Treptow, accompanied by eight mechanics led by Master Gunnery Sergeant Wilbur Stuckey as noncommissioned officer in charge (NCOIC). Two weeks later, NAPs Master Technical Sergeants Joe Palko and Alexander Thomson joined them at Henderson. Two days after Palko and Thomson arrived, nine more pilots arrived aboard an R4D, including Second Lieutenants Sam Folsom, David K. Allen, Hugo A. Olsson, Jr., Roy M.A. Ruddell, Edward P. Andrews, Donald L. Clark, Lowell D. Grow, Frank H. Presley, and Paul S. Rutledge.

Squadron leader Davis led 20 pilots including XO Joe Foss, First Lieutenants Otto H. Brueggeman, Jr., Edwin C. Fry, and Gregory M. Loesch, along with Second Lieutenants Koller C. Brandon, John W. Clark, Wiley H. Craft, Cecil H. Doyle, William B. Freeman, Thomas W. Furlow, Roger A. Haberman, Joseph L. Narr, Arthur N. Nehf, Jr., John E. Schuler, Wallace G. Wethe, William P. Marontate, and Robert F. Simpson aboard *Copahee* on October 6. All but Simpson got off the little carrier successfully on October 9 and landed at Henderson that afternoon. The last three pilots, NAP Staff Sergeant James A. Felton and Second Lieutenants Oscar M. Bate Jr. and Donald G. Owen, arrived the next day in the R4D that brought the rest of the squadron mechanics and armorers.

Shortly after landing on Henderson's main strip, Major Davis was informed in no uncertain terms by VMF-223's John Smith that they had landed on the wrong airfield; the pilots climbed back into their cockpits, took off and landed over on Fighter One's runway. When he reported to air command headquarters, Davis learned that Lieutenant Treptow had been killed in action on October 2 while intercepting the daily raid with VMF-223.

Tom Mann, 23, had opted for a Marine commission when he received his Wings of Gold on March 14, 1942. Initially assigned to VMF-122, he had been transferred to VMF-121 four days before the squadron sailed to New Caledonia. As one of the first squadron pilots sent up to Guadalcanal, he was attached to VMF-224, with which unit he was credited with half a Betty on September 28, two Bettys of his own on October 11, and a Zero on October 13. He was thus one of newly arrived VMF-121's most experienced pilots when he was credited with half a Zero on October 18 and achieved ace status with a Betty bomber on October 23.

Lieutenant Mann later recalled his and the squadron's time on the island:

Our fighters were operating from a dirt runway – Fighter-One – with absolutely no maintenance facilities. The maintenance crews can only be praised for the outstanding job they did keeping us flying. Living conditions were horrible: shellings, air raids, snipers, and horrible food. Few of us peons had any knowledge or realized how precarious our tactical situation was. Flight operations on the Canal were primitive. Pilots generally sat on benches or around picnic tables at the edge of the jungle, waiting for a scramble. The alert came from coastwatchers hiding out in the Solomons north of us. We took off when they saw Japanese planes heading down the Slot toward us. It was always a mad scramble, with the hope and prayer that we could get into a decent position to launch our attacks. Briefing and debriefing were nonexistent. It just happened that an alert from the coastwatchers usually gave us just enough time to get up to 20,000 feet by the time the Japanese arrived. VMF-121 could not be considered a well-organized, cohesive flying unit. I had no squadron duties during my tour on Guadalcanal. The pilots and enlisted personnel found their way to the Canal in increments from September on. The last increment landed from a transport on November 11. However, we had excellent leaders: Major John Smith, Major Bob Galer, Major Duke Davis, Captain Joe Foss, Lieutenant Colonel Joe Bauer, and others, who were able to train us on the job and set wonderful examples for us kids to follow.

On October 10, the "Green Knights," as VMF-121 were known, flew their first mission, when Davis led XO Foss, First Lieutenant

Fry, and Second Lieutenants Furlow, Rutledge, Nehf, Farr, Loesch, Doyle, Marontate, Brandon, and NAP Palko to escort nine SBDs on a strike against destroyers waiting at the "bomb line" for their run to Guadalcanal. One destroyer was hit; the fighter pilots were fortunate that there was no air cover to contest the mission.

Once the squadron had their own airplanes at Henderson, they worked hard to learn what they needed to know to survive. Sam Folsom later recalled that:

> The first few days of combat were rough. In training the highest we had ever flown was roughly 10,000 feet and most of us had only fired our guns once in a training exercise. The second day we were there, we were sent on an interception and got all the way up to 30,000 feet. The enemy bombers were at 22,000 feet and their escorts were at 24–25,000 feet. When we dived down to attack, I lost control. After recovering and regaining control, I closed in on the bombers and pulled the trigger only to find out my guns wouldn't fire. Due to our lack of flying experience at this altitude, we didn't realize that lubricating the weapons before flying would freeze the lubricant at this high of an altitude.

October 11 was a bad day for the Cactus defenders due to a change in Japanese tactics that saw the enemy send two missions, with the first being missed by the coastwatchers due to the poor weather. The Bettys in the first raid got past the defenders and were able to successfully bomb both Henderson and the Cow Pasture, tearing gashes in the pierced-steel planking (PSP) with which both runways had been recently covered to deal with the problem of mud, while also setting fire to 5,000 gallons of avgas. Several F4Fs did manage to scramble and Lieutenants Freeman and Narr scored VMF-121's first victories when each got a Betty, though Narr had to "swim home" when his engine failed due to a mechanical problem and he was forced to ditch in Ironbottom Sound. However, he was quickly pulled from the water by a passing Higgins boat and returned to the squadron at the end of the day.

The Wildcats were in the midst of being refueled by hand when the enemy returned two hours later. Fifteen Bettys lined up to bomb the helpless aircraft on the field. Joe Foss led a dozen Wildcats that scrambled to intercept the 15 Bettys and 17 Zeros. In his first combat, he failed to spot the enemy fighters diving on the Wildcats as the others peeled away from the attacking Zeros and found himself suddenly alone and surrounded by the enemy. He scored his first victory when the enemy leader pulled out of his gunnery pass right in front of him, firing a quick burst that disintegrated the Zero. He was almost instantly the target of three others, and his engine was badly shot up. With the Wildcat dripping oil from the windmilling engine, he was lucky to make it back to land dead-stick at Fighter One. Climbing out of his cockpit, he saw the hits all over the fighter and realized he was lucky to be alive. He turned to the others and declared, "You can call me 'Swivel-Neck Joe' from now on." He soon gained a reputation for aggressive close-in fighting and uncanny gunnery skills.

The squadron's ground crews soon learned the problems of keeping their airplanes ready for combat on Guadalcanal. Folsom recalled that:

The climate was particularly hard on anything made of rubber, like hoses and wheels. The dust fouled fuel pressure diaphragms, as well as blower and cooler parts. Operations on the muddy field took their toll on props and wings when the airplanes slid into each other or vehicles. There were lots of operational accidents, and it was a never-ending job for the crews to keep the airplanes ready to go.

For the pilots, this meant that there was no such thing as a personal airplane. "We climbed in the first one that worked." Joe Foss' logbook listed no fewer than 34 different F4Fs that he flew during his time at Cactus.

On October 14, following the devastating battleship bombardment the night before, the Japanese sent an air raid at midday to finish things off, though the bombing accomplished little. Again, they used the tactic of sending a second raid soon after the first. The coastwatchers were able to provide sufficient warning for the defenders from VMF-121 and 224 and VF-5 to get airborne in time to get to altitude. Foss got a Zero while NAP Palko scored a Betty, but Lieutenant Koller C. Brandon was shot down, though he managed to bail out and was rescued. Sadly, Lieutenant Paul Rutledge was shot down and killed by enemy AA while escorting the SBDs that went out to attack the oncoming "Tokyo Express" and Technical Sergeant Alexander Thomson, one of the prewar squadron members who had participated in the 1941 war games, died when his Wildcat crashed soon after takeoff when the engine seized.

The squadron's best day since they arrived on Guadalcanal came on October 17, when Major Davis and Lieutenants Haberman, Loesch, Narr, and Wethe claimed eight Bettys between them, while Lieutenant Freeman shot down two of the Zero escorts. The next day, Joe Foss joined the ranks of Guadalcanal aces when he shot down number five, another Zero, while Marine Thomas Mann shared a Betty with VF-71 survivor Ensign Norman Brown.

At 1100 hours on October 23, Major Davis led 13 VMF-121 pilots, ten from VMF-212 and five from VF-71 to intercept in a mission that saw the "Green Knights" score against the enemy fighters, while Foss proved he had become "Swivel-Neck Joe." By this time the squadron XO had formed what became known as "Foss's Flying Circus," two divisions of Wildcats, known respectively as the "Farm Boys" and "City Slickers." Leading the eight F4Fs in a dive from 30,000 feet into the Zero escorts, Foss demonstrated his "shooting eye" when he knocked down two on his first pass. In the fight that followed, Foss shot down two more Zeros while Davis nailed another Zero and Tom Mann dropped a Betty. Loesch and Haberman each shot down a Zero and shared a third. Lieutenant Doyle scored two Zeros and Ruddell got another Zero. The VMF-212 and VF-71 pilots claimed ten fighters and bombers among them.

As a result of their combat experience, Foss and several other pilots in the squadron had their Wildcats set up so that their primary weapons were the four inner guns, using the outer two for "get-home insurance." He had the two inner guns bore-sighted for 250 yards, the next two at 300 yards and the outer two at 350 yards. While many pilots disliked the F4F-4's armament, which spread the same ammunition supply as carried by the four-gun F4F-3 among six guns and reduced total firing time by 30 seconds – a lifetime in combat – Foss held that with the defective ammunition they were receiving, a pilot using six guns had a 50 percent better chance of keeping enough guns working to accomplish the job.

The "shooting eye" Foss had developed in his youth was never on better display than on October 25, when he claimed five Zeros during the morning interception, while Lieutenant Narr scored a Zero and a

Betty. The first midday raid saw Major Davis shoot down a Zero and a Betty while Lieutenants Doyle and Wethe got a Zero each. While the enemy mounted raids over the final week of October, the squadron didn't score again.

On November 7, Joe Foss tied John L. Smith's 19 victories during a battle with the Rufes and Petes from the Shortland Islands in which he managed to knock down two of the highly maneuverable Petes and set a Rufe on fire. As he turned away from the burning Rufe, he spotted a third Pete, but when he attacked it, the rear gunner put several bullets into his engine. As he struggled with the failing engine, he became separated from the rest of the squadron in the rain and his radio died. The iron rule in that situation was to head for home. Unfortunately, because of a series of squall lines between the location of the fight and Guadalcanal that he had to maneuver to avoid, he missed his landmarks and failed to check his compass. When he finally did take a look, he found he was 30 degrees off course.

At that moment the engine coughed and quit; the gas gauges registered empty. Too low to bail out successfully, he ditched off Malaita, the big island just north of Guadalcanal. The F4F quickly sank as he struggled to get out of the cockpit, having hit his head on the gunsight when he pancaked into the water. The Wildcat was completely underwater when he managed to free himself and swim to the surface. The battle to survive continued, as he swam for five hours in an unsuccessful attempt to get to shore. At dusk, with his strength nearly gone, he was found by Solomon Islanders who were working for the local coastwatcher. They had watched him set down in the water and were searching for him. They took him to the camp, where a message was sent to Henderson that he was safe. He spent the night with the coastwatchers before General Geiger's PBY showed up the next morning and returned him to Henderson. He was back in the air on November 10.

The "Green Knights" were reinforced by five pilots from *Wasp*'s VF-71. In addition, perhaps the most inspirational leader of the Cactus fighter pilots, Lieutenant Colonel Harold W. Bauer, CO of VMF-212, was attached to VMF-121 on Special Temporary Aviation Duty (STAD) for their four-week stay on the island. Born in Kansas, he was raised in Alma, Nebraska, and appointed to Annapolis in 1926, where he received the nickname "Indian Joe" for his prowess as a football player. A member of the class of 1930, he took a commission as a second lieutenant in the Marines. Following two years as a company officer in the 6th Marine Regiment, he returned to Annapolis in 1932 as assistant basketball and lacrosse coach. Following promotion to first lieutenant, he reported to Pensacola in December 1934 for flight training. Graduating in 1936 with his Wings of Gold, he served with several squadrons at Quantico including Marine Scouting Squadron 1 (VMS-1) and Marine Fighting Squadron 1 (VMF-1). In June 1941, he became XO of VMF-221 when the squadron was formed out of VMF-2. One of the other pilots who served in the unit was Marion Carl. At the time of Pearl Harbor, VMF-221 was preparing to go aboard *Saratoga* for transport to Hawaii. The squadron became part of the relief force for Wake Island, but when the relief operation was canceled, it went ashore as the air defense of Midway Island.

Bauer was appointed CO of VMF-211 in February 1942 when that squadron was re-formed after the fall of Wake, and then became commander of VMF-212 when it was formed from VMF-211 cadre, where he was promoted to major when the squadron went to New Caledonia in April. Bauer spent most of the spring and summer of 1942 training his young Marine pilots, who nicknamed him "the Coach" for his unstinting effort to pass on everything he knew about flying fighters. His training was so good that when VMF-223 arrived on its way to Guadalcanal as the first Marine fighter squadron on the island, eight of his best pilots were transferred to John Smith's squadron, while he undertook to give the final polish to Smith's eight least-experienced squadron members.

The "Coach" Bauer finally arrived on Guadalcanal the last week of September, when he went up to see conditions for himself before taking the squadron into combat. On September 28, flying with Smith's division on an interception, he shot down a Zero when the Marines came under attack from the enemy. Returning to his squadron at Efate, he was back a few days later when he flew a second interception with his friend Bob Galer's VMF-224 where he showed that his reputation as a fighter pilot's fighter pilot was well-deserved, shooting down four Zeros and damaging a fifth in a wild fight over Ironbottom Sound. On October 16, when he led 16 VMF-212 pilots to Henderson, the formation arrived just as the McFarland came under air attack. Bauer shot down four of the attacking Val dive bombers.

The pace of combat over Cactus was such that the pilots of VMF-212, who had been sent as relief on October 16, were relieved due to exhaustion and returned to Espiritu on November 11 after Major Paul J. Fontana's VMF-112 arrived to take their place that afternoon. Their commander could have left with them, but Bauer believed he was needed at Guadalcanal and remained behind for the next three crucial days, which were considered the most dangerous of the campaign.

"The Coach" downed numbers ten and eleven at dusk over the Slot, 100 miles north of Guadalcanal on November 14 in a fight with Zeros protecting the transport force from the SBDs that he and the other Marine pilots were escorting to strike the enemy. The Zeros fell on the Wildcats as they were strafing the transports. As his last victory fell away toward the darkening sea trailing smoke and flame, Bauer came under attack from the wingman. When his engine caught fire, he pulled back the canopy, rolled inverted, and fell out. Joe Foss saw him shuck out of his parachute when he hit the water and circled as he saw Bauer quickly inflate his Mae West and swim out of a large oil slick. "The Coach" waved at him. Foss tried to drop his life raft but couldn't. He radioed to Henderson that Bauer was down, then flew back to Henderson where he jumped in the J2F-5 Duck flown by Captain Joe Renner. By the time they got to the site where Bauer had gone down, dusk was falling and they couldn't spot him in the dark waters below. The next morning at dawn, Renner took the J2F, escorted by Foss and five other Marines, to search for Bauer. Despite looking for several hours, the waters of the Slot were empty. Natives from the Russell Islands put out in their canoes hoping to find Bauer. "The Coach" was never seen again. Under his command, VMF-212 were officially credited with shooting down 92 enemy aircraft in the five weeks they were on the island, as well as assisting in sinking two destroyers. Bauer had already been recommended for the Medal of Honor for his leadership and fighting ability as seen on October 2 and October 16; he was one of three Marine aviators at Guadalcanal who would receive the nation's highest honor.

Major Paul J. Fontana, whose squadron replaced Bauer's, was born in Lucca, Italy, on November 27, 1911. His family came to the United States in 1914 and he grew up in Sparks, Nevada. Fontana went to the University of Nevada at Reno after completing high school and graduated in 1934 with a Bachelor of Science degree in electrical engineering. After working two years for the Department of the Interior, he resigned his ROTC Army Reserves commission to accept appointment as a Marine second lieutenant on July 6, 1936. After a year aboard the heavy cruiser USS *Salt Lake City* (CA-25), and another at Marine Barracks, Mare Island, California, he received orders to Pensacola for flight training in January, 1939. Winning his Wings of Gold on January 25, 1940, he spent six months at NAS North Island before returning to Pensacola in November, 1940 as a flight instructor. In July 1941 he finally received orders to fighters, joining VMF-3 at Quantico, where he was promoted to captain in October. After Pearl Harbor, he went to San Diego, where he became a "plank owner" in newly formed VMF-112, taking command of the squadron that May.

Fontana later recalled the summer of 1942:

Just after Midway, we were filled out with brand new grads from Pensacola, who all had around 250 hours total, and nobody had more than 30 in fighters. I spent as much time in the air with them as possible over the next two months. We only had 12 F4Fs, but by the time we received orders to head to the South Pacific in September, they had an average of around 40-45 hours each, and we had concentrated on gunnery training. I was really proud of them when we got to Henderson at one of the most difficult times in the whole campaign, and they were able to step right into operations.

The pilots who had arrived in October thought they had seen the most difficult days possible, but they were wrong. November would see the high tide of the enemy's attempt to retake Guadalcanal.

18

AND THEN THERE WAS ONE

October 27–28

Following the defeats at the Battle of the Eastern Solomons and Edson's Ridge, a fundamental shift took place in Japanese strategy. Rejecting war's traditional principles that the defenders – in this case the US Navy – must be first destroyed to obtain the goal, the Japanese came to see that the key to success on Guadalcanal was taking Henderson Field from the Marines in order to immediately begin operating from the field with aircraft flown in from Rabaul and the carriers against Allied naval forces, which would lead to their defeat. Their reasoning was based on the realization that so long as the Americans held Henderson, they could prevent the Imperial forces from building up sufficient force to remove the Americans from the area altogether.

As the result of this change in strategy, the Japanese began landing General Hyakutake's 17th Army on the island, with the goal of taking the airfield. Despite the US victory in the night battle off Cape Esperance, more than 15,000 troops had gone ashore over the nights between October 1 and 17. The Army's plan was that the final offensive to take Henderson would start on October 20, with success by October 25. There was, however, a fatal flaw in the plan: Japanese intelligence believed there was a maximum of 10,000 Marines on the island when in fact there were 23,000, two and a half times the force General Hyakutake expected to fight. To support the Army offensive, Admiral Yamamoto ordered the Imperial Navy's carriers and other warships to take position near the southern Solomons in order to block any American attempt at reinforcement. The admiral's ultimate hope was to engage any Allied naval forces that responded to the offensive and defeat them as he had expected to accomplish at the Battle of the Eastern Solomons.

The 17th Army's main force moved out on October 20 to position itself to attack the Marine positions, scheduled to commence the night of October 23. The troops found the going difficult in the heavy jungle and in the face of the difficulties experienced in getting the attack force into position by October 23, the attack was pushed back 24 hours by General Hyakutake to October 24. However, the general's order did not make it to all the forward units. At dusk on October 23, the Marine position at the mouth of the Matanikau River was attacked by two battalions of the 4th Infantry Regiment, supported by nine tanks of the 1st Independent Tank Company. Although the Marines had no warning of the approaching Japanese, their positions were well dug in and Marine artillery fire destroyed all nine tanks, while the heavy and light machine-gun positions slaughtered most of the attacking soldiers when they attempted to cross the river. The Marines suffered only light casualties in was later known as "the Battle of the Matanikau."

The next night, Major General Masao Maruyama's main force attacked Marine positions on the Lunga River beginning around 2300 hours. The planned naval gunfire support failed to appear. That night and the next, the enemy launched several frontal assaults on the positions held by Lieutenant Colonel Lewis B. "Chesty" Puller's 1st Battalion, 7th Marine Regiment and Lieutenant Colonel Robert Hall's 3rd Battalion of the recently arrived Army 164th Infantry Regiment, fighting in a driving downpour. The enemy was so close that crews of the 37mm anti-tank guns fired cannister grapeshot directly into the oncoming attackers, while some units held their position in hand-to-hand fighting. Over the two nights, approximately 500 Imperial Army troops were killed in return for a total of 60 killed and wounded between the Marines and soldiers. The next few days were spent hunting down and killing a few small groups of enemy soldiers that broke through the American lines. During the day, Wildcats and Airacobras risked takeoffs from the muddy Fighter One to find their way in the poor weather and provide support strafing

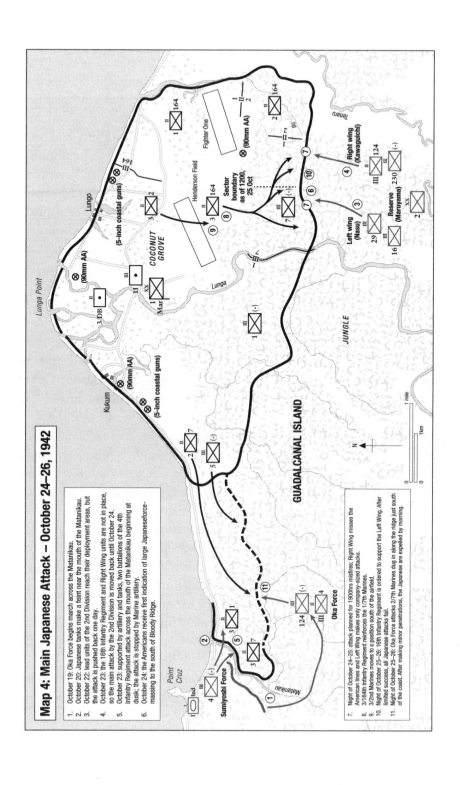

Map 4: Main Japanese Attack – October 24–26, 1942

1. October 19: Oka Force begins march across the Matanikau.
2. October 20: Japanese tanks make a feint near the mouth of the Matanikau.
3. October 22: lead units of the 2nd Division reach their deployment areas, but the attack is pushed back one day.
4. October 23: the 16th Infantry Regiment and Right Wing units are not in place, so the main attack by the 2nd Division is moved back until October 24.
5. October 23: supported by artillery and tanks, two battalions of the 4th Infantry Regiment attack across the mouth of the Matanikau beginning at dusk; the attack is stopped by Marine artillery.
6. October 24: the Americans receive first indication of large Japanese force massing to the south of Bloody Ridge.
7. Night of October 24–25: attack planned for 1900hrs misfires; Right Wing misses the American lines and Left Wing makes only company-sized attacks.
8. 3/164th Infantry Regiment reinforces the 1/7th Marines.
9. 3/2nd Marines moves to a position south of the airfield.
10. Night of October 25–26: 16th Infantry Regiment is ordered to support the Left Wing. After limited success, all Japanese attacks fail.
11. Night of October 25–26: Oka Force attacks 2/7th Marines dug in along the ridge just south of the coast. After making minor penetrations, the Japanese are expelled by morning.

GUADALCANAL ISLAND

JUNGLE

Lunga Point

Point Cruz

Lungo

Kukum

Lunga

Henderson Field

Fighter One

COCONUT GROVE

Tenaru

Sector boundary as of 1200, 25 Oct

Right wing (Kawaguchi)

Left wing (Nasu)

Reserve (Maruyama)

Sumiyoshi Force

Oka Force

Matanikau

(90mm AA)

(5-inch coastal guns)

(90mm AA)

(5-inch coastal guns)

3.DB

1 Mar

11

164

164

164

N

0   1 mile

0   1km

the enemy. Following the battle, the Marines were very impressed by the firepower of the M-1 Garand semiautomatic rifle that the Army troops carried, which proved its superiority over the bolt-action 1903 Springfield rifle that the Marines used. In the confusion of battle on the night of October 24–25, a Japanese lookout mistakenly reported green–white–green flares, the signal that the airfield had been captured. General Hyakutake, who was aware of Admiral Yamamoto's impatience over holding the fleet in the vicinity, immediately radioed the news of the victory to Imperial Army Headquarters at Rabaul. However, within hours, the Army backed off the early, optimistic report as messengers from the Matanikau front reached Hyakutake's headquarters with the real news. In the meantime, however, Yamamoto ordered the Imperial naval forces to swing into action and "annihilate" any and all American naval forces in the region.

The morning of October 24, the "Tokyo Express" headed toward Guadalcanal to apply the *coup de grâce* to the airfield in the mistaken belief that the troops ashore should then be able to complete their occupation. Six VMSB-241 pilots had managed to get airborne in the pouring rain and managed to give warning. Three destroyers were spotted 40 miles from the island by one, while another found five destroyers led by the old light cruiser *Yura* another ten miles up the Slot. Five Dauntlesses led by VS-71's John Eldridge took off at 1145 hours to deal with the second group. At 1300 hours, they found *Yura* and the destroyers. Eldridge planted his bomb on *Yura's* main deck, while the next two dropped near misses that brought the cruiser to a stop. While Eldridge's force returned to Henderson to refuel and rearm, the ships were attacked by a flight of bomb-carrying P-39s. At 1500 hours, Bombing 6's Lieutenant Commander Ray Davis and two wingmen found the ships and Davis bombed the destroyer *Akizuki* while his two wingmen hit *Yura* again. At 1630 hours, Eldridge returned with four SBDs, four P-39s, and three F4Fs. One Airacobra pilot hit *Yura* while *Akizuki* suffered two more near misses. *Yura* finally sank while the other surviving destroyers escorted *Akizuki* back north. Henderson would not be shelled.

Although US intelligence was unable to read any enemy messages, the specialists predicted in mid-October that the enemy was operating a force at least the size of that which had fought at Eastern Solomons, based on "traffic analysis." After the sinking of *Wasp*, only the *Hornet* was in the South Pacific. *Enterprise* had entered the Pearl Harbor navy yard on September 10 and the repair crews had immediately set to work on it, 24 hours a day, seven days a week. Not only were its wounds repaired, its 1.1-inch "Chicago piano" antiaircraft guns were replaced with 40mm Bofors guns that delivered what the "Chicago pianos" couldn't: the hitting power to knock a dive bomber or torpedo plane out of the sky before it had a chance to drop its weapon. An even dozen more 20mm light AA guns were also installed. In the face of the mortal threat in the South Pacific, the work was rushed and the "Big E," the new fast battleship *South Dakota* that was replacing *North Carolina*, and their escorts, departed Pearl Harbor on October 16, four weeks earlier than originally estimated.

Steaming at high speed, the veteran carrier rendezvoused with *Hornet* 273 miles northeast of Espiritu Santo on the evening of October 23. Task Force 17 was commanded by Rear Admiral George Murray aboard *Hornet*, while Task Force 16 was led by Rear Admiral Thomas Kinkaid aboard *Enterprise*. Kinkaid, Commander Task Force 16/Senior Officer Present Afloat (SOPA) was in overall command of the two task forces. The two carriers were escorted by *South Dakota* (BB-57), heavy cruisers *Portland* (CA-33), *Northampton* (CA-26), *Pensacola* (CA-24), and anti-aircraft light cruisers *San Juan* (CLAA-54), *San Diego* (CLAA-53), and *Juneau* (CLAA-52) with 14 destroyers.

South of Guadalcanal, Rear Admiral Willis Lee commanded Task Force 64 in the battleship *Washington* (BB-56), with the cruisers *San Francisco* (CA-38), *Helena* (CL-50), and *Atlanta* (CLAA-51), with six destroyers, ready to move in and intercept any enemy transports. With none sighted, Lee withdrew for fueling on October 24.

Despite the Army's failure on Guadalcanal and the loss of *Yura*, Vice Admiral Nobutake Kondō kept the Mobile Fleet south of the Solomons, hoping the plan to force a fleet action might yet bear fruit. Once again, as at Eastern Solomons, Imperial forces were divided into three separate fleet units. Kondō commanded the Advanced Force with his flag aboard *Atago*, with the carrier *Junyō*, battleships *Kongō* and *Haruna*, and their escorts. The Main Force, centered on the veteran *Shōkaku* and *Zuikaku*, and the light carrier *Zuihō* were again commanded by Vice Admiral Chuichi Nagumo. Rear Admiral Hiroaki Abe led the Vanguard Force aboard the battleship *Hiei* with its sister *Kirishima*, three heavy cruisers, one light cruiser, and seven destroyers.

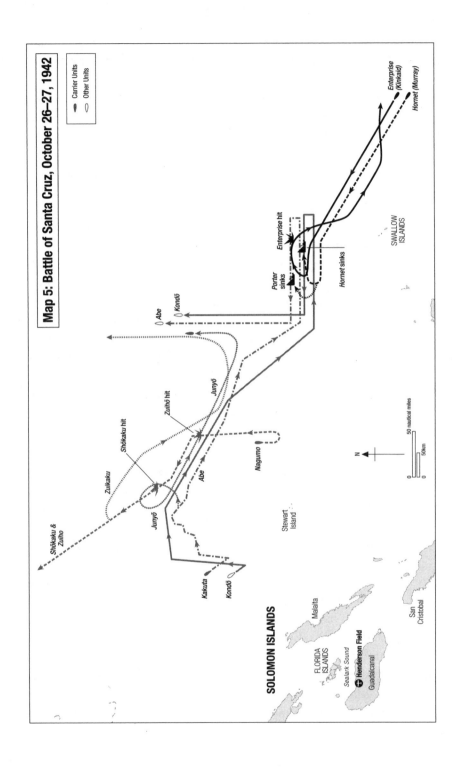

Map 5: Battle of Santa Cruz, October 26–27, 1942

Carrier Units
Other Units

Enterprise (Kinkaid)
Hornet (Murray)

SWALLOW ISLANDS

Enterprise hit
Porter sinks
Hornet sinks

Kondō
Abe

Zuihō hit
Junyō
Shōkaku hit
Zuikaku
Shōkaku & Zuihō

Nagumo

Abe
Junyō

Kakuta
Kondō

Stewart Island

N

0   50km
0   50 nautical miles

SOLOMON ISLANDS

Malaita
FLORIDA ISLANDS
Sealark Sound
Henderson Field
Guadalcanal

San Cristobal

Forty days after *Wasp* was lost, American and Japanese carriers met on October 26, 1942, in the Battle of Santa Cruz, the final carrier action of the opening phase of the Pacific War.

A VP-23 PBY spotted the Japanese Main Force at 1103 hours on October 25, 355 miles from Task Force 61, just beyond strike range. Admiral Nagumo, knowing his fleet had been spotted though he did not know the enemy's location, turned north to remain beyond range of the force that he believed was somewhere south of him. When he received the sighting report, Kinkaid ordered Task Force 61 north at top speed to close the range. *Enterprise* launched a 23-plane strike at 1425 hours, but by the time the planes returned it was dark, and the inexperienced pilots of Air Group 10 were forced to make night landings. The first plane crashed on *Enterprise's* flight deck. Most of the remaining aircraft made it aboard safely, but three Dauntlesses and three Avengers ditched when they ran out of gas after each pilot had taken several wave-offs. Lieutenant Frank Miller was lost when his Avenger sank before he could escape the cockpit.

At 0250 hours on October 26, Nagumo reversed course. The Japanese carriers were 200 miles from Task Force 61 by dawn. Task Force 61 went to General Quarters at 0550 hours on October 26. Fifteen minutes later, just before sunrise, *Enterprise* launched 16 Dauntless scouts to patrol in pairs out to 200 miles, from the southwest to due north. A few minutes after the last SBD cleared the deck, the sun rose, revealing a glorious tropical day: long gentle swells and a breeze from the southeast at six to ten knots, with puffy cumulus clouds and occasional rain squalls. However, with the exception of the squalls, the weather favored the enemy: scattered clouds offered shelter to approaching attackers, while *Enterprise* and *Hornet* were forced by the wind to turn away from the enemy to launch or land their planes.

Both forces discovered the other at nearly the same time. At 0645 hours, the Japanese carriers *Shōkaku* and *Zuikaku* were spotted by Scouting 10 commander Lieutenant Commander James R. Lee and wingman Ensign William E. Johnson. They didn't spot *Zuihō*. The two attempted to attack the enemy after sending their spotting report, hoping to damage at least one flight deck before the enemy could launch a strike. Before they could close, they were intercepted by eight defending Zeros; the American rear seaters shot down three of the enemy fighters and the two managed to escape. As they headed back to *Enterprise*, a *Shōkaku* Kate spotted *Hornet* at 0658 hours.

Each force immediately launched strikes as soon as it received the reports. *Zuikaku*, *Shōkaku*, and *Zuihō* launched a combined force of 21 D3A2 Vals, 20 B5N2 Kates, and 21 A6M2 Zeros at 0740 hours. *Zuihō* was spotted minutes after the strike force disappeared over the horizon by VS-10 pilots Lieutenant Stockton Strong and Ensign Charles Irvine. After quickly reporting the sighting, they attacked the carrier while the CAP was chasing other scouts. Both of their 500-pound bombs hit *Zuihō*, damaging the flight deck and putting the ship out of the battle, though too late to stop the carrier's launch. *Shōkaku* followed up with a second strike of 19 Vals and eight Zeros at 0810 hours, while *Zuikaku* launched 16 additional Kates 30 minutes later. There were now 110 aircraft headed toward Task Force 61.

Unfortunately, due to US operating procedure that had carrier task forces operate independently of each other, *Enterprise* and *Hornet* launched individual, uncoordinated strikes. *Hornet*'s 15 SBDs, six TBF-1s, and eight F4F-4s lifted off at 0800 hours, led by Lieutenant William "Gus" Widhelm, who was known for his battle cry on climbing into his airplane: "Widhelm is ready! Prepare the Japs!" Three SBDs, seven TBF-1s, and eight F4F-4s left *Enterprise* at 0810 hours. *Hornet* followed up with nine SBDs, eight TBF-1s, and seven F4F-4s 30 minutes later. Because of the extreme range, the aircraft were unable to waste valuable gasoline and time assembling their forces. The result was the most disorganized US Navy air strike of the war.

The two American carriers and their 169 aircraft faced four Japanese carriers: the now-damaged *Zuihō*, as well as *Shōkaku*, *Zuikaku*, and *Junyō*, carrying 212 aircraft, accompanied by a potent surface force of four battleships and eight heavy cruisers.

At 0830 hours, the opposing formations sighted each other. *Enterprise*'s group was attacked by *Zuihō*'s nine Zeros while they were climbing for altitude. In a swirling fight, four Zeros, three Wildcats, and two Avengers were shot down, while a Wildcat and two Avengers were so badly damaged they were forced to return to *Enterprise*.

Lieutenant (jg) Clayton Fisher was "tail-end Charlie" of *Hornet*'s Bombing 8 formation. Fisher had been with the squadron since it was formed, and had survived the ill-fated "flight to nowhere" at

Midway on June 4. Looking out at the four F4Fs that constituted the formation's sole defense, he had a bad feeling about the lack of escort, later recalling, "I really thought I was on a suicide mission. I think we all did. Four fighters? We knew they couldn't handle the Zeros." As *Hornet*'s bombers continued to climb steadily to altitude, Fisher was alerted by his section leader to look up. "I looked up and here's this beautiful big flight of Japanese planes – dive bombers and Zeros above them, tight formation, and they went over the top of us."

The Vanguard Force was sighted by *Hornet*'s strike at 0850 hours; ten minutes later, they found the Main Force carriers. As the Dauntlesses neared the Japanese fleet, Fisher's group came under attack by the enemy CAP. The Zeros from *Zuihō* engaged the Wildcats, which drew them away from the 15 Dauntlesses. The surviving Wildcats turned around and headed for home. The Dauntlesses pressed on alone. Moments later, more Zeros, this time from *Shōkaku*, attacked. Fisher watched as a skilled Zero pilot made a high-side run on Widhelm: "I watched his 20 millimeters go off, big blue flames, and he hit Gus in the engine and pretty soon we were flying through his oil smoke." Widhelm's SBD went down, but the intrepid pilot and his rear seater survived to be picked up later on. Three other Dauntlesses went down, but the 11 survivors soon caught sight of their target. Fisher recalled: "My plane had been hit, my gunner had been hit, and I didn't have any dive brakes. So, when we rolled into the attack, I had to go straight down. With no dive brakes."

At 0927 hours, ten SBDs attacked *Shōkaku*. Fisher's bomber dropped like a rock as it shot downward toward the carrier. Because of the speed of his dive, Fisher overshot and was forced to jettison his bomb harmlessly in the sea. The other nine scored six hits that wrecked *Shōkaku*'s flight deck and put the carrier out of action. The 11th near-missed the destroyer *Teruzuki*, which suffered minor damage. The six Avengers got separated from the rest and made an unsuccessful attack on the heavy cruiser *Tone*.

With his SBD leaking hydraulic fluid and becoming progressively harder to control, Fisher pulled out and headed for the nearest cloud. Before he could reach safety, his retreat was cut off by a Zero that cut loose with a burst of 20mm fire that barely missed Aviation Radioman 3/c George Ferguson, Fisher's gunner, and smashed into the armor plate behind Fisher's head. "The concussion in a closed cockpit was such that it felt like I got hit over the head. At the same time, I felt like I had a hot rod go through my shoulder and I was stunned. All the fight went out of me and I couldn't move." Fisher managed to regain his senses, pulled up, looked over, and realized the enemy fighter was on his wing, waiting for him to go down. Ferguson swung his twin .30-caliber gun mount around and fired a long burst at the Zero that chased the enemy pilot away and left the two young fliers to fend for themselves all the way back to *Hornet*.

The *Enterprise* strike, which had been badly weakened in the encounter with the Zeros, had mixed results. With the Wildcat escorts low on fuel as a result of the earlier scrap, the dive bombers attacked the first enemy ships they came across, which turned out to be Admiral Abe's Vanguard Force centered on the battleships *Hiei* and *Kirishima*. Dauntless pilots Lieutenant (jg) Henry Ervin, Ensign John Ritchey, and Lieutenant (jg) George Estes reported two hits on *Kirishima*, but the Japanese only logged them as near misses. At the same time, the five Avengers attacked a cruiser, but scored no hits. Only ten of the total 75 strike aircraft attacked and damaged *Shōkaku*, while two scouts damaged *Zuihō*. *Zuikaku* was completely unharmed.

About ten minutes after the Japanese strike group passed Clay Fisher's formation, they came within visual range of *Hornet*'s task force. The strike had been picked up on radar at 0830 hours, but the radar operators aboard *Enterprise* belatedly identified the incoming enemy because of the confusion caused by the many groups of planes from both forces that were now northwest of the task force. With the enemy planes only 45 miles from Task Force 61, the CAP – 38 Wildcats, controlled by *Enterprise* – had little time to react. The inexperienced FDO on *Enterprise* mistakenly positioned the defenders too low and too close to the task force.

Unluckily, *Hornet* was spotted by an enemy scout at 0852 hours, just after *Enterprise* entered a rain squall. At 0855 hours radar reported that the enemy was 35 miles away and the Wildcats on CAP were vectored to engage. Four *Hornet* F4Fs made first contact, knocking down two Vals 20 miles from the task force. Minutes later, *Enterprise* pilots Lieutenant Albert D. Pollock and Ensign Steve G. Nona each downed a bomber. As other fighters struggled to gain altitude and advantage over the incoming strike, at 0857 hours *Enterprise* turned and headed for a rain squall, where the ship took shelter. In a matter of a few minutes, the single high-frequency radio net was swamped with calls and only a few of the defenders managed to get to the enemy. *Hornet* and the surrounding escorts opened fire at 0909 hours when the untouched 20 Kates and 16 Vals commenced their attacks.

At 0912 hours, a 551-pound semi-armor-piercing bomb dropped by a Val hit the carrier's flight deck dead center across from the island and penetrated three decks before killing 60 when it exploded. This was followed moments later by a high-explosive bomb that hit the flight deck and detonated on impact, killing 30 and creating an 11-foot hole. A minute later, *Hornet* was hit by a second armor-piercing bomb that penetrated three decks before exploding.

At 0914 hours *Hornet*'s defensive fire hit a Val and set it afire. The plane continued its dive and hit the stack, spreading burning fuel over the signal bridge and killing seven.

Unfortunately, the defending Wildcats had been positioned to stop an American-style low-level/low-speed torpedo attack. The deadly Kates maneuvered for a classic "hammer and anvil" attack from ahead of *Hornet*, their 250 miles per hour speed making them impossible for the defenders to climb up and catch before they dropped their torpedoes from 2,500 feet. Defensive fire from *Hornet*'s escorts knocked down several, but still two Type 91 torpedoes hit the carrier in its engineering compartments at 0913 and 0917 hours, knocking out all power and bringing the ship to a stop. When defensive AA set one Kate on fire, the pilot deliberately crashed into the hangar deck starting a fire close to the main aviation fuel tanks. At 0922 hours, the surviving attackers departed. *Hornet* was dead in the water and on fire. Ten miles to the northeast, *Enterprise* emerged from the rain squall in which the carrier had hidden. *Hornet*, afire and adrift, was clearly visible from *Enterprise*: Unfortunately for *Enterprise*, one of the last enemy attackers spotted the carrier emerging from the squall and sent a report.

Among the fighter pilots defending the fleet was Ensign Donald Gordon, a native of Fort Scott, Kansas, who had earned his Wings of Gold at NAS Jacksonville, Florida, the previous March and been assigned to the newly formed VF-10 in July. Unlike many of the new pilots who first fought in 1942, Gordon had about 500 flight hours in his logbook, more than twice that of most Navy ensigns and Marine second lieutenants who had preceded him during the first ten months of the war. He recalled that the day began early for him:

> I was one of about a dozen VF-10 pilots who were carrier night qualified – I had thirteen night landings by then – so I was assigned to the pre-dawn launch on October 26. We flew a three-hour CAP mission. When we recovered aboard the *Enterprise*, our attack group had just departed to hit the Japanese fleet.

Gordon's Wildcat was refueled while he grabbed something to eat:

> I quickly refueled and immediately took off at 0940 hours with Ensign Gerry Davis on my wing. Everything was pretty expedited, but this was not an all-out scramble. Gerry and I were vectored to the north-northwest. On the way, I could see the *Hornet* to my right; she was about 20 miles northeast of the *Enterprise*, and both ships were heading south. I ran into a rain squall and flew northwest for about five miles. At that point, the *Enterprise* fighter director told me that there were bogies at my one o'clock.

Gordon spotted a formation of five Kate torpedo bombers:

> They were not more than two miles from us, flying right above the horizon, and letting down to commence their attack on the *Hornet*. Gerry and I were between 12,000 and 15,000 feet. I dropped my nose to the right and started down in what would eventually amount to a nearly full 180-degree turn.

In his first combat, Gordon came out of his turn and took a bead on the nearest Kate just as the enemy formation spread apart to drop their torpedoes:

> I was at 10,000 feet, so I held my fire for what seemed like ages. I was executing a low-side run, coming in at the Kate from the four o'clock position from about ten degrees above the beam. When I opened fire, I was still about two miles away. Of course, I didn't hit anything. When I got down to about 5,000 feet, I fired again. But, of course, I was still out of range. I felt really stupid; we had been

drilled and drilled to fire only when we were right on top of our target, when it was impossible to miss with six guns. Man, I was *way* out! I was excited. I wanted to kill. I was more concerned with that than with saving my ammo. I finally realized that my gunsight pipper was covering the entire Kate I was trying to hit. I suddenly woke up to what I was doing. I knew that the red meatball on the side of the Kate was two mils wide and that my pipper was two mils wide. The pipper would have just covered the meatball from 1,000 feet away, which was the proper range. But the pipper was covering the whole airplane! It finally dawned on me that I was way out of range, so I decided to hold my fire.

Gordon pulled out of his dive when he reached the Kate's altitude and continued his gunnery pass:

I was well within 700 feet of him, coming in from five o'clock from his tail. My pipper was ahead of his nose, and I was drawing a 50- to 75-mil lead to account for my angle of approach and the difference in our speeds. I was trying to hit him in the engine, but he caught fire at the right wing root forward of the cockpit. I'm sure I got him, but I didn't see the airplane crash.

Gordon recovered above and astern of the first Kate he had tried to shoot, then dropped down on the second-nearest enemy bomber:

This brought me to the same position from which I had fired on the first one. I drew the same lead and fired again, and the Kate immediately started pouring smoke and flame from the right wing root forward of the cockpit. As I broke off astern of him, the rear gunner appeared to be dead; his gun was straight up in the air. I didn't see the second Kate actually hit the water either.

Gordon was three miles north-northwest of *Hornet*:

I started looking around for the other three Kates. I don't know what happened to them. I never saw them again, but I am sure they didn't hit the *Hornet*; if they had, they'd had to have hit her on her port side, and she was not hit by any torpedoes on that side.

Gordon and Davis turned back to the *Enterprise*, which had just disappeared in the rain squall:

> I saw another F4F, which had the numeral 12 on its side. As I prepared to join him, I looked up and saw a Zero just as it made an overhead run on the F4F. The Zero fired, and one of the F4F's landing gear dropped. Then I saw the canopy explode, and then the other wheel dropped. The F4F spiraled into the water. I don't even know if it was an *Enterprise* airplane or a *Hornet* airplane. I was only 500 feet off when the Zero started its run, so I took a bead on it and pulled my trigger. One round went out. I had used over 1,600 rounds getting the two Kates, mostly firing from out of range.

Out of ammo, Gordon led his wingman over to *Enterprise*. The carrier was not under attack at the moment:

> I led Gerry down to get in the traffic pattern. Without ammo, we were no good in the air. As we came around in the groove, the F4F in front of me went into the starboard catwalk and messed up the flight deck for several minutes. As I took my wave-off to the right, another pack of enemy aircraft were coming in and a destroyer on my three o'clock position took a bomb hit on the bow. I got my gear up in a hurry and pulled away, but Gerry Davis never came out of the AA. I later heard that the AA gunners on the stern of the destroyer that got hit shot down an F4F.

Fisher and Ferguson finally neared Task Force 61:

> It was apparent that we would not be able to land aboard with the attack going on. When I finally picked up the *Hornet*, she was dead in the water. It really shocked me, foam all over the flight deck, yellow foam all over, and she was listing pretty bad.

Both Fisher and Ferguson were wounded. The Dauntless was running low on fuel and was badly damaged:

> I realized the plane wouldn't make it to *Enterprise* in the distance. Chopping throttle, I pulled ahead of what I thought was a destroyer,

pulled up the nose, dragged the tail and plopped neatly into the Pacific. Fortunately, we were able to get out before it sank.

The antiaircraft cruiser *Juneau* threw a line and snatched the two out of the water as the ship passed by at high speed. Suffering critical wounds to his elbow and arm, Clay Fisher's Santa Cruz ordeal was finally over.

Having escaped the AA unscathed, Ensign Gordon flew out five miles west to a holding pattern where other *Enterprise* aircraft were waiting for an opportunity to land. He found his friend, Ensign Chip Redding, sole survivor of one of the two VF-10 divisions that had escorted the strike force.

> Chip joined up on me, but his radio had been shot up so he signaled to ask how much ammo I had. I signaled that I had no ammo. He then pointed to the aft end of his aircraft and I checked it out. He was really shot up bad.

Gordon spotted a Kate as it pulled away from its attack on *Enterprise*, heading west low on the water:

> I was afraid he would try to shoot me down and my only escape was to head right for him. I got down on the water and aimed my airplane right at him. I wasn't going to run into him, but I figured I could get past him. Apparently, the pilot wasn't paying attention to what was in front of him. I thought I saw him looking back over his left shoulder at the *Enterprise*. He must have been startled by me when he turned back to face the front. All of a sudden, he dropped his left wing to avoid me and cartwheeled into the water. I got credit for that one!

At 1030 hours, ten minutes after the ship emerged from the rain squall, *Enterprise* turned into the wind to recover the returning SBDs of VS-10, as well as both its own and *Hornet*'s CAP. The flight deck crew worked hard to prepare a second strike, to be led by Lieutenant Commander James Thomas, for launch as soon as possible. Unfortunately, at about 1055 hours, the blips of the second Japanese strike began to flicker on *Enterprise*'s radar, dangerously near and closing fast. Landing operations ceased and the remaining airborne planes were ordered out of the area while the ships of the task force prepared to defend Round Two. With the firefighting assistance of three destroyers that came alongside the carrier, *Hornet*'s fires were under control. Despite the impending attack, the heavy cruiser *Northampton* continued preparations to take *Hornet* under tow.

The second strike force arrived over Task Force 61 at 1105 hours. Judging *Hornet* to be sinking, they concentrated on *Enterprise* at 1108 hours. Due to bad radar information, which had missed the attackers' altitude, the defending Wildcats were positioned too low and were unable to get high enough before *Enterprise* came under attack. The new 40mm AA knocked down two Vals as they initiated their attack, but two 551-pound bombs soon struck the "Big E" with a third attacker's bomb a near miss. The first bomb plunged through the forward flight deck and reemerged to explode just off the ship's bow. Shrapnel peppered the carrier, creating 160 holes between the waterline and forecastle. The explosion set one Dauntless on fire, and blew another overboard, killing Aviation Machinist's Mate 1/c Sam Presley, who was manning the machine guns in the plane's rear seat. The second bomb struck just aft of the forward elevator, breaking in two. One half of the bomb exploded on the hangar deck, wiping out seven planes, while the other half detonated two decks below, wiping out a repair party and a medical party. Forty were killed and 75 wounded.

The near miss created a geyser of water next to the carrier, rocking the entire ship and caving in hull plating by three inches, breaching two fortunately empty fuel tanks. The blast knocked a second Dauntless overboard while another tumbled into the 20mm gun galleries. Worse, the explosions jammed the midships elevator in the "down" position, which stopped flight deck operations. Despite the wounds and a list to starboard, *Enterprise* maintained speed and position while the new faster-firing 40mm Bofors cannons and *South Dakota*'s anti-aircraft guns until the order to cease fire came at 1120 hours, shooting down many of the attackers as they pulled out of their dives.

At 1123 hours, Pearl Harbor and Coral Sea veteran Lieutenant Commander Shigeharu Murata arrived with 15 Kates from *Shōkaku*. Lieutenant Stanley "Swede" Vejtasa had just shot down two escaping Vals from the first wave. He spotted Murata's force headed toward *Enterprise* at 250 knots, ten miles out. With wingman Lieutenant Dave Harris, Vejtasa climbed to 13,000 feet, then dived on Murata's Kates, shooting down five while Harris shot down a sixth before they ran out of ammunition; three more were shot down by other Wildcats. With the two Vals he had shot down just before this fight, Vejtasa had just set the Navy record to date of seven enemy planes shot down in a single day. The pilot of one Kate that Vejtasa set afire deliberately crashed into the destroyer *Smith*, which lost 57 crewmen in the explosion and the fire that broke out. *Smith*'s captain steered the destroyer into *South Dakota*'s enormous wake, which put out the fires.

Murata's six surviving Kates lined up for a "hammer and anvil" attack at 1144 hours. The planes to starboard dropped first. *Enterprise*'s Captain Osborne Hardison ordered full right rudder and the ship combed the torpedoes. This was followed by an order for full left rudder to miss *Smith* and more torpedoes. Moving at 28 knots, the carrier's stern shuddered with each radical turn. The maneuvers forced five Kates maneuvering to attack into a long turn to get into position. Three of the five were shot down by *Enterprise* and *South Dakota*; the fourth attempted to drop its torpedo while the plane was in a stall off the stern – torpedo and bomber fell into the sea. The last Kate managed a good drop, but Hardison paralleled the torpedo as it ran past the "Big E" 50 feet away.

With the attack over at 1159 hours, *Enterprise* prepared to land the planes collecting overhead, regardless of the huge hole created by the damaged midships elevator. After a momentary disruption when *South Dakota*'s gunners mistakenly opened fire on six SBDs, LSO Lieutenant Robin Lindsey only managed to bring a few planes aboard before the ship's guns roared back to life. The 18 Vals and 12 Zeros belatedly launched by *Junyō*, led by Lieutenant Maseo Yamaguchi, had finally arrived. *Enterprise* took a near miss, but *South Dakota* was hit on its heavily armored No. 2 16-inch gun turret; shrapnel from the blast killed one and wounded 50, including the battleship's commander, Captain Thomas Gatch. *San Juan* was hit by a bomb that went completely through the ship before it exploded beneath the hull and damaged the rudder. Six Vals escaped the hail of defending fire to return to *Junyō*.

Enterprise's VF-10 claimed 17 shot down against seven Wildcats lost and four pilots killed while *Hornet*'s VF-72 claimed 28 for five pilots killed and ten Wildcats lost as they defended their carriers through the three attacks. *South Dakota* shot down 26. *Enterprise*'s gunners claimed 46, the record for any American carrier in the Pacific War. Nine Zeros from the second strike returned to land aboard *Zuikaku* in serviceable condition; only two of the 27 Vals and Kates which attacked *Hornet* returned. *South Dakota's* claim of shooting down nearly 100 attackers was initially believed, with the unfortunate effect being that for the rest of the war, battleships would be seen primarily as antiaircraft defense for carriers.

Ensign Gordon received credit for shooting down the first Kate, and for the one he scared into crashing into the sea; the second was scored a "probable" since he didn't see anything after he shot at it. "When I got to my stateroom that night, I found that a mess cook who had been killed by one of the bombs had been put in my bunk. He was still there when I returned."

Lieutenant Commander Masatake Okumiya, *Junyō's* air staff officer, described the strike group's return:

> We searched the sky with apprehension. There were only a few planes in the air in comparison with the numbers launched several hours before. The planes lurched and staggered onto the deck, every single fighter and bomber bullet-holed. As the pilots climbed wearily from their cramped cockpits, they told of unbelievable opposition, of skies choked with antiaircraft shell bursts and tracers.

The survivors claimed that they had sunk three carriers, one battleship, one cruiser, one destroyer, and one "unidentified large warship" while the Mobile Fleet claimed 79 American aircraft shot down.

At 1235 hours, *Enterprise* turned into the wind and commenced recovering aircraft. Ship's LSO Lieutenant Robin Lindsey had joined the "Big E" in July 1941, learning the difficult and demanding "paddles" trade from the ship's prewar LSOs. He was assisted in the task by air group LSO Lieutenant (jg) James G. Daniels, a pilot who had survived VF-6's trial in Pearl Harbor on the night of December 7 when three *Enterprise* Wildcat pilots were killed by panicked gunners who shot at anything in the sky. In the finest LSO performance in the history of naval aviation, Lindsey and Daniels brought plane after plane aboard at 20-second intervals.

With the deck forward blocked by the hole where the central elevator was jammed in the down position and unable to strike aircraft below with the forward elevator jammed "up," the "pack" inevitably moved steadily aft as the *Hornet* overflow meant that aircraft were parked over the "three" wire, then the "two." With close to 100 planes crowded onto the deck, Daniels bet Lindsey a dime for every plane "cut" onto the "one" wire.

Lindsey's sound phone talker reported receiving an order from the bridge to cease the landing operation to prevent a major accident putting the last American carrier in the Pacific out of action. Not knowing if he was about to disobey an order from Captain Hardison or Rear Admiral Kinkaid, Lindsey ordered his talker to pull the plug: "I don't want to hear anything from anybody." He continued giving the "cut" to plane after plane, each tailhook grabbing the last available wire.

Finally, only "Swede" Vejtasa's Wildcat was overhead. Vejtasa later recalled that, as he turned final over the carrier's wake and looked at a deck filled with airplanes from bow to nearly stern, "There didn't look to be any space left, but I trusted Robin, he was the best 'waver' in the business. He gave me a 'roger' pass and I made the best landing of my life." Lindsey gave the "cut" with the Wildcat eight feet in the air over the stern. Vejtasa chopped throttle and dropped onto the deck with his hook holding the "one" wire. Crewmen in the catwalks on the deck's edge applauded and cheered as Vejtasa shut down, dismounted and warmly shook hands with Lindsey.

Sadly, Lindsey's incredible performance was unappreciated on the flag bridge. Non-aviator Admiral Kinkaid gave orders for Lindsey to be put "in hack" – confined to his stateroom – for having disobeyed a direct order. The admiral said nothing to fellow-aviator Captain Hardison, who kept *Enterprise* steaming into the wind so the landing operations could continue. That evening, former Air Boss (in charge of coordinating activity on the flight decks) now *Enterprise* XO Commander John Crommelin brought an "unauthorized beverage" to Lindsey, and asked what he could do for his friend. Lindsey replied that he would love to have the battle flag *Enterprise* flew that day. The prize was delivered the next morning, and can be seen today at the National Naval Aviation Museum in Pensacola.

Surmising correctly that the enemy could still launch strikes, as Vejtasa crossed the flight deck, Admiral Kinkaid ordered Task Force 17 to withdraw. *Hornet's* Task Force 17 got orders to retreat as soon as the fate of their carrier was resolved. Kinkaid made the right decision. At 1300 hours, when the damaged *Zuihō* and *Shōkaku* departed the fleet and headed for Truk, Mobile Fleet commander Admiral Kondō ordered his Advanced and Vanguard Forces to prepare for a night engagement and head toward the last reported American position. *Junyō* launched seven Kates and eight Zeros, while *Zuikaku* launched seven Kates, two Vals, and five Zeros at 1306 hours, with *Junyō* following up at 1535 hours with a final launch of four Kates and six Zeros.

With preparations finally complete, *Northampton* commenced towing *Hornet* at 1445 hours, at a speed of 5 knots. While *Hornet* was close to restoring partial power, the chances of being successfully towed to safety with the fleet so far from a friendly port were nil in the face of continued enemy action.

At 1515 hours, *Hornet* and *Northampton* were sighted by *Junyō*'s strike. Without air defense, the seven Kates maneuvered for optimum position as the defenders filled the sky with antiaircraft fire. Even with their care in set-up, the first six torpedoes missed; at 1523 hours, No. 7 hit *Hornet* amidships, with the sea flooding into the gaping hole. The newly restored electrical system failed again and the carrier took on a 14-degree list. In response to a message from force commander Admiral Murray regarding the situation and with communications intelligence having spotted the approaching enemy fleet, Halsey reluctantly ordered *Hornet* scuttled. As the crew went into the water, with Captain Mason the last man to climb over the side, *Zuikaku*'s third strike arrived overhead. The first Kate dropped a torpedo that scored the final hit at 1720 hours, while shipboard AA drove off the others. As the enemy flew off, *Hornet* showed no sign of sinking. Admiral Murray ordered destroyers *Mustin* and *Anderson* to dispatch the carrier. Despite their firing several torpedoes and more than 400 5-inch shells, the ship remained afloat. Finally, with the enemy 20 minutes distant, the burning hulk was abandoned at 2040 hours.

The Japanese surrounded *Hornet* at 2220 hours. When Admiral Kondō realized this was the carrier that had launched the Doolittle Raid, he gave orders to take the ship for a war trophy, but it proved impossible to organize a tow in the darkness as the fires spread. At 0135 hours on October 27, *Makigumo* and *Akigumo* fired four Type 93 torpedoes and *Hornet* finally sank in 17,000 feet of water. Since the retreating Americans could not be pursued due to fuel shortage, Kondō ordered the fleet north, where they met oilers in the Bismarck Sea north of Bougainville and finally dropped anchor in Truk Lagoon on October 30.

After ten and a half months of unrelenting combat, finally only *Enterprise* and *Saratoga* were left of the seven carriers that the US Navy had so carefully created over the previous 15 years. *Hornet* lasted 371 days from the ship's Commissioning Day and would be the last American fleet carrier sunk by enemy action.

Admiral Kinkaid's report to Admiral Nimitz claimed two Shōkaku-class fleet carriers hit and eliminated along with hits on a battleship, three heavy cruisers, and a light cruiser, and possible hits on another heavy cruiser. Actual US losses were *Hornet* and the destroyer *Porter* (torpedoed during the first attack on *Enterprise*), and damage to *Enterprise*, light cruiser *San Juan*, destroyer *Smith*, and the battleship *South Dakota*, while 74 planes were lost, and over 400 men killed or wounded.

For the Americans, the fact that Nagumo's carriers and Kondō's battleships were turned away from Guadalcanal, which gave the Marines and soldiers there some much needed relief, made the losses worthwhile. Though plane losses were high on both sides – 74 American and 92 Japanese – the loss of airmen pointed to a Japanese catastrophe. Nearly 70 Japanese aircrews were lost at Santa Cruz, while all but 33 American airmen shot down were rescued.

Tactically – and for a short time strategically – the Battle of Santa Cruz was an Imperial Navy victory, but it was pyrrhic. Both *Shōkaku* and *Zuihō* suffered such severe damage that *Shōkaku* was under repair until March 1943 and did not reunite with *Zuikaku* until July, while *Zuihō* returned to duty in late January. *Zuikaku*, though undamaged, returned to Japan without sufficient aircrew to man the air group. Crucially for the outcome of the Pacific War, losses among the elite fliers of the Imperial Naval Air Force came to 148 pilots and aircrew, most importantly including two dive-bomber squadron leaders, three torpedo squadron leaders, and 18 section or flight leaders. This was more than the total losses in the previous three carrier battles. In less than a year, 409 of the 765 elite fliers who had attacked Pearl Harbor were dead, a loss that could never be replaced.

On October 28, *Enterprise* arrived at New Caledonia sporting a large sign that the crew had erected on its flight deck: "*Enterprise* vs. Japan." Over the next two weeks, emergency repairs by Seabees and the repair ship *Vulcan* allowed the carrier to sortie from Nouméa with a full air group on her flight deck, ready to fight. By then, the only Japanese carriers in the region were *Hiyō* and *Junyō*, both slow converted ocean liners. They stayed well north of Guadalcanal, out of range of the Cactus Air Force. While *Enterprise* and her task force faced significant threat from land-based air forces and submarines, the simple fact that two weeks after Santa Cruz, an American carrier was off the Solomons, battered but ready for action, while there was not a single enemy carrier to challenge the ship was proof the battle had proven a strategic defeat for the Japanese.

Having now failed to defeat the enemy three times, Admiral Nagumo was reassigned to shore duty. The conclusion of his report to Admiral Yamamoto stated: "This battle was a tactical win, but a shattering strategic loss for Japan. Considering the great superiority of our enemy's industrial capacity, we must win every battle overwhelmingly in order to win this war. This last one, although a victory, unfortunately, was not an overwhelming victory."

Even more than Midway, the Battle of Santa Cruz marked the inflection point in the Pacific War. Over the remaining 34 months of the Pacific War, the Imperial Navy would never undertake another independent offensive action, and only grow weaker, while the Americans remained on the offensive throughout those months, growing from strength to strength.

19

THE DARKNESS BEFORE DAWN

November 1–15

Despite the defeat they had suffered in the offensive to take Henderson Field, the Imperial Army remained committed to the goal of defeating the Marines and expelling them from Guadalcanal. Another attack was planned to take place in November. Before this could proceed, there was a need for further reinforcements. Eleven large transports were provided by Admiral Yamamoto to move the 38th Infantry Division's 7,000 troops from Rabaul to Guadalcanal with ammunition, food, and heavy equipment. On November 9, Admiral Hiroake Abe's battleships *Hiei* and *Kirishima* were ordered to deliver a second heavy bombardment of Henderson Field the night of November 12–13 to provide cover and allow the transports to unload safely in daylight the next day. There was doubt the Marines could hold Guadalcanal against the coming offensive. The Imperial Navy was known to be on the move. What was left of the U.S. Navy was badly outnumbered by its Imperial Navy opponents.

The "changing of the guard" at Henderson continued. Conditions and operation levels were such that a squadron was mostly used up in terms of losses, exhaustion of aircrews, and wear and tear on aircraft over a tour of four to five weeks. Marine Air Group 11 had arrived at New Caledonia on October 30; on November 1, Major Joe Sailer's 18 SBDs of VMSB-132 arrived at Henderson. The next day, an R4D delivered Major Paul Fontana and nine pilots of VMF-112. VMF-112, VMF-122, and

VMSB-142 were all operational at Henderson by November 12 when they were finally joined by Lieutenant Colonel Paul Moret's VMSB-131 TBF-1s, the first Marine unit to operate the Avenger.

Throughout the last week of October and the first week of November, Admiral Turner's small scale resupply convoys continued to arrive at Guadalcanal. Running these convoys was difficult and dangerous, due to the constant threat posed by enemy ships and aircraft. Because of this, Turner's convoys were limited in number of ships, because they were forced to arrive shortly after dawn and needed to be unloaded in order to depart before darkness. In early November, radio traffic analysis of the Imperial Navy and decoded Imperial Army radio messages revealed the enemy's preparation of another round on Guadalcanal. Halsey demanded that Turner make an all-out resupply effort. On November 11, Task Force 67, the largest reinforcement and resupply convoy sent to Guadalcanal since the invasion on August 7, arrived shortly after dawn. Two task groups commanded by Rear Admirals Daniel Callaghan and Norman Scott provided cover against an attack by the Imperial Navy, while aircraft from Henderson Field provided air cover.

In all, about 6,000 men were to be put ashore on Guadalcanal, including the Army's 182nd Reinforced Regiment; Battery "L," 11th Marines, with their 155mm howitzers; the Army 245th Field Artillery Battalion; the 101st Medical Regiment; 1,300 officers and men of the 4th Marine Replacement Battalion; Company "A," of the Army 57th Engineers; one quartermaster company; one ordnance company; and 372 naval personnel, as well as considerable ammunition. The ships coming from Espiritu Santo carried the 1st Marine Aviation Engineer Battalion, Marine replacements, ground personnel of the 1st Marine Air Wing, aviation engineering and operating material, ammunition, and food.

Unloading was delayed by two raids that day from Japanese aircraft based at Buin and it was soon obvious that unloading could not be completed by dusk. Unloading continued through the night; many ships were empty by dawn, but more air attacks were expected, which meant the force would have to withdraw out of range and return, making it impossible to complete unloading before that night.

The task force maintained battle stations throughout the day of November 12 as waves of enemy planes attacked. Shortly after Turner's transports arrived, Henderson was warned by Bougainville coastwatcher

Paul Mason that 25 Bettys with eight Zero escorts were heading down the Slot. At 0915 hours, VMF-121's Major Davis led Lieutenants Sam Folsom, Bob Simpson, Donald Owen, Joe Narr, Frank Presley, David Allen, Tom Mann, Roy Ruddell and Wallace Wethe, along with VMO-251's visiting CO Major William R. Campbell, VMF-212's First Lieutenant John Sigman, and one of Paul Fontana's VMF-112 pilots on his first mission, on a scramble to intercept a formation of Vals escorted by Zeros. In the fight, Loesch scored a Val while Allen and Presley each bagged a Zero; Sam Folsom claimed a Val for which he received credit for a "probable." A Zero creased Davis' cheek with a 20mm shell in a burst that also hit his engine, but the 121 CO got back to Henderson safely. After Dave Allen got his Zero, the wingman got him; with his engine smoking, Allen pushed back the canopy and went over the side, to be picked up off Lunga Point. Unfortunately, Bob Simpson, Joe Narr, and Roy Ruddell fell victim to either the enemy or the task force flak, and were listed as Missing In Action when they failed to return.

Tom Mann later described the events of November 11 in a letter to his wife:

I spotted a flight of 12 dive bombers at 12,000 feet, starting their run on the ships. Approximately half of them had started their dives by the time I got in position. The remaining six or seven started their dives when I started shooting. I opened fire on the last one in a diving tail position. It smoked, then flamed and fell off. I then shot down the leader of that echelon, then picked up a third in its dive. I opened fire and it smoked and streamed fire. The bomb dropped as I fired, but I stuck with it and closed to about 300 feet. The bomb landed just to the north of a destroyer, and the bomber hit beside the explosion. I don't remember the ship's AA, but they had to be firing like blazes!

As I pulled out of my dive, I saw another one heading north after it pulled out of its dive. I closed on his tail. The pilot fish-tailed as he tried to give his gunner a shot at me. I fired a short burst and it exploded in mid-air. I then noticed another one and went after it. Our speeds were pretty close and it took a long time to close on him. As I closed in I noticed he was really hugging the deck, so low his propwash was leaving a wake in the water. I opened fire and then I noticed another bomber to my left. The first one went down and I turned toward the one beside me, but his gunner opened fire. I got hit in the oil cooler under the left wing and in the cockpit and got shrapnel in my left arm and leg. My throttle got hit and was useless. I headed south toward home, but my engine quit midway between Savo and Tulagi and I made a dead-stick landing in the ocean. It must have knocked me out, because I came to and there was water in the cockpit. I hit the gunsight and broke some teeth. I got out but couldn't inflate my boat. I inflated my Mae West and started swimming toward Tulagi. I was swimming from around 0930 to dusk.

I landed on an island north of Tulagi and two natives found me and took me to a larger island, where I stayed for seven days while they treated my wounds. On November 18, I was returned to our base at Tulagi in a large dugout canoe rowed by 22 islanders. The entire trip was approximately 45 miles and was made in eight hours without a stop. The islanders chanted or sang religious songs for the entire trip. I returned wearing a Japanese dungaree uniform that the islanders gave me in exchange for my flight suit. They told me that the uniform was from one of three Japanese they had killed on their island. The doctors at the base removed six or eight pieces of shrapnel, up to an inch in size, from my left hand, left arm, and left leg.

Mann later received the Navy Cross for his efforts with VMF-121 and for shooting down a total of nine enemy aircraft. November 11 was both the high point and the worst day of his tour.

At 1030 hours, Joe Foss and his "Flying Circus" managed to get to 29,000 feet in time to intercept the enemy, except that they failed to show up. The incoming raid was lost by Cactus radar when it was near the eastern tip of Florida Island. This was because the bombers dived to execute a torpedo attack on the transports. Foss spotted the Bettys low over Ironbottom Sound through a break in the clouds. The Flying Circus executed a wild dive to catch them. As the Wildcats dived into the warmer air at lower altitude, frost glazed their canopies. The wild dive created such terrific pressure that the plexiglass of Foss' canopy was blown out and the walk strips were peeled off the Wildcat's wings. Just as the Bettys began their attack run, Foss dropped into position 100 yards behind the trailing Betty. Opening fire, he set its right engine afire and it careened into the water below. Foss lined up a second Betty but was interrupted by a Zero; he turned on the fighter and exploded it just above the water. With these two victories, he had beaten John Smith's score and was the leading American ace, with 21 shot down.

Unfortunately, NAP Master Technical Sergeant Joe Palko, who had taken off with Foss, was shot down and killed. His Wildcat crashed on Tulagi; when would-be rescuers got to the plane, he was found in the cockpit shot through the throat. Palko had been almost a father figure to the young pilots when they were first assigned to the squadron.

Major Paul Fontana led VMF-112 on their first interception. In a wild fight low over the waters of the sound, he shot four of the bombers into the water before they could drop their deadly torpedoes. The P-39 Airacobras of the 67th Squadron also hit the attackers before they could drop, splashing the big green bombers into the water below.

Despite the intervention of the fighters, both Admiral Callaghan's flagship *San Francisco* and the destroyer *Buchanan* were hit, killing 30 and wounding 50. When a Betty was hit on its torpedo run by *San Francisco*'s gunners, setting it afire, the pilot deliberately crashed into its after machine-gun platform, starting a fire. Boatswain's Mate First Class Reinhardt Keppler led the firefighting while also supervising treatment of the wounded and removal of the dead, saving several lives.

In the wild fight over the transports, the Marines claimed 17 Betty torpedo bombers and five Zeros for the loss of three Wildcats and an Airacobra. The transports continued unloading.

On November 12, the Japanese sent three raids over the course of the day. VMF-121 claimed two Zeros and ten Bettys in two interception missions. Shipboard AA claimed another ten.

Late in the afternoon of November 12, ComSoPac radioed a warning that a large enemy force had been spotted headed down the Slot. These were the ships that Allied intelligence had been tracking. At the same time as they came through Indispensable Strait into the Slot, Admiral Tanaka's "Tokyo Express" transport force carrying the troops and equipment of the 38th Infantry Division departed the Shortlands. It was estimated that the enemy would arrive at Guadalcanal shortly after midnight.

Admiral Turner ordered the two cover forces commanded by Admirals Callaghan and Scott combined into Task Group 67.4 with Callaghan in overall command. This unfortunate decision was made despite the fact Scott was the victor at Cape Esperance and had the experience to command in a night battle because Callaghan was senior in rank by two days; he had never held a combat command, having been chief of staff to Admiral Ghormley. The orders were to stop the Japanese at all costs.

Sisterships *Hiei* and *Kirishima*, two of the first dreadnoughts to join the Imperial Fleet at the outset of World War I, were supported by the light cruiser *Nagara* and 11 destroyers. Fortunately for the Americans, both battleships carried only high-explosive shells for the planned bombardment of Henderson Field.

The night of November 12–13 was the dark of the moon. Across Ironbottom Sound there were rain squalls and thunderstorms in all quadrants. It was perfect weather for the Imperial Navy's night fighters. The American battle line placed Admiral Scott's flagship *Atlanta* in the lead, followed by Callaghan in *San Francisco*, then heavy cruiser *Portland*, with light cruisers *Helena* and *Juneau* at the rear. The inexperienced Callaghan placed *Helena* and the brand-new destroyer *Fletcher* (DD-445), the two ships carrying new SG radar that was less affected by the weather, at the rear, while the others, equipped with temperamental SC radar that would be blinded at important moments by the lightning that surrounded the force, were in the lead. Only Scott's ships had operated and trained together. Worst of all, Callaghan failed to provide his captains with a battle plan.

At 0124 hours, *Helena's* radar picked up the oncoming enemy but it was unable to pass the word to Callaghan since the weather affected radio communications. When Callaghan did get the message, he wasted time as radar reported ships not in sight, trying to command visually from the bridge where he was unable to follow what the radar was telling him.

Abe's fleet passed through an intense rain squall and his confusing orders split the formation into several small groups just before they emerged out of the storm into what the Japanese called "Savo Sound" from the west side of Savo Island instead of from the Slot; thus they entered from the northwest, rather than the north as the Americans expected.

The opponents closed, each unseen by the other.

Callaghan ordered a turn to cross the enemy's "T" as Scott had done at Cape Esperance. Moments later, both formations stumbled into squalls that affected the US radar. Callaghan was uncertain of his ships' positions when *Cushing* (DD-376) at the front of the formation

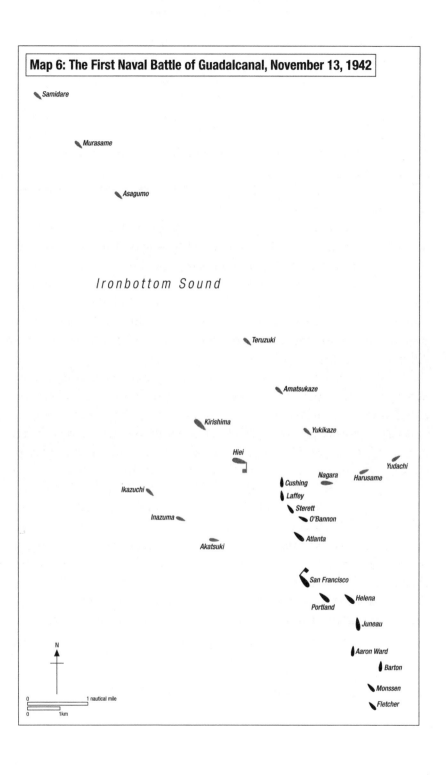

Map 6: The First Naval Battle of Guadalcanal, November 13, 1942

Samidare

Murasame

Asagumo

Ironbottom Sound

Teruzuki

Amatsukaze

Kirishima

Yukikaze

Hiei

Yudachi

Cushing   Nagara   Harusame

Ikazuchi   Laffey

Sterett

Inazuma   O'Bannon

Akatsuki   Atlanta

San Francisco

Portland   Helena

Juneau

N

Aaron Ward

Barton

Monssen

0   1 nautical mile

Fletcher

0   1km

visually confirmed radar contact. Callaghan refused to order "Open fire," fearing that the targets were American. His indecision was fatal.

Both forces emerged from the squalls almost simultaneously. Abe was surprised to discover an unexpected American force in point blank range. Like Callaghan, he hesitated, unsure of the ships' identity. The delay by both admirals allowed the two formations to overlap as individual captains on both sides awaited the order to commence firing. At 0148 hours, *Akatsuki* and *Hiei* turned on their searchlights, revealing *Atlanta* 3,000 yards distant. Ships in both forces opened fire and the two formations completely disintegrated.

Callaghan ordered, "Odd ships fire to starboard, even ships fire to port." The next moments were described by one of *Monssen's* surviving officers as "a barroom brawl after the lights had been shot out." Intermingled, both sides fought in an utterly confused close-range mêlée in which the Imperial Navy's 20 years of night battle training was deadly. All 13 Japanese destroyers were armed with the deadly Type 93 torpedo, and almost all American losses were due to this weapon they didn't know existed.

Cushing took fire from *Nagara* and several destroyers, stopping the destroyer dead in the water. *Nagara* and destroyers *Inazuma*, *Ikazuchi*, and *Akatsuki* then heavily damaged *Atlanta* with gunfire and torpedoes. With all engineering power cut by a torpedo hit, the light cruiser drifted into *San Francisco's* line of fire; Admiral Scott and many of the bridge crew were killed by "friendly fire." *Atlanta* drifted out of control, taking more hits until the ship drifted out of the battle.

Destroyer *Laffey* narrowly missed a collision when passing 20 feet from *Hiei*, which couldn't depress any guns low enough to fire. *Laffey* raked *Hiei's* superstructure with 5-inch and machine-gun fire, wounding Admiral Abe and killing his chief of staff. *Laffey's* No. 3 gun mount was knocked out by fire from an enemy destroyer. With *Hiei* to port, *Kirishima* astern, and two destroyers on the port bow, *Laffey* fought a no-quarter duel, taking a 14-inch shell hit from *Hiei*, which fortunately wasn't armor-piercing. One torpedo hit the fantail, putting the destroyer out of action. As Lieutenant Commander William B. Hank ordered "Abandon ship," *Laffey* was ripped in two by a violent explosion and sank immediately. Of the 247 in the crew, 59 were killed, including Captain Hank, with 116 wounded. *Laffey* was later awarded the Presidential Unit Citation.

When *San Francisco* passed 2,500 yards from *Hiei*, the heavy cruiser came under fire from Abe's flagship along with *Kirishima*, *Inazuma*, and *Ikazuchi*. In two minutes, 15 major hits and 25 lesser ones turned the bridge into Swiss cheese, killing Admiral Callaghan, Captain Cassin Young, and most of the bridge crew while setting fires on the decks. Fortunately, *Hiei* and *Kirishima*'s shots were the special fragmentation bombardment shells and *San Francisco* was saved from being sunk outright. The cruiser landed one shell in *Hiei*'s steering gear room, which severely inhibited the battleship's maneuverability. In five minutes, command of *San Francisco* devolved to Lieutenant Commander Herb Schonland, the damage control officer, who kept at his work of saving the ship in waist deep water lit by lanterns as his men restored watertight integrity. He would be awarded the Medal of Honor for his leadership in the desperate situation below decks.

Wounded Marine Gunnery Sergeant Tom MacGuire climbed down from the signal bridge, where he was the only survivor, to the navigating bridge. Fifty years later, he recalled the scene of devastation: "There was blood everywhere, the bulkheads looked like Swiss cheese. The Admiral died as I touched him. Then I saw someone stir, and I went to him." Lieutenant Commander Bruce McCandless, the communications officer, had been knocked unconscious when thrown against a bulkhead by an explosion. MacGuire helped him to his feet and McCandless' orders saved the ship during the wild charge through the battle. His citation for the Medal of Honor reads:

Faced with the lack of superior command upon his recovery, and displaying superb initiative, he promptly assumed command of the ship and ordered her course and gunfire against an overwhelmingly powerful force. With his superiors in other vessels unaware of the loss of their admiral, and challenged by his great responsibility, Lieutenant Commander McCandless boldly continued to engage the enemy and to lead our column of following vessels to a great victory. Largely through his brilliant seamanship and great courage, the *San Francisco* was brought back to port, saved to fight again in the service of her country.

During the out-of-control course through the enemy fleet, Boatswain's Mate Keppler, who had led the fight to put out the fire caused by the crash of the Betty earlier that day, led the firefighters when the ship's hangar was set afire. His Medal of Honor citation reads:

> Later, although mortally wounded, he labored valiantly in the midst of bursting shells, persistently directing firefighting operations and administering to wounded personnel until he finally collapsed from loss of blood. His great personal valor, maintained with utter disregard of personal safety, was in keeping with the highest traditions of the US Naval Service. He gallantly gave his life for his country.

International News Service correspondent Ira Wolfert, ashore on Guadalcanal, later wrote:

> The action was illuminated in brief, blinding flashes by Jap searchlights which were shot out as soon as they were turned on, by muzzle flashes from big guns, by fantastic streams of tracers, and by huge orange-colored explosions as two Jap destroyers and one of our destroyers blew up. From the beach it resembled a door to hell opening and closing, over and over.

Portland was hit by a torpedo from *Inazuma* or *Ikazuchi* that jammed the rudder over and forced the ship to steam in a circle. As the cruiser completed the first loop, *Hiei* was spotted and hit with four salvoes, after which the crew was fully occupied regaining control and *Portland* took no further part in the battle.

Juneau and the four destroyers at the rear were attacked by *Yudachi* and *Amatsukaze*, which used their deadly Type 93 torpedoes with terrible purpose. *Barton* was hit by two torpedoes and blew up, taking most of its crew down with it. *Amatsukaze* also torpedoed *Juneau*; the fatally damaged cruiser slowly crept away to the east. *Monssen* avoided the wreck of *Barton*, but was spotted by *Asagumo*, *Murasame*, and *Samidare* just after they sank *Laffey*. They opened fire and hit *Monssen* so badly that the crew was forced to abandon ship.

Amatsukaze spotted *San Francisco* and approached with torpedoes ready. No one aboard saw *Helena* until the light cruiser opened fire with a 15-gun broadside that seriously damaged *Amatsukaze*. *Helena* was then distracted by *Asagumo*, *Murasame*, and *Samidare*, chasing them off with a radar-directed barrage that damaged all three.

After nearly 40 minutes of close range ship-versus-ship fighting that hadn't been seen since the Age of Sail, both sides broke contact and ceased fire at 0226 hours. On the American side, only *Helena* and *Fletcher* could still offer resistance, while *Kirishima*, *Nagara*, and the destroyers *Asagumo*, *Teruzuki*, *Yukikaze*, and *Harusame* were only lightly damaged.

At that moment, it seemed that Callaghan's do-or-die effort had failed, since the enemy could still continue on to bombard Henderson Field and allow Tanaka's fleet to land the troops and supplies safely in the morning. However, Abe ordered his fleet to retire. *Hiei* was badly damaged and both battleships had expended most of the special bombardment ammunition, which meant they might not destroy Henderson. The admiral did not know the enemy's losses, while his ships were scattered and would take considerable time to re-form. As they turned back, *Kirishima* attempted to take *Hiei* under tow, but the hull was flooded and the rudder was jammed hard over, which made it impossible. *Yukikaze* and *Teruzuki* remained behind to assist the battleship's withdrawal, while *Samidare* found and picked up *Yudachi's* survivors at 0300 hours before retiring.

Dawn revealed a terrible sight in Ironbottom Sound: *Portland*, *San Francisco*, *Aaron Ward*, and *Sterett* were badly damaged but were eventually able to restore power and withdraw for later repair. *Atlanta* sank that night at 2000 hours. *Helena's* Captain Hoover, the senior surviving commander, ordered the fleet to depart for Espiritu Santo at 1200 hours. At 1100 hours, the badly damaged *Juneau* was 800 yards off *San Francisco's* starboard forward quarter, with the bow down 13 feet as waves washed over the forecastle. The Japanese submarine I-26 fired two torpedoes at *San Francisco* which both passed ahead; one hit *Juneau* in the same place the light cruiser had been torpedoed the night before. The ship exploded, broke in two and disappeared in 20 seconds. Captain Hoover wrongly concluded there were no survivors; fearing a second attack, he ordered the fleet to leave without trying to rescue anyone.

More than 100 of *Juneau's* 697-man crew went into the water, including two of the five famous Sullivan brothers of Boston, who had gained considerable publicity when they all joined the Navy and were assigned together aboard *Juneau*. The survivors were left for eight days at the mercy of the sharks before ten were spotted in separate rafts five miles apart by passing aircraft; USS *Ballard* (DD-267) rescued them on November 20. Both of the surviving Sullivans were among the missing. Hoover's decision to depart in order to save the fleet was bitterly criticized in the press and the Navy; Halsey immediately relieved Hoover of command. Writing after the war, the admiral criticized his own decision, and said that Hoover's decision to save the fleet was right.

The Navy announced that seven enemy ships were sunk and that the enemy withdrawal was a significant victory. When the Imperial Navy's records became available after the war, the Navy found it had suffered one of the worst defeats in the service's history. Despite this, the outcome was strategically important.

Dawn on November 14 found *Enterprise* steaming through squalls, low clouds and rain 270 miles south of Guadalcanal. At 0615 hours, the carrier launched ten SBD scouts to search for the enemy. At 0810 hours, it was decided to reduce the number of planes aboard since the damaged No. I elevator was still out of commission; if fewer aircraft were on hand, flight operations would be facilitated in case of attack. Nine Torpedo 8 Avengers led by squadron commander Lieutenant Albert P. Coffin and six Fighting 10 Wildcats were ordered to proceed to Guadalcanal for temporary duty with the land-based air force. The aircraft were airborne by 0830 hours. Fortuitously, eight of the nine TBFs were armed with torpedoes.

Shortly after dawn, the badly damaged *Hiei* was discovered by planes from Guadalcanal, circling to starboard at five knots, accompanied by the two escorts. At 1030 hours, B-17Es of the 11th Bomb Group made an unsuccessful attempt to sink the battleship. At 1100 hours, the Air Group 10 flight from *Enterprise* arrived over the sound and spotted *Hiei* and the escorts. The Avengers launched an attack from both sides of the ship's bow. Two hits were scored on the port side, one on the bow, one on the stern, and a final hit on the starboard side amidships. *Hiei* circled north and seemed dead in the water as the TBFs and their escorts proceeded to Henderson Field. At 1130 hours, two Avengers from newly arrived VMSB-131 torpedoed *Hiei*, but the ship still refused to go down.

At 1430 hours *Hiei* was again attacked by six TBFs, eight SBDs, and eight F4Fs from both Marine squadrons and the *Enterprise* group. One torpedo hit amidships on the starboard side and another on the stern, with a third on the port side. Two other torpedoes were duds which struck the battleship and bounced off the armor belt. Around 1500 hours, three VT-8 and two VMSB-131 TBFs scored two more torpedo hits, while

Marine SBDs hit the warship with three direct 1,000-pound bomb hits and two near-misses. All told, *Hiei* was subjected to seven torpedo, five dive bombing, and two strafing attacks. In addition to torpedo damage, the ship had received at least four 1,000-pound bomb hits. At 1830 hours *Hiei* was reported still afloat and making slow headway, escorted by five destroyers. By the next morning, the dreadnought had disappeared, and an oil slick two to three miles wide was observed in the sound near Savo. *Hiei* was the first Imperial Navy battleship lost in the Pacific War.

The sacrifice by Callaghan, Scott, and their sailors delayed the Japanese by a day. Admiral Yamamoto, furious over Abe's poor performance, immediately removed him and ordered Admiral Kondō to resume the mission. Kondō was later described by officers he had served with as "an English sort of officer, very gentlemanly, and good with his staff, but better suited for training command than battle." Admiral Mikawa's cruiser force from the Eighth Fleet, which included the heavy cruisers *Chōkai*, *Kinugasa*, *Maya*, and *Suzuya*, the light cruisers *Isuzu* and *Tenryū*, and six destroyers, had been originally assigned to cover the landing on November 13; they rendezvoused with Kondō's flagship *Kirishima* and the escorting destroyers to finish the Henderson Field bombardment.

Having turned back with Abe's decision to withdraw, Admiral Tanaka's transports and their escorts turned south again during the afternoon of November 13 and headed for Guadalcanal, planning to land the troops early in the morning of November 14.

Following Yamamoto's orders, Admiral Kondō, with his flag in *Kirishima* and accompanied by heavy cruiser *Takao*, light cruisers *Nagara* and *Sendai*, and destroyers *Asagumo*, *Hatsuyuki*, *Shirayuki*, *Shikanami*, *Uranami*, and *Teruzuki*, rendezvoused with *Atago*, *Samidari*, and *Inazuma* that evening, but stayed out of range of Henderson's aircraft.

With the US naval defenders having withdrawn, Admiral Mikawa's force entered Ironbottom Sound uncontested late that night. At 0155 hours on November 14, the heavy cruisers *Suzuya* and *Maya* bombarded Henderson for 35 minutes; the rest of the force remained near Savo Island to cover them if there was an American attempt to intervene. Unlike "the Bombardment," this action caused some damage to aircraft and field facilities, but Henderson was not put out of action. With the shelling finished, Mikawa withdrew his ships to Rabaul.

At 0712 hours that morning, *Enterprise* launched ten SBDs to search for Mikawa's force. At 0915 hours, the carrier received a message from Lieutenant (jg) Robert D. Gibson that he and Ensign R.M. Buchanan had spotted two battleships and two cruisers at 0850 hours. In fact, he had found Mikawa's force, 230 miles north of Guadalcanal, and misidentified two of the heavy cruisers. *Enterprise* immediately put together a strike force and launched 17 SBDs at 0945 hours.

Gibson and Buchanan shadowed Mikawa's cruisers force until 0930 hours, at which time they popped out of the clouds and dive bombed *Kinugasa*. Gibson's 500-pound bomb hit just forward of its bridge; shrapnel from the explosion killed its captain and XO. Buchanan's near miss dished in the left rear side and the cruiser soon listed ten degrees to port. The ships had fired as soon as they spotted the two SBDs in their dives; Buchanan's Dauntless was discovered to have an 8-inch hole in the fuselage when he landed at Henderson Field at 1220 hours.

Maya was soon the victim of Ensigns R.A. Hoogerwerf and P.M. Halloran who showed up at 1000 hours in response to Gibson's report. Unfortunately, Ensign Halloran pulled out too low and clipped the mainmast, crashing into the cruiser's port side and setting off ready stowage 4.7-inch shells from the secondary battery. *Maya* lost 37 dead but was able to maintain position and speed in the formation. At 1045 hours, 17 SBDs launched by *Enterprise* in response to Gibson's report arrived and attacked the force. Near misses flooded *Chōkai's* boiler room, while a hit on the light cruiser *Isuzu* knocked out the ship's steering. The already damaged *Kinugasa* suffered more damage to the engines from close misses that also jammed its rudder. The cruiser capsized and sank at 1122 hours, taking down 511 crewmen.

Other scouts found Tanaka's transports at 1300 hours and Dauntlesses from *Enterprise* and Henderson made repeated attacks throughout the afternoon. *Enterprise* launched eight SBDs and 12 VF-10 F4Fs led by Squadron CO Lieutenant Commander Jimmy Flatley at 1412 hours. They sighted the transport force at 1630 hours northwest of the Russell Islands. Seven transports appeared undamaged, while three or four others that had been hit were burning in the distance. Five Zeros attacked Lieutenant (jg) W.C. Edwards, Lieutenant (jg) M.D. Carmody, and Lieutenant (jg) R.F. Edmondson. Aviation Radioman 2/c Colley, Edwards' rear seat gunner, shot down two while Aviation Radioman 2/c Reames, Edmondson's rear seat gunner, finished off a third.

Each of the SBDs then scored a direct hit on a separate transport. Ensign N.E. Wiggins scored a near hit ten feet from the starboard side of a transport. Ensign D.H. Frissell dived on another ship and released at 1,900 feet. His 1,000-pound delayed action bomb struck the extreme port side of the well deck, and likely passed through the ship's side before it exploded in a geyser of water with large pieces of debris. Lieutenant (jg) B.A. McGraw released at 2,500 feet and pulled out low over the water. His bomb hit on the target port side amidships, blowing out the side of the ship, which lay dead in the water. Lieutenant (jg) F.R. West chose a transport that another pilot had missed and released at 1,800 feet, striking directly amidships and starting a serious fire. His rear seat gunner fired about 150 rounds at a light cruiser which had the range and was firing at them. A Zero made a run on Ensign Wiggins as he pulled out at 300 feet, but he turned into the attacker, forcing it to pass by his starboard side. His rear seater, Aviation Radioman 3/c Mayer, got some hits. The last three transports bombed were around 2,000 to 15,000 tons and crowded with soldiers.

The escorting Wildcats strafed the two remaining undamaged transports, which were heavily loaded, and left them burning. Flatley's flight then strafed a destroyer. Ensign E.B. Coalson became separated and was jumped by four Zeros, one of which he managed to shoot down. The strike force then flew to Henderson, where they arrived around 1700 hours to become part of the Cactus Air Force. They reported six 1,000-pound bomb hits on five transports, and that two other ships had been set on fire. Four Zeros had been shot down.

At 1630 hours an attack group was launched from Henderson Field which included seven VB-10 Dauntlesses, led by squadron CO Lieutenant Commander James A. Thomas. About ten miles northeast of the Russell Islands they sighted ten transports and three destroyers. They approached from the southwest at 12,000 feet and were immediately attacked by defending Zeros covering the convoy. Aviation Chief Radioman Gardner, Thomas' rear seat gunner, shot down one of them. Thomas dived on a transport and released his 1,000-pound bomb at 2,000 feet, pulling out at 800 feet. The bomb struck amidships, but no fire was observed and Gardner strafed it during withdrawal. Lieutenant (jg) Gibson's rear seat gunner, Aviation Radioman 2/c Schindele, saw ten Zeros come in on the formation's left side. Two attacked and Schindele hit one of them; smoke poured out of its engine. Gibson's SBD was badly shot up and he went into a spin, but he recovered and managed to get back to Henderson Field. Ensign E.J. Stevens was attacked by several Zeros as he pushed over following Thomas. Releasing at 2,500 feet, he pulled out low over the water. His bomb hit amidships a moment after Thomas' hit. During withdrawal, Stevens and his rear seat gunner, Aviation Radioman 2/c Nelson, strafed two transports.

Lieutenant Wakeham and Ensign Robinson were attacked by a Zero that made a head-on run. Robinson opened fire with his fixed guns, but a Zero that attacked from astern hit both aircraft, which were close together. Robinson pulled away to avoid a collision with Wakeham. At that moment the Zero put a 20mm shell into his engine; it cut out and burst into flames. Robinson side slipped, which put out the fire in the engine and one that had started in the rear cockpit. He pushed over into a steep dive and the engine started up again. The Zero followed and kept on firing. Robinson aileron rolled to the right as the Zero hit him again. He continued his dive, with his 1,000-pound bomb still in place to give speed. When he pulled out at 2,500 feet, he was doing 320 knots, but the Zero came up astern again. He made a split-S from 2,500 feet to 300 and recovered at about 240 knots. Once more, the Zero got on his tail. He flew low among the coconut trees on one of the Russell Islands till he got to a hill, where he was forced to pull up as the Zero continued firing. Robinson dived to gain speed then zoomed up toward some clouds. The Zero rocked its wings and turned away toward the ships. When Robinson returned to Henderson Field at about 1630 hours, the ground crews counted 68 holes in his plane.

Ensign Carroum dropped his bomb at 1,500 feet, and was then struck by AA fire that damaged the engine. The Dauntless hit the water and the impact knocked Carroum unconscious for a moment, but he and his rear gunner, Aviation Radioman 3/c Hynson, managed to get out before the dive bomber sank and reached their rubber boat; however, the plane's tail fouled the boat and took it under. Carroum was caught by his gun belt and pulled down to a depth of ten feet before he could free himself. He popped the CO_2 cartridges on his Mae West which carried him to the surface. He and Hynson swam together all night but lost contact shortly after dawn. Alone, Carroum swam and floated for 73 hours till he made it to one of the Russell Islands. Natives found and cared for him till he was picked up by a PBY on November 26 and brought to Tulagi.

At 1645 hours, VS-10's Lieutenant (jg) C.G. Estes took off from Henderson with three Marine dive bombers to attack the transports. He scored one direct hit at about 1745 hours. By 1800 hours, the surviving transports were milling around about 60 miles northwest of Savo. All told, four transports and cargo vessels were damaged so badly that they sank, four were set on fire and completely burned out, and three cargo ships and one transport, which were less damaged, were still headed toward Tassafaronga on Guadalcanal.

At mid-morning, the submarine USS *Trout* (SS-202) had spotted Kondō's ships as they refueled and attempted an attack that was upset by two of the destroyers, which forced the submarine to break off. Late that afternoon, while the Japanese task force headed toward Guadalcanal, it was unsuccessfully attacked by planes from Henderson. As the planes disappeared, the fleet was spotted by USS *Flying Fish* (SS-229). The submarine closed and fired five torpedoes but failed to score. However, its contact report made clear to Admiral Halsey that there was still a serious threat posed by this force.

Following the initial reports of Callaghan's engagement with Abe's force, Halsey had ordered *Washington* and *South Dakota* to depart *Enterprise*'s task force on November 13 and provide reinforcement as Task Force 64. Task force commander Rear Admiral Willis A. "Ching Chong" Lee, a chain-smoking, approachable commander who relieved tension by reading lurid novels or swapping sea stories with the enlisted men standing watch duty on the bridge, was considered the Navy's leading gunnery expert. When Kondō's force was reported on the morning of November 14 by *Flying Fish*, the two battleships were 100 miles south of Guadalcanal. Halsey ordered Lee to enter Ironbottom Sound and confront the enemy. Only the destroyers *Walke* (DD-416), *Benham* (DD-397), *Preston* (DD-379), and *Gwin* (DD-433) were available for support. None of the ships in the scratch force had ever operated or trained together. After dinner that evening, Lee went over his expectations and explained how he intended to fight the battle. Task Force 64 entered Ironbottom Sound and arrived off Savo Island at dusk.

Kondō's force entered the sound shortly after 2200 hours. Shortly after, the ships were spotted and reported by PT boats from Tulagi. Kondō split his force, sending *Sendai*, *Shikinami*, and *Uranami* to sweep the Savo's east side while *Ayanami* swept the southwest side in search

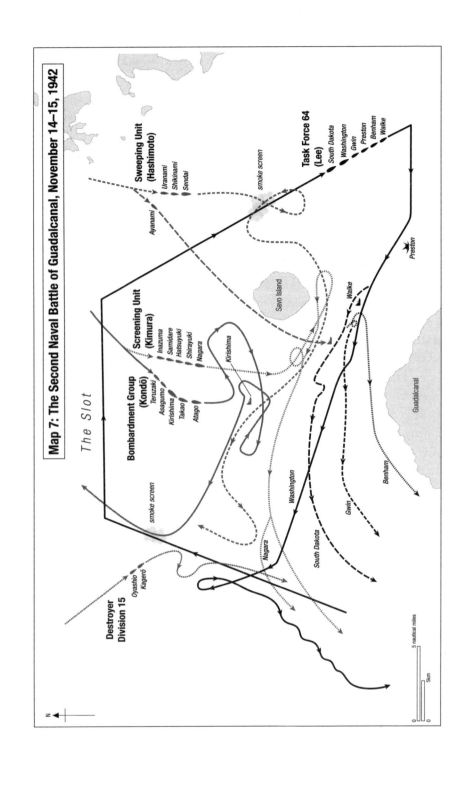

Map 7: The Second Naval Battle of Guadalcanal, November 14–15, 1942

The Slot

Destroyer
Division 15

Oyashio
Kagerō

Bombardment Group
(Kondō)
Teruzaki
Asagumo
Kirishima
Takao
Atago

smoke screen

Nagara

South Dakota

Washington

Screening Unit
(Kimura)
Inazuma
Samidare
Hatsuyuki
Shirayuki
Nagara

Kirishima

Sweeping Unit
(Hashimoto)
Uranami
Shikinami
Sendai

Ayanami

smoke screen

Savo Island

Walke

Gwin

Benham

Guadalcanal

Task Force 64
(Lee)
South Dakota
Washington
Gwin
Preston
Benham
Walke

Preston

N

5 nautical miles

5km

of Allied ships. The searchers spotted Lee's ships at 2300 hours, though they misidentified the battleships as cruisers. Kondō ordered *Sendai* and the accompanying destroyers to join *Nagara*'s force to engage the enemy before he brought *Kirishima*, *Atago*, and *Takao* into position for the bombardment.

Washington's radar spotted the *Sendai* force, but failed to detect the *Nagara* force. *Washington* and *South Dakota* opened fire on *Sendai*, *Uranami*, and *Shikinami* with radar control at 2317 hours. Lee ordered cease fire at 2322 hours when radar lost the ships. The three warships were undamaged.

The four American destroyers engaged *Ayanami* and the *Nagara* group. *Walke* and *Preston* were badly hit with gunfire and torpedoes. At 2336 hours, *Preston*'s captain ordered "Abandon ship" a minute before the destroyer rolled to starboard the bow hung in the air for ten minutes before the destroyer sank, taking 117 men and the captain. At 2332 hours, *Gwin*'s engine was hit and the destroyer was put out of the battle. *Walke* was preparing to fire torpedoes, when a Type 93 torpedo hit the destroyer at 2338 hours in the No. 2 magazine; the explosion blew off the bow. Power and communication failed as fires spread and the captain ordered "Abandon ship" minutes later; when *Walke* sank, the depth charges aboard exploded, killing 80 men in the water including Captain Fraser. *Benham*'s bow was blown off by another torpedo; the ship withdrew before sinking the next day. The four destroyers had successfully screened the battleships despite their losses.

Most of the destroyer survivors drowned when *Washington* steamed through the wreckage of *Walke* and *Preston* while opening fire with the secondary battery at *Ayanami*, setting the enemy destroyer on fire. Suddenly, *South Dakota*, close behind, suffered a series of electrical failures when the chief engineer mistakenly locked down a circuit breaker; radar, radios, and almost all the gun batteries lost all power. Despite this, *South Dakota* followed *Washington* toward the western side of Savo Island. At 2355 hours, *Washington* turned left to pass behind the burning destroyers. *South Dakota* was forced to turn starboard to avoid *Benham* and was silhouetted between the fires and the enemy.

Receiving reports that the enemy destroyers were sunk, Admiral Kondō headed toward Guadalcanal in the belief that the Americans had been defeated. His ships and the two American battleships were on a collision course.

Just before midnight, the silhouetted *South Dakota* was spotted and *Kirishima* opened fire while the destroyers launched torpedoes. Nearly blind, *South Dakota* managed a few hits on *Kirishima*, while taking 26 hits that knocked out communications and what was left of the fire control system; fires broke out on its upper decks and the battleship was forced to turn away at 0017 hours on November 15.

While the Japanese concentrated their fire on *South Dakota*, *Washington* approached without being spotted. With the range at 9,000 yards, Lee determined that the target was not *South Dakota*. *Washington* opened fire on *Kirishima* at exactly midnight, hitting the enemy warship with at least nine and possibly 20 16-inch shells; 17 5-inch hits from the secondary battery hit below the waterline. *Kirishima*'s main battery was disabled and the ship was set afire while the 5-inch hits caused major flooding and jammed the rudder, forcing the battleship to circle to port, out of control.

The other ships in Kondō's force were unable to locate *Washington* in the darkness since they had no radar. Lee set course toward the Russell Islands to draw the enemy away from Guadalcanal and *South Dakota*. *Washington* was spotted at 0050 hours; the destroyers launched several torpedoes which Lee avoided as he withdrew. Kondō ordered his ships to break off at 0104 hours in the belief that it was now clear for the transports and departed the sound at 0130 hours.

At 0155 hours, *South Dakota* managed to extinguish all fires and a few minutes later was back in communication with Washington. Lee ordered the warship to retire at best speed.

Uranami scuttled the badly damaged *Ayanami* with a torpedo at 0200 hours, then rescued survivors. Though badly battered, *Kirishima* was still afloat. Like sistership *Hiei*, the ship's engines still worked, but the rudder was jammed ten degrees starboard. Captain Sanji Iwabuchi ordered the magazines flooded when the fire spread but that only worsened conditions. At 0230 hours, *Nagara* was able to rig a tow with *Kirishima* listing to starboard; it was to no avail. Captain Iwabuchi ordered the emperor's portrait transferred to *Asagumo* at 0300 hours. At 0325 hours, the dreadnought rolled over and sank northwest of Savo Island, the second Imperial Navy battleship lost in two days and the first enemy battleship sunk by an American battleship since the Battle of Santiago Bay in the Spanish-American War. *Asagumo*, *Teruzuki*, and

Samidare rescued the survivors. *Kirishima* and *Hiei* both lie upside down in Ironbottom Sound, only a few miles from each other.

The four surviving transports beached themselves at Tassafaronga at 0400 hours. Admiral Tanaka's destroyers unloaded their troops and raced back up the Slot to safer waters. Aircraft from Henderson spotted the beached transports at 0555 hours; they were battered by aircraft and Marine field artillery. USS *Meade* (DD-602) crossed from Tulagi and shelled them for nearly an hour, destroying all equipment that had yet to be unloaded and setting them afire, turning them into twisted wreckage wracked by internal explosions. Only some 2,000–3,000 troops of the 7,000 originally embarked made it ashore, having lost most of their ammunition and food. *Meade* then cruised the waters between Savo and Guadalcanal, rescuing 266 survivors from *Preston* and *Walke*.

Guadalcanal had been saved.

20

END OF THE BEGINNING

November 15 – December 31

As dark as the future had appeared to those on Guadalcanal on the night of November 10, daylight on November 15 really was the dawn at the end of a dark night. Literally, over four days, the fortunes of war had turned 180 degrees. It wasn't immediately apparent to those on the ground, but they were now in a different reality from where they had been at dusk the night before. There would be other dark nights, but none as dark as these. It was not just the dawn of a new day – it was the dawn of a new era in the South Pacific.

On the morning of November 15, Cactus Fighter Command could muster three P-39s and 38 airworthy Wildcats with the arrival the day before of VF-10's 24 fighters. Just before noon, seven P-38Gs from the 339th Fighter Group's 503rd Fighter Squadron flew up from Espiritu Santo and landed on Henderson, the first Lightnings to operate at Guadalcanal. More of them were on the way, while back in the United States VMF-124 had taken delivery of the first of the new F4U-1 Corsair, and the pilots were getting used to their new mounts as the Marines became the beneficiaries of the Navy's inability to mate the new air superiority fighter to a carrier deck successfully.

In a bit more than 11 weeks of fighting, six Wildcat-equipped squadrons – five Marine and one Navy – had flown from Henderson Field. The Marines claimed 305 enemy aircraft shot down, while VF-5 added another 45; the IJNAF admitted losing a total of 260. Even using the admitted Japanese losses, the Americans had compiled a victory ratio of approximately 2.5-to-1 – the saying "Grumman saved Guadalcanal" wasn't advertising hype.

That same day, their Japanese opponents on Rabaul counted a total of 30 Zero fighters and 66 Betty bombers; had they been fully equipped, there would have been over 250 Zeros, but the Rabaul units had never been at full strength. Unlike the Americans, who were able to rescue 80 percent of their downed fliers, only a handful of the Imperial Navy's sea eagles who failed to return to base were ever seen again. On top of the losses at Midway, the IJNAF losses over Guadalcanal and at Eastern Solomons and Santa Cruz had ripped out the elite force's heart.

On November 19, VMF-121 was relieved and the squadron personnel flew to Espiritu Santo courtesy of the R4Ds of VMD-451. From there, the pilots were flown to Sydney, Australia, for leave while the ground crews took liberty in Nouméa. By the end of the month, most fighter operations moved from the Cow Pasture to Fighter Two, located on higher ground and not subject to flooding as the old field was. All of the 503rd Squadron's P-38s were now based at Fighter Two and the first of the Lightnings from the 504th and 505th squadrons had arrived. The Cactus Air Force grew in strength and capability daily. Six Lockheed Hudson twin-engine patrol bombers of the Royal New Zealand Air Force (RNZAF) No. 3 Bomber-Reconnaissance Squadron took up residence at Henderson in the week after the naval actions, providing increased capability for searching out the enemy throughout the Solomons as far north as Bougainville.

The Japanese failure in the two desperate sea battles on November 12–13 and 14–15 removed the threat of another offensive to take Henderson Field. Over the two weeks left of November, the enemy appeared to abandon the surviving troops on the island to slow but inevitable extinction. What had happened was that General MacArthur had activated the other part of the Allied "pincer" campaign in New Guinea. Lieutenant General Hitoshi Imamura had taken command of the newly formed 8th Area Army at Rabaul; his responsibilities included General Hyakutake's 17th Army on Guadalcanal and the 18th Army in New Guinea. While Imamura initially planned to organize another attempt to retake Henderson Field, his plans were disrupted by the opening of the Allied offensive at Buna in New Guinea, which was seen as a more severe threat to Rabaul. Further major reinforcement for

Guadalcanal was suspended while the Imperial Army concentrated on the crisis in New Guinea.

In the weeks after the naval Battle of Guadalcanal, the new RNZAF search planes and the veteran Catalinas of VP-23 found fewer ships in the Buin-Faisi area, while General Vandegrift's reports for the period listed only minor encounters with enemy troops as the soldiers and Marines disposed of the surviving enemy units threatening Henderson Field. Rumors began to spread among the Marines that they would soon be relieved. At the end of the month, the arrival of the rest of the American Division confirmed the rumors of relief as fact. The American was soon joined by the 25th "Tropic Lightning" Infantry Division and the US Army XIV Corps formally relieved the 1st Marine Division on December 7, the first anniversary of the attack on Pearl Harbor that had initiated the Pacific War.

A period of bright moonlight which resulted from the extended period of good weather after the dark nights in mid-month saw cloudless skies at night that made intercepting surface ships easier. The Imperial Navy could no longer use slow cargo ships to deliver provisions to the starving Imperial Army forces. In these conditions, the Imperial Navy was forced to resort to supply by submarines, which were incapable of bringing more than a small portion of the supplies required by the troops of the 17th Army. Admiral Tanaka's "Tokyo Express" developed a plan to deliver supplies using large oil drums that were cleaned out and filled with supplies and food, leaving enough air inside to provide buoyancy. The plan saw the drums tied together and put over the side to drift ashore; there a swimmer brought the buoyed end of the rope to the beach, where working parties would haul in the supplies. Doing this kind of operation with only a few destroyers at a time wasn't enough. On November 26, General Hyakutake reported that many front-line units had not been resupplied for six days and rear-area troops were on one-third rations. Admiral Tanaka waited for the weather to change while the drums were cleaned out and supplies were gathered.

Two weeks after Lee's victory, on November 30, the Americans finally learned how mistaken they were to discount the power and effectiveness of the Type 93 torpedo. The Battle of Tassafaronga, or in Japanese history, the Battle of Lunga Point, took place the night of November 30/December 1, 1942, and disproved every lesson that the US Navy declared it had learned over the previous four months.

With a forecast for overcast skies and the phase of the moon turning to darkness, Admiral Mikawa ordered Tanaka's Guadalcanal Reinforcement Group to make the first of five expanded runs to Guadalcanal on the night of November 30/December 1. *Kuroshio*, *Oyashio*, *Kagerō*, *Suzukaze*, *Kawakaze*, and *Makinami* would each carry 240 drums, the largest attempted resupply since November 11. The six drum-carrying destroyers left their torpedo reloads behind, carrying only eight each in their tubes, while escorts *Naganami* and *Takanami* carried reloads. All were Solomons combat veterans.

On November 24, Admiral Kinkaid was ordered to form Task Force 67 at Espiritu Santo with recently arrived heavy cruisers *Pensacola* and *Northampton* and the now-veteran *Fletcher*. They were joined on November 27 by heavy cruisers *Minneapolis* and *New Orleans*, light cruiser *Honolulu*, and destroyers *Drayton* (DD-366), *Maury* (DD-401), and *Perkins* (DD-377) fresh from Pearl Harbor. Before Kinkaid could go over his plans with his captains, he was replaced on November 28 by Rear Admiral Carleton H. Wright, who commanded the newcomers in *Minneapolis*. Wright was a well-regarded officer who had been captain of *Augusta* when it took President Roosevelt to his first meeting with Prime Minister Churchill in August 1941. Promoted to rear admiral the previous May, great things were expected of him in his first combat command. With the exception of *Fletcher*, the others were newcomers to a surface battle task force, having spent their time since Pearl Harbor as escorts for aircraft carriers, providing antiaircraft support.

While US intelligence could no longer read the Imperial Navy traffic, that of the Imperial Army was an open book. When the message informing General Hyakutake of the coming supply run was decoded on November 29, at 1940 hours Admiral Halsey ordered Admiral Wright to depart at the earliest possible moment, and intercept an enemy group identified as six destroyers and six transports off Guadalcanal. Just before 2400 hours that night, Task Force 67 departed Espiritu Santo for Guadalcanal. En route to Guadalcanal on November 30, the force encountered three transports escorted by five destroyers returning from Guadalcanal. Destroyers *Lamson* (DD-369) and *Lardner* (DD-487) were ordered to reinforce Task Force 67. Commander Laurence A. Abercrombie, who commanded the two, was suddenly SOPA for destroyers; he had no knowledge of Wright's battle plan.

Paul Mason, the Bougainville coastwatcher, reported the departure of Tanaka's destroyers from their base in the Shortlands at 0005 hours on November 30; his message was passed to Wright. During the day of November 30, Tanaka attempted to evade air patrols from Guadalcanal, heading northeast through Bougainville Strait before turning south and entering the Slot through Indispensable Strait shortly after sunset; He informed his captains that he expected action that night.

Task Force 67 entered Lengo Channel at 2140 hours on November 30 and went to General Quarters. They exited into Ironbottom Sound just after 2200 hours. That night, unlike the clear skies of the previous ten days, was very dark and overcast. Maximum surface visibility was under two miles. At 2240 hours, Tanaka's destroyers passed south of Savo and slowed to 12 knots near the unloading area. At the same time, Task Force 67 turned towards Savo.

At 2306 hours, Tanaka's ships were picked up by *Minneapolis'* SG radar near Cape Esperance 23,000 yards distant. *Fletcher* picked up two targets 14,000 yards off the destroyer's port bow. The task force radars located five ships, four approximately a mile and a quarter off Guadalcanal, the fifth half a mile further out. At 2316 hours, the enemy was 7,000 yards away and *Fletcher's* Commander Cole requested permission to fire torpedoes. Two minutes later, Wright responded that the range was too great. At 2320 hours, Wright finally gave permission to fire. In the time between initial query and permission to fire, the targets escaped from an optimum firing setup ahead to a marginal position passing abeam. *Fletcher* fired two five-torpedo salvos, at 2320 hours. *Perkins* launched eight in one salvo and *Drayton* launched two. All 20 missed.

New Orleans' radar did not spot the enemy until 2314 hours, at a range of 14,000 yards. *Pensacola* lacked radar and made no contacts until *Minneapolis* opened fire. *Honolulu* spotted nothing until the flagship opened fire, while *Northampton* depended on the others' reports. At 2321 hours, Wright ordered all ships to open fire; the destroyers fired 5-inch armor-piercing shells and starshells. *Fletcher* fired 60 rounds using radar before ceasing fire and retiring around Savo, with the other three destroyers following.

Minneapolis fired four main battery salvos at what was identified as a "transport," though none were present. The first salvo was over, but the next three were directly on; the target "violently disintegrated" after the fourth salvo. *New Orleans* opened fire a minute later on an enemy destroyer 8,700 yards distant, which blew up after the fourth salvo. *Pensacola* had difficulty locating a target, but with starshells from either *Honolulu* or *Northampton*, opened fire at a "light cruiser" 10,000 yards away. *Honolulu* and *Northampton* fired at the same target which was seen to sink after *Pensacola's* fifth salvo landed.

At 2224 hours, *Honolulu* spotted an enemy destroyer and commenced rapid fire with the 6-inch main battery for 30 seconds, producing several hits. After firing starshells and another minute of gunfire, the enemy destroyer sank and the light cruiser checked fire.

All the cruisers engaged in rapid fire of starshells and main battery salvos. The blinding flashes, smoke, and splashes made it impossible to see the Japanese formation clearly. At 2326 hours, the cruisers checked fire since the night was so dark, visibility so limited, and flashes and smoke in the target area so confusing it was impossible to see what was taking place.

At the same time that *Minneapolis* had initially spotted them, Tanaka's ships split into two groups and put their drums overboard. *Takanami* reported a visual sighting of the Americans at 2312 hours; at 2316 hours, Tanaka ordered unloading halted.

Takanami, the target for most of the initial American fire, returned fire and launched eight Type 93 torpedoes just before the ship was destroyed. Tanaka's flagship, *Naganami*, reversed course and laid a smoke screen, then opened fire. At 2323 hours, *Suzukaze*, *Naganami*, and *Kawakaze* each fired eight torpedoes toward the American gunflashes. The four destroyers at the head of the column maintained their heading and Wright's cruisers passed on the opposite course. Once they were clear, *Kuroshio* fired four and *Oyashio* fired eight torpedoes at *Minneapolis* at 2328 hours; 44 Type 93 torpedoes now headed straight at the American force.

Minneapolis had just fired a ninth salvo when two torpedoes hit at 2327 hours; the first touched off the aviation fuel storage forward of turret No. 1 while the second knocked out three of four firerooms. The entire bow forward of turret No. 1 folded down at a 70-degree angle and the cruiser lost power and steering. The waves raised by the explosions were so high that when they fell they put out the forecastle fires, while flooding the navigating bridge. As *Minneapolis* shuddered and rolled drunkenly, the entire bow tore loose at frame 22. Amazingly, the three forward turrets resumed fire; all power was lost after the 11th salvo and steering was momentarily lost as the heavy cruiser rapidly slowed. Effective damage control saved *Minneapolis* while oil was pumped overboard to correct a four-degree list and all heavy objects above the main deck were jettisoned. Admiral Wright passed command to Admiral Mahlon Tisdale in *Honolulu*.

At 2328 hours, *New Orleans* was hit beside turret No. 1; the forward ammunition magazines and aviation gas storage exploded and severed the entire bow forward of turret No. 2. All crews in turrets Nos 1 and 2 were killed and the ship was forced to reverse course to starboard; after which steering and communications were lost and the main deck was wrecked back to frame 42. The second deck was completely missing forward of frame 31, and flooded aft to frame 42. Everything below the second deck forward of frame 31 had been blown out in the explosion.

Seaman Herbert Brown described the scene after the torpedo hit:

> I had to see. I walked alongside the silent turret two and was stopped by a lifeline stretched from the outboard port lifeline to the side of the turret. Thank God it was there, for one more step and I would have pitched head first into the dark water 30 feet below. The bow was gone. One hundred and twenty five feet of ship and No. 1 main battery turret with three 8-inch guns were gone. Eighteen hundred tons of ship were gone. Oh my God, all those guys I went through boot camp with – all gone.

Seeing *Minneapolis* and *New Orleans* hit, *Pensacola* passed the stricken cruisers to port. At 2329 hours, a torpedo hit abreast the mainmast. The explosion spread flaming oil through the cruiser's interior and across the main deck, ripping away the port outer shaft and killing 125 crewmen. *Pensacola* quickly lost power and communications, and took a 13-degree list.

Honolulu turned to pass *Minneapolis* and *New Orleans* to starboard, increasing speed to 30 knots and somehow managing to avoid being hit while firing at the disappearing enemy ships. *Northampton* followed *Honolulu* past the damaged cruisers but did not increase speed or maneuver. At 2348 hours, two of *Kawakaze's* torpedoes were seen close aboard on the port bow, traveling very close together. The captain barely had time to order hard left rudder before the cruiser took two hits so close together that many on board felt only one explosion. One torpedo hit at frame 108 causing ten degree list to port while the ship caught fire. The other exploded in the after engine room, which stopped three of four propeller shafts. Shortly after, the list increased to 20 degrees. The captain stopped in hopes the ship would right itself, but the list reached 23 degrees, at which point he ordered the bridge abandoned, the firerooms secured, and all personnel brought topside.

At 2344 hours, Tanaka ordered his destroyers to break contact and retire. *Kuroshio* and *Kagerō* fired eight more torpedoes, but all missed. *Takanami*, the only ship seriously damaged by all the American gunfire, was abandoned at 0130 hours on December 1. In his after-action report, Admiral Tanaka claimed to have sunk a battleship and two cruisers.

Northampton was abandoned at 0130 hours when the crew was unable to contain the fires. When the list reached 35 degrees at 0240 hours, the salvage party was forced to abandon ship. Just past 0300 hours, *Northampton* rolled over and sank stern first. By 0400 hours *Fletcher* and *Drayton* had rescued all 57 officers and 716 men.

At dawn, three fleet tugs were able to take *Minneapolis*, *New Orleans*, and *Pensacola* under tow, arriving at Tulagi shortly after 0800 hours. *Pensacola*'s fires were finally put out shortly before 1200 hours. Otherwise undamaged, the ship departed on December 6 for Espiritu Santo and further repair. *Minneapolis* and *New Orleans* were anchored close to shore and camouflaged to protect them from air attack while temporary bows made of coconut logs were constructed. They departed for Espiritu Santo on December 12. All three warships required lengthy and extensive repairs in the United States.

Tassafaronga was the third-worst defeat suffered by the US Navy in World War II, after Pearl Harbor and Savo Island. However, despite the heavy losses, the battle set the stage for the Imperial Navy's increasing difficulty resupplying the troops. Tanaka led ten destroyers back to Guadalcanal on December 3 and successfully dumped 1,500 drums of provisions. Nevertheless, the drums were not ashore by dawn and American aircraft sank all but 310 of them by strafing as the starving enemy looked on from the jungle. PT boats thwarted a third attempt by 12 destroyers on December 7 off Cape Esperance, forcing the destroyers to abandon their mission.

After this, the Imperial Navy informed General Imamura that it was stopping all destroyer runs to Guadalcanal. The 17th Army on the island was losing 50 men a day to starvation and tropical diseases for which it had no medicines. Imamura protested the decision and

Admiral Yamamoto agreed to one last run. On December 11, Tanaka's destroyers were ambushed by five PT boats off Guadalcanal and his flagship was torpedoed, with the admiral wounded in the blast. The destroyer was scuttled and the wounded Tanaka transferred to another. Only 220 of the 1,200 drums released were recovered, with the rest strafed by aircraft from Henderson following their discovery in the morning.

On December 12, Admiral Yamamoto proposed abandoning Guadalcanal to establish a new defensive line in the central Solomons. Admiral Tanaka was relieved of command and returned to Japan on December 29. While the Army opposed Yamamoto's proposed retreat, Imperial Headquarters in Tokyo agreed to his plan on December 31. Over the next six weeks, the Imperial Navy would carry out an audacious withdrawal of the 17th Army from Guadalcanal, under the noses of the Americans who only discovered what was happening when it was over.

While the "official narrative" of the Pacific War holds that the Battle of Midway was the turning point in the Pacific Theater, this claim relies on the belief that, following that battle, the Japanese changed over to the strategic defensive while the Allies took the unending initiative in the Pacific War. While it may seem that this is what happened, given that Imperial Japan never experienced a battlefield victory that was strategic in importance against the Allies following Midway, the facts don't really support that view.

What happened during the four months of the critical Guadalcanal campaign was what Admiral Yamamoto had in mind when he warned that if he was to go to war in the Pacific, he would run wild for six months and be able to "promise nothing" past that. At Guadalcanal, Japan lost the ability to replace its losses. After Guadalcanal, the nation whose industrial output was 15 percent of its opponent's could no longer maintain its forces in combat. In the air campaign of attrition over Guadalcanal, the Americans were able to rescue 80 percent of the fliers who were shot down, to fly again; the Imperial Navy's losses were nearly 100 percent. Not only were the airmen rescued, but the pilots who arrived after the initial force were increasingly better trained than those they replaced. That was not the case for the enemy; the replacements in the IJNAF were instead increasingly poorly trained. The IJNAF lost over 1,200 experienced pilots and aircrew members, and 683 aircraft between August 7 and December 31, 1942. Saburo Sakai later wrote that the worst trainees in his prewar training class who washed out were better than the majority of those who came onto operations after the Guadalcanal campaign,

Guadalcanal, not Midway, marked the irreversible tide of victory for the Allies in the Pacific.

After Guadalcanal, the armed forces of Imperial Japan never grew stronger, while those of the United States went from strength to strength over the rest of the war.

GLOSSARY

AA	antiaircraft
AirSoPac	Aircraft South Pacific
APD	destroyer-transport
CAG	Commander Air Group
CAP	Combat Air Patrol
CinCPac	Commander in Chief Pacific
CNO	Chief of Naval Operations
ComAirGuadalcanal	Commander Aircraft Guadalcanal
COMINCH	Commander-In-Chief
ComSoPac	Commander South Pacific Theater
CUB	Advanced Base Aviation Construction Battalion
FDO	fighter direction officer
FMF	Fleet Marine Force
IJNAF	Imperial Japanese Naval Air Force
JCS	Joint Chiefs of Staff
MAG	Marine air group
MAW	Marine air wing
MCAS	Marine Corps air station
NAP	Naval Aviation Pilot

NAS	Naval air station
NGVR	New Guinea Volunteer Rifles (Australian)
RAAF	Royal Australian Air Force
RNZAF	Royal New Zealand Air Force
ROTC	Reserve Officers Training Corps
SoPac	South Pacific Area
USAAC	United States Army Air Corps
VB	Bombing Squadron (Navy)
VF	Fighter Squadron (Navy)
VMF	Marine Fighter Squadron
VMO	Marine Observation Squadron
VMR	Marine Transport Squadron
VMSB	Marine Scout-bomber Squadron
VS	Scouting Squadron (Navy)
VT	Attack Squadron (Navy)
buntaicho	division leader
chutai	squadron
hikotaicho	air group commander
shotai	flight

INDEX

References to maps are in **bold**.